The Many Faces of Christianism

Political and Public Theologies

COMPARISONS – COALITIONS – CRITIQUES

Editor-in-Chief

Ulrich Schmiedel (*Lund University*)

Editorial Board

Julie Cooper (*Tel Aviv University*)
Vincent Lloyd (*Villanova University*)
Tommy Lynch (*University of Chichester*)
Esther McIntosh (*York St John's*)
Sturla Stålsett (*Norwegian School of Theology, Religion and Society, Oslo*)
Fatima Tofighi (*University of Religions, Qom*)

Advisory Board

Seforosa Carroll (*World Council of Churches, Geneva*)
Stephan van Eerp (*KU Leuven*)
Elaine Graham (*University of Chester*)
Kristin Heyer (*Boston College*)
Catherine Keller (*Drew University, Madison, NJ*)
Brian Klug (*University of Oxford*)
Valentina Napolitano (*University of Toronto*)
Joshua Ralston (*University of Edinburgh*)
Thomas Schlag (*University of Zurich*)
Sohaira Zahid Siddiquin (*Georgetown University, Ar-Rayyan*)
Robert Vosloo (*University of Stellenbosch*)

VOLUME 7

The titles published in this series are listed at *brill.com/ppt*

The Many Faces of Christianism

The 'Russian World' in Europe

Edited by

Marietta van der Tol
Sophia R.C. Johnson
Petr Kratochvíl
Zoran Grozdanov

BRILL

LEIDEN | BOSTON

 This is an open access title distributed under the terms of the CC BY-NC 4.0 license, which permits any non-commercial use, distribution, and reproduction in any medium, provided the original author(s) and source are credited. Further information and the complete license text can be found at https://creativecommons.org/licenses/by-nc/4.0/

The terms of the CC license apply only to the original material. The use of material from other sources (indicated by a reference) such as diagrams, illustrations, photos and text samples may require further permission from the respective copyright holder.

Harold C. Smith Foundation (2019), DAAD-Cambridge Hub for German Studies (2021), Alfred Landecker Foundation (2025).

Cover illustration: The wall of a Christian church damaged by shelling in Ukraine. Photographer: Baranov Oleksandr. Shutterstock Photo ID 2384419475.

The Library of Congress Cataloging-in-Publication Data is available online at https://catalog.loc.gov
LC record available at https://lccn.loc.gov/2025018212

Typeface for the Latin, Greek, and Cyrillic scripts: "Brill". See and download: brill.com/brill-typeface.

ISSN 2666-9218
ISBN 978-90-04-73188-2 (paperback)
ISBN 978-90-04-73189-9 (e-book)
DOI 10.1163/9789004731899

Copyright 2025 by Marietta van der Tol, Sophia R.C. Johnson, Petr Kratochvíl, and Zoran Grozdanov.
Published by Koninklijke Brill BV, Plantijnstraat 2, 2321 JC Leiden, The Netherlands.
Koninklijke Brill BV incorporates the imprints Brill, Brill Nijhoff, Brill Schöningh, Brill Fink, Brill mentis, Brill Wageningen Academic, Vandenhoeck & Ruprecht, Böhlau and V&R unipress.
Koninklijke Brill BV reserves the right to protect this publication against unauthorized use.
For more information: info@brill.com.

This book is printed on acid-free paper and produced in a sustainable manner.

Contents

Foreword VII
Acknowledgements IX
List of Figures and Tables XI
Notes on Contributors XII

1 The Many Faces of Christianism: The 'Russian World' in Europe 1
   Marietta van der Tol, Petr Kratochvíl, Sophia Johnson, and Zoran Grozdanov

2 Populism and Religion: Why the Twain Will Always Meet 17
   Petr Kratochvíl

3 When a Light Cloak Turns into a Pious Cage: Thinking National Identity with Karl Barth and John Paul II 41
   Zoran Grozdanov

4 Fratelli Tutti: A Failed Battle against Christian Nationalism? 60
   Anne Guillard

5 The Russian World, The Hungarian World, and Make America Great Again: Political Imaginaries and Their Spaces 80
   Marietta van der Tol

6 Russian World, Holy Russia: Towards a New Ideology? 107
   Veronica Cibotaru

7 Putinism and Alexander Solzhenitsyn's Religious Motifs 125
   Dmytro Bintsarovskyi

8 From St. Paul and Carl Schmitt to Alexander Dugin: The Katechon as a Political Category in Empire Building 143
   Dustin J. Byrd

9 Between Religious Nationalism and Universal Familism: Anti-Gender Movement Values in Croatia and Serbia 169
   Ivan Tranfić

10 The Orthodox Church and the Greek Solution Party: A Stunted Political Relation between Adjacent Ideological Platforms 194
    Konstantinos Papastathis and Anastasia Litina

11 Belonging without Attending? National Identity and Contemporary Religious Patterns in Serbia 210
    Marko Veković

12 The Danish People's Party and the Heritage of Tidehverv: A National Example of a European Tendency 230
    Erik Sporon Fiedler

13 Christianity, Religion and Christian Democracy 250
    Katharina Kunter and Leon van den Broeke

14 The European Union as a Space of (In)Securities: Analysing Political Reasoning by Lithuanian Catholics 273
    Rosita Garškaitė-Antonowicz

15 Theopolitical Visions of National Belonging: Resisting the Totalising Tendencies of Inclusion 290
    Jenny Leith

16 The Contested Meanings of the Anglican Parish in Multireligious England 308
    Lauren Morry

17 Concluding Reflection: The Call for Political Theologies after Christendom 325
    Marietta van der Tol, Petr Kratochvíl, Sophia Johnson, and Zoran Grozdanov

Appendix 1: A Declaration on the "Russian World" (Russkii Mir) Teaching 336
Appendix 2: A statement of solidarity with the Orthodox Declaration on the "Russian World" (Russkii Mir) Teaching, and against Christian Nationalism and New Totalitarianism 342
Index 345

Foreword

It seems, as I write, that the world is facing an exceptional level of instability and threat. The ongoing conflict in Gaza, triggered by the actions of Hamas on 7 October 2023, but after decades of tension and war in the region, currently risks escalation into a much wider conflict. That crisis has come, however, on the back of other conflicts, not least the war in Ukraine. The Russian invasion of Ukraine in February 2022, following on from its earlier actions in the Donbas region, brought the risks of nuclear escalation, and widespread suffering, death and dislocation. It caused an energy and food supply crisis, fuelling inflation and food shortages across the world. One can only shudder, contemplating the scale of reparation and aid which will be needed in the wake of a just peace settlement in the region, a settlement for which we must earnestly hope and pray. Hundreds of thousands have been killed or wounded on both sides, and millions more forced to flee their homes.

In all this, religion is inevitably caught up. Whatever its transcendent source, religion is also a part of human life and experience, and no person of faith is abstracted from the many complexities of human society which strain and break in times of conflict. The faith I profess, Christianity, is centred on a person whose very divinity was gifted into and lived in the messiness of human history. Jesus was a man of peace and love, whose resistance to violence was so uncompromising it led him to a criminal's abject death. Yet his followers, for all their efforts to live up to his teaching, themselves have often become aggressive, violent enforcers of one point of view, of the lust for domination, of the often overbearing and overweening conviction that one nation or people has a God-given destiny which includes the subjugation of others. We see this in the conflict in Ukraine, in no uncertain terms, with the weaponisation of religion and its deployment in apologetic argument supporting the Russian action.

Christians can do, and have been doing, many things to ameliorate the situation – receiving and supporting refugees, sending aid, supporting proposals for a just peace, above all praying for peace. But they can also promote and support the careful dissection of the arguments used by those who twist religion to their own purposes. Theology and faith have much to say to political situations, and a profound critique to offer of human ideologies of power.

And so, I welcome this rich and bracing collection of essays on the ways in which religion has been appropriated to narrow and often authoritarian political ends. The term 'Christianism' is a relatively new one to me, but surely, we all recognize that political ambitions which privilege one perspective and one community at the cost of others often clothe themselves – especially in the

West – in pseudo-Christian language, and make appeal to concepts of Christian tradition and identity. These are dangerous strategies which need unmasking. Albeit with a particular focus on the ideology of the 'Russian world' and the political affiliations of some Orthodox thinkers, there is a great variety of perspectives and arguments on offer here, and many readers will no doubt find themselves disagreeing with some and agreeing with others. The editors are to be congratulated on assembling such a diverse and distinguished body of authors. Church leaders such as I am, as much as politicians, are inevitably in the business of managing human institutions, with all the expectations and indeed temptations which go with that, and we need the critical interrogation of scholars and theologians to highlight our own enmeshing in the, often conflicting, pressures of civil society, and to help us navigate a better way through. So, I am grateful for what is offered here, and commend it.

The Most Revd Justin Welby, Archbishop of Canterbury
Lambeth Palace, London, 4 September 2024

Acknowledgements

This volume arises from the networking project *Protestant Political Thought: Religion, State, Nation,* hosted at the University of Cambridge (2019–2021) and the University of Oxford (2021–2023). A series of workshops, reading groups, conferences, and collaborative publication projects sought to stimulate academic reflection on the relationship between religion and the rise of the transnational Far Right. The project had just begun engaging Orthodoxy when the Russian invasion of Ukraine materialised, giving reason to specifically bridge conversations about right-wing populism and the role of religion in Putin's Russia. Consecutive international conferences examined the role of space and the sacred, as well as the potentiality of 'Political Theologies after Christendom', considering 'theology after' a range of political atrocities: the Holodomor, the Holocaust, Apartheid, Srebrenica, Gulag, Bucha.

In the wake of the Russian invasion of Ukraine, several scholars took the initiative to a Statement of Solidarity with dissenting Orthodox scholars (Appendix 1), calling upon the scholarly community to come alongside them in critiquing the role of religion in Russia. The initiative came up in the context of Cyril Hovorun's keynote at the University Church in Oxford, part of one of the PPT-conferences, and took shape with contributions from Cyril Hovorun, Marietta van der Tol, Sophia Johnson, Petr Kratochvíl, John Heathershaw, Brendon Gallaher, Miroslav Volf, Ryan McAnnally-Linz, and Katharina Kunter. The first signatory, Jürgen Moltmann, signed with a special message 'In the name of the Confessing Church I am supporting your statement with my signature'. His recent passing gives pause to reflect on his international contribution to political theology, as well as on what it means to carry the post-war legacy into the 21st century.

The project's events, which has welcomed the participation of more than 250 scholars from 41 states, was made possible by generous seed-funding from the Harold C. Smith Foundation and has over the years benefited from supportive funding from a range of sources, including the Arts and Humanities Research Council Doctoral Training Programme, the DAAD-Cambridge Research Hub for German Studies, the Cambridge Faculty of Theology, Wesley House (Cambridge), the Woolf Institute (Cambridge), the Huffington Ecumenical Institute at Loyola Marymount University, the Alfred Landecker Programme at the Blavatnik School of Government (Oxford), the Inez and Julius Polin Institute for theological research at Åbo Akademi (Turku), and the Anabaptist Mennonite Network UK.

The project has produced several special issues: on Old Testament imaginaries of the nation, published in *The Journal of the Bible and its Reception;* on the role of space and the sacred in *Religion, State, Society,* and on nationalism and history in *The International Journal of Religion*. In 2024, Routledge published the first volume of *A Global Sourcebook in Protestant Political Thought,* providing a window into the early Protestant world in 200 historical sources that shed light on the ways in which Protestants wrestled with politics and religion in the wake of the Reformation. This edited volume on *The many faces of Christianism*, comparing the Russian World and Christian nationalism comes as the final output of the initial sources of funding.

Editors of this volume have benefited from individual funding. Petr Kratochvíl was supported by Metropolitan University Prague research project no. 100-3 "International Relations and Territorial Studies" (2023) based on a grant from the Institutional Fund for the Long-term Strategic Development of Research Organizations. Sophia Johnson's work was supported by the Memorial Foundation for Jewish Culture and grant project 492891937 "Josua Postkolonial" of the German Research Foundation as part of the Chair for Literary History of the Old Testament (Prof. Dr. Joachim J. Krause). Marietta van der Tol's research was enabled by a Postdoctoral Research Fellowship with the Alfred Landecker Chair for Values and Public Policy (Prof. Jonathan Wolff) at the Blavatnik School of Government (University of Oxford) and a Leverhulme Early Career Fellowship at the Faculty of Divinity (University of Cambridge), supported by the Leverhulme Trust and Isaac Newton Trust. She received funding from the Alfred Landecker Foundation for the Landecker Lectureship "Imagining Sacred Lands: the Russian World, Hungarian World and Holy Serbia" at the University of Cambridge (2025), which supports the Open Access publication of this volume.

Editors express their gratitude to a few scholars whose insights have particularly benefited this volume, including Regina Elsner, Cecilia Nahnfeldt, Cyril Hovorun, Gionathan Lo Mascolo, Philip Gorski, and Beatrice de Graaf. Special thanks go to our Ukrainian colleagues, who invited us to their Summer Schools and seminar series, especially Roman Soloviy, Ksenia Trofymchuk, Valerii Sekisov, Valentin Siniy, Dmytro Vovk. The final shape of the conclusion fell in its place after a seminar hosted by the McDonald Distinguished Fellowship Programme at the Center for the Study of Law and Religion at Emory University, for which we like to thank John Witte, Christian Green, Whittney Barth, Pamela Slotte, and Isidoros Katsos. We thank research assistants Yelizaveta Raichynets, Ben Davidson, and Andrej Bukovac-Mimica. Finally, our thanks go to the series editor Ulrich Schmiedel.

Marietta van der Tol
Cambridge, October 2024

Figures and Tables

Figures

- 9.1   Anti-gender smo values in Croatia   180
- 9.2   Anti-gender smo values in Serbia   184
- 10.1 Church attendance and anti-immigrant attitudes in Greece   202

Tables

- 10.1 Religious attendance and radical right voting-2019 (1)   204
- 10.2 Religious attendance and radical right voting-2019 (2)   205
- 11.1 Religious person: Data showing how people in Serbia identify in terms of religiosity, including categories such as religious, non-religious, or convinced atheist   218
- 11.2 Belief in God: Data showing the percentage of people in Serbia who believe in God   219
- 11.3 Belief in life after death: Data showing the percentage of people in Serbia who believe in life after death   219
- 11.4 Belief in hell: Data showing the percentage of people in Serbia who believe in hell   220
- 11.5 Belief in heaven: Data indicating the percentage of people in Serbia who believe in heaven   220
- 11.6 How often do you attend religious services: Data reflecting the frequency of church attendance in Serbia, showing how often individuals participate in religious services   221

Notes on Contributors

Dmytro Bintsarovskyi
is a post-doctoral researcher at the Theologische Universiteit Kampen/Utrecht, the Netherlands. He received his PhD degree (cum laude) in 2019 from the Theologische Universiteit Kampen. A more accessible version of his dissertation was published as a book under the title *Hidden and Revealed: The Doctrine of God in the Reformed and Eastern Orthodox Traditions* in the series Studies in Historical and Systematic Theology, published by Lexham Press.

Dustin J. Byrd
is professor of philosophy and religion at The University of Olivet in Michigan, USA. He is also a visiting professor of religious studies at Michigan State University. A specialist in the critical theory of religion and psychoanalytic political theory, he is the founder and co-director of the Institute for Critical Social Theory and has published numerous books on political religion and political philosophy.

Veronica Cibotaru
is a postdoctoral research fellow at the University of Tübingen, College of Fellows – Center for Interdisciplinary and Intercultural Studies. She works in the fields of philosophy of religion, language and artificial intelligence. She has published several articles devoted to the relationship between ethics and the idea of God, the phenomenology of religious experience, the difference between religion and spirituality and to the possibility of interreligious dialogue. Previously she has also worked as a journalist for the Orthodox French website Orthodoxie.com, and has published articles and given interviews for other newspapers such as *Le Monde* and *Le Point*.

Rosita Garškaitė-Antonowicz
is an assistant professor at the Institute of International Relations and Political Science, Vilnius University. She recently defended her dissertation on the relationship between Catholicism and the popular support for European integration. Her research interests include the intersection of religion and politics, Euroscepticism, the Far Right, post-communist transformation, and interpretive methodologies.

Zoran Grozdanov
is an associate professor at the University Centre for Protestant Theology Matthias Flacius Illyricus in Zagreb. As an author or an editor, he has published

ten volumes, and recently he has coedited and contributed to the volume *Balkan Contextual Theology: An Introduction* (Routledge, 2022) which is the first attempt of the contextual Balkan theology, giving voices to Islamic, Orthodox, Protestant, Catholic and secular voices. His books include *Harsh Word: The Death of God in Early Hegel and Early Moltmann* (Belgrade, 2016, in Croatian) and *Homeland Painted with the Incense: Theology of National Identity* (Rijeka, 2023, in Croatian).

Anne Guillard
is doing post-doctoral research at the University of Oxford (United Kingdom) funded by the Swiss National Science Foundation. Her research focuses on the political theory of public reason and the religious claims to integrate it. She explores the use of religious experience and Christian reference in public discourse. She analyses the underlying types of political theology mobilised by political and religious leaders in France, Italy and Hungary. She holds a double doctorate in Political Theory from Sciences Po Paris and in Christian Theology from the University of Geneva.

Sophia R. C. Johnson
is a postdoctoral researcher in Hebrew Bible at Ruhr-Universität Bochum in Germany. Her research centres on the political uses of and influences on interpretation of the Hebrew Bible/Old Testament, both in its original ancient context and in modern reception history. Sophia received her PhD from the University of Cambridge where she was also lecturer at the Faculty of Divinity and researcher at the Centre for Geopolitics. Sophia currently works with Prof. Dr. Joachim J. Krause on the project "Josua Postkolonial" funded by the Deutsche Forschungsgemeinschaft, which uses postcolonial theories to re-examine the biblical book of Joshua in its ancient imperial context. She has published in journals such as *Journal of the Bible and Its Reception, Journal of Biblical Literature,* and most recently *Zeitschrift für die alttestamentliche Wissenschaft.*

Petr Kratochvíl
is a full professor at the Faculty of Philosophy of Charles University, a senior researcher at the Institute of International Relations in Prague, and lecturer at Metropolitan University Prague. He also teaches at Sciences-Po in Paris and at Metropolitan University of Prague. His research interests include the religion-politics nexus, theories of international relations, European integration, and Russian foreign policy. He has published extensively on all these topics, with dozens of books, book chapters and scholarly articles, including in top journals such as *Journal of Common Market Studies, Cooperation and Conflict, Geopolitics,* and the *Journal of European Integration.* In 2023, his co-authored

article won the award offered by American Political Science Association for the best article about religion and politics.

Katharina Kunter
is professor of contemporary church history at the Faculty of Theology at the University of Helsinki (Finland). Her research focuses on the intersections between political history and the history of religion and culture. In her first book *Die Kirchen im KSZE-Prozess 1968–1978* (2000), she examined the role of the churches in the period of Détente in the 1970s. Further studies examined Christian political opposition and conformance in communist Central and Eastern Europe, especially in Protestantism in the GDR: *Erfüllte Hoffnungen und zerbrochene Träume. Evangelische Kirchen in Deutschland im Spannungsfeld von Demokratie und Sozialismus 1980–1993* (2004) and *'Es gibt keinen Gott!' Kirchen und Kommunismus. Eine Konfliktgeschichte* (2016). She is currently working on a study on the geopolitical role of Christianity in the twentieth century.

Jenny Leith
is lecturer in Christian ethics at Westcott House, Cambridge. Her research brings together political theology, ecclesiology, and spirituality, and she is the author of *Political Formation: Being Formed by the Spirit in Church and World* (SCM Press, 2023). Her interest in the relationship between Christian faith and participation in political life grew out of several years spent working as a parliamentary researcher and in social policy.

Anastasia Litina
is an associate professor in the School of Economics and Regional Studies, Department of Economics, at the University of Macedonia, Thessaloniki, Greece. She holds a Ph.D. in Economics (University of Macedonia, 2009), has visited Brown University as a visiting researcher for a semester, and worked as a post-doctoral researcher in the Department of Economics and Management at the University of Luxembourg. Her main research interests lie in the field of economic growth, comparative development, the economics of culture, environmental economics and cultural economics. Her publications appeared in the *Journal of Economic Growth*; *Research Policy*; *Harvard Business Review*; *Journal of the Economic Behavior and Organization*; and in *Religion, State and the Society*.

Lauren Morry
is a post-award visitor at the University of Oxford's Faculty of Theology and Religion. She completed her DPhil in 2023 with the thesis *The Palace and*

the Parish: The Church of England's Approach to Interreligious Relations With Muslims Nationally and Locally, 2005–2021. Her research interests include the anthropology of religion, Muslim-Christian relations, and questions of church and state.

Konstantinos Papastathis
is an assistant professor in the Department of Political Science at Aristotle University of Thessaloniki. With a research background that spans internationally academic institutions such as the Hebrew University of Jerusalem, the University of Luxembourg and Leiden University, his expertise lies in politics and religion, populism, church history, and Middle Eastern studies. Dr. Papastathis has made significant contributions to top field academic journals including *Religion, State and Society*; *Politics, Religion and Ideology*; *Middle Eastern Studies*; *British Journal of Middle Eastern Studies*; *Journal of Eastern Christian Studies*; and *Jerusalem Quarterly*, along with several collective volumes.

Erik Sporon Fiedler
is a postdoctoral fellow at the Department of Cross-Cultural and Regional Studies, University of Copenhagen, Denmark. He is currently working on the individual research project 'Paternal Care? A Contemporary Intellectual History of Lutheranism, Welfare, and Gender' funded by the Carlsberg Foundation. He has previously been HM Queen Margrethe II's Distinguished Postdoctoral Fellow at the Danish Academy in Rome, where he worked on the research project 'Economic Religion' also funded by the Carlsberg Foundation.

Ivan Tranfić
holds a PhD in political science and sociology from the Scuola Normale Superiore and is a member of the Center of Social Movement Studies (COSMOS) in Florence, Italy. He holds a BA and an MA degree in Political Science from the University of Zagreb, and an MA in Nationalism Studies from Central European University, Budapest. His research explores the role of lay activists, churches, and parental associations in movement mobilization for traditional family values. Specifically, his PhD project examined radical-right opposition to 'gender ideology' and abortion in Southeast Europe.

Leon van den Broeke
is professor in theology of law and church polity at the Theological University Utrecht, the Netherlands. Until recently, he also worked at the Vrije Universiteit Amsterdam. His teaching and research includes church-state relations.

Marietta D.C. van der Tol
is Landecker Lecturer at the University of Cambridge, specialising in the comparative study of religion in constitutional law, politics, and society. She is author of the book *Constitutional Intolerance: The Fashioning of the Other in Europe's Constitutional Repertoires* (2025). Previously she was the inaugural Alfred Landecker Postdoctoral Research Fellow at the Blavatnik School of Government, and College Lecturer in Politics at St Peter's and Lincoln College, and Leverhulme Early Career Fellow at the University of Cambridge. She obtained graduate degrees in law, history (Utrecht University), and religion (Yale University) before completing her doctorate in politics at the University of Cambridge.

Marko Veković
is associate professor of religion and politics at University of Belgrade, Faculty of Political Science, Serbia. He has been appointed as a visiting scholar at Temple University (2014), Columbia University (2016), and as a post-doctoral scholar at University of Erfurt (2019). His work has been published in *Democratization, Journal for the Scientific Study of Religion, Journal of Church and State, Nordic Journal of Religion and Society,* and his most recent book is *Democratization in Christian Orthodox Europe: Comparing Greece, Serbia and Russia* (Routledge, 2021).

CHAPTER 1

The Many Faces of Christianism: The 'Russian World' in Europe

Marietta van der Tol, Petr Kratochvíl, Sophia Johnson, and Zoran Grozdanov

Is the war in Ukraine a 'Holy War'? Two years after the start of the Russian invasion of Ukraine, Patriarch Kirill of Moscow and All Rus' seemed to be thinking so, at least according to the Mandate of the xxv World Russian People's Council "The Present and Future of the Russian World".[1] The Council is Russia's largest public forum, including many public figures from the world of politics, commerce, culture, and the church, and is chaired by the head of the Russian Orthodox Church.[2] The mandate references "the onslaught of Western globalism", the Russian aspirations in a multipolar world order, family policies, and migration, and as such echoes the familiar codewords of European populists. After the mandate was adopted at its annual congress in 2023, held in the State Kremlin Palace, and at which President Vladimir Putin spoke, Patriarch Kirill approved it in March 2024. Although Patriarch Kirill's repeatedly referenced the imaginaries of Holy Rus' and the Russian World, it was on this occasion that the World Council of Churches responded that the language of a "Holy War" was incompatible with its values, and indeed with previous statements of the Patriarch.[3]

In *The Godless Crusade,* Tobias Cremer illuminated how religious leaders responded differently to the appropriation of religious repertoires by far-right populist movements in Germany, France, and the USA.[4] Similarly to *The Claim*

---

1 andate of the xxv World Russian People's Council 'The Present and Future of the Russian World'", the Moscow Patriarchate, accessed 6 June 2024, http://www.patriarchia.ru/db/text/6116189.html.
2 For more information, see the website of the World Russian People's Council, accessed 6 June 2024, https://vrns.ru/.
3 World Council of Churches General Secretary, "wcc statement on the Decree of the xxv World Russian People's Council", World Council of Churches, accessed 6 June 2024, https://www.oikoumene.org/resources/documents/wcc-statement-on-decree-of-xxv-world-russian-peoples-council.
4 Tobias Cremer, *The Godless Crusade. Religion, Populism and Right-Wing Identity Politics in the West* (Cambridge: Cambridge University Press, 2023).

© MARIETTA VAN DER TOL ET AL., 2025 | DOI:10.1163/9789004731899_002
This is an open access chapter distributed under the terms of the CC BY-NC 4.0 license.

to Christianity: Responding to the Far Right by Hannah Strømmen and Ulrich Schmiedel, it underscored the sensitivity of far-right parties to critiques leveraged from within the main Christian churches.[5] Such critiques were deemed most effective if they were clearly articulated and relatively centralised, conditions that have become more difficult to meet with the declining church membership and the at times awkward positioning of the church in political discourse. Both books raise the question of ownership: who gets to define and defend Christianity? And, why can political leaders call for crusades on behalf of ('Christian') traditional values?

A crusader mentality is certainly visible in the diffuse forums that populate the transnational Right.[6] Examples of this are the St Basil the Great Foundation, the Tradition, Family, Property Movement, the World Congress of Families, the Alliance Defending Freedom, the Conservative Political Action Conference Foundation, the Heritage Foundation (from Project 2025), as well as lesser-known organisations such as Civitas Christiana, Ordo Iuris, the Edmund Burke Foundation/National Conservatism, the Danube Institute and the Mathias Corvinus Collegium.[7] Former Prime Minister of the UK, Liz Truss, launched her book *Ten Years to Save the West: Lessons from the Only Conservative in the Room* at CPAC Washington in February 2024.[8] These spaces are deliberately devised as transnational spaces and deploy the bridge frames of civilizational decline, globalism, the family, and migration, as issues that may interest a diffuse

---

5 Hannah Strømmen and Ulrich Schmiedel, *The Claim to Christianity: Responding to the Far Right* (London: SCM Press, 2020).
6 Neil Datta, "Modern-day crusaders in Europe. Tradition, family and property": Analysis of a transnational, ultra-conservative, catholic-inspired influence network", *Political perspectives: journal for political research* 8, no. 3 (2018): 69-105.
7 Jeanne Smits, "The international Russophile Movement's Second Congress: Behind the Fight for 'Multipolarity' is a Hatred of the West", 12 March 2024, https://www.tfp.org/the-international-russophile-movements-second-congress-behind-the-fight-for-multipolarity-is-a-hatred-of-the-west/; Kristina Stoeckl, "The rise of the Russian Christian Right: the case of the World Congress of Families", *Religion, State & Society* 48, no. 4 (2020): 223-238; BNNVARA, "Gods Lobbyisten", 2 March 2025, https://www.bnnvara.nl/zembla/artikelen/gods-lobbyisten; Rita Abrahamsen and Michael Williams, "CPAC and NatCon: Uniting a Transnational Radical Right", https://canopyforum.org/2024/10/25/cpac-and-natcon-uniting-a-transnational-radical-right/; Gábor Halmai and Andrew Ryder, "The Battle for Hearts and Minds in Hungarian Academia, *Verfassungsblog*, 15 January 2025, https://intr2dok.vifa-recht.de/servlets/MCRFileNodeServlet/mir_derivate_00018108/The%20Battle%20for%20Hearts%20and%20Minds%20in%20Hungarian%20Academia.pdf; Edward Knudsen, "Hungary. Country Report", in Helmut K. Anheier and ifa, ed., *The External Cultural Policy Monitor* (Stuttgart: ifa 2025); Szabolcs Panyi, "Renaming the EU, Dismantling the Commission: Polish, Hungarian Illiberals seek US backing", *VSquare,* 10 March 2025, https://vsquare.org/heritage-foundation-mcc-ordo-iuris-russia-european-union-european-court-of-justice/.
8 Liz Truss, *Ten Years to Save the West: Lessons from the Only Conservative in the Room* (Hull: Biteback Publishing, 2024).

audience, from ordinary conservatives to nationalists, and even the Extreme Right. Moreover, the transnational Right operates increasingly professionally and benefits from significant (and sometimes hidden) funding streams, including from oligarchs like Konstantin Malofeev and Vladimir Yakunin.[9]

The extent to which these bridge frames are used to rally conservative Christians behind illiberal purposes is increasingly documented, for example in the books *The Moralist International: Russia in the Global Culture Wars* by Kristina Stoeckl,[10] in *The Christian Right in Europe* by Gionathan Lo Mascolo,[11] and in *Defending Democracy from its Christian Enemies* by David Gushee.[12] However, although anti-liberal orientations can certainly be found among conservative Christians, it would be a mistake to assume that therefore, they are more likely to be illiberal or anti-democratic, as is sometimes inferred. Rather, the bridge frames are designed to create political alliances among a range of constituencies, which are sometimes relatively successful, but in all cases contested, including from within Christian communities. Moreover, the overall growth of the Far Right cannot solely be attributed to conservative Christians. While 'evangelicals' were politically significant in the election of Donald Trump in 2016 and 2024, Christian voters form only a modest portion of the electorate in many European countries, where other constituencies outnumber religious conservatives in accounting for the growth of the Far Right. This is reflected in the political priorities of far-right parties, which often tend to more general issues, such as migration and the demonization of the political left.

The successes of far-right parties and movements and the influence of Russia as a champion of illiberalism are different, yet intertwined phenomena. Some pro-Russian sentiments were visible as early as in the campaigns against the Ukraine-European Association Agreement in 2016, triggering a Dutch referendum even after Russia first annexed Crimea in 2014 and a passenger airplane from Malaysia Airlines, MH17, had been shot down above the Donbass.[13]

---

9   Lovenduski, Joni. "Funding anti-gender politics in Europe." *The Political Quarterly* 93, no. 3 (2022): 530-532; Harm Ede Botje, "Ultraconservatievee organisaties steeds machtiger: 'Leidt tot een uitholling van de Europese democratie'", 11 May 2025, https://www.ftm.nl/artikelen/ultrarechts-aast-op-lhbti-en-vrouwenrechten.

10 Kristina Stoeckl and Dmitry Uzlaner, *The Moralist International: Russia in the Global Culture Wars* (New York: Fordham University Press, 2022).

11 Gionathan Lo Mascolo, ed., *The Christian Right in Europe: Movements, Networks, and Denominations* (New York: Transcript, 2023).

12 David Gushee, *Defending Democracy from its Christian Enemies* (Grand Rapids, MI: Eerdmans, 2023).

13 Marcel van Herpen, "The Rise of Kremlin-Friendly Populism in the Netherlands", *Cicero Foundation Great Debate Paper* 18/04 (2018), accessed 6 June 2024, https://www.cicerofoundation.org/wp-content/uploads/Van_Herpen_Kremlin-Friendly_Populism_Netherlands.pdf.

Despite hundreds of Dutch casualties, Geert Wilders went to Russia in 2018 on the invitation of politician Leonid Slutsky, chair of the foreign affairs committee of the Russian Duma and chair of the far-right Russian Peace Foundation. According to *Follow the Money*, he is "part of a network that seeks to influence and bribe Western politicians, and regularly invites them to Russia".[14] It is perhaps no accident that ever since the start of the war in 2014, several far-right parties have been reluctant to condemn the war in Ukraine or unwilling to support Ukraine militarily, and according to Czech intelligence, specific individuals appear to have accepted bribes from Russian actors to echo pro-Russian propaganda in Europe's parliaments.[15] All this raises concerns about the instrumentalization of the war in Ukraine by many far-right parties for electoral purposes domestically and about their discernment of the consequences of this behaviour for Europe, NATO, and even the international political order.

These issues, along with the spread of disinformation in the context of elections by Russian-backed actors, have given rise to credible concerns about Russian influence in European and American elections – such as in Romania in 2024. Less attention, however, has developed for Orbán's political aspirations for Central Europe and his influence in the region. These aspirations are mediated through significant satellite parties in neighbouring states, including in Croatia, Serbia, and Romania, a reported uptick in media campaigns and intelligence activity in Slovakia, and according to VSquare, online campaigns in other European states, including in Germany, Belgium, and Italy.[16] This is compounded by the work of a transnationally active think-tank, the Mathias Corvinus Collegium, which was endowed with more than Hungary's annual budget for Higher Education, and which styles itself as an alternative academy.[17] They also operated as a focal point for the Farmers' Protests against the

---

14 Sophia Twigt, "Gelekte documenten bewijzen tot nu toe onbekende connecties tussen Rusland en de PVV", *Follow the Money*, 19 October 2023, accessed 6 June 2024, https://www.ftm.nl/artikelen/de-banden-tussen-pvv-en-rusland-zijn-sterker-dan-gedacht.

15 "BIS odhalila ruskou vlivovou síť. Aktéři skončili na sankčním seznamu", Security information service (BIS), accessed 6 June 2024, https://www.bis.cz/aktuality/bis-odhalila-ruskou-vlivovou-sit-akteri-skoncili-na-sankcnim-seznamu-ff8aacba.html.

16 Szabolcs Panyi, "How Orbán flooded Central Europe with Millions of Ads during Election Season", *VSQUARE*, 29 February 2024, accessed 6 June 2024, https://vsquare.org/orban-central-europe-online-ads-election-season/.

17 On the MCC's funding, see Valerie Hopkins, "Campus in Hungary is Flagship of Orban's Bid to Create a Conservative Elite", *New York Times*, 28 June 2021, accessed 6 June 2024, https://www.nytimes.com/2021/06/28/world/europe/hungary-orban-university.html; Andras Gergely, Andrea Dudik, and Marton Kasnyik, "Inside Viktor Orban's $1 billion Academy for Tomoorow's Nationalists", *Bloomberg UK*, 23 November 2023, accessed 6 June 2024, https://www.bloomberg.com/news/features/2023-11-23/hungary-orban-s-school-is-training-a-new-generation-of-nationalists.

European Union in the Spring of 2024, months before Hungary would assume the Presidency of the Council of the European Union.[18]

The Russian invasion of Ukraine has nevertheless thrown into sharp relief how Russia envisions a different kind of Europe, and potentially, a different kind of world order.[19] President Vladimir Putin's historical excursions focus on the post-Soviet space, especially on the alleged artificiality of Ukraine's statehood, but they also connect the regional issues with the broader argument about the Western interference. The 'collective West' has become a central figure of speech in Russian state propaganda and Russian public figures accuse it of everything ranging from warmongering to Satanism.[20] Orbán has toyed with similar ideas, for example, talking about new agreements with the EU, Russia, America, and China.[21] Both the war in Ukraine and Orbán's reorientation on the major world powers reflects the declining dominance of the United States and its *Pax Americana* in the context of Europe.[22] However, it is important to note that despite the overlapping bridge frames, the European Far Right is diffuse and fundamentally divided in their geopolitical orientation on the changing world order. Nicola Guerra characterises this as the "opposing influences of Steve Bannon and Aleksandr Dugin", leading to a most crucial distinction between factions that eventually orient themselves on the power of the United States and NATO, and factions that orient themselves on Russia in a multipolar world order.[23]

---

18 Marta Kasztelan, Claire Carlile, and Joey Grostern, "Orbán-backed think-tank courts farmers linked to far-right ahead of elections", *EU Observer*, 2 May 2024, accessed 6 June 2024, https://euobserver.com/green-economy/ar506ca561; Sarah Wheaton and Eddy Wax, "Viktor Orbán brings culture war to Brussels", *Politico*, 15 November 2023, https://www.politico.eu/article/viktor-orban-hungary-culture-war-woke-brussels/.

19 John Heathershaw, *Security after Christendom: Global Politics and Political Theology for Apocalyptic Times* (Eugene, OR: Wipf and Stock 2024).

20 andate of the XXV World Russian People's Council 'The Present and Future of the Russian World'".

21 Viktor Orbán, "Some things last forever!", Tusványos Summer University, 23 July 2022, accessed 9 April 2024. https://2015-2022.miniszterelnok.hu/speech-by-prime-minister-viktor-orban-at-the-31st-balvanyos-summer-free-university-and-student-camp/.

22 John Ikenberry, *Liberal Leviathan: The Origins, Crisis and Transformation of the American World Order* (Princeton: Princeton University Press, 2011); John Mearsheimer, "Bound to fail: the rise and fall of the liberal international order", *International Security* 43, no. 4 (2019): 7–50; Stephen Brooks and William Wohlforth, *World out of Balance: International Relations and the Challenge of American Primacy* (Princeton: Princeton University Press, 2008).

23 Nicola Guerra, "The Russian-Ukrainian war has shattered the European far right. The opposing influences of Steve Bannon and Aleksandr Dugin". *European Politics and Society* 25, no. 2 (2024): 421–439.

It is precisely in this geopolitical context that the notion of Russkii Mir (Русский мир), in this book translated as the Russian World, has emerged as a competitor of the *Pax Americana,* and could be understood as Russian-shaped World, Order, or Peace. This notion has emerged from complex and at times contradictory discourses. Over the last few decades, the idea of the Russian World was sometimes understood as cultural or linguistic kinship and sometimes as Russia's "tentacles" in exerting influence over post-Soviet states.[24] Recently, the idea of the Russian World has increasingly aligned with Russia's expansionist policies. A politicized version of Christianity, and Russian Orthodoxy in particular, is highly influential in shaping the idea of the Russian World, partially through the canonical claims of the Russian Orthodox Church, but mostly through popularised notions of Holy Rus' and Ancient Rus' that imply the unity of Russians, Ukrainians and Belarussians as 'brothers'.[25] In this sense, the Russian World refers to an "organically unified transnational orthodox Christian Russian civilisation that includes the territories and people of Russia, Ukraine, Belarus and sometimes other nations".[26]

The religious repertoires of the Russian World nod to the changing meaning of Christianism. As defined by Rogers Brubaker, the concept of Christianism initially referred to "a secularist posture, a philosemitic stance, and an ostensibly liberal defence of gender equality, gay rights, and freedom of speech", as exemplified in Western European populist movements.[27] The phenomenon of Christianism, in its wider context from Moscow to the Midwest, can also be anti-Western, anti-liberal, anti-LGBT, anti-elitist, and anti-democratic, and is less obviously definable as a fundamentally secularist posture.[28] Christianism has thus emerged as a powerful geopolitical phenomenon that transcends the secular-sacred divide: in culture, in identity, and in new political ideologies. It

---

24   Mikhail Suslov, "Russian World Concept: Post-Soviet Geopolitical Ideology and the Logic of Spheres of Influence", *Geopolitics* 23, no. 2 (2018): 330–353.

25   Regina Elsner, "Ideological Pillow and Strategic Partner: The Russian Orthodox Church and the War", *Russian Analytical Digest,* no. 286 (2022): 2–4; Mikhail Suslov, "Holy Rus: The Geopolitical Imagination in the Contemporary Russian Orthodox Church", *Russian Politics & Law* 52, no. 3 (2014): 67–86; Thomas Bremer, "Diffuses Konzept: Die Russische Orthodoxe Kirche und die 'Russische Welt'", *Osteuropa* 66, no. 3 (2016): 3–18.

26   "Statement of Solidarity", see appendix 2 of this volume; Aristotle Papanikolaou, *The Mystical as Political: Democracy and Non-Radical Orthodoxy* (Notre Dame, IN: University of Notre Dame Press 2012).

27   Rogers Brubaker, "Between Nationalism and Civilisationalism: The European populist movement in comparative perspective", *Ethnic and Racial Studies* 40, no. 8 (2017), 1191–1226.

28   András Sajó, Renáta Uitz, and Stephen Holmes, eds., *The Routledge Handbook of Illiberalism* (London: Routledge, 2022).

is a disparate political movement that builds on repertoires that are both secular and religious, while religion is no longer constitutive of political notions of the sacred, and even contests what the secular and the sacred mean.[29] In this sense, Christianism may be transliminal: as existing on the edge of the secular as well as of religion, thus defying one of the main binaries of European modernity.[30] What unites all these disparate fields is not only that Christianity serves in all of them as an effective political tool, but, essentially, that the roles Christianity seems to adopt in politics are all (allegedly) defensive, related to the perceived need for a return to (cultural) Christianity as bulwark against other religious traditions, migrants, societal decadence, or as a protection against civilizational collapse.

This supposedly defensive role is complemented by the return of the apocalyptic: the future, be it in the liberal guise or otherwise, offers nothing but destruction and ultimately the end of civilization.[31] This is expressed in the notion of the eschatological 'katechon', or the 'restrainer', which the Mandate of the xxv World Russian People's Council ascribes to Russia:

> From a spiritual and moral point of view, the special military operation is a Holy War, in which Russia and its people, defending the unified spiritual space of the Holy Rus', fulfils the mission of the "Holder", protecting the world from the onslaught of globalism and the victory of the West that has fallen into Satanism.

Apocalyptic repertoires also appear in far-right narratives, which on the one hand sacralise the past (i.e. a 'lost golden age') and on the other hand ascribe a cosmic clash of good and evil to the present, while asserting themselves as those who curb the 'evil' forces.[32] The strongly felt presence of millenniarist tendencies among some nativists can paradoxically draw strength not only

---

29   Markus Balkenhol, Ernst van den Hemel, and Irene Stengs, *The Secular Sacred: Emotions of Belonging and the Perils of Nation and Religion* (Cham: Palgrave Macmillan, 2020); Edith Clowes, *Russia on the Edge: Imagined Geographies and Post-Soviet Identity* (Ithaca, NY: Cornell University Press, 2011).

30   Marietta van der Tol and Philip Gorski, "Secularisation as the fragmentation of the sacred and of sacred space", *Religion, State, Society* 50, no. 5 (2022), 495–512.

31   Chip Berlet, "Christian identity: the apocalyptic style, political religion, palingenesis and neo-fascism", in *Fascism, totalitarianism and political religion*, ed. Roger Griffin (Abingdon: Routledge, 2013), 175–212.

32   Marietta van der Tol and Matthew Rowley, "A posture of protest? The search for Christian identity in a post-secular society: between secularised eschatology and a sacralisation of history", *International Journal of Religion* 2 (2021): 101–113.

from the conservative critique of liberalism, but also from the accelerating environmental problems and the politicised discourses about predictions of climatic collapse.[33] The emergence of Christianist narratives thus cannot be discarded as merely a response to the erosion of the global liberal order or as a purely political phenomenon, as it reveals a deeper anxiety about the most fundamental aspects of human civilization.

References to (cultural) Christianity have contributed to (geo)political forms of sacralisation, causing the category of religion to re-emerge as one of the central unresolved issues of post-secular European politics. The re-appropriation of Christianity has also offered space for the contestation of secular politics by Christian and religious actors, some of whom regard Christianist movements as possible allies or vehicles to gain greater political influence. Perhaps under the influence of secularisation, individualisation, and globalisation, Western politics has shown itself to be relatively blind to the cultural, political, and sometimes even religious significance of Christianity. This has become especially apparent in the shocked cluelessness with which European political leaders observe the populist re-appropriation of the religious language, the story of illiberal Christian democracy in Hungary, the election of President Trump in 2016 and 2024, and the official support of the Russian Orthodox Church's hierarchy for the Russian war against Ukraine.[34]

In all of this, the bulwarks of present-day anti-liberalism, such as the notions of Holy Rus' or the Russian World, nationalist and populist movements in Europe, as well as the Make America Great Again-campaign feature major political imaginaries: they assert a timeless connection between certain territories, certain people, and cultural or civilizational exceptionalism.[35] All of these build on a connection of these political imaginaries with (selected aspects) of religious tradition. However, what we are witnessing is not a new re-assertion of an old political identity or a simple re-emergence of the alliance between the throne and the altar. Instead, we can see two parallel, interrelated developments. One is the return of territoriality to politics and even the contestation of borders, the other is the sacralization of such (re-)territorialized

---

33 Daniel Nilsson DeHanas, "The spirit of populism: sacred, charismatic, redemptive, and apocalyptic dimensions," *Democratization* (2023): 1–21.

34 For this, see one of the most recent documents signed by Patriarch Kirill, "The Present and the Future of the Russian World", the Moscow Patriarchate, 27 March 2024, http://www.patriarchia.ru/db/text/6116189.html?fbclid=IwAR0aH7kPV_rPt8LUz8R0G09uh v7RNSVnLAunximFEHoZloT_s2DUsoEzbmM_aem_AZQrY1KLTqPWOjDuGc7SMA4Aw JrQuY2wIX5vg-rh_YLbGry9KFURftUiw_BoKRcCcDdQr8sE-lVWaUo-DjO0bW_u.

35 Niklas Bernsan and Barbara Törnquist-Plewa, *Cultural and Political Imaginaries in Putin's Russia* (Leiden: Brill 2019).

politics and the particular communities tied to it.[36] Against the narratives of post-national politics and post-territorial political networks, it may seemingly attractively (and successfully) invoke the community defined by the political space it occupies, by its solidity, but also by the spatially defined others, the 'enemies' one must defend oneself from.

This volume explores Christianism as a complex phenomenon which can be observed, in its many formations, across the European continent and beyond. It sheds light on the various ways in which religious (neo-)traditionalism builds alliances with illiberal forces. The following studies show that there are multiple elements that all these attempts share – the deep distrust towards the liberal hegemony, the stress on the local against the global, and the central role of 'othering', i.e. of seeing 'our' political community as increasingly stressed by a hostile *alter*. The similarities are not accidental – all these attempts react to the same processes of secularization as well as to the weakening of the liberal hegemony. Increasingly, there is evidence of intentional cooperation among these like-minded movements with growing transnational circulation of ideas, emulation of political strategies, but also financial ties.

Chapters in this volume enter the space of public and political theology from several disciplines: international relations, political theory, anthropology, history, and theology. This interdisciplinary approach was developed over a series of conferences organised under the umbrella of the Protestant Political Thought project at the University of Oxford from 2022–2024. This project has provided a platform for reflection on the rise of populism in Europe and its connections to American and Russian politics. The chapters in this volume also enter the space of public and political theology from several religious angles, including Protestantism, Roman Catholicism and Orthodoxy. This interdenominational perspective was shaped by the reflections of Cyril Hovorun, who lectured on the ideology of the Russian World and Putinism at Oxford's University Church, just weeks after the full-scale invasion had begun.[37] While the Statement of Solidarity (Appendix 2) called attention to the many features that nationalism, populism, and the notion of the Russian World share, it was obvious that a more fundamental intellectual critique of the Russian World required sustained scholarly work – which this volume seeks to offer.

---

36 Chris Park, *Sacred Worlds: An Introduction to Geography and Religion* (London: Routledge 1994).
37 Cyril Hovorun, "Orthodoxy political theology between national identity and empire" (conference keynote lecture, Christian identity in national, transnational, and local space, University of Oxford, 4–5 April 2022), accessed 6 June 2024, https://www.youtube.com/watch?v=Fk2GL8YrCoA.

These concerns are reflected in the order of the chapters. The volume opens with several theoretical chapters on the relationship between the sacred and political imaginaries, followed by chapters that engage with the Russian World, a variety of European populism(s), or both. They represent as it were a continuum of religious engagement with illiberal politics: from the endorsement of a brutal war to illiberal majorities, populists in comfortable coalitions, and to the more awkward relationships between Christian democracy and populism in Denmark, Germany, and the Netherlands. Whereas the salience of illiberal politics has long been ascribed to Central and Eastern Europe, the super election year of 2024 has yielded a far-right victory in the USA, and shows that the influence of transnational illiberalism is likely to grow across these spaces. If one should believe the aspirations of CPAC and other conferences of National Conservatism, this growing influence must be taken seriously, as it may significantly undermine the structures of mutual protection that democracy and the rule of law offer.

The first chapter is Petr Kratochvíl's study "Populism and Religion: Why the Twain will Meet", which argues that there are deep intrinsic similarities between (a certain type of) religion and populism: They both share a similar political temporality, and they expound similar views of the sacred and of the natural. For Kratochvíl, the recent wave of populism can thus be seen as the main carrier of the politics of faith at the time of culturalised religion. Herein lies the real strength of populism – in its ability to express the popular dissatisfaction in a quasi-religious manner, thus evoking deep affection and loyalty, but also a strong feeling of existential anxiety and an urgent need to act.

If religion and populism are intertwined, so are religion and nationalism. The linkage between the national identity and religious belonging is the main theme of Zoran Grozdanov's chapter titled "When a Light Cloak Turns into a Pious Cage: Thinking National Identity with Karl Barth and John Paul II". In his fascinating analysis, Grozdanov shows that these two highly influential theologians offer strikingly different approaches to national identity. John Paul II, whose work must be understood in the context of Polish independence after the Soviet occupation, was quite appreciative of national identity as a theological category, a persistent and even natural part of God's plan with humankind. Karl Barth, on the other hand, whose work is deeply shaped by the legacy of the Nazi-era, had offered an incisive critique of most forms of Christian nationalism.

Anne Guillard continues with the exploration of the critiques of Christian nationalism in her chapter "Fratelli Tutti, or, The Battle Against Christian Nationalism". In her intriguing study, Guillard argues that the late Pope Francis offers a trenchant critique of Christian-inspired nationalism. In contrast with his two predecessors, Pope John Paul II and Pope Benedict XVI, he stresses the importance of biblically inspired fraternity and human dignity so as to overcome excessive othering. However, the author also warns that the Pope's approach is not without its risks, as it posits against the nationalist appropriation of Christianity another version of repoliticized religion, which comes to the fore in the deep rifts among conservative and progressive Catholics.

In "The Russian World, the Hungarian World, and Make America Great Again: Political Imaginaries and their Spaces", Marietta van der Tol explores the conceptual similarities and dissimilarities between political imaginaries and the spatial claims they sustain in the context Russia, Hungary, and in the United States. This chapter explains how these political imaginaries engage in the sacralisation of spatial politics, even if in a hybrid secular-sacred way. Extracts from speeches by Vladimir Putin and Patriarch Kirill, Viktor Orbán, Capitol insurrectionists and Donald Trump show how their political imaginations contest and coexist with reality. This contemporaneity of the spatially and temporally irreconcilable poses a profound challenge to constitutional democracies.

The book then delves deeper into the fabric of the 'Russian World' and its relationship with adjacent concepts, such as Holy Rus' and civilisational exceptionalism.[38] In the chapter "Russian World, Holy Russia: Towards a New Ideology", Veronica Cibotaru illuminates the theological-political correlation of the ideological discourse of the Russian Orthodox Church and the Russian state, highlighting their shared anti-Western discourse and their interest in common spiritual and religious heritage. This chapter argues that the notion of 'Holy Rus' bears a specific mythical, ahistorical reading of the history of contemporary nations, bolstering a spiritual justification of the war in Ukraine. Whereas technically distinct from the notion of the Russian World, the notion of Holy Rus' functions as an important bridge frame between civilisationist and intra-Orthodox discourses.

In the chapter "Putinism and Alexander Solzhenitsyn's Religious Motifs", Dmytro Bintsarovskyi expounds on the anti-imperialistic orientation of the famous Russian novelist and dissident Solzhenitsyn (1918–2008), even as Putin has borrowed from his religious motifs. While Solzhenitsyn largely shared the anti-Western and conservative sentiments prevalent in Russia today, his appeals to religion differed from the prevailing patterns. To demonstrate the affinity between Putinism and Solzhenitsyn's general worldview, the chapter discusses two recent instances when Putin referred to Solzhenitsyn, implicitly

---

38 John Burgess, *Holy Rus: The Rebirth of Orthodoxy in the New Russia* (New Haven, CT: Yale University Press 2017); Papanikolaou, *The Mystical as Political*.

or explicitly, for vindicating his aggression against Ukraine and his cultural crusade against the West. The chapter then demonstrates that despite this affinity, Solzhenitsyn did not use religion to promote aggressive policies but rather to challenge Russia's expansionism, to develop a civic spirit in Russian society, and to bring his compatriots to critical self-reflection.

In "From St Paul and Carl Schmitt to Alexander Dugin: The Katechon as a Political Category in Empire Building", Dustin Byrd illuminates the notion of the 'katechon', or the restrainer, in Alexander Dugin's extremist take on Putin's geopolitical and neo-imperialist aspirations. Dugin's work is profoundly apocalyptic in that it frames the war, or 'special military operation', as an eschatological collision between good and evil, Christ and Satan, thus asserting the war on Ukraine as spiritually and existentially necessary for the future of Russia. The category of the 'katechon' derives from St. Paul's Second Epistle to the Thessalonians, but also shaped the work of Nazi jurist Carl Schmitt, as explored in this chapter. Byrd argues that Dugin's notion of the restrainer sanctions the possibility of a 'total war' (*Totaler Krieg*) and transforms eschatological hope to an ideology of conquest in the name of the Russian World.

Having studied the notions of the Russian World and Holy Russia, the volume then turns to the phenomenon of Christianism in Europe, where religion too, has shaped nationalism-based exceptionalism. In the chapter "Between Religious Nationalism and Universal Familism: Anti-Gender Movement Values in Croatia and Serbia", Ivan Tranfić compares the salience of the anti-gender bridge frame in anti-gender movements in Serbia and Croatia. Whereas Serbian anti-gender movements exist in familiar nationalist frameworks owing to its preoccupation with territoriality, sovereignty, and reproduction of the nation, equivalent Catholic-inspired movements in Croatia are less inclined towards ethnonationalism and front a universal form of illiberalism and antipluralism. As such, they appear as two kinds of radical-right mobilisation against 'gender ideology': one that fronts the political over the theological, and one that fronts the theological over the political. For this reason, the chapter argues that scholarship must pay attention to doctrine and political theology as, depending on context, constitutive of anti-gender activism.

In "The Orthodox Church and the Greek Solution Party", Konstantinos Papastathis and Anastasia Litina turn to the use of religion by the populist and pro-Russian Greek Solution Party. Similarly to other countries in the region, such as Serbia, there is a strong nexus between ethnicity and religion, with religion functioning as a marker of belonging and non-belonging, here vis-à-vis Islam and migration. The authors convincingly show that a linkage between religiosity and some of the basic tenets of the Greek Solution party exists, such as the correlation between religiosity and Islamophobia. However, they also argue that the competition among multiple radical right parties and increased volatility of the party spectrum make predictions about voter alignment with a particular party more difficult.

The chapter "Belonging Without Attending? National Identity and Contemporary Religious Patterns in Serbia" by Marko Veković discusses the importance of the Serbian Orthodox Church to populism in Serbia, as Serbs overwhelmingly self-identify as Serbian Orthodox, even as churches remain mostly empty for the Sunday liturgy. Veković sheds light on the tension between the ethnonationalist priorities of the church hierarchy and their involvement in anti-liberal, anti-Western politics on the one hand, and the struggles of local priests on the other hand. His chapter shows that local priests recognise this discrepancy and that they are more worried about intergenerational irreligiosity owing to the Communist past, which has broken the transmission of tradition from one generation on the other.

In "The Danish People's Party and the Heritage of Tidehverv: A National Example of a European Tendency", Erik Sporon Fiedler discusses the story of the nationalist Danish People's Party in what might be considered the laboratory for the use of religious repertoires in European populist movements, especially in Poland, Hungary, and Sweden. Fiedler traces the religious nationalism of the new leader Morten Messerschmidt back to the legacy of the antimodernist Tidehverv movement since the 1920s. Fiedler explores how the Tidehverv movement developed from a countercultural into a culture-war minded movement, eventually transforming into a political movement through the affiliation of several Tidehverv leaders with the right-wing populist party the Danish People's Party (*Dansk Folkeparti*), which shaped the ideological position of the Danish People's Party significantly.

In "Christianity, Religion, and Christian Democracy", Katharina Kunter and Leon van den Broeke argue that the decline of Christian Democracy in Germany and the Netherlands is not simply a matter of secularisation. They suggest that the decreasing visibility of Christianity in these parties is inherent to the co-existence of Christian and non-Christian influences within Christian Democracy. However, this relative inclusivity has rendered the meaning of 'Christian' in Christian Democracy more elusive, while Christians and Christianity may also be co-opted by other parties. This co-optation is most obvious in right-wing parties, whose growth has rendered Christian Democracies to the margins of the political Centre. At the same time, should right-wing parties fail to form stable governments, perhaps Christian Democracy might have a fresh opportunity to re-articulate its values as a Centrist or Centre-Right political force.

In the following chapter, "The European Union as a Space of (In)Securities: Analysing the Political Reasoning of Lithuanian Catholics", Rosita

Garškaitė-Antonowicz focuses on contradictions in the views of Lithuanian Catholics. What makes the chapter especially relevant is Garškaitė-Antonowicz's focus on the most devout segment of voters and not the 'cultural' Catholics who are typically studied in this context. The author shows that the devout Catholics' views cannot be simply reduced to a one-sided narrative about a political alliance between the far right and Catholicism. Instead, Lithuanian Catholics take diverse positions to navigate the complexities of seeing the EU both as an area of existential security and ontological insecurity.

The two final chapters of the volume are dedicated to different aspects of Anglicanism. Jenny Leith, in her fascinating study entitled "Theopolitical Visions of National Belonging: Resisting the Totalising Tendencies of Inclusion" draws on the seminal study of 'the boundaries of Home' by Susannah Ticciati. Based on her reading, the author identifies two failed attempts at national community building in England, one described as 'expanding container' and the other as 'despatialised values'. However, the analysis does not stop there as Leith offers a novel perspective on how belonging can be understood differently, as a process of 'disruptive joining'.

This analysis is mirrored in the last chapter, "The Contested Meanings of the Anglican Parish in Multireligious England", in which Lauren Morry engages the experience of Anglican priests whose parishes are predominantly non-Christian. Morry focuses on the tension between nationally produced reports and strategies and the diverse approaches in concrete Anglican parishes. Here, she highlights the possibility for multiple layers of meaning making on the level of the parish, which may or may not derive from Anglican ecclesiology. By doing this, the chapter also highlights the importance of studying local practices and local spatio-political imaginaries as a welcome corrective to an excessive focus on central institutions and their pronouncements.

Thus, this volume shows two contrasting movements: on the one hand a Christianity that is predominantly cultural and emboldens populist and imperialist politics, and on the other hand, a Christianity that becomes less and less expressed in traditional measures of religiosity. These contrasting movements are both expressions of secularisation and simultaneously a defensive reaction to it, giving rise to complex amalgamations of the secular-sacred, and taking shape within their immediate political context. Taken together, the chapters in this volume show that interdisciplinary reflection on public and political theology is crucial to a better understanding of the conflicted role of religion in politics in Russia, across Europe, and the USA. We hope that this deeper understanding of the confluences of the sacred and the secular across varieties of Christianism will enable both academics and religious traditions to confront the ensuing challenges for democracy in contemporary politics and society.

Bibliography

Abrahamsen, R., and M. C. Williams. (2023). "Transnational Nationalists: Building a Global Radical Right". *Political Insight* 14, no. 3: 28–31.

Balkenhol, M., E. van den Hemel, and I. Stengs. (2020). *The Secular Sacred: Emotions of Belonging and the Perils of Nation and Religion*. Cham: Palgrave Macmillan.

Berlet, C. (2013). "Christian identity: the apocalyptic style, political religion, palingenesis and neo-fascism". In: R. Griffin (ed.). *Fascism, totalitarianism and political religion*. Abingdon: Routledge. Pp. 175–212.

Bernsand, N., and B. Törnquist-Plewa. (2019). *Cultural and Political Imaginaries in Putin's Russia*. Leiden: Brill.

Bremer, T. (2016). "Diffuses Konzept: Die Russische Orthodoxe Kirche und die 'Russische Welt'". *Osteuropa* 66, no. 3: 3–18.

Brooks, S., and William W. (2008). *World out of Balance: International Relations and the Challenge of American Primacy*. Princeton: Princeton University Press.

Brubaker, R. (2017). "Between Nationalism and Civilisationalism: The European populist movement in comparative perspective". *Ethnic and Racial Studies* 40, no. 8: 1191–1226.

Burgess, J. (2017). *Holy Rus: The Rebirth of Orthodoxy in the New Russia*. New Haven CT: Yale University Press.

Clowes, E. (2011). *Russia on the Edge: Imagined Geographies and Post-Soviet Identity*, Ithaca NY: Cornell University Press.

Cremer, T. (2022). "Defenders of the Faith? How shifting social cleavages and the rise of identity politics are reshaping right-wing populists' attitudes towards religion in the West". *Religion, State and Society* 50, no. 5: 532–552.

Elsner, R. (2022). "Ideological Pillow and Strategic Partner: The Russian Orthodox Church and the War". *Russian Analytical Digest*, no. 286: 2–4.

Guerra, N. (2024). "The Russian-Ukrainian war has shattered the European far right. The opposing influences of Steve Bannon and Aleksandr Dugin". *European Politics and Society* 25, no. 2: 421–439.

Gushee, D. (2023). *Defending Democracy from its Christian Enemies*. Grand Rapids, MI: Eerdmans.

Heathershaw, J. (2024). *Security after Christendom: Global Politics and Political Theology for Apocalyptic Times*. Eugene OR: Wipf and Stock.

Hovorun, C. (2024). "Orthodox political theology between national identity and empire". Christian identity in national, transnational and local space. Conference keynote lecture, University of Oxford, 4–5 April 2024.

Ikenberry, J. (2011). *Liberal Leviathan: The Origins, Crisis and Transformation of the American World Order*. Princeton: Princeton University Press.

Koch, T. (2024). "Family ties and ethnic lines: ethnopluralism in the Far Right's mobilization in Europe". *Ethnic and Racial Studies* 47, no. 9: 1791–1811.

Lo Mascolo, G., ed. (2023). *The Christian Right in Europe: Movements, Networks, and Denominations*. New York: Transcript.

Mearsheimer, J. (2019). "Bound to fail: the rise and fall of the liberal international order". *International Security* 43, no. 4: 7–50.

Nilsson DeHanas, D. (2023). "The spirit of populism: sacred, charismatic, redemptive, and apocalyptic dimensions". *Democratization*: 1–21.

Papanikolaou, A. (2012). *The Mystical as Political: Democracy and Non-Radical Orthodoxy*. Notre Dame IN: University of Notre Dame Press.

Park, C. (1994). *Sacred Worlds: An Introduction to Geography and Religion*. London: Routledge.

Sajó, A., R. Uitz, and S. Holmes. (2022). *The Routledge Handbook of Illiberalism*. London: Routledge.

Stoeckl, K., and D. Uzlaner. (2022). *The Moralist International: Russia in the Global Culture Wars*. New York: Fordham University Press.

Strømmen, H., and U. Schmiedel. (2020). *The Claim to Christianity: Responding to the Far Right*. London: SCM Press.

Suslov, M. (2014). "Holy Rus: The Geopolitical Imagination in the Contemporary Russian Orthodox Church". *Russian Politics & Law* 52, no. 3: 67–86.

Suslov, M. (2018). "Russian World Concept: Post-Soviet Geopolitical Ideology and the Logic of Spheres of Influence". *Geopolitics* 23, no. 2: 330–353.

Truss, L. (2024). *Ten Years to Save the West: Lessons from the Only Conservative in the Room*. Hull: Biteback Publishing.

Van der Tol, M.D.C., and M. Rowley. (2021). "A posture of protest? The search for Christian identity in a post-secular society: between secularised eschatology and a sacralisation of history". *International Journal of Religion* 2: 101–113.

Van der Tol, M.D.C., and Philip Gorski. (2022). "Secularisation as the fragmentation of the sacred and of sacred space". *Religion, State and Society* 50, no. 5: 495–512.

Van Herpen, M. (2018). "The Rise of Kremlin-Friendly Populism in the Netherlands". *Cicero Foundation Great Debate Paper* 18/04. Accessed 6 June 2024. https://www.cicerofoundation.org/wp-content/uploads/Van_Herpen_Kremlin-Friendly_Populism_Netherlands.pdf.

CHAPTER 2

Populism and Religion: Why the Twain Will Always Meet

Petr Kratochvíl

1 Introduction

There can be no doubt that liberal democracy is going through a difficult time.[1] In more than half of the world's liberal democracies, the quality of democracy has been declining for six consecutive years.[2] The popular (dis)satisfaction with democracy mirrors findings about the decrease in democratic performance: Even in some of the well-established democracies, such as the United States, the legitimacy of key political institutions has also decreased to the lowest figures in recent history.[3] Academics concur: One scholarly study after another argues that liberal democracy is under attack.[4] Political entrepreneurs capitalize on the sentiment and those who have built their careers on assaulting liberal democracy are experiencing impressive successes; the critical voices do not solely come from the populist fringe anymore. As a result, the doubts about liberal democracy cannot be heard in non-democratic countries only,

---

1   This chapter is the result of Metropolitan University Prague research project no. 100-3 "International Relations and Territorial Studies" (2023) based on a grant from the Institutional Fund for the Long-term Strategic Development of Research Organizations.
2   "The Global State of Democracy 2023", Global State of Democracy Initiative, International IDEA, published 2 November 2023, https://www.idea.int/publications/catalogue/global-state-democracy-2023-new-checks-and-balances.
3   Domenico Montanaro, "There's a toxic brew of mistrust toward U.S. institutions. It's got real consequences," NPR, 3 March 2023, https://www.npr.org/2023/05/03/1173382045/americans-arent-thrilled-with-the-government-the-supreme-court-is-just-one-examp.
4   Clayton Crockett, *Radical Political Theology: Religion and Politics after Liberalism* (New York: Columbia University Press, 2013); Carl A. Raschke, *Force of God: Political Theology and the Crisis of Liberal Democracy* (New York: Columbia University Press, 2015); Ziya Öniş, "The Age of Anxiety: The Crisis of Liberal Democracy in a Post-Hegemonic Global Order", *The International Spectator* 52, no.3 (2017): 18–35; Manuel Castells, *Rupture: The Crisis of Liberal Democracy*, trans. Rosie Marteau (Cambridge: Polity Press, 2019); Jacques Rupnik, "Explaining Eastern Europe: The Crisis of Liberalism", *Journal of Democracy* 29, no. 3 (2018): 24–38; David Owen, "A Global Crisis of Liberal Democracy? On Autocratic Democracy, Populism and Post-Truth Politics", *Journal of Social and Political Philosophy* 1, no. 1 (2022): 30–46.

© PETR KRATOCHVÍL, 2025 | DOI:10.1163/9789004731899_003
This is an open access chapter distributed under the terms of the CC BY-NC 4.0 license.

but this criticism is now commonplace in democratic countries themselves: not only the Chinese President Xi and the Russian President Putin are the leading critics in this respect, but also influential politicians in the United States, Brazil, India, and elsewhere. As a result, the crisis of liberal democracy is not only a domestic problem anymore and one might even argue that it has never been *primarily* a domestic problem: liberalism is a core element of the hegemony on which the global order is built,[5] and which is now under assault as well.[6] The crisis of liberalism thus has the potential to not only transform the way we think about our societies, but also global politics.[7]

There are weighty reasons underpinning the validity of the anti-liberal critique related either to the acceleration of the climate crisis or to the growing global inequalities both within and across countries; and also to the inability or unwillingness of liberal democracies to address these challenges in an effective manner. But there are two more fundamental, intrinsic reasons why the critique is so appealing intellectually and so effective politically, and why it has become the core element of the new wave of populist politics. First, these new populists succeeded in linking output legitimacy issues with the perennial internal tension in liberal democracy itself: the tension between the liberal and the democratic dimension thereof. As a consequence, the current attack on liberal democracy primarily aims at uncoupling democratic policymaking from its liberal companion. In other words, it argues that we need to reassert the rights of the community as a whole and push through majoritarian decisions, to which the liberal insistence on the rights of minorities is a major obstacle. This focus on the community as a whole, on the people, typically defined in a civilisational or a nativist way, is the hallmark of the new populist movements which have been mushrooming all across the planet in recent decades.

Second, populism is so appealing these days because it can boast a strong *political theology* where liberalism's offer is scant and its political theology, if any, often implicit.[8] Against the more individualistic narrative of the liberals, populism offers the affectively alluring offer of redemption and of belonging

---

5 By liberalism, I generally understand the large group of theories that are concerned with the limits to the scope of state power and the related defence of individual and collective rights of citizens (cf. the definition in William A. Galston, "Why the new liberalism isn't all that new, and why the old liberalism isn't what we thought it was", *Social Philosophy and Policy* 24, no. 1 (2007): 289–305).
6 Amitav Acharya, "After Liberal Hegemony: The Advent of a Multiplex World Order", *Ethics & International Affairs* 31, no. 3 (2017): 271–85.
7 Alexander Cooley and Daniel Nexon, *Exit from Hegemony: The Unravelling of the American Global Order* (New York: Oxford University Press, 2020).
8 But see, for instance, Nicholas Michelsen, "Liberalism, Political Theology and Suicide Bombing", *Millennium* 42, no. 1 (2013): 198–223.

to a sacralised community. Populism, old and new, has always had a strong affinity to religion. By this affinity I do not mean the superficial observation that religion serves as a tool for some populists who aim at instrumentalising it to reach a specific segment of the electorate, as important as that sometimes is. I argue that even those types of populism that do not forge explicit alliances with religious actors share a structural similarity to religion: populism has always been a kind of *politics of faith*, to use the famous phrase of Michael Oakeshott.[9] The populist resurgence at a time when liberalism is undergoing a crisis of credibility is not accidental; it is this deep structural similarity to religion that makes populism so attractive.

The similarity between populism and a certain type of religious tradition deserves much more sustained attention. This is so because by seeing the resurgence of religion in (global) politics and the rise of populism as two largely independent phenomena we risk underestimating the challenge which liberal democracy is currently facing. We need to focus on the shared root causes of these trends as they are essential for understanding why a certain political temporality is suddenly becoming so appealing, why the 'natural' is making a comeback to the political lexicon, but also what transformations of our political milieu we should expect as a result of these changes.

The aim of my study is thus to shed light on the hidden depths of the alliance between populists and religious conservatives that go beyond the simple instrumentalization of religion for political purposes. To achieve this end, I will proceed in three steps. First, I will explain why I believe that populists see liberalism as their archenemy, and not democracy as such. This will allow me, in the second step, to elucidate the structural affinity between the populist and the religious versions of anti-liberalism, elaborating on populist *politics of faith* and the three distinct expressions of the resemblance between this *politics of faith* and some religious traditions. I will conclude with a discussion about the future of liberalism, stressing the importance of it developing its own political theology.

This intrinsic relationship between populism and a certain type of religious thought is also the reason why this study appears in a book dedicated to Christianism. Christianist and other religious-nativist movements indeed blur the boundary between the sacred and the secular, one of the most pervasive dichotomies in modern Western political thought. But they do this so successfully and so effortlessly exactly because the dichotomy was more of a theoretical construct than lived experience in Western societies. At a time when

---

9 Michael Oakeshott, *The Politics of Faith and the Politics of Scepticism*, ed. Timothy Fuller (New Haven, CT: Yale University Press, 1996).

the liberal guardians of secularism are weakening, the hidden linkage between religion and the re-emerging populism can come forth with full force and the implicit connection between the two can be again publicly declared. Needless to say, this move cannot be but seen as a fundamental challenge to the way liberals understand the relationship between politics and religion. As such, it deserves our utmost attention.

2   The Populist Attack on Liberalism

It is liberal democracy's main strength as well as its key weakness that it accommodates several competing principles. There are multiple ways in which these key principles can be described. Galston talks about "the republican principle, democracy, constitutionalism, and liberalism",[10] but out of these principles the two least readily reconcilable are the liberal and the democratic one. Indeed, it can be even argued that liberal democracy is based on the contradiction between democracy and liberalism.[11] While democracy is based on the majoritarian rule, liberalism is concerned with the protection of the individual and minorities. A functioning liberal democracy then seeks to find the right balance between the will of the majority and the protection of the rights of minorities.

The conundrum of how to enforce democratic, majoritarian decisions while maintaining a societal pluralism can be answered in multiple ways. Rawlsian liberalism, to apply one of the most influential views, would argue that citizens adhere to various moral or religious doctrines, but they also realize that their doctrines should not be simply imposed on those members of the society who do not profess the same. As a result, citizens will try to establish such rules which can in principle be acceptable to all reasonable members of the society, irrespective of their own individually held doctrines. According to John Rawls, the shared principles on which such a political conception can be erected are equality, freedom and fairness, the underlying principles of the society's public political culture.[12] Religious doctrines do not constitute the foundation of a

---

10   William A. Galston, "The Populist Challenge to Liberal Democracy", *Journal of Democracy* 29, no. 2 (2018): 9.
11   As famously formulated, for instance, by C. Mudde and C. R. Kaltwasser, "Exclusionary vs. Inclusionary Populism: Comparing Contemporary Europe and Latin America", *Government and Opposition* 48, no. 2 (2013): 147–74; for the older formulation, see Michael Freeden, *Ideologies and Political Theory: A Conceptual Approach* (Oxford: Clarendon, 1996).
12   John Rawls, *Political Liberalism* (New York: Columbia University Press, 1996).

public political culture, but they can, subsequently, endorse the idea of justice that arises from this culture. Rawls' notion of overlapping consensus serves this exact function: diverse comprehensive doctrines can support the idea, let us say, of equality of citizens from within themselves. While originally independent of any particular doctrine, the idea's legitimacy is strengthened due to its compatibility with these diverse doctrines. In this sense, a comprehensive doctrine (for example, a Christian one) is never seen as a foundation of the liberal political order but plays only the secondary role of affirming the order as reasonable.

The liberal argument of this type has long been criticised by both conservative and populist thinkers (compare the analysis of J. Skorupski for the former, and Paul Blokker, for the latter),[13] but the recent emergence of the new populism renders this disagreement more politically acute than ever.[14] There are two basic directions in which the proponents of this position radically disagree with the liberal position. Firstly, they contest the argument that the foundations of a public political culture can be defined without a recourse to a religious tradition. Instead of using a religious argument in favour of a pre-existing conception of justice, they argue that their conception of justice originates in a religious tradition (such as Christianity). That is why traditional values have made such a forceful comeback in the public sphere; they constitute an attempt at reversing the Rawlsian argument: instead of having a conception of justice that precedes various religious doctrines, such a view builds its conception of justice on a specific interpretation of a religious tradition, claiming that the overlapping consensus still exists as other moral or religious doctrines can reasonably affirm the validity of the religion-derived conception of justice. Secondly, and relatedly, the populist critics of liberalism, such as the Hungarian Prime Minister Viktor Orbán, argue that the liberal conception of justice can no longer be endorsed by the Christian (or another religion's) moral doctrine. Instead of endorsing the liberal conception of justice, (conservative) religious citizens do not find the current conception of justice reasonable and the overlapping consensus does not emerge.

Neither argument is novel, but what makes the anti-liberal critique more relevant today is the fact that the argument about a democracy without liberalism

---

13   J. Skorupski, "The Conservative Critique of Liberalism", in *The Cambridge Companion to Liberalism*, ed. S. Wall (Cambridge: Cambridge University Press, 2015), 401–22; Paul Blokker, "Populism and illiberalism", in *Routledge Handbook of Illiberalism*, eds. András Sajó, Renáta Uitz, and Stephen Holmes (New York: Routledge, 2021), 261–79.

14   Ivan Krastev, "The populist moment", *Критика и хуманизъм* 23_EN (2007), 103–8; Marco Revelli, *The New Populism: Democracy Stares into the Abyss* (London: Verso, 2019).

has moved from academia to politics. In a sense, the argument is plausible. It is easy to conceive of a democracy "unmodified by any adjectives"[15] which would still retain its key feature, namely the decision-making process based on voting and the popular will. Majoritarian politics, perhaps detrimental to the interests of minorities, can still be essentially democratic. While this anti-liberal tendency has always been present in populist movements, the most recent wave of populism, which emerged in the last two decades, elevated anti-liberalism to one of its core principles. The reasons for this are again linked to the contraposition of the sacred in the new populism against liberalism, or, put simply, to the re-enchantment of politics.[16] For the new populists, liberalism is thus not simply an inconvenient obstacle in enacting the popular will, but it becomes an archenemy which obstinately refuses this re-enchantment.

Until the 1990s, European populism remained a marginal phenomenon, and it only became a substantial political force following the start of the Great Recession in 2008.[17] While European populists were reacting to the growing socio-economic inequalities and the strict austerity programmes introduced by governments across the EU, the concrete expressions of populist protest were rather diverse, building on both the Left critique of global capitalism and the Right critique of structural budget imbalances and state regulation. Hence, for some time, the only common denominator for the many varieties of European populism was the discursive construction of 'the people' by populists.[18] This is the argument Cas Mudde famously made when claiming that populism is a "thin-centered" ideology.[19] Populism is thus not a full-fledged ideology akin to socialism or liberalism; the only relevant substantive element of populism is its insistence on the absolute distinction between two clearly separated groups: the people and the elite. Populist leaders, no matter how rich they are or how elitist their background is, claim to always stand with the people and argue that the elites are corrupt. As no compromise between the virtuous people and the immoral elites is possible, the only solution is to replace these elites with leaders who will listen to the *volonté générale*, which will allow the community to finally become fully self-ruling, fully democratic.

This focus on the homogeneous people leads directly to the stress on the majoritarian decision and the suppression of minority views. In general,

---

15 Galston, "The Populist Challenge", 9.
16 J.P. Zúquete, "Populism and Religion", in *The Oxford Handbook of Populism*, eds. Cristóbal Rovira Kaltwasser et al. (Oxford: Oxford University Press, 2017), 445–66.
17 Abdul Noury and Gerard Roland, "Identity Politics and Populism in Europe", *Annual Review of Political Science* 23, no. 1 (2020): 421–39.
18 Ernesto Laclau, *On Populist Reason* (London: Verso, 2005).
19 Mudde and Kaltwasser, "Exclusionary vs. Inclusionary Populism".

populism exhibits the tendency to see the will of the people as consensual, as the result of the introduction of *common sense* into politics.[20] Hence, minority opinions are not accepted as just different, yet still reasonable positions, but as unnatural deviations. The dissenters are not innocent, as they typically serve the elites, thus betraying the people from which they arose. It is only logical to conclude that "populism is a threat not to democracy per se but rather to the dominant liberal variant of democracy".[21] Multiple influential studies of populism arrive at the same conclusion: liberalism, not democracy, is the main target. The most famous is perhaps Fareed Zakaria's concept of 'illiberal democracy',[22] but other, not less pertinent studies follow suit. For instance, an influential study by Papas claims that liberalism is "the opposite of populism",[23] while arguing that "modern populism points directly to its two negative poles, that is political liberalism and nondemocratic autocracy".[24] Galston argues that populism may be hostile to constitutionalism, but that it "takes an even dimmer view of liberal protections for individuals and minority groups".[25] This reasoning is distinct from, but still related to the position advocated by the second group of scholars (such as Margaret Canovan, or Chantal Mouffe when speaking about 'Left Populism'),[26] who argue that populism is in fact not a threat to democracy at all, as it aims at redressing the democratic deficit within existing liberal democracies.

There are of course many additional pragmatic reasons for targeting liberalism as well. To directly attack democratic elections would require a conceptual severing of popular will from elections. While this can be achieved (for instance, via the argument that the leader knows what people want and that there is no need for this costly democratic procedure), such a move is difficult to make and even such regimes as President Putin's in Russia maintain the façade of a democratic constitutional arrangement.[27] Multi-party elections may be regularly held, while the elections are manipulated by the state-controlled

---

20 Cf. William Mazzarella, "The Anthropology of Populism: Beyond the Liberal Settlement", *Annual Review of Anthropology* 48 (2019): 45–60.
21 Galston, "The Populist Challenge", 11.
22 Fareed Zakaria, "The Rise of Illiberal Democracy", *Foreign Affairs* 76, no. 6 (1997): 22–43.
23 Takis S. Pappas, *Populism and Liberal Democracy: A Comparative and Theoretical Analysis* (Oxford: Oxford University Press, 2019), 41.
24 Pappas, *Populism and Liberal Democracy*, 35.
25 Galston, "The Populist Challenge", 11.
26 Margaret Canovan, "Trust the People! Populism and the Two Faces of Democracy", *Political Studies* 47 (1999): 2–16; Chantal Mouffe, "The populist moment", *Simbiótica. Revista Eletrônica* 6, no. 1 (2019): 6–11.
27 Alexei Trochev and Peter H. Solomon Jr., "Authoritarian constitutionalism in Putin's Russia: A pragmatic constitutional court in a dual state", *Communist and Post-Communist*

media, by unequal distribution of financial support, and by legislative limitations on the activities of the opposition party. Democracy can thus be turned into a "managed democracy",[28] while the formal primacy of the popular will is asserted. The liberal elements of democracy, on the other hand, are comparatively much easier to attack and empirical evidence supports this claim: The civil liberties such as freedom of speech, free access to the media, and freedom of association and of protest are typically the first targets in the attempts to transform liberal democracies into hybrid regimes. In particular, the supposedly excessive rights of minorities are often the first to be suppressed, both in terms of legislative changes and on the symbolical level.

3 Populism and Religion

Among the most distinctive features of the most recent wave of European (right wing) populism is its affinity with a certain type of Christianity.[29] Almost everywhere in Europe, more or less explicit alliances have been forged between populist parties and Christian conservatives. From Matteo Salvini waving a rosary at public rallies to the ultra-conservative Catholicism of the Law and Justice Party in Poland, from UKIP's Christian Manifesto to the National Front's mascot Joan of Arc—all these features indicate that European populists share a special proximity to (a type of) Christianity which is often reciprocated by Christian leaders and voters alike.[30] While this connection is not entirely surprising, the research on populism started to seriously catch up with this development only in the last ten years.[31] In spite of these academic contributions, much confusion about the exact relationship between populism and religion

---

Studies 51, no. 3 (2018): 201–14; cf. also Tom Casier, "Russia and the diffusion of political norms: The perfect rival?" *Democratization* 29, no. 3 (2022): 433–50.

28 Richard Sakwa, *Russia's Futures* (John Wiley & Sons, 2019).

29 I provided above a discussion about the definition of populism, so here is my working definition of religion: I define religion as *a religious tradition*, i.e., lived experience related to the ultimate aspects of existence that extends both in space and time. A religious tradition cannot be reduced to beliefs only; it transcends the simple ideas-matter dichotomy, involving norms, institutions, and practices, as well as material objects.

30 See the excellent study by Luca Ozzano, *The Masks of the Political God: Religion and Political Parties in Contemporary Democracies* (Rowman and Littlefield, 2020).

31 See, for instance Nadia Marzouki, Duncan McDonnell, and Olivier Roy, eds., *Saving the People: How Populists Hijack Religion* (Oxford University Press, 2016); R. Brubaker, "Between Nationalism and Civilizationism: The European Populist Moment in Comparative Perspective", *Ethnic and Racial Studies* 40, no. 8 (2017): 1191–226; Galston, "The Populist Challenge"; D.N. DeHanas and M. Shterin, "Religion and the Rise of Populism", *Religion,*

remains. Most importantly, two different phenomena, which are related to populism and religion, but in distinct ways, continue to be mixed up. The first is the political instrumentalization of religion by populists, and the second is the deeper linkage between populism and religion that often escapes unnoticed, hidden behind the more eye-catching alliance between populists and religious conservatives.

However, these two phenomena are fundamentally different. The fact that populists strike alliances with religious actors is not intrinsic to populism, as populists easily can be, and often have been, anti-clerical, and religious voters from different parts of Europe have different attitudes to populism.[32] The fact that these alliances emerge even in the most secularised countries of Europe should be revealing in this sense: populists simply attack mainstream politics and mainstream political elites, which happen to be liberal and secular. Many religious actors have always been uncomfortable with the outspokenly secular and liberal outlook of these elites and so they emerge as seemingly natural allies of populists. But this is misleading, as these kinds of alliances are primarily built upon the shared distrust towards the elites. In those countries where populists remain on the margin and religious actors work with the elites, populists tend to criticise the religious elites as well, as we know from the study of Latin American Left Populism.[33] To put my argument differently, the alliances of populists with religion depend on the context, and on the role the religious actors play in that context. Typically, if they are part of the secular ruling elites, the populists will likely be anti-religious; if the religious actors oppose the elites, populists will often cooperate with these religious actors.[34] Religious

---

State & Society 46, no. 3 (2018): 177–85; Nicholas Morieson, *Religion and the Populist Radical Right: Secular Christianism and Populism in Western Europe* (Vernon Press, 2021).

[32] Timothy Peace, "Religion and the ideology of populism", in *The Routledge Handbook of Religion, Politics and Ideology*, ed. Jeffrey Haynes (Abingdon: Routledge, 2021), 138–52; Kamil Marcinkiewicz and Ruth Dassonneville, "Do religious voters support populist radical right parties? Opposite effects in Western and East-Central Europe", *Party Politics* 28, no. 3 (2022): 444–56.

[33] Jeffrey Klaiber, "The Catholic Church and the Leftist Populist Regimes of Latin America: Venezuela, Ecuador, and Bolivia", in *Democracy, Culture, Catholicism: Voices from Four Continents*, eds. Michael J. Schuck and John Crowley-Buck (New York: Fordham University Press, 2015), 219–32.

[34] But there are exceptions: see, for instance, Zoran Grozdanov, "From Incarnation to Identity: The Theological Background of National-Populist Politics in the Western Balkans", in *The Spirit of Populism*, eds. Ulrich Schmiedel and Joshua Ralston (Leiden: Brill, 2021), 149–63.

actors can as easily provide legitimation to the populists as to the ruling class.[35] In other words, the alliances with religious conservatives are common, but not ubiquitous and certainly not an essential, defining feature of populism. There are, after all, clear examples of European populists, such as Syriza in Greece or Podemos in Spain, who have not forged such religious alliances.

However, there is a second connection between religion and populism. This connection is not a matter of political expedience; it is not accidental but rather based on a shared set of fundamental principles. Put simply, populism and religion are in some ways phenomena of a similar kind. Hence, the affinity between populism and religion is not based only on the above-mentioned instrumentalization of religion, but also on the mutual recognition of these shared principles. Three of these deep-seated similarities are politically particularly relevant and these are (a) the centrality of the sacred for politics, (b) the return of the natural, and (c) the shared political temporality. Before we proceed to the analysis of these three shared principles, I want to draw attention to what I believe are two serious limitations of the current research on populism and religion. First, the argument is often heard that "the connection between populism and religion must be viewed as part of a subtype of populism".[36] This, I believe, is an error derived from the conflation of the instrumentalization of religion by populists (which I discussed above) and the shared religious-populist principles.[37] Of course, some populists work with religious actors, but others do not. Some instrumentalise religion in their favour, others instrumentalise the fight against religion, and yet others do not care about religion at all. In this sense, religious populism is indeed a subtype of populism. However, I am convinced that even the most vocally anti-religious or leftist populists share a proximity to religion exactly because populism as a whole is akin to religion in some respects (see below). For this reason, it is deeply misleading to claim that only one specific type of populism is related to religion.

---

35 And I do not want to complicate this analysis by pointing to situations where the populists and the ruling class become one and the same, as is the case in Hungary.
36 Zúquete, "Populism and Religion".
37 To be fair, Zúquete is aware of this fallacy. In one of his excellent studies, he argues that "[n]o wonder that, and to a greater extent than in relation to other parties and movements, scholars on populism, or at least a fair number of them, have noted populism's affinity with religion not in terms of essence but in terms of resemblance" ("Populism and Religion", 451). While I would argue that the distinction between "essence" and "resemblance" is misleading, as there is an essential similarity between the two, Zúquete's claim points in the right direction.

While this first flaw conflates the instrumentalization of religion with the similarity of populism to religion, the second problem misidentifies this similarity. Very often, those analysing populism argue that populism is a surrogate religion.[38] This claim is readily understandable, for the scholars dealing with religion and politics through the concept of surrogate religion (and scholars with similar notions of implicit and civil religion) have recently become quite fashionable. The notion is based on the functionalist definition of religion, which claims that a surrogate religion can replace traditional religion as long as it can fulfil similar functions. Hence, nationalism can be seen as a surrogate religion in its veneration of the nation, but even sports, let us say, football, can gain some features of a religion, and so can other phenomena such as pop music. While I see the merit in this argument, I believe it is wrong to apply the notion, without further qualification, to populism. The key problem lies in the assumption about the relationship between the traditional and the surrogate religion. The whole argument is predicated upon the assumption that as a consequence of ongoing secularisation, traditional religion is losing its strength. Its functions are then transferred to other social phenomena which can partially fill in the void. Traditional religion and surrogate religion are thus, at least on the conceptual level, in a competitive relationship, and the weaker the former becomes, the more the latter grows. This is not true of the relationship between religion and populism though. In fact, I argue that because of the intrinsic similarities, the return of religion to the public sphere in the last twenty years and the rise of populism in the same period are not accidental. There is more to the alliance between the two than just political expediency; instead, our late modern societies are turning towards the exact principles which populism and religion share—hence their parallel rise.

4   The Religion-Politics Nexus: Three Shared Axioms

The proximity between religion and populism is not a result of the reservations populist and religious leaders have about liberal democracy. It is the other way around. Their critique of liberalism is the product of their shared axioms: the political importance of the sacred, the political importance of the natural and the past-oriented political temporality. Both religious actors and populists criticise liberalism because it is an antithesis to these three axioms, and both religion and populism desire the return of these three principles to

---

38   DeHanas and Shterin, "Religion and the Rise of Populism".

politics. However, the validity of my argument is predicated upon another axiom that underlies these three, especially in the European context: the Christianist redefinition of religion. While Christianism is a term made famous by Rogers Brubaker, I use it slightly differently: Christianism is not a specific civilizational, identitarian populism which is opposed to the more traditional nationalist populism, as Brubaker would have it.[39] Instead, it is the redefinition of religion in cultural and political terms. Christianism claims that, to be a good Christian, one does not have to go regularly to church; in fact, one does not have to believe even in the most fundamental tenets of the Christian faith. Neither religious observance nor a personal faith in Jesus is required. Instead, Christianism is a culturalised religion, a defence of the values of the Christian civilisation (whatever this may mean for populists). Christianism is Christianity transformed into the cultural and political myth about the bedrock of Western societies, as it is lived out in a myriad of everyday practices, or so the advocates of Christianism claim.

Brubaker argues that there are two types of populism in Europe: one is the Christianist Western European one, and the other the authoritarian nationalist populism of Central and Eastern Europe. In his distinction, the Christianist populism is based on the defence of the Western civilisation, instead of the more narrowly defined defence of the nation. Christianist populists, in the view of Brubaker, have accepted gender equality and LGBT+ rights as part of the Western civilisation, claiming that European women and LGBT+ people also need to be protected from external enemies (typically represented by Islam and Muslim migrants). Authoritarian populists from Russia, Hungary, and Poland, on the other hand, use a more explicit linkage to Christianity and Christian churches, connecting it in a more traditional fashion with the defence of their national or even ethnic communities against alleged enemies. Gender ideology and the LGBT+ movement are not accepted by them and instead become the target of the populist attack.[40]

While this distinction sounds nice on the conceptual level, the problem is that in reality, the populism of the first type is substantially less present even in Western Europe than Brubaker's distinction would seem to imply. Indeed, there are some populist parties which meet his criteria (notably in the Netherlands, the case Brubaker studied most closely). But most others do not fit the pattern. Giorgia Meloni's Brothers of Italy are well-known for both gender conservatism and homophobic attacks and so is the UKIP in Great Britain. In spite of the pinkwashing strategies of France's *Rassemblement national*, the party

---

39   See Brubaker, "Between Nationalism and Civilizationism".
40   Brubaker, "Between Nationalism and Civilizationism".

members as well as its electorate also exhibit a high level of homophobia.[41] It is also not true that a clear-cut distinction can be made between the populists who focus on the defence of European civilisation and those defending the nation. In fact, as my previous research shows, Central European populists resort to the civilizational discourse very frequently as well. For all these reasons, I believe that there is just one dominant Christianist populism that is defined against liberalism. This means that Christianist populism is targeting all the elements liberals defend, from gender equality to LGBT+ issues to the inclusive approach to Muslim migration. There are of course national and regional variations across Europe, with some populists being less hostile to LGBT+ rights than others, but overall, their positions are quite similar. In other words, the cases to which Brubaker points are exceptions rather than the rule.

Christianist populism, the way I understand it, that is, as populism that builds on the culturalised version of Christianity, has one additional substantial advantage. It skilfully decouples Christianity from actual Christian faith, while not denying it. This means that Christianist populism can thrive both in a religious context and in a highly secular one, as is typical for many European countries. Hence, it works very well in countries like Poland, where cultural Christianity is combined with support by the Catholic Church. But even more importantly, it works in countries where the support by churches is politically less relevant, such as in France or in the Czech Republic. In all these very secularised countries, Christianism can be easily tapped by populists who frame their position as the defence of normalcy, common sense, 'our traditions', etc. This is also the reason why 'traditional values' are so highly relevant for the populists, no matter how vague, as these are an extremely useful political shortcut for Christianist populists. Needless to say, these values very often do not overlap with the values professed by Christians, and, as the critique of this type of populism by Pope Francis shows, they are in fact frequently directly opposed to Christianity.[42]

4.1 *The Return of the Sacred*

The first and most fundamental similarity of religion and politics is their shared commitment to the role of the sacred. Liberal politics is based on continuous

---

41 Nicholas Vinocur, "National Front Defector Blasts Homophobic Insults", *Politico*, 7 December 2016, accessed 6 September 2023, https://www.politico.eu/article/national-front-defector-blasts-homophobic-insults/.

42 Anna Momigliano, "Papa, Don't Preach", *Foreign Policy*, 20 June 2019, accessed 6 September 2023, https://foreignpolicy.com/2019/06/20/papa-dont-preach-italy-matteo-salvini-pope-francis-vatican-immigration-league-lega/.

negotiation with the aim of reaching a mutually acceptable position that would meet some of the requirements of all the involved parties. Liberal politics is thus a process of pragmatic compromise-seeking which eschews clear-cut good and evil categories, and instead operates with the potential acceptance of all reasonable positions if they can be accommodated within the constitutional framework. Populism's starting point is the exact opposite. In its case the political world is reenchanted. In particular, 'the people' is defined as sacred as it transcends and encompasses its members; it is the ultimate all-powerful decision-maker who is infallible and whose will must not be questioned but followed. The sacred community is then contrasted with the evil elites, those who are trying to seduce the people and deny their right to self-rule. It is this Manichean distinction between the people and the elites, between the entirely pure and the entirely corrupt, that lies at the heart of the populist project.[43]

But the reliance on the sacredness of the collective and of the communitarian is not the only sacralising aspect of populism.[44] Populism is not only about what the people is, but also about what the people can attain. Again, in a way reminiscent of Oakeshott's "politics of faith",[45] populism aims at a radical transformation of the political system. While often vague as far as the concrete steps are concerned, populism nonetheless bases its appeal on the 'obvious' corruption of the current system and the possibility of, and indeed the need for, its replacement.[46] In other words, the attraction of populism is founded not only on the sacralisation of the political community, but also on the redemptive redefinition of politics. If citizens are tired of the never-ending political haggling of liberalism, populism offers a once-and-for-all solution. To

---

43 DeHanas and Shterin, "Religion and the Rise of Populism".
44 Cf. also J.P. Zúquete, "Missionary Politics—A Contribution to the Study of Populism", *Religion Compass* 7, no. 7 (2013): 263–71.
45 Oakeshott, *The Politics of Faith*.
46 It is important to note that for Oakeshott, the politics of faith is distinct from, and often even opposite to, the traditional religious beliefs that are typically sceptical of the possibility of a radical transformation of the political order or of the establishment of an earthly utopia. However, this distinction is based on Oakeshott's reduction of religion to "traditional religious beliefs" and their contraposition to Pelagianism. Throughout history, religiously inspired movements attempted to establish an earthly paradise or at least overthrow corrupt, ungodly tyrants. Oakeshott, as a true conservative, tries to save religion from its own children, maintaining that they are not related. But the very term Oakeshott uses—the "politics of faith"—betrays the deep similarity between the two and undermines his own argument to the contrary. At the very best, he may be right in terms of arguing that the radical religious movements aiming at social transformation draw from a different understanding of faith in politics than religious conservatives, but nothing more.

put it briefly, populism itself is a "political journey of redemption":[47] it starts with positing a situation of crisis, preferably the ultimate crisis of our time, implying the urgent need for its solution. The populist redemptivism directly or indirectly draws on the chiliastic conviction of the end of time, the coming of the Antichrist and the fight of the just against the hosts of Satan.[48] One highly visible corollary of this process is the contestation over the sacred/secular nature of space and public space in particular. The attempts to claim public space fully as either sacred or secular are, however, seldomly successful.[49] This inability to fully reclaim public space as sacred then easily leads to the perpetuation of the conflict, boosting the legitimacy of the populist calls for the continued contestation over public space.

The final step in this sacralisation is the preeminent role assigned to the leaders of the populist movements. This aspect of sacralisation is more visible in the Latin American research on populism than in the European scholarship. The mainstream European understanding of populism is the one mentioned above: populism understood as a thin ideology based on the distinction between the people and the elites. Latin American scholars typically define populism as a political strategy, not an ideology, albeit a weak one: "a political strategy through which a personalistic leader seeks or exercises government power based on direct, unmediated, uninstitutionalized support from large numbers of mostly unorganized followers".[50] This leader is often seen as a heroic saint, a prophet, a single holy warrior who is willing to stand against all the might of the elites. It is fully in line with this understanding that populist movements are much more frequently built upon the principle of charismatic leadership, verging on a cult, rather than the bureaucratic authority which is typical for mainstream political parties.

---

47 Franscisco Panizza, "What Do We Mean When We Talk about Populism?" in: *Latin American Populism in the Twenty-First Century*, eds. Carlos de la Torre and Cynthia J. Arnson (Baltimore: John Hopkins University Press, 2013), 114.

48 Canovan, "Trust the People!"

49 See the analysis of the trans-liminality of space in M.D.C. Van der Tol and P.S. Gorski, "Secularisation as the fragmentation of the sacred and of sacred space", *Religion, State and Society* 50, no. 5 (2022): 495–512.

50 Kurt Weyland, "Clarifying a Contested Concept: Populism in the Study of Latin American Politics", *Comparative Politics* 34 (2001): 14; see also Ihsan Yilmaz and Nicholas Morieson, "A Systematic Literature Review of Populism, Religion and Emotions", *Religions* 12, no. 4 (2021): 272.

4.2 *The Return of the Natural*

The second principle is the populist insistence on the political importance of the *natural, normalcy,* and *common sense*—a principle that is central to much religious conservative thought[51] as well as various natural law theories.[52] The reliance on the natural order of things is a powerful defence of populists against the liberal attempts at deliberation. For populism in its pure form, discussing political differences is nonsensical, as a compromise is not possible; either you fight for the firmly given natural order of things or you are against it: there is no middle ground between the two. The stress on the natural and the common sense of ordinary people can be easily linked to the people/elite distinction. As we have seen in the previous analysis, populism always starts with a critique of the liberal, decadent, corrupt elites whose corruption is evident from their excessive lifestyles, and the natural/unnatural dichotomy is virtually always applied here as well.

The construction of this normalcy extends not only to economic phenomena (with slogans such as 'normal people work' or 'ordinary people deserve a fair salary'), but also to broader cultural considerations. Hence, certain social conventions and communities are 'naturalised' and presented as the commonsensical bulwark against the deviancy of the liberals: marriage, the family, the church, the nation, and civilisation. There is an analogy between the populist critique of liberal pluralism and the populist critique of liberal decadence that has now become so prevalent in Russia and elsewhere.[53] Exactly as the liberal goal of searching for political compromises among diverse social groups leads to corruption and 'dirty politics', so does the liberal permissiveness lead to the distortion of universally valid moral principles. The defence of the natural is thus based on the belief that the liberal, progressive elites aim at the destruction of the laws of nature themselves. The liberals cast doubt on the very distinction between a man and a woman, they redefine marriage in unacceptable ways, and they want to destroy any natural bond between people, replacing it with artificial constructs. In the populist discourse, the nation can

---

51 See, for instance, Catholic integralism in Xavier Foccroulle Ménard and Anna Su, "Liberalism, Catholic Integralism, and the Question of Religious Freedom", *BYU L. Rev.* 47 (2021): 1171.

52 Ronald M. Dworkin, *Taking Rights Seriously* (Cambridge, MA: Harvard University Press, 1977); John Finnis, *Natural Law & Natural Rights* (New York: Oxford University Press 2011); Heinrich A. Rommen, *The Natural Law*, trans. Thomas R. Hanley (Indianapolis: Liberty Fund, 2012).

53 Petr Kratochvíl and Gaziza Shakhanova, "The Patriotic Turn and Re-Building Russia's Historical Memory: Resisting the West, Leading the Post-Soviet East?" *Problems of Post-Communism* 68, no. 5 (2021): 442–56.

be such a natural phenomenon, and the post-national ideology of European integration is then seen as a direct challenge to the nation, particularly in the countries of Eastern Europe, where independent statehood is a relatively novel phenomenon. Under the same guise, the liberals can also be accused of trying to destroy Christianity, push it out of the public space, and marginalise its influence in the society.

As a result, the populist would argue, all natural communities—the family, the nation, and the church—are under attack. The sacred and the natural are firmly connected in the populist discourse: to follow common sense is to be on the right side of history and to fight for the natural order. While this order is mainly represented by the existence of the *natural community*, it is conceptually of secondary relevance whether this community is defined as a nation or as a civilisation. That the nation is recast as a natural, qua sacred, community is not really surprising, as this corresponds with the Durkheimian argument about society's veneration of itself. But the entire civilisation (Christian or otherwise) can also attain a similar status of an uncontested good. We are naturally part of a greater whole, a civilisation, populists would claim; and to protect our civilisation against the barbarians that desire its destruction is a sacred duty. What matters is thus not the decision of which type of collectivity we are part of, but that this collectivity is seen as going beyond the mere sum of its members (that is, it is transcendental). Needless to say, populist discourses often freely combine both national and civilizational aspects in one comprehensive narrative.

Given this particularistic focus on the nation or civilisation, it may be surprising that populists add one more element to the mix: along with the natural and the sacred, they also extoll the universal. It is something of a paradox: The liberal elites are accused of spreading their post-national, post-Christian ideology, which is imposed universally—no exception is allowed. Christianist populists such as Viktor Orbán claim that what they are fighting for is the right of their nation, their country, and their Christian families to resist this liberal hegemony. What lies behind this advocacy of the illiberal exception is, in fact, a hidden claim to the true universality the populists represent. The populists present their own universality, a universality of the natural relationship between a man and a woman, of communitarian bonds, and of distinct local cultures and religious traditions, none of which can be reduced, as they would argue, to the artificial universalism of the liberals.

4.3 *The Return of the Past*
The third element that unites all the populist strands with religion is the strong stress on the past political temporality. The critique of the immanent present,

of the non-functioning political system and of the corrupt elites is always contrasted with a utopia.[54] It is not only that populism contrasts the current situation with alternative systems, but it is also revolutionary as it argues that these alternatives can be achieved and are in fact within the grasp of this very generation, thus creating a specific secular eschatology. The verisimilitude of this claim does not lie in the future (as hopeful as future-oriented temporalities are), but mainly in the past. By arguing that there used to be a different system, a system of justice and harmony, or a golden past, the proposed transformation of the current system gains the air of plausibility. The utopia (which is, literally, "nowhere") is translated into a eu-topia ("a good place"), and this place can be found in the past. The sacralisation of the past thus spills over to the re-sacralisation of the space in that we live as well. The stress on the past is one of the features of populism that are becoming more relevant: Donald Trump's 'Make America Great Again' and the Brexiteers' 'Take back control' are purely past-oriented. The central importance of the past temporality for the current wave of populism is connected with the populists' political strategy built around ontological insecurity and the fear of the future, be it related to globalization, climate change, global epidemics or the increasing likelihood of a great power war.

Another way of shedding light on the affinity of populism to the past temporality is by exploring Paul Taggart's concept of the heartland. For Taggart, the heartland is central to the populist understanding of politics, representing the imaginary space where the virtuous people reside. This space contains both a spatial and a temporal political dimension, as it defines the community as a place that has to be protected, but it also connects the past with the future in a specific way: It is "a version of the past that celebrates a hypothetical, uncomplicated and non-political territory of imagination".[55] While the heartland forges a political link between the imaginary past and the future, the past and the future are not symmetrical in the account, as the future is derived from the past. The prioritisation of the past is then also reflected in the structure of the populist discourse itself: the glorification of the past is the primary discursive

---

54 Filipe Carreira Da Silva and Mónica Brito Vieira, "Populism and the politics of redemption", *Thesis Eleven* 149, no. 1 (2018): 10–30.

55 Paul Taggart, "Populism Has the Potential to Damage European Democracy, but Demonising Populist Parties Is Self-defeating", EUROPP (blog), LSE, 13 December 2012, accessed 6 September 2023, https://blogs.lse.ac.uk/europpblog/2012/12/13/populism-has-the-potential-to-damage-european-democracy-paul-taggart/; see also Paul Taggart, *Populism* (Buckingham, PA: Open University Press, 2000); Paul Taggart, "Populism and Representative Politics in Contemporary Europe", *Journal of Political Ideologies* 9, no. 3 (2004): 269–88.

element and the future a replication of the lost glory (again, as exemplified by the Hungarian or Russian populists). The focus on the heartland also brings to light the bifurcation of the two types of populist-religious affinity that I mentioned above (the first being the more superficial instrumentalization of religion for political purposes, and the other being the structural similarity between the two): the secularised populist utopia is often entirely detached from a concrete (let us say Christian) eschatological content, but it still bears the structural resemblance to it.[56]

The focus on the past brings with it a double advantage. Firstly, it creates a link between the past, the sacred, and the natural. For populists, the triangular connection between these three elements is absolutely essential, as the arguments about the natural and the universal only make sense if an (imagined) past can be rendered politically believable, a past when the world was still in order, when common sense ruled the world, a world in which we could call our children boys and girls (this is a paraphrase of what the speaker of the Russian Ministry of Foreign Affairs Maria Zakharova said at a Russian war rally). Secondly, the focus on the past yet again renders liberalism, with its clear future-oriented temporality and its contempt for the past, the archenemy. The liberal version of political temporality also offers a utopia, a future-oriented one. But the liberal future is entirely novel; it has shaken off all the vestiges of the past, such as racial prejudice. Populists, on the other hand, construct their future differently, namely as a replication of the glorious past, which allows them to criticise the current system while retaining those elements from the past which they favour (such as religion or nationalism, etc.).

5 Conclusion

The global rise of populism in the last two decades is a serious warning that liberal democracies may be losing the hearts and minds of a significant segment of their citizens. This development also casts doubt over the belief that politics can be based on non-affective rationality and that people will support liberal democracy simply because it offers more effective solutions than its alternatives. It is clear by now that populist leaders, from Donald Trump to the Brexiteers to Viktor Orbán, do not provide magical solutions to the problems of ordinary people, but rather often worsen their situation. However, what they

---

56 Cf. M.D.C. Van der Tol and M. Rowley, "A Posture of Protest? The Search for Christian Identity in A Post-Secular Society: Between Secularised Eschatology and A Sacralisation of History", *International Journal of Religion* 2, no. 2 (2021): 101–13.

offer is a political narrative which exerts such a powerful attraction that it is difficult for their opponents to match it. I argue that this powerful attraction is mainly due to a single key feature of populism—its similarity to religion. This similarity is sometimes misunderstood and reduced to the alliances of populists with explicitly religious actors, such as churches or religiously oriented political parties. However, the populist-religious alliances, as useful as they may be in some cases, detract our attention from the real, much deeper affinity of religion and populism.

I believe that this affinity with religion, even though it is not new, now has a stronger effect than in past populist movements due to what I call the culturalization of religion. Explicit religion may or may not be taken seriously by populists, but they remain staunch advocates of religion expressed in terms of sacralised cultural phenomena, and in terms of belonging to a (sacred) community. Culturalised religion is thus not about religious observance, but about the resistance of essentialized culture against technocracy, and about "traditional values", values that have themselves forgotten their religious roots. The recent wave of populism can thus be seen as the main carrier of the *politics of faith* at the time of culturalised religion. Populism has always been akin to religious devotion, but the process of the culturalisation of religion (which itself is a form of secularisation) has rendered the religious in populism much more easily recognisable and much more attractive for voters than before.

The three most politically relevant structural similarities between religion and populism are the stress on the sacred, on the natural and on the past. The centrepiece of the populist attention is the people, and the people becomes, in a Durkheimian fashion, both the ultimate sovereign and the infallible deity. The people live virtuously, they never err, and they would make things right if only they were given the opportunity to enforce the general will. The people is also a unified, single organism. All these are the reasons why liberalism with its defence of individual freedoms and minority rights is the most hated element of the liberal democratic arrangement. But the sacred features extend beyond the people as the populist leader also becomes a warrior saint, a divine hero who fights the righteous fight against the corrupted elites. The sacralisation also includes populist policies: The more acute the crisis, the more the redemption that populism offers is needed. Populists claim that the people is not only untouchable, but that it also ensures a natural bond among the citizens, a bond that liberalism has forgotten. The stress on the natural and the almost automatic conflation of the natural and the good is another key connection between populism and religion. Populism offers the final restitution; it fights for the natural and just order of things. Again, the decadent elites, with their depraved lifestyles and unnatural excesses, are the main target.

Finally, against the liberal devaluation of tradition and its orientation towards a future fully cut-off from the past, populists rehabilitate time, and especially the past. The past, exactly like in religion, becomes the source for the future. The Christian eschatological promise about the wolves and the *lambs* feeding together is—not accidentally—a variation on the paradisiacal situation which is described in the myth about the Fall. This is the exact function the populist past temporality serves. The glorious future is not contrasted with the injustices of the past as is the case with the liberal narrative, but it is rather a model based on the replication of the imagined golden past; the promised future utopia is the mythical past recreated. Populism thus follows the religious fundamentalists' attempt to replicate the original state (as in the various apostolic movements in Christianity or Salafism in Islam). Populism is, to put it shortly, a form of political fundamentalism, with all its strengths and weaknesses.

Despite some recent setbacks experienced by populist leaders, the success of populist politics will continue. Populism will not vanish if—miraculously—the current socio-economic problems disappear; the 'populist moment' is likely to transform into a more protracted populist period. Although the cause of the populist resurgence certainly is, on some level, the growing socio-economic inequalities, the true strength of populism lies in its ability to express this dissatisfaction in a quasi-religious manner, thus evoking deep affection and loyalty, but also a strong feeling of existential anxiety and an urgent need to act. Liberal democratic politics is in crisis because it struggles with maintaining the same level of allegiance as the politics of faith, the politics of sacralisation. In short, liberal democracy struggles because it does not offer a similarly compelling political theology with a correspondingly deep political loyalty. The future of the populist cause thus depends not only on its own viability, but also on the ability of liberal democracy to take seriously the lesson offered by populists. But the most fundamental question remains: whether such a liberal political theology can be created that would become at least as attractive for the disaffected citizenry as the one offered by liberalism's populist challengers.

Bibliography

Acharya, A. (2017). "After Liberal Hegemony: The Advent of a Multiplex World Order". *Ethics & International Affairs* 31, no. 3: 271–85.

Blokker, P. (2021). "Populism and illiberalism". In: A. Sajó, R. Uitz, and S. Holmes (eds.). *Routledge Handbook of Illiberalism*. New York: Routledge. Pp. 261–79.

Brubaker, R. (2017). "Between Nationalism and Civilizationism: The European Populist Moment in Comparative Perspective". *Ethnic and Racial Studies* 40, no. 8: 1191–226.

Canovan, M. (1999). "Trust the People! Populism and the Two Faces of Democracy". *Political Studies* 47: 2–16.

Casier, T. (2022). "Russia and the diffusion of political norms: The perfect rival?" *Democratization* 29, no.3: 433–50.

Castells, M. (2019). *Rupture: The Crisis of Liberal Democracy*. Translated by Rosie Marteau. Cambridge: Polity Press.

Cooley, A., and D. Nexon. (2020). *Exit from Hegemony: The Unravelling of the American Global Order*. New York: Oxford University Press.

Crockett, C. (2013). *Radical Political Theology: Religion and Politics after Liberalism*. New York: Columbia University Press.

Da Silva, F.C., and M.B. Vieira. (2018). "Populism and the politics of redemption". *Thesis Eleven* 149, no. 1: 10–30.

DeHanas, D.N., and M. Shterin. (2018). "Religion and the Rise of Populism". *Religion, State & Society* 46, no. 3: 177–85.

Dworkin, R. M. (1977). *Taking Rights Seriously*. Cambridge, MA: Harvard University Press.

Finnis, J. (2011). *Natural Law & Natural Rights*. New York: Oxford University Press.

Freeden, M. (1996). *Ideologies and Political Theory: A Conceptual Approach*.Oxford: Clarendon.

Galston, W.A. (2007). "Why the new liberalism isn't all that new, and why the old liberalism isn't what we thought it was". *Social Philosophy and Policy* 24, no. 1: 289–305.

Galston, W.A. (2018). "The Populist Challenge to Liberal Democracy". *Journal of Democracy 29 no. 2: 5–19*.

Grozdanov, Z. (2021). "From Incarnation to Identity: The Theological Background of National-Populist Politics in the Western Balkans". In: U. Schmiedel and J. Ralston (eds.). *The Spirit of Populism*. Leiden: Brill. Pp. 149–63.

Klaiber, J. (2015)."The Catholic Church and the Leftist Populist Regimes of Latin America: Venezuela, Ecuador, and Bolivia". In: M.J. Schuck and J. Crowley-Buck (eds.) *Democracy, Culture, Catholicism: Voices from Four Continents*. New York: Fordham University Press. Pp. 219–32.

Krastev, I. (2007). "The populist moment". *Критика и хуманизъм* 23_EN: 103–8.

Kratochvíl, P., and G. Shakhanova. (2021). "The Patriotic Turn and Re-Building Russia's Historical Memory: Resisting the West, Leading the Post-Soviet East?" *Problems of Post-Communism* 68, no. 5: 442–56.

Laclau, E. (2005). *On Populist Reason*. London: Verso.

Marcinkiewicz, K., and R. Dassonneville. (2022). "Do religious voters support populist radical right parties? Opposite effects in Western and East-Central Europe". *Party Politics* 28, no. 3: 444–56.

Marzouki, N., D. McDonnell, and O. Roy, eds. (2016). *Saving the People: How Populists Hijack Religion*. Oxford University Press.

Mazzarella, W. (2019). "The Anthropology of Populism: Beyond the Liberal Settlement". *Annual Review of Anthropology* 48: 45–60.

Ménard, X.F., and A. Su. (2021). "Liberalism, Catholic Integralism, and the Question of Religious Freedom". BYU *L. Rev.* 47: 1171.

Michelsen, N. (2013). "Liberalism, Political Theology and Suicide Bombing". *Millennium* 42, no. 1: 198–223.

Momigliano, A. (2019). "Papa, Don't Preach". *Foreign Policy*, 20 June 2019. https://foreignpolicy.com/2019/06/20/papa-dont-preach-italy-matteo-salvini-pope-francis-vatican-immigration-league-lega/.

Morieson, N. (2021). *Religion and the Populist Radical Right: Secular Christianism and Populism in Western Europe*. Vernon Press.

Mouffe, C. (2019). "The populist moment". *Simbiótica. Revista Eletrônica* 6, no. 1: 6–11.

Mudde, C., and C. R. Kaltwasser. (2013). "Exclusionary vs. Inclusionary Populism: Comparing Contemporary Europe and Latin America". *Government and Opposition* 48, no. 2: 147–74.

Noury, A., and G. Roland. (2020). "Identity Politics and Populism in Europe". *Annual Review of Political Science* 23, no. 1: 421–39.

Oakeshott, M. (1996). *The Politics of Faith and the Politics of Scepticism*. Edited by T. Fuller. New Haven, CT: Yale University Press.

Öniş, Z. (2017). "The Age of Anxiety: The Crisis of Liberal Democracy in a Post-Hegemonic Global Order". *The International Spectator* 52, no. 3: 18–35.

Owen, D. (2022). "A Global Crisis of Liberal Democracy? On Autocratic Democracy, Populism and Post-Truth Politics". *Journal of Social and Political Philosophy* 1, no. 1: 30–46.

Ozzano, L. (2020). *The Masks of the Political God: Religion and Political Parties in Contemporary Democracies*. Rowman and Littlefield.

Panizza, F. (2013). "What Do We Mean When We Talk about Populism?" In: C. de la Torre and C.J. Arnson (eds.). *Latin American Populism in the Twenty-First Century*. Baltimore: John Hopkins University Press. Pp. 85–115.

Pappas, T.S. (2019). *Populism and Liberal Democracy: A Comparative and Theoretical Analysis*. Oxford: Oxford University Press.

Peace, T. (2021). "Religion and the ideology of populism". In: Jeffrey Haynes (ed.). *The Routledge Handbook of Religion, Politics and Ideology*. Abingdon: Routledge. Pp. 138–52.

Raschke, C. A. (2015). *Force of God: Political Theology and the Crisis of Liberal Democracy*. New York: Columbia University Press.

Rawls, J. (1996). *Political Liberalism*. New York: Columbia University Press.

Revelli, M. (2019). *The New Populism: Democracy Stares into the Abyss*. London: Verso.

Rommen, H.A. (2012). *The Natural Law*. Translated by Thomas R. Hanley. Indianapolis: Liberty Fund.

Rupnik, J. (2018). "Explaining Eastern Europe: The Crisis of Liberalism". *Journal of Democracy* 29, no. 3: 24–38.

Sakwa, R. (2019). *Russia's Futures*. John Wiley & Sons.

Skorupski, J. (2015). "The Conservative Critique of Liberalism". In: S. Wall (ed.). *The Cambridge Companion to Liberalism*. Cambridge: Cambridge University Press. Pp. 401–22.

Taggart, P. (2000). *Populism*. Buckingham, PA: Open University Press.

Taggart, P. (2004). "Populism and Representative Politics in Contemporary Europe". *Journal of Political Ideologies* 9, no. 3: 269–88.

Taggart, P. (2012). "Populism Has the Potential to Damage European Democracy, but Demonising Populist Parties Is Self-defeating". EUROPP (blog). LSE, 13 December 2012. https://blogs.lse.ac.uk/europpblog/2012/12/13/populism-has-the-potential-to-damage-european-democracy-paul-taggart/.

Trochev, A., and P.H. Solomon Jr. (2018). "Authoritarian constitutionalism in Putin's Russia: A pragmatic constitutional court in a dual state". *Communist and Post-Communist Studies* 51, no. 3: 201–14.

Van der Tol, M.D.C., and M. Rowley (2021). "A Posture of Protest? The Search for Christian Identity in A Post-Secular Society: Between Secularised Eschatology and A Sacralisation of History". *International Journal of Religion* 2, no. 2: 101–13.

Van der Tol, M.D.C., and P.S. Gorski. (2022). "Secularisation as the fragmentation of the sacred and of sacred space". *Religion, State and Society* 50, no. 5: 495–512.

Vinocur, N. (2016). "National Front Defector Blasts Homophobic Insults". *Politico*, 7 December 2016. https://www.politico.eu/article/national-front-defector-blasts-homophobic-insults/.

Weyland, K. (2001). "Clarifying a Contested Concept: Populism in the Study of Latin American Politics". *Comparative Politics* 34: 1–22.

Yilmaz, I., and N. Morieson. (2021). "A Systematic Literature Review of Populism, Religion and Emotions". *Religions* 12, no. 4: 272.

Zakaria, F. (1997). "The Rise of Illiberal Democracy". *Foreign Affairs* 76, no. 6: 22–43.

Zúquete, J.P. (2013). "Missionary Politics—A Contribution to the Study of Populism". *Religion Compass* 7, no. 7: 263–71.

Zúquete, J.P. (2017). "Populism and Religion". In: C.R. Kaltwasser, P. Taggart, P.O. Espejo, and P. Ostiguy (eds.). *The Oxford Handbook of Populism*. Oxford University Press. Pp. 445–66.

CHAPTER 3

When a Light Cloak Turns into a Pious Cage: Thinking National Identity with Karl Barth and John Paul II

Zoran Grozdanov

1   Introduction

'Pilgrim clothing', 'light cloak', 'national identity', 'external goods' – it is almost impossible not to notice the strong resemblance between thinking about Weberian 'external goods' and Karl Barth's comment on 'national identity': "This [national identity] belongs only to his pilgrim clothing which he has put on and will put off again".[1] In fact, Max Weber had expressed in so many words that "the care for external goods should only lie on the shoulders of the 'saint like a light cloak, which can be thrown aside at any moment'".[2] However, Weber added to this that "fate decreed that the cloak should become an iron cage".[3]

Has fate also decreed that national identity, which Barth claims belongs to pilgrim clothing that can be put on and off at will, also becomes the iron cage that traps human existence such that other identities are irrelevant, even religious ones? In fact, does national identity, bounded and bordered as it is, define human existence? This notion of an iron cage resembles what sociologist Siniša Malešević described as a "super-thick ideology, metaideological doctrine" that it is more than political ideology, and is rehearsed in "the social practice embedded in the everyday life of modern societies".[4] For many people, their national identity is important to their self-understanding, perhaps as Scots, Germans, Poles, or Croats. According to Zygmunt Bauman, national identity often functions as an *a priori* determination of the relationship between the self and one's community, rather than the fruit or the consequence of belonging.[5]

---

1   Karl Barth, *Church Dogmatics* III/4 (Peabody, MA: Hendrickson Publishers, 2010), 302.
2   Max Weber, *The Protestant Ethic and the Spirit of Capitalism* (London and New York: Routledge, 2010), 123.
3   Weber, *The Protestant Ethic*, 123.
4   Siniša Malešević, *Grounded Nationalisms: A Sociological Analysis* (Cambridge: Cambridge University Press, 2019), 4.
5   Zygmunt Bauman, *Liquid Modernity* (Cambridge: Polity Press 2000), 178.

This chapter compares the notion of national identity in the work of the German theologian Karl Barth and the Polish-born Pope John Paul II. Within their context, Karl Barth (1886–1968) contended with the legacy of Nazism in the German Church and especially the phenomenon of the German Christian nationalism, which he understood as "heretical".[6] In the third volume of his *Church Dogmatics,* he introduced the notions of "near and distant neighbours".[7] Pope John Paul II, born as Karol Józef Wojtyła in 1920, in the early days of Polish independence, and Primate of the Roman Catholic Church during the end of the Soviet Union, attached great weight to the idea of national identity, even as part of the created order. In his book *Memory and Identity*, which greatly influenced the rise of post-Soviet nationalisms, he emphasises the idea of nation as a "permanent reality".[8] While their immediate context is foundational to the analysis of their views, their ideas also transcend their particular contexts, and both were eager to set the tone in theological debates on national identity.

In the comparison of their work, this chapter will focus on their diverging theologies of national identity. Barth's systematic thinking is especially instructive for contemporary debates about national identity, not simply as an example from history, but as a mode of thinking that can shape religious critiques of nationalism. Moreover, Barth's thought is instructive insofar as religious and national identities tend to be fused in scholarship on Eastern Europe.[9] Many scholars will make an equation between being a Pole and being a Catholic, or a Croat and a Catholic, or being Hungarian and Christian.[10]

Elsewhere, I have written about the theological presuppositions required for such an equation, and how they came about.[11] Religion is not an "innocent bride seduced by a manipulative and crafty groom who, clad in an elegant suit,

---

6   Barth, *Church Dogmatics* III/4, 305.
7   Barth, *Church Dogmatics* III/4, 285–323.
8   Pope John Paul II, *Memory and Identity: Conversations at the Dawn of a Millennium* (Rizzoli: New York, 2005), 66; Zoran Grozdanov, "From Incarnation to Identity: The Theological Background of National-Populist Politics in the Western Balkans", in *The Spirit of Populism: Political Theologies in Polarized Times*, eds. Ulrich Schmiedel and Joshua Ralston (Leiden: Brill, 2022), 149–63.
9   Vjekoslav Perica, *Balkan Idols: Religion and Nationalism in Yugoslav States* (Oxford: Oxford University Press, 2004).
10 Anna Grzymala-Busse, *Nations under God: How Churches use Moral Authority to Influence Policy* (Princeton: Princeton University Press, 2015), 145–227.
11 Grozdanov, "From Incarnation to Identity"; Zoran Grozdanov, "IncarNation: On the Possibility of Balkan Contextual Theology", in *Balkan Contextual Theology: An Introduction*, eds. Stipe Odak and Zoran Grozdanov (London and New York: Routledge, 2023).

promises her a bright future",[12] but is much more of a partner in creating this 'bright future'. And more than a merely passive partner, religion is an active participant in national identity.[13] As such, it is a mistake to refer to national identities as 'hijacked' religious identities, as these phenomena are historically intertwined. This chapter then questions how, theologically speaking, national identity constitutes a pilgrim's clothing or an iron cage, and how the one can become the other? This chapter examines the doctrinal presuppositions required for evaluating the importance of national identities for religious identities. These presuppositions are well grounded in the work of Barth and Pope John Paul II, although from completely different perspectives and yielding different outcomes.

One of the issues that emerges, is to what extent the notion of national identity invokes the image of creation as well as of incarnation, and the possible analogies between the Divine and humans that derive from it. The very old issue between Protestant and Catholic theology, that of *analogia entis* (analogy of being), thus comes into play in the issues of national identity, patriotism and nationalism.[14] Or, stated somewhat differently, did God create nations, since with the creation of the human being God also created our social nature, which makes a nation a "natural society"?[15] Or are these just historical contingencies from which the human being is "originally free"?[16] Alternatively, is national identity a light cloak which can be put on and off whenever one likes, or is it an iron cage from which we must *necessarily* think—and even a revelation of God Godself? Or, again, how can we reconcile what Barth calls "wholly and utterly belonging to his own people" with the fact that human being is originally free from such belonging?

2   Barth's Light Cloak of National Identity

Barth begins his "Near and Distant Neighbours" with the distinction between the inner and outer circles of human connections in this world. In the first, inner circle he puts (biological) family—the "creaturely nature of every man"

---

12   Zoran Grozdanov, "We the (Catholic) People! Is Populism Hijacking Christianity? An Eastern European Perspective", *Concilium* 1 (2021): 84–90.
13   See Grozdanov, "From Incarnation to Identity: The Theological Background of National-Populist Politics in the Western Balkans", 149–163.
14   Carys Moseley, *Nations and Nationalism in the Theology of Karl Barth* (Oxford: Oxford University Press, 2013), 98.
15   Pope John Paul II, *Memory and Identity*, 70.
16   Barth, *Church Dogmatics* III/4, 302.

as a father, mother, man and woman, or as a child.[17] However, there is a second, outer circle which springs from this inner one, since there is a "greater nexus which is grounded in nature and fashioned in history and to which every man belongs and is bound and committed by derivation and birth".[18] Barth calls this outer circle that of near neighbours, the ones who are closer to particular human beings "by nature and with the fact of his historical existence", that is as part of "his own particular race and people".[19] Consequently, since he considers that these are "one's own" race and people, it is presupposed that there are different races and peoples from one's own, and he calls these "distant neighbours" or foreigners.[20] In the same sense that the human being is committed to "his race and people" because of shared race (ethnicity), history, and so on, so there is also a commitment to distant neighbours, "as a fellow human being".[21]

So, there are two kinds of commitments: first, the historically bounded commitments, gained through shared culture, language, and customs, which a human being has with his near neighbours. Second, the fact of creaturely existence gives rise to commitments to distant neighbours, those who do not belong to one's nation, ethnicity, or race. However, on the level of commitment, Barth places near and distant neighbours on the same level. Although a human being stands with his near neighbours "in deep connection which is determinative for his whole existence, and supremely effective and binding for his whole being", both types of neighbours "inevitably call[s] him to obedience and sanctif[y] him".[22] As Barth puts it, his own race and people are his home and it is hardly possible to imagine that we can "breathe or think or feel or act or live at all without them".[23] In his description of near neighbours, Barth uses language, culture and history as those aspects that determine human existence. He does not escape from determining the human being within these frameworks, and the same is affirmed by John Paul II.

However, Barth relativizes the theological foundations of national identity. While he believes that people derive their identity from their existence alongside their near neighbours, he also questions the boundaries of that (national) belonging. Barth plays here with the notions of obedience and call, which the

---

17   Barth, *Church Dogmatics* III/4, 285.
18   Barth, *Church Dogmatics* III/4, 286.
19   Barth, Church Dogmatics III/4, 286. The term "race" in Barth's usage was disputed, but according to his usage of the word *Rasse*, he was employing this term as used by the German Christians and their theology of race (Moseley, *Nations and Nationalism*, 98).
20   Barth, *Church Dogmatics* III/4, 286.
21   Barth, *Church Dogmatics* III/4, 286.
22   Barth, *Church Dogmatics* III/4, 287.
23   Barth, *Church Dogmatics* III/4, 287.

human being receives as a command from God with reference to their near neighbours. As such, it "includes definitive affirmation of home, motherland and people".[24] Humans are bounded by that setting insofar as they have a *responsibility* for it, but they are decisively not bounded by its claims definitive belonging. Human existence, in this account, is not grounded in culture and national belonging. This notion of responsibility plays a huge role in Barth's grounding of national identity. For him, such responsibility for one's own homeland and culture disallows one from becoming a pure cosmopolitan without any boundaries, belonging here and there as one wishes, since "none of us can really manage to be so".[25] On the contrary, with the notions of command, call and the human being's obedience, Barth places the human being within a concrete environment for which he bears responsibility.

Yet command and call are also subordinated to the extensions of our environment. The identities of 'my people' and 'other people', as Barth says, are dynamic, not static: they are fluid.[26] The borders which are naturally given, no matter whether they are geographical, linguistic, or cultural borders, are fluid, since the command of God which summons the human being to his own setting is necessarily marked by extensions towards other people. These extensions are the consequence of a call and a command from God, and not of our determination by culture, language, or national belonging. As Barth would say, identity is not determined by one's natural environment, but primarily by the call and obedience to God. "There is no slightest doubt", Barth would explain, "that where the command of God is sounded and heard the concepts of home, motherland and people, while they must retain their original sense, will prove capable of extension. If we live in obedience, we can be at home even in other lands without being disloyal".[27] To emphasise his point, Barth states that "wherever we are called to do good, we can find again our motherland".[28]

With these statements, Barth is entering the arena of the definition of national (and also ethnic) identities and the discussions that dominate contemporary sociology and political science. Without going into a lengthy discussion on the many positions taken on these issues, they are concerned with the definitions of national identity as constructed, "imagined" as Benedict

---

24 Barth, *Church Dogmatics* III/4, 292.
25 Barth, *Church Dogmatics* III/4, 286.
26 Barth, *Church Dogmatics* III/4, 294.
27 Barth, *Church Dogmatics* III/4, 293.
28 Barth, *Church Dogmatics* III/4, 293.

Anderson would say,[29] or as primordial.[30] According to the first position, nations and national identities are the inventions of modern times, attached to the rise of the modern state. They are "constructs and cultural artefacts" that shape the organisational unity of people in the context of nation states.[31] This is in contrast to a 'primordial' position which states that "the world consists of natural nations ... that nations and their characters are organisms that can be easily ascertained by their cultural differentiae; that the members of nations may, and frequently have, lost their national self-consciousness along with their independence; and that the duty of nationalists is to restore that self-consciousness and independence to the 'reawakened' organic nation".[32]

Whilst Barth is not concerned with these typologies, his work on nations and national identity resembles these discussions. Whether nations are constructs or not, whether God created nations, to translate the primordial position into theological language is not Barth's primary concern, although he touches upon these issues in the very content of his argument. He does not start with that question, but with the theological question of the nature of the human being and its relationship towards "quotidian identities", or everyday, immediate identities to borrow from David Kelsey.[33] Where can these quotidian identities be grounded in the human being, and what role does national identity play in the determination of human existence? Barth is quite novel here, especially considering the discussions he had with the German Christians with their primordial view of national identities.

In this sense, Barth makes very strong distinctions between orders of creation. For Barth, within the orders of creation, or as he has it, "immutable orders",[34] natural determination belongs to the human being. This includes being a man or a woman, a parent, brother or sister, or a child. For him, these identities belong to "permanent orders", "natural determinations".[35] They are permanent and natural because they belong to the creation of God. However, with the help of a lengthy exegesis of Genesis 1–9, realities such as economic systems, social systems, or cultural, political and religious factors that determine

---

29 Benedict Anderson, *Imagined Communities: Reflections on the Origin and Spread of Nationalism* (London: Verso, 1983).
30 Anthony Smith, *Nationalism and Modernism: A Critical Survey of Recent Theories of Nations and Nationalism* (London and New York: Routledge, 1998).
31 Smith, Nationalism and Modernism, 146.
32 Smith, Nationalism and Modernism, 146.
33 David Kelsey, *Eccentric Existence: A Theological Anthropology*, vol. 1 (Louisville: Westminster John Knox Press, 2009), 190ff.
34 Barth, *Church Dogmatics* III/4, 301.
35 Barth, *Church Dogmatics* III/4, 301.

a human being's existence are "historical realities", but such determinations are transient for Barth.[36] "As a man", Barth will emphasise, "he is necessarily male or female and free to be the other or without the other ... As a man, however, he is not necessarily but only factually though perhaps very ardently, a citizen of Basel, or a Swiss, or a Spaniard".[37] In this essay, he uses his well-known wit and humour to explain that culture and language (or as he names it, dialect) depend on historical contingencies, and that markers of ethnic or national identity are changeable and subjugated to historical processes – such that one cannot ascribe these identities to nature or biology.

We might say that historical constructions are the framework for one's obedience, but they constitute a very loose framework from which human beings can (and must, since God commands them!) move and return, making all borders fluid. Therefore, "we must not confuse the contrast of near and distant neighbours with the creation of God and its immutable orders".[38] God's command plays a huge role in Barth's thinking about national identities. He differentiates between the specific content of the command, which he ascribes to the "immutable orders"—that is, what scripture commands and demands obedience to, located on the level of "the woman, parents and children", while on the level of historical construction, there is "no special form of command of God".[39] Consequently, a human being's national identity for Barth is "a fact" and no more than that. It is a fact with which he or she is "wholly bound and wholly free".[40] This fact is just "pilgrim clothing which he has put on and will put off again".[41]

3   Pope John Paul II's Pious Cage of Culture and Nation

John Paul II's theology of national belonging holds a prominent place within his papal thought, expressed in various encyclicals and a posthumously published book of interviews with him under the title *Memory and Identity*.[42] However, his thought is deeply shaped by the fate of Poland, as a state that emerged from imperial and Soviet rule. He became pope while Poland still was under communist rule, with the imposition of a culture and ideology foreign to

---

36   Barth, *Church Dogmatics* III/4, 294.
37   Barth, *Church Dogmatics* III/4, 302.
38   Barth, *Church Dogmatics* III/4, 301.
39   Barth, *Church Dogmatics* III/4, 303.
40   Barth, *Church Dogmatics* III/4, 303.
41   Barth, *Church Dogmatics* III/4, 302.
42   John Paul II, *Memory and Identity*.

the Polish people, and in this context, John Paul II became a major spokesman of the nations that were either in the process of gaining national independence or in the process of finding their own resources for establishing their own national distinctiveness.[43]

This concern with national identity comes with an emphasis on ethnicity and the ethnicization of human existence, which in his thought became indispensable ingredients for understanding identity, even Christian identity. In his very first encyclical after becoming Pope, *Redemptor hominis*, John Paul II started to build his theology of national belonging. The reference to 'theology of' is intentional, since the Pope clearly treated nationality as a theological category in this encyclical.[44] In this work, he connects national identity for the first time with the "mystery of the incarnation" in which Christ has assumed not "the 'abstract' man, but the real, 'concrete', 'historical' man" with the membership of the nation.[45] A historical human being, as he will later term them, "combines his deepest human identity with membership of a nation".[46] For John Paul II, national belonging is not only a category that inevitably defines human beings, but it is also a theological category in which he grounds in the mystery of incarnation.

The foundational argument for making national identity a theological category derives from his views on human nature itself. He defines human nature through the social teaching of the Catholic Church, which claims that human nature is communal and social, created in the image of the communal and social nature of the triune God. For the Pope, this social and communal nature defines both human nature and national belonging: "Catholic social doctrine", says John Paul II, "holds that the family and the nation are both natural societies, not the product of mere convention".[47] Furthermore, he adds to this that the "*patria* (homeland) is intimately linked with the idea of 'generating'; but

---

43 Zoran Grozdanov and Branko Sekulić, "Christ's Ethnonationalist Crucifixion: Sacralization of Ethnonationalist Agendas within Croatian Catholicism and Serbian Orthodoxy—Cases and Effects", *Occasional Papers on Religion in Eastern Europe* 40, no. 9 (2020): Article 2.

44 Dorian Llywelyn, *Towards a Catholic Theology of Nationality* (Lanham: Lexington Books, 2010), 159.

45 John Paul II, *Redemptor Hominis* [Encyclical], The Holy See, 4 March 1979, pg. 13, accessed 6 September 2023, https://www.vatican.va/content/john-paul-ii/en/encyclicals/documents/hf_jp-ii_enc_04031979_redemptor-hominis.html.

46 John Paul II, *Laborem Exercens* [Encyclical], the Holy See, 14 September 1981, pg. 10, accessed 5 September 2023, https://www.vatican.va/content/john-paul-ii/en/encyclicals/documents/hf_jp-ii_enc_14091981_laborem-exercens.html.

47 John Paul II, *Memory and Identity*, 70.

the word 'nation' is also etymologically linked with birth".[48] To connect the concept of nation to birth, the Pope relates it to the notion of family, in which the father (*pater*) along with the mother who gives birth together create a new human being. However, birth is here not only a biological process, but through this birth the *pater* transfers to the child the heritage and culture that he has inherited and cherished. Such logic allows John Paul II to state that patriotism belongs to God's fourth commandment which "obliges us to honour our father and mother".[49]

Honouring mother and father, so the logic goes, not only means honouring them in person, but also honouring the culture that they transfer to us and which becomes a crucial ingredient of our nature. We are not born into the culture and nation, as Barth would say, but *with* culture and nation. Furthermore, since Wojtyła connects patriotism to the word *pater* (as well as mother), as a state of honouring our forebearers, he is able to state that "patria truly resembles a mother" and the obligations toward this *patria*, homeland, "provides the basis for our corresponding duty of *pietas*".[50] This *pietas* for the Pope, accordingly, is not limited to a biological father and mother, but also entails love towards everything that makes this heritage: its history, tradition, language and its natural features. *Pietas*, of course, also includes sacrifice, which is born out of the love towards our compatriots, and "every danger that threatens the overall good of our native land becomes an occasion to demonstrate this love".[51]

Such love for one's culture, language, and tradition, is shown and testified by the "many tombs of soldiers who fought for Poland".[52] The homeland demands duty, the Pope would say, and since we are completely bounded by the values of the homeland, and since those values we inherit and cherish by birth belong to our nature, to sacrifice for one's homeland is naturally to fight for the preservation of our nature. It is interesting to note, within the context of such sacrifice for the goods of the homeland, that the Pope mentions some moments in history where this "readiness to accept sacrifice" for the promotion of the values and ideals of the homeland were weakened by "individualism" that has manifested itself as a "disruptive factor".[53]

---

48 John Paul II, *Memory and Identity*, 69.
49 John Paul II, *Memory and Identity*, 65.
50 John Paul II, *Memory and Identity*, 65.
51 John Paul II, *Memory and Identity*, 66.
52 John Paul II, *Memory and Identity*, 66.
53 John Paul II, *Memory and Identity*, 66. On this kind of sacrifice to the homeland and the place of Mary in such piety, see Cathelijne de Busser and Anna Niedźwiedź, "Mary in Poland: A Polish Master Symbol", in: *Moved by Mary: The Power of Pilgrimage in the*

So, the Pope equates human nature and homeland, and along with homeland, culture. He mentions, but does not explain how he came to this concept of the nation in his essay on patriotism and homeland. For him, the nation is the community which is "based in a given territory and distinguished from other nations by its culture".[54] Nation, he further adds, is not the same as the state but the "nation tends naturally to establish itself as a State".[55] He sees the state as a different order from the nation since the state can have different forms and is not strictly defined, in contrast to the nation which is defined by its culture and territory and belongs to the field of theological anthropology.[56] Thus, he asserts an organic link between human nature and culture that forms the homeland and the nation.

Pope John Paul II repeatedly mentions that culture is a spiritual entity and that therefore the nation itself has a "spirit" which is awakened every time its rights are under threat.[57] This resembles the notorious idea of nationhood in the work of Johann Gottfried von Herder (1744–1803), with specific reference to its origin and 'the spirit of the nation'. Herder's idea of nationhood features in many Eastern European theories of nationhood, and the Polish Pope is not immune to such theories. For him, nations belong to the natural order and are not imagined communities, but formed through the rise of organisational apparatus in modern times.

This kind of corporealisation of human identity through culture and nation allows the Pope to give to culture and nation a much wider theological scope than Barth. Speaking at a UNESCO conference in 1980, Pope John Paul II firmly stated that Western societies are organically linked to the message of the gospel and that this message formed the culture of these societies. In that address he said that "there is no doubt that the first and fundamental dimension of culture is healthy morality: *moral culture*".[58] Culture is the educator of the human being, and where culture is crucially influenced by Christianity, this in turn means that the proper moral education of human beings must be through the Christian message and values. These statements also allow him to speak about evangelisation in such corporate terms—not only is the human being

---

    Modern World, eds. Anna-Karina Hermkens and Willy Jansen (London-New York: Routledge, 2009).

54 John Paul II, *Memory and Identity*, 70.
55 John Paul II, *Memory and Identity*, 70.
56 Llywelyn, *Catholic Theology of Nationality*, 160.
57 John Paul II, *Memory and Identity*, 61.
58 John Paul II, "Address to UNESCO" [Speech], the Holy See, 2 June 1980, accessed 6 September 2023, https://inters.org/John-Paul-II-UNESCO-Culture.

evangelised but also entire cultures and consequently the nation that was formed through this culture.[59]

What is distinctive in the work of Pope John Paul II, is his effort to ground national belonging in theology, and specifically the mystery of the incarnation.[60] The incarnation grounds nation, and here the Pope uses the doctrine of the incarnation to emphasise that in the event of God becoming human, God has not assumed human nature in general, but the concrete humanity of Jesus Christ, and by the logic of this argument concrete human nature is primarily marked by culture and nation. Consequently, what is assumed stretches further into each human being which is, through union with Christ, also assumed with all his natural qualities. The Pope states that in the incarnation, we are dealing with concrete, historical man. National belonging, as well as one's culture, becomes a theological category in the precise sense that both culture and nation become the object of redemption. In this sense, as we have already mentioned, the late Pope is able to speak about the evangelisation of entire cultures and nations, since these categories are not just an 'add-on' to human nature, but lie at the very core of it, and in assuming human flesh God made these categories the subject of divine judgement and divine redemption.

In his short theological deliberations on the issues of theology and nation, the Pope also uses the example of Israel, claiming that in the Bible we find "elements of an authentic theology of the nation".[61] For him, Israel's becoming the elect people of God was preceded by their becoming a nation in the ethnic sense. Israel was not formed through election, but was already formed as the "nation", as the Pope would say, "in biological terms", after which came God's election with its "spiritual dimension". Such election affected only Israel's "spiritual life" and not its identity in both senses, natural and spiritual.[62] Israel is a messianic people not because of its election, but because "from that nation Messiah was to come", and with this Messiah, the entire Israelite identity was assumed in the person of Messiah, Jesus Christ.[63] Therefore, following Athanasius' statement that "what has not been assumed has not been redeemed", we might draw the conclusion along with the Pope that the "history of all nations is invited to enter in the history of salvation".[64] Nations are also under judgement,

---

59 John Paul II, *Slavorum Apostoli* [Encyclical], the Holy See, 2 June 1985, pg. 21, accessed 6 September 2023, https://www.vatican.va/content/john-paul-ii/en/encyclicals/documents/hf_jp-ii_enc_19850602_slavorum-apostoli.html.
60 John Paul II, *Memory and Identity*, 71.
61 John Paul II, *Memory and Identity*, 70.
62 John Paul II, *Memory and Identity*, 70–71.
63 John Paul II, *Memory and Identity*, 70.
64 John Paul II, *Memory and Identity*, 71.

not just individuals, and nations have to build a culture that is heavily marked by Christianity, and reversely, such culture is the basis of the nation. This culture, and consequently the nation, must rest on "healthy morality".[65]

4 How Christ Became Ethnicised

The theology of the orders of creation marks the crucial difference between Barth's and John Paul II's theologies of national belonging, with far-reaching consequences. In the final part, we will describe the differences and possible consequences of these two theologies in contemporary manifestations of nationalism and national populism. Their starting points for theology are different, let alone their views of temporal identities, including national identity. Indeed, one might say that Wojtyła's view of the nations is as divinely willed, with guaranteed persistence, something which, on Barth's view, "is quite arbitrary and even laughable".[66]

Barth's theology of national identities depends on his theology of the orders of creation. Within these orders he differentiates between orders and ordinances of God. Such differences rest on what Barth would say is created by God and what is created by human beings, which is the area of human responsibility and calling. Createdness belongs to biological features—mother, father, daughter, son, brother and sister. This is the area of the command of God that has its definitive form and content attested in the scriptures. Since there is no special command in the sphere of the peoples, says Barth, "so there is no specific obedience".[67] What is a command and what is obedience? Barth was specific regarding both of these activities on the part of God and the human being. "Special command" refers to what is strictly commanded in the scriptures and what is not specifically commanded belongs to the sphere of freedom. In this sense, Barth strongly affirms that within the sphere of the near and distant neighbours, those who are not our biological family, "there is obviously no special form of the command of God in respect of the existence and relationship of the peoples".[68]

National identity, however, does play a huge role in the formation of identity: since one utterly belongs to this sphere, one has responsibility for it, but is casually and generally free from that sphere. Why? Because national identity

---

65   John Paul II, "Address to UNESCO".
66   Barth, *Church Dogmatics* III/4, 302.
67   Barth, *Church Dogmatics* III/4, 304.
68   Barth, *Church Dogmatics* III/4, 303.

does not belong to the order of creation with its specific commands (of how to form a relationship, of how to behave, with more or less strict instructions). The area of the national is, in this sense, contingent, and represents what a human being is responsible for, to shape it in view of the command of God and not in the view of historical demands. The national has no value in and of itself. As Barth would say, the fact of national belonging is "just a fact, nothing more", and we must relate to it in that way.[69] What happened that caused Barth to have such a distanced view towards national identity?

Certainly, it was the rise of the German Christians and their *ordo* of creation in which they placed race, people and nation. His criticism of Wojtyla would be very similar to his criticism of the German Christians. Instead of filling the content of the command exclusively with what is strictly commanded by the gospel, namely duties to man and woman, parents and children, Barth says, there came about the "free discovery" that the nation belongs to the order of creation and therefore lies under the specific command and specific obedience. He continues: "On this free discovery there is then erected an *ordo* of nation and nationality which is supposed *to be immanent in human nature* and therefore to be originally and finally determinative and binding". The consequence of this free discovery is very simple and devastating, the inevitable introduction of "foreign deity, a national God from which this specific command proceeds". All this Barth just simply calls "false doctrine", and we "must avoid maintaining and reaching it".[70]

This national God in Pope John Paul II's theology is confusing. He confirms that love of country (not the state, but people and homeland) is an act of piety. One's death for the homeland is very close to the martyr's death, and it is very obvious why he says so. If nationhood is essential to human existence as created by God, then dying for one's nation would potentially be a pious act, since it honours God. However, Wojtyla relativizes national identities with the universality of Christian message, drawing very strong boundaries between nations that accept the Christian message and are redeemed by it. The human being accepts the gospel, within the context of their culture and nation, and therefore it would be natural to claim that in the history of salvation, the "history of all nations is invited". Human beings are trapped within his national identity, certainly not free from it, and have the obligation to participate in it, hold its values dear and transform them in the light of the gospel.

---

69 Barth, *Church Dogmatics* III/4, 305.
70 Barth, *Church Dogmatics* III/4, 305.

This theology,[71] as we said earlier, had enormous influence on the Eastern European nationalisms that appeared at the twilight of Communism, from the end of 1970s onwards, but also on the religious populist movements of the 2000s in Eastern European countries marked by Catholicism. Eastern Europe, especially the Balkans, was not previously known as home to "religious nationalism". Although religious nationalisms have different faces and definitions,[72] Balkan Catholic nationalism was under the strong influence of the theological grounding and primordial view of ethnic identities presented by John Paul II. The 1980s saw the rise of national consciousness in the countries that were either in the Communist bloc (Poland) or in a multinational state (Yugoslavia) under communist rule. In these countries the church had a huge influence on the lives of ordinary people, but also, as time would show in the 1990s, on politics, since it was the only institution independent of the regime.[73]

This independence enabled it to promote political and social agendas that were based on the dignity of the human person, human rights, and freedom of speech; and such freedoms were soon accompanied by the freedom of national self-determination. However, nations were understood in the ethnic sense since in the Eastern Europe, ethnicity, language and citizenship were always mixed in such a way that the idea of the nation state emerges from ethnic community.[74] So, beside the church's fight against communism as an ideology, for instance in Yugoslavia, the struggle was supported by the claims for national (ethnic) liberation. "Religious beliefs", as was stated, "are associated with the new ethno-national projects to which they have brought a feeling of historical continuity with the pre-communist past".[75]

In this vein, Croatian theologians started to speak about homeland, defined in John Paul II's terms, as a territory and community of people that share the same culture. In the Yugoslav context, which was very multicultural and multinational, the demand for homeland lost its anti-communist stance and became the marker of national liberation, in contrast to other cultures (Serbian Orthodox or Muslim, primarily) present in this multinational state. Discussions of

---

71 See the article by Kunter and Van den Broeke "Christianity, Religion, and Christian Democracy" in this volume.
72 Atalia Omer and Jason A. Springs, eds., *Religious Nationalism* (Santa Barbara: ABC-Clio, 2005).
73 Grozdanov and Sekulić, "Christ's Ethnonationalist Crucifixion".
74 See for example Rogers Brubaker, "Religion and Nationalism: Four Approaches," *Nations and Nationalisms* 18, no. 1 (2012): 2–20.
75 Ivan Iveković, "Nationalism and the Political Use and Abuse of Religion: The Politicization of Orthodoxy, Catholicism and Islam in Yugoslav Successor States", *Social Compass* 49, no. 4 (2002): 534.

the homeland did not lack religious associations, for example in the works of the most prominent Croatian Catholic theologians who stated that "homeland is the place of human being's supernatural realization", that "the concept of nation comprises in itself common biological origin, common history, common social organization, common culture and common homeland".[76]

Even the most progressive Croatian theologian almost enthusiastically, with maternal symbolism, stated that "we call our homeland a mother since it is a maternal womb in which one can safely grow" and that "one can find a mature state of freedom in the homeland".[77] These statements were fully in accord with John Paul II's views of natural communities and religious belonging, and they carry with them the strong anti-gender rhetoric[78] that is apparent in the recent religio-populist movements throughout the Eastern Europe.[79] On these views, one cannot be Christian without being fully identified with one's community of culture and nation. In the same vein, when they spoke about the homeland, they were speaking about *ethnos* not *demos*.[80] The Catholic Church itself has to be fully enculturated with the ethnic community, to the point that "with my baptism, Jesus in me became a Croat".[81]

Were these theologians, along with Pope John Paul II, nationalists? They will say definitively and emphatically "no!". All of them repeatedly distanced themselves from nationalism and they condemned nationalism,[82] whilst praising patriotism, 'healthy nationalism' and love for country. However, what is really meant by the term 'nationalistic'? Siniša Malešević points out that nationalist ideology assumes that "the nation is a natural and principal form of human solidarity",[83] and that its "discursive repertoire is much more attuned to the

76 Rudolf Brajčić, *Bit i suvremenost Crkve: Putovi vjerničke svijesti danas* (Zagreb: FTI, 1986), 198.
77 Tomislav Janko Šagi Bunić, *Katolička Crkva i hrvatski narod* (Zagreb: Kršćanska sadašnjost, 1983), 17.
78 See Ivan Tranfić's text in this volume, "Between Religious Nationalism and Universal Familism".
79 Grozdanov, "From Incarnation to Identity".
80 Živko Kustić, *Hrvatska: mit ili misterij?* (Zagreb: Minerva, 1995), 234.
81 Darko Hudelist, *Rim, a ne Beograd: Promjena doba i mirna ofenziva Katoličke Crkve u Hrvatskoj u Titovoj SFR Jugoslaviji (1975–1984)* (Zagreb: Alfa, 2017), 233.
82 "Clearly, one thing must be avoided at all costs: the risk of allowing this essential function of the nation to lead to unhealthy nationalism" (John Paul II, *Memory and* Identity, 67); "Every nationalism is suspicious in the eyes of the Catholics" (Šagi Bunić, *Katolička Crkva i hrvatski narod,* 13). Their view of nationalism is strictly aggressive, chauvinistic, describing the desire to subjugate and conquer other nations in "cultural, political, national or economic terms" (Šagi Bunić, *Katolička Crkva i hrvatski narod,* 13).
83 Siniša Malešević, *Nation-States and Nationalisms: Organization, Ideology and Solidarity* (Cambridge: Polity Press, 2013), 112.

intimate metaphors of family, friendship and community".[84] Barth meanwhile would use a much broader definition of nationalism according to which even the demand that nations have the right for their own state is a nationalistic demand.[85]

The language and the symbols that the Polish Pope and Croatian theologians used are astonishingly similar to those used by the German theologians in the 1930s who paved the way for the theological support of Hitler.[86] Beside the Herderian notion of the 'spirit of the nation', which is common to all these theologies, it might be said that the greatest similarity between German and post-communist national theology rests in the view of the orders of creation. "We recognize in race, ethnicity, and nation orders of life given and entrusted to us by God, who has commanded us to preserve them"—so said the "Guidelines of the German Christian Faith Movement" in 1932.[87] "Family and nation are natural societies", said John Paul II, which in turn became "nation, as family, is the primarily natural community. Nationalism should be understood as an important feature of the human being in concrete history ... Religions and Churches, as an important part of the spirit of the people are spontaneously accepted since they are embedded in the peoples' being in a spiritual and cultural way".[88]

5 Conclusion

The diverging notions of national identity in the work of Karl Barth and Pope John Paul II are echoed in the support and critique of contemporary nationalism and populism in Europe. An interesting fact, especially from Eastern European perspectives, is that the rise of many nationalisms and national populisms all over Europe and the USA are seen as something very recent. Nationalism and various levels of emphasis on national belonging are wrongly considered ideologies of the past. National belonging, at least in the Eastern European context, has proved to be a most persistent ideology, capable of subsuming, and even overarching religious discourse.

---

84 Malešević, *Nation-States and Nationalisms*, 87.
85 Moseley, *Nations and Nationalism*, 96.
86 See for instance arguments by Emmanuel Hirsch in Robert P. Ericksen, *Theologians Under Hitler* (New Haven: Yale University Press, 1985).
87 Christine Tietz, *Karl Barth: A Life in Conflict* (Oxford: Oxford University Press, 2021), 211.
88 Drago Šimundža, *Crkva i demokracija* (Split: Crkva u svijetu, 1995), 154–5.

It is well-documented that iconography of John Paul II is widely used in the Eastern European national and religious populist movements.[89] When religious actors in the public sphere protest or advocate against something that has to do with an anticipated loss of moral or national identity, whether it be March for Life rallies, or manifestations for the canonisations of national saints, Pope John Paul II's face and quotes appear on posters and banners. How did it come about that religion became so supportive of national belonging to the point of the irreplaceability of Christianity when speaking about communal identity? The key-issue is the notion of "inculturation" that Vatican II introduced into the Church's mission, which in the late Pope's theology became an inculturation of Christianity in ethnic, or cultural identity.[90] But, more importantly, it has to do with equating orders of creation with the social identity of human beings, which is primarily marked by culture that a community shares, and it shares it according to common descent, meaning ethnicity.

Such appropriation of identity by ethnic and national categories placed a huge emphasis on the preservation of national identity, and even more so did the preservation of national identity that is primarily marked by Christianity, since in late Pope's view, the link between "the Gospel and man in his very humanity" is "a creator of culture in its very foundation".[91] In this view we have the logic of reducing national belonging, which springs out of culture, to its Christian foundations and Christian identity. In his later work, John Paul II described the state of Western societies as at a "stage which could be defined as a 'post-identity'"[92] due to their obliviousness to the fact that nation is founded upon common culture. The fight for national identity and belonging is in this way reduced to the morality of culture and Christian values that ground and preserve the culture, and such Christian values are inextricably linked with the very being of the nation. Whether or not there is any place for the autonomy of culture or national belonging that has no direct link to Christian identity is a problem that Barth is able to solve by the very fact that he places the orders

---

89 Zoran Grozdanov and Nebojša Zelič, "From Catholic Church to Religious-Populist Movements: Religious Populism Coming of Age in Croatia", in *The Christian Right in Europe: Movements, Networks and Denominations*, ed. Gionathan lo Mascolo (Bielefeld: Transcript Verlag, 2023).

90 John Paul II chapter "Thinking 'My Country'" in his *Memory and Identity* is filled with strong connections between incarnation and inculturation. He locates culture almost exclusively within the ethnic and national boundaries, calling the nation as a carrier of the culture and the one that exists "primarily throughout the culture" (*Memory and Identity*, 84–85).

91 John Paul II, "Address to UNESCO".

92 John Paul II, *Memory and Identity*, 86.

of creation 'above' the ordinances of creation, which avoids placing a definitive mark on human beings and their social identity.

With freedom from national or cultural identity, Barth was able to 'de-Christianise' culture and place it on a plane of free human activity that should not (and must not) be linked to Christian, or even national, values. For him this is a command of God, not only a recommendation for a multicultural world.

Bibliography

Anderson, A. (1983). *Imagined Communities: Reflections on the Origin and Spread of Nationalism*. London: Verso.

Barth, K. (2010). *Church Dogmatics* III/4. Peabody, MA: Hendrickson Publishers.

Bauman, Z. (2000). *Liquid Modernity*. Cambridge: Polity Press.

Brajčić, R. (1986). *Bit i suvremenost Crkve: Putovi vjerničke svijesti danas*. Zagreb: FTI.

Ericksen, R.P. (1985). *Theologians Under Hitler* (New Haven: Yale University Press).

Grozdanov, Z. (2021). "We the (Catholic) People! Is Populism Hijacking Christianity? An Eastern European Perspective". *Concilium* 1: 84–90.

Grozdanov, Z. (2022). "From Incarnation to Identity: The Theological Background of National-Populist Politics in the Western Balkans". In: U. Schmiedel and J. Ralston (eds.) *The Spirit of Populism: Political Theologies in Polarized Times*. Leiden: Brill. Pp. 149–63.

Grozdanov, Z. (2023). "IncarNation: On the Possibility of Balkan Contextual Theology". In: S. Odak and Z. Grozdanov (eds.). *Balkan Contextual Theology: An Introduction*. London and New York: Routledge.

Grozdanov, Z., and B. Sekulić. (2020). "Christ's Ethnonationalist Crucifixion: Sacralization of Ethnonationalist Agendas within Croatian Catholicism and Serbian Orthodoxy—Cases and Effects". *Occasional Papers on Religion in Eastern Europe* 40, no. 9: Article 2.

Grozdanov, Z., and N. Zelič. (2023). "From Catholic Church to Religious-Populist Movements: Religious Populism Coming of Age in Croatia". In: G. lo Mascolo (ed.). *The Christian Right in Europe: Movements, Networks and Denominations*. Bielefeld: Transcript Verlag.

Grzymała-Busse, A. (2015). *Nations under God: How Churches use Moral Authority to Influence Policy*. Princeton: Princeton University Press.

Hudelist, D. (2017). *Rim, a ne Beograd: Promjena doba i mirna ofenziva Katoličke Crkve u Hrvatskoj u Titovoj SFR Jugoslaviji (1975–1984)*. Zagreb: Alfa.

Iveković, I. (2002). "Nationalism and the Political Use and Abuse of Religion: The Politicization of Orthodoxy, Catholicism and Islam in Yugoslav Successor States". *Social Compass* 49, no. 4: 523–36.

Kelsey, D. (2009). *Eccentric Existence: A Theological Anthropology.* Vol. 1. Louisville: Westminster John Knox Press.

Kustić, Ž. (1995). *Hrvatska: mit ili misterij?* Zagreb: Minerva.

Llywelyn, D. (2010). *Towards a Catholic Theology of Nationality.* Lanham: Lexington Books.

Malešević, S. (2013). *Nation-States and Nationalisms: Organization, Ideology and Solidarity.* Cambridge: Polity Press.

Malešević, S. (2019). *Grounded Nationalisms: A Sociological Analysis.* Cambridge: Cambridge University Press.

Moseley, C. (2013). *Nations and Nationalism in the Theology of Karl Barth.* Oxford: Oxford University Press.

Omer, A., and J.A. Springs, eds. (2005). *Religious Nationalism.* Santa Barbara: ABC-Clio.

Perica, V. (2004). *Balkan Idols: Religion and Nationalism in Yugoslav States.* Oxford: Oxford University Press.

Pope John Paul II. (1979). *Redemptor Hominis* [Encyclical]. The Holy See, 4 March 1979. https://www.vatican.va/content/john-paul-ii/en/encyclicals/documents/hf_jp-ii_enc_04031979_redemptor-hominis.html.

Pope John Paul II. (1980). "Address to UNESCO" [Speech]. The Holy See, 2 June 1980. https://inters.org/John-Paul-II-UNESCO-Culture.

Pope John Paul II. (1981). *Laborem Exercens* [Encyclical]. The Holy See, 14 September 1981. https://www.vatican.va/content/john-paul-ii/en/encyclicals/documents/hf_jp-ii_enc_14091981_laborem-exercens.html.

Pope John Paul II. (1985). *Slavorum Apostoli* [Encyclical]. The Holy See, 2 June 1985. https://www.vatican.va/content/john-paul-ii/en/encyclicals/documents/hf_jp-ii_enc_19850602_slavorum-apostoli.html.

Pope John Paul II. (2005). *Memory and Identity: Conversations at the Dawn of a Millennium.* Rizzoli: New York.

Šagi Bunić, T. J. (1983). *Katolička Crkva i hrvatski narod.* Zagreb: Kršćanska sadašnjost.

Šimundža, D. (1995). *Crkva i demokracija.* Split: Crkva u svijetu.

Smith, A. (1998). *Nationalism and Modernism: A Critical Survey of Recent Theories of Nations and Nationalism.* London and New York: Routledge.

Tietz, C. (2021). *Karl Barth: A Life in Conflict.* Oxford: Oxford University Press.

Weber, M. (2001). *The Protestant Ethic and the Spirit of Capitalism.* London and New York: Routledge.

CHAPTER 4

Fratelli Tutti: A Failed Battle against Christian Nationalism?

Anne Guillard

1   Introduction

The question of fraternity towards migrants shakes up the relationship between religion and politics in Europe. The rise of populism supports the emergence of a nationalism that feeds on the issue of migration and Islam.[1] Religion seems "first and foremost as a marker of identity, enabling populist parties to distinguish between the good 'us' and the bad 'them'".[2] Religion, here, is to be understood in its loose meaning: as a historical heritage rather than a set of creeds and practices. The working definition of religion used here is a set of shared convictions, symbols and ritual actions that enable believers to experience what they have in common and thereby help to forge the unity of their faith and their Church. Religion is a culture that forges attitudes that evoke that on which humans depend, that which transcends the meaning and power of human action. Christianity in this sense is a symbolic material. Christianity appears as a symbol of true Europeanness binding Western nations against the 'others', roughly designated as Muslims who have settled in Europe, who practice an exogenous religion, and are therefore considered as unassimilable to the dominant population.[3] Muslims are blamed for cultivating norms of life regarding dress, food, and sexuality that "alter the assumed cultural homogeneity of the host society, and for fuelling insecurity and terrorism".[4] Christianity becomes consequently a matter of belonging, of cultivating certain codes, instead of believing.

This rise of national populism is posing as a powerful symbol of an alternative to liberal democracy, at the cost of astonishing collusions with religion.

---

1 Alain Dieckhoff, Christophe Jaffrelot, and Elise Massicard, eds., *Contemporary Populists in Power* (Cham: Palgrave Macmillan, 2022).
2 Olivier Roy, "Beyond Populism", in *Saving the People: How Populists Hijack Religion*, eds. Nadia Marzouki, Duncan McDonnell, and Olivier Roy (London: Hurst, 2016), 186.
3 Alain Dieckhoff and Philippe Portier, "Populist movements and the Religious. Toward a Return of the Theo-Political?", *Journal of Religion in Europe* 16 (2023): 113–124.
4 Dieckhoff and Portier, "Populist movements and the Religious", 119.

Religion reactivates a political cleavage: it is no longer uncommon to see political figures converging their adherence to the Christian faith with their political support for nationalist policies. They merge different topics such as anti-migration and traditional family values to address overlapping concerns.[5] This civilizational Christianity is intensely asserted, for example, in Italy by Fratelli d'Italia of Georgia Meloni or the Lega of Matteo Salvini, the former publicly self-describing as a Christian,[6] the latter putting the Italian people under the protection of the Virgin of Fatima. It is also the case in Poland with the Law and Justice Party (PiS), in Austria with the Freedom Party (FPÖ), in Hungary with the Fidesz Party, in Switzerland with the Union of the Center (UDC), in Germany with the Alternative for Germany (AfD), in France with the National Rally (RN) and the Reconquest Party, in Sweden with the Sweden Democrats, and in Finland with the True Finns Party.[7]

Under the papacy of the late Pope Francis (the Pope), the Catholic Church tried to respond to the rise in all-out nationalism. In his encyclical *Fratelli Tutti*, published in 2020, the Pope critiques the rise of nationalism in Western democracies.[8] Public debate is increasingly structured around the question of identity, and religious identity in particular, but this religious appropriation is not simply the work of political actors. Salvini, for example, has found support in some religious associations. Donald Trump's candidacy in 2016 was also strongly relayed by many prominent Evangelical churches, even as Evangelical support has disintegrated since. Vladimir Putin's aggressive war on Ukraine asserts a transnational or civilizational identity in contrast with 'the West', with overt support from the Patriarchate of Moscow.[9] Aware of the possibility that national or political identity can be nourished by religious foundations, as was the case under

---

5   Timo Koch, "Family Ties and Ethnic Lines: Ethnopluralism in the Far Right's Mobilization in Europe", *Ethnic and Racial Studies* (2024): 1–21.
6   When becoming prime minister in October 2022, Georgia Meloni described herself with her attachment to traditional elements of normativity, at once gendered, familial, national and religious: "I am Georgia. I am a woman, I am a mother, I am Italian, I am Christian".
7   Rogers Brubaker, "Between Nationalism and Civilizationism: The European Populist Moment in Comparative Perspective", *Ethnic and Racial Studies* 40, no. 8 (2017): 1191–1226.
8   Matteo Salvini bypasses the teaching of Pope Francis. For the leader of the Lega, religion is not a message of universal love, which would make no difference between citizens from here and populations from elsewhere.
9   Kathy Rousselet, "Russian Orthodox Imaginaries and Their Family Resemblance to Populism", *Journal of Religion in Europe* 16 (2023): 172–198; Mikhail Suslov, "Holy Rus: The Geopolitical Imagination in the Contemporary Russian Orthodox Church", *Russian Politics & Law* 52, no. 3 (2014). For a better understanding of the ideological discourse shaped by Russian Orthodox Church and Russian Government, see in this volume Van der Tol's and Cibotaru's chapters.

Pope John Paul II,[10] Francis responds to the rise of nationalism with a word of warning, that it is dangerous to merge one's religious with their national identity.

The very origin of the encyclical *Fratelli Tutti* is the fruit of the meeting and dialogue between the Pope and the Grand Imam Ahmad Al-Tayyeb in Abu Dhabi. This meeting, wrote the Pope, "was no mere diplomatic gesture, but a reflection born of dialogue and common commitment. The present Encyclical takes up and develops some of the great themes raised in the Document that we both signed".[11] The following paragraph clarifies its purpose:

> I offer this social Encyclical as a modest contribution to continued reflection, in the hope that in the face of present-day attempts to eliminate or ignore others, we may prove capable of responding with a new vision of fraternity and social friendship that will not remain at the level of words. Although I have written it from the Christian convictions that inspire and sustain me, I have sought to make this reflection an invitation to dialogue among all people of good will.[12]

Francis urges a swift reaction when nationalist rhetoric begins to infiltrate religious circles because, he declares with the Great Imam Ahmad Al-Tayyeb, "God, the Almighty, does not need to be defended by anyone and does not want His name to be used to terrorise people".[13]

This encyclical marks a major departure from the conception of the nation formed by previous popes, John Paul II and Benedict XVI. Despite the attempt of the Second Vatican Council (1962–65) to definitively break the identification of nations with the Church – which had taken the form of a nationalist Catholicism in certain countries such as Spain and Portugal at the time and France earlier in the 1930's – John Paul II started to reintroduce an ambiguity in the conception of nation.[14] In his view, nation is, as family, a natural society and not a political artefact. Nation is thus seen as an anthropological category; nation is defined by culture and territory. In his encyclical *Redemptor hominis* (1979) he delineates the first features of its thought on national identity: there,

---

10 See Grozdanov's chapter in this volume, "When a light cloak turns into a pious cage: Thinking national identity with Karl Barth and John Paul II".
11 Pope Francis, *Fratelli Tutti* [Encyclical Letter on Fraternity and Social Friendship], the Holy See, 3 October 2020, accessed 7 September 2023, https://www.vatican.va/content/francesco/en/encyclicals/documents/papa-francesco_20201003_enciclica-fratelli-tutti.html, 5.
12 Pope Francis, *Fratelli Tutti*, 6.
13 Pope Francis, *Fratelli Tutti*, 6.
14 For a detailed analysis of the theology of the nation developed by John Paul II, see in this volume Grozdanov's contribution.

he makes a strong emphasis on the component of ethnicity in the understanding of identity, namely Christian identity.[15] What emerges is a concept of nation founded in a natural law that "organically" ties human nature and culture to homeland.[16]

Although Pope Benedict XVI has not made the nation a major theme of his pontificate as John Paul II did, he is nevertheless following in the footsteps of the latter.[17] In a speech given in Lourdes in 2008 on "The Church and the Nation", Benedict XVI took up the words of John Paul II's address to the UNESCO conference in 1980:

> "The Nation is in fact"—to take up the words of Pope John Paul II—"the great community of men who are united by various ties, but above all, precisely by culture. The Nation exists 'through' culture and 'for' culture, and it is therefore the great educator of men in order that they may 'be more' in the community" (Address to UNESCO, 2 June 1980, no. 14). From this perspective, drawing attention to France's Christian roots will permit each inhabitant of the country to come to a better understanding of his or her origin and destiny. Consequently, within the current institutional framework and with the utmost respect for the laws that are in force, it is necessary to find a new path, in order to interpret and live from day to day the fundamental values on which the Nation's identity is built.

---

15   John Paul II, *Redemptor Hominis*, The Holy See, 4 March 1979, accessed 12 May 2024, https://www.vatican.va/content/john-paul-ii/en/encyclicals/documents/hf_jp-ii enc 04031979 redemptor-hominis.html, 13.

16   It should nevertheless be noted that John Paul II, despite of his rather perilous way of grounding national belonging in a theology of natural law that emphasizes the role of national identity and patriotism in the formation of religious identities—and vice versa—also made a vibrant appeal to beware of nationalism; In 1994, in a speech to members of the diplomatic corps, Pope John Paul II asserts that "History has shown that nationalism quickly becomes totalitarianism, and that when states are no longer equal, people are no longer equal either. In this way, the natural solidarity between peoples is destroyed, the sense of proportion perverted, and the principle of the unity of the human race scorned. The Catholic Church cannot accept such a vision of things. Universal by nature, she knows herself to be at the service of all and never identifies with a particular national community. She welcomes into her bosom all nations, all races, all cultures" (see: John Paul II, "Address of His Holiness John Paul II to the Diplomatic Corps Accredited to the Holy See", speech, the Holy See, 15 January 1994, accessed 7 December 2023, https://www.vatican.va/content/john-paul-ii/en/speeches/1994/january/documents/hf_jp-ii_spe_19940115_corpo-diplomatico.html).

17   Let us not forget that John Paul II called Cardinal Ratzinger, the future Benedict XVI, already in 1981 to his side to work together on a "doctrinal rearmament" of the Church at a time when Catholicism was experiencing a historic crisis with the definitive accentuation of the secularisation process.

The reference to the Christian roots of a nation – here France – and the discourse at the UNESCO conference are a firm statement that Western societies are organically linked to the message of the gospel and that this message formed the culture of these societies. It also emphasizes how in Benedict XVI's view inherited from John Paul II's, culture as the moral educator of humans is – and ought to be – crucially influenced by Christianity, by its message and values.[18]

Francis' position contrasts sharply with that of his predecessors. However, he preaches in the knowledge that he is going against the ideas of part of his Church. In many Western countries, certain intellectuals, Catholic or otherwise, are claiming to rely on the Church and its tradition to denounce the changes taking place in Western nations. It is striking to see how Catholic new conservatives are reclaiming John Paul II' and Benedict XVI's legacies for that purpose.[19] The centre of traditionalism is no longer exclusively French-speaking Catholicism in Europe, but conservative Catholicism in the United States.[20] This neo-traditionalism, which is superimposed on 'Catholic Trumpism' in the United States, manifests itself in the opposition of bishops – led by Cardinal Burke, Cardinal Sarah, Cardinal Müller, Archbishop Carlo Maria Vigano, etc. – and lay intellectuals who oppose Pope Francis, accusing him of wanting to break up the Church. Taking over anti-gender rhetoric to justify their desire for the sovereignty of the people and Western Christian civilisation, this national identity crisis demonises cultural liberalism and multiculturalism; and it is part of the culture war that is tearing the Catholic Church apart.

Culture war as a protest movement aims to wage a moral crusade against societal changes, particularly related to the cultural and legislative promotion of gender and sexual equality, and the transformation of family models that appears to threaten Christianity's anthropological heritage.[21] The issue of safeguarding this view of gender relations and family models seems crucial for the Catholic Church, as evidenced by the anti-gender campaigns that have swept across Europe, with the *Manif pour tous* (Protest for Everyone) in France in

---

18   Benedict XVI, "Meeting with French Episcopal Conference. Address of His Holiness Benedict XVI", speech, the Holy See, 14 September 2008, accessed 12 May 2024, https://www.vatican.va/content/benedict-xvi/en/speeches/2008/september/documents/hf_ben-xvi_spe_20080914_lourdes-vescovi.html.

19   Peter A. Kwasniewski, ed., *From Benedict's Peace to Francis's War. Catholics Respond to the Motu Proprio "Traditionis Custodes" on the Latin Mass* (New-York: Angelico Press, 2021).

20   Massimo Faggioli, *The Liminal Papacy of Pope Francis: Moving toward Global Catholicity* (New-York: Orbis, 2020).

21   See Van der Tol's chapter in this volume for a detailed analysis of the demonisation of liberalism in the USA, Hungary and Russia by religious and political leaders.

2013 remaining a memorable symbol.[22] According to this perspective, undermining the "natural" conception of family would amount to destroying the fundamental unit of society and, consequently, the last defence against political tyranny.[23]

This is how the theme of immigration and campaigns against sexual rights and marriage for all became two equally important factors explaining the rise of far-right movements within Catholic ranks. The intertwining of these two elements, the fight against gender and the fight against immigration, in a tendency towards conspiratorial discourse, helps to understand the rapid advancement of discourse on the protection of national identity. It is no coincidence that Georgia Meloni, Mike Pence, former Vice President of Donald Trump, Serbian President Aleksandar Vučić, Czech Prime Minister Andrej Babis, Slovenian Prime Minister Janez Jansa, and two French figures from the far-right, Éric Zemmour and Marion Maréchal Le Pen, participated in the "European Demographic Summit" held in Budapest in September 2021 by Hungarian Prime Minister Viktor Orbán, which endorsed the merging of two theories, that of 'gender ideology' and that of the 'Great Replacement'. The 'demographic winter' faced by Europe and the fertility issues of its population are thus attributed to the 'gender ideology' advocating contraception, abortion, and homosexuality. This demographic void, combined with the arrival of migrants, provides the background for the language of the 'Great Replacement'. While Pope Francis is also critical of gender-related issues, he takes the opposite stance on the issue of migration. His defence of migrants has aroused disapproval among the most conservative fringes of the Church; Francis clearly reminds in his encyclical *Fratelli Tutti* that the Catholic Church cannot be used as the guardian of any national identity.[24]

If it seems necessary for the Catholic Church to prevent 'old demons' to coming back, the encyclical nevertheless invites us to ask whether the Pope's arguments and the type of positioning adopted in this text really enable him to achieve his aim: to thwart the identification of religious identity with national

---

22 Roman Kuhar, David Paternotte, eds., *Anti-Gender Campaigns in Europe* (London: Rowman & Littlefield International, 2018).

23 Sociologists of religion agree that this discourse on gender is a political strategy on the part of the Church to reassert the role of religion in the public arena. See Yann Raison Du Cleuziou, *Une Contre-révolution catholique: aux origines de la Manif pour tous* (Paris: Le Seuil, 2019); Philippe Portier and Jean-Paul Willaime, *La Religion dans la France contemporaine : entre sécularisation et recomposition* (Paris: Armand Colin, 2021).

24 This is the case in France, for example, with Eric Zemmour, Michel Onfray, Pierre Manent and Chantal Delsol; in Italy with Giorgia Meloni and Matteo Salvini; in Hungary with Viktor Orbán and in Poland with Ryszard Legutko and Jarosław Kaczyński.

identity. Does the political theology of this encyclical fundamentally delegitimise the fusion of religious and political identities? This paper argues that despite its good intentions, this strategy fails because of the (re-)politicisation of theology. There is therefore a contemporary need for a general reflection on the nature of political theology, and in particular its purpose, insofar as it can renew fundamental reflection on the nature and function of religious phenomena in society. This chapter intends to study how the encyclical goes to great lengths to thwart Christian nationalism by sharply criticising its deployment and proposing a biblical reading of fraternity to fight against the resurgence of nationalism. It also deepens the analysis by questioning the relevance of the political theology suggested by the Pope in this encyclical. It particularly outlines the risk of developing a political theology that is potentially a repoliticised theology of religion.

2 An Encyclical to Thwart Christian Nationalism

2.1 *A Fierce Critique of Nationalism*

In *Fratelli Tutti*, Francis proposes to reflect on three related themes: the sovereignty of states, the nation, and war. These three elements relate to each other and are reflected in the phenomenon of nationalism, which he criticises fiercely. The fact that Francis tackles this issue in the very first chapter, entitled "Dark Clouds over a Closed World", is indicative of the importance he attaches to this scourge, from which his own flock is no longer immune: "In some countries", he writes, "a concept of popular and national unity influenced by various ideologies is creating new forms of selfishness and a loss of the social sense under the guise of defending national interests".[25] In this chapter, he denounces the conflicts disguised as the defence of national interests, which are evidence that "instances of a myopic, extremist, resentful and aggressive nationalism are on the rise".[26] The terms used are strong. Pope Francis makes Christianity's view of nationalism, xenophobia, violence and contempt extremely clear: these are expressions of unacceptable feelings of domination and destruction. The Church, he acknowledges, took too long to denounce the system of slavery based on the same affects; and it can no longer side with the oppressors. This mentality of oppression and closure is therefore unacceptable for Christianity because it jeopardises the development of human brotherhood.[27] Yet it seems

---

25   Pope Francis, *Fratelli Tutti*, 11.
26   Pope Francis, *Fratelli Tutti*, 11.
27   Pope Francis, *Fratelli Tutti*, 39.

that the experience of war does not serve as an opportunity for societies to learn about brotherhood. Pope Francis asks, is this due to collective laziness? A loss of memory?

The Pope puts forward the hypothesis of a loss of a sense of history, a lack of transmission and even contempt for the wealth of past generations. According to him, the culture of capitalism is largely responsible for eroding the links between generations.[28] It produces societies in which people become rootless and easily fall into the trap of ideologies.[29] It is a disguised form of cultural colonisation that contributes to people abandoning their own traditions, letting themselves be "robbed of their soul" as they seek to imitate another culture. The consequences are devastating: these societies lose "their spiritual identity, their moral consistency and, finally, their ideological, economic and political independence".[30] Without a sense or knowledge of history, nationalism proliferates, seizing on this ignorance to rewrite history by twisting it to suit a political agenda.

As well as liquefying historical consciousness, this capitalist culture sows division: "this culture unifies the world but divides persons and nations".[31] In a very sharp manner, Francis expresses how capitalist economy imposes a single cultural model that exploits local conflicts to impose the interests of transnational economic powers. It is therefore easy to understand how global capitalism serves as a support for the rise of nationalism, he explains. Nationalism feeds on this disintegration of historical consciousness and on the feeling of powerlessness in the face of economic powers with bellicose methods that political powers struggle to regulate. In a barely veiled way, the Pope denounces the hegemonic power of the United States and the "infrastructure strategies"[32]

---

28 Among the important factors mentioned by the Pope to explain the end of historical consciousness is the idea of the "cultural penetration of a kind of 'deconstructionism', in which human freedom claims to build everything from scratch". Note the vagueness surrounding his use of the term "deconstructionism". It seems to be a tendentious criticism of the theory of deconstruction used in the social sciences and philosophy in the wake of French theory. The Vatican's critique of the concept of gender, for example, invokes the same type of deconstructionist argument that the Church's magisterium condemns because it promotes an all-powerful human freedom unbound by the natural limits of creation.
29 Pope Francis, *Fratelli Tutti*, 12, 13, 14.
30 Cardinal Raúl Silva Henríquez, Homily at the Te deum in Santiago de Chile, 18 September 1974.
31 Pope Francis, *Fratelli Tutti*, 12.
32 The walls built at the borders of the United States, Hungary and Poland bear witness to this. To protect themselves from the enemy outside, the migrant, and from the enemy within, the liberal culture and Brussels, these latter two countries are pursuing tough poli-

of that country and others in Europe, such as Hungary and Poland, which have succumbed to the "the temptation to build a culture of walls, to raise walls, walls in the heart, walls on the land, in order to prevent this encounter with other cultures, with other people".[33] Nationalists, turning in on themselves, "err in thinking that they can develop on their own, heedless of the ruin of others, that by closing their doors to others they will be better protected. Immigrants are seen as usurpers who have nothing to offer".[34]

Nationalist rhetoric plays on the spread of despair, discouragement, and distrust of liberal democratic institutions.[35] Under the guise of defending traditional values and using critical and declinist rhetoric, nationalist leaders deny, in various ways, the right of others to exist and weaken the principle of fraternity. Differences of opinion about the norms and values that structure society, particularly those that shape family models, have become tools in the hands of populists. Of course, the Pope would not risk defending emerging sexual and family models that contradict the moral doctrine of the Catholic Church, but he does insist that everyone should be vigilant with regard to the use of social networks on the internet, which encourage and capitalise on users' penchant for controversy by creating binary divisions between 'them' and 'us' on the fringes of conspiracy thinking, which nationalist leaders know perfectly well how to exploit.[36] The Pope sees this binary principle as one of the reasons for

---

cies: the construction of border walls that are becoming no-rights zones to prevent the arrival of foreigners (already built in Hungary and a project approved in Poland), and an extremely effective pro-natalist policy since 2010 to perpetuate the national culture (in Hungary, 5% of GDP is devoted to this pro-natalist policy).

33   Pope Francis, *Fratelli Tutti*, 27.
34   Pope Francis, *Fratelli Tutti*, 141.
35   Poland's Law and Justice party and Hungary's Fidesz are mobilising around a declinist discourse, that of a Europe and its civilisation affected by a cultural and demographic depression generated by liberalism. According to the speeches of their leaders, particularly the one given by Orbàn during his victory in the 2019 European elections, Brussels' plan is to put an end to Christianity and nations through mass immigration. Aware of this plan, the political leaders of Hungary and Poland present themselves as the sole defenders of European civilisation, nation states and the Christian faith. For Ryszard Legutko, leader of the Law and Justice party in the European Parliament, "the nation states are the bulwark of protection against the destruction of European Christian culture by Brussels", and for Orbàn, "every country in Europe has the right to protect its Christian culture, it has the right to reject the ideology of multiculturalism".
36   Posts and threads on social media are the favourite mode of communication of populist leaders. It allows producing a message that is both emotional and immediate, unfiltered by radios and media of the elites in place. See: Rita Marchetti, Nicola Righetti, Susanna Pagiotti, and Anna Stanziano, "Right-Wing Populism and Political Instrumentalization of

the success of nationalism and warns repeatedly in the encyclical against this simplistic way of thinking, recalling the unfortunate lessons of history.

2.2 Biblical Brotherhood to Fight the Scourge of Nationalism

But once Francis has so fiercely criticised nationalism and its capitalist support, how does he respond to the underlying anxieties that motivate a growing public support for a dangerous ideology? The Pope's response is to draw on the concept of biblical brotherhood to overcome these anxieties. The result is a detailed reflection on the link between the need for peoples to put down roots and the universalism of fraternity. Francis insists as much on the importance of being rooted in one's own tradition as he does on welcoming foreigners when they come peacefully. It is only in this articulation of the particular and the universal that authentic encounters and mutual enrichment can take place:

> Just as there can be no dialogue with 'others' without a sense of our own identity, so there can be no openness between peoples except on the basis of love for one's own land, one's own people, one's own cultural roots. I cannot truly encounter another unless I stand on firm foundations, for it is on the basis of these that I can accept the gift the other brings and in turn offer an authentic gift of my own. I can welcome others who are different, and value the unique contribution they have to make, only if I am firmly rooted in my own people and culture. Everyone loves and cares for his or her native land and village, just as they love and care for their home and are personally responsible for its upkeep.[37]

The Church, he says, defends the fact that peoples are attached to their language, their culture, their faith and their roots, as long as this resistance is peaceful and opposed to a hollow and superficial cosmopolitanism that ultimately favours the globalisation of capitalist culture: "There can be a false openness to the universal, born of the shallowness of those lacking insight into the genius of their native land or harbouring unresolved resentment towards their own people".[38] The Church approves of the desire of peoples to maintain their languages, customs and traditions, but at the same time affirms that all human beings created by the same creator are entitled to equal dignity

---

Religion. The Italian Debate on Matteo Salvini's Use of Religious Symbols on Facebook", *Journal of Religion in Europe* 16 (2023): 144–171.

37 Pope Francis, *Fratelli Tutti*, 143.
38 Pope Francis, *Fratelli Tutti*, 145.

and respect: "All individuals, whatever their origin, know that they are part of the greater human family, without which they will not be able to understand themselves fully".[39] It is here, at the turn of the family metaphor, that the concept of biblical brotherhood emerges. What does it consist of?

The family metaphor is rooted in biblical tradition: God made a special covenant with Abraham and his descendants after him, with a view to linking him with all the nations, called "families". As the verse in Genesis says: "in you all the families of the earth shall be blessed" (12.3b, NRSV). The particularity of the covenant calls for the universality of salvation and, in so doing, for brotherhood between families, between nations. The biblical foundation of brotherhood is therefore God, as creator and parent of all creatures. There is also a Christological foundation: Christians recognise "Christ in every abandoned brother and sister". Relations with strangers are built on the ability to "recognise the face of Christ in the other".

But the meaning of this biblical fraternity takes on its full significance in the encyclical's constant reference to the parable of the Good Samaritan, which serves as the common thread running through the Pope's reflections. What does this stranger have to say when, on a journey, he changes all his plans in order to help a stranger whom others have abandoned on the side of the road, asks Francis. The Good Samaritan did not try to find out who his neighbour was, what people or religion he came from, but simply made himself the neighbour of the man on the ground, dying. This parable, as Paul Ricoeur read it, shows that "the neighbour is the double requirement of the near and the far".[40] He, the stranger from a faraway land, became close to this person in need. This is where neighbour meets fraternity, unconditional solidarity: it means turning the attention to ever greater singularity and universality. And it is in how, according to the Pope, the feeling of fraternity, the idea of anonymous charity, is an essential political feeling.

Pope Francis has therefore made the principle of fraternity the subject of an entire encyclical. From the very first lines, he describes a fraternity that is defined by space:

> "FRATELLI TUTTI". With these words, Saint Francis of Assisi addressed his brothers and sisters and proposed to them a way of life marked by the flavour of the Gospel. Of the counsels Francis offered, I would like to select the one in which he calls for a love that transcends the barriers of geography and distance, and declares blessed all those who love their

---

39   Pope Francis, *Fratelli Tutti*, 149.
40   Paul Ricoeur, "Le socius et le prochain", in *Histoire et vérité* (Paris: Seuil, 1954).

brother "as much when he is far away from him as when he is with him". In his simple and direct way, Saint Francis expressed the essence of a fraternal openness that allows us to acknowledge, appreciate and love each person, regardless of physical proximity, regardless of where he or she was born or lives.[41]

At a time of a renewed culture of walls at state borders, defining fraternity by space is highly significant: in the papal text, fraternity is a space of conviviality for the sake of the common good. It is a political proposal of experiencing fraternity and social friendship. The Pope's thinking is shaped in a cosmopolitan imaginary; he starts from the principle that to be human, i.e. to learn to see oneself in others, implies welcoming one another. He thus challenges the demographic imagination of nationalism, which is rooted in a nativist perspective that assumes that one population will replace another.

If the Pope is so careful to define the contours of the concept of biblical brotherhood, it is in order to be able to resist the old demons of nationalism in concrete terms. In the face of the tragedies of migration and identitarian withdrawal, Francis defends a resolute concept of brotherhood that is a response to the rise of nationalism in Europe. He urges to make fraternity a voluntary policy, namely to be someone's neighbour, to consider the parable of the Good Samaritan, implies a political praxis. By taking up the ethical consequences of the parable of the Samaritan, the Pope questions the political scope of the text:

> What would be the reaction to that same story nowadays, in a world that constantly witnesses the emergence and growth of social groups clinging to an identity that separates them from others? How would it affect those who organize themselves in a way that prevents any foreign presence that might threaten their identity and their closed and self-referential structures? There, even the possibility of acting as a neighbour is excluded; one is a neighbour only to those who serve their purpose. The word 'neighbour' loses all meaning; there can only be 'associates', partners in the pursuit of particular interests.[42]

In a climate of unabashed xenophobia, of ever harsher migration policies, of ever more alarming situations of distress and precariousness, these questions are an appeal to the faith of Catholics tempted by the extreme nationalist

---

41   Pope Francis, *Fratelli Tutti*, 1.
42   Pope Francis, *Fratelli Tutti*, 102.

right: "rather than expressing your anxieties in the ballot papers, anchor yourself in your faith", the Pope seems to be saying.

However, if this controversy over migration runs through the Church, it goes much further, touching the very foundations of democratic societies. Disregard for fraternity undermines both equality and liberty. On the one hand, equality is not achieved by pure incantation: "it is the result of the conscious and careful cultivation of fraternity".[43] On the other hand, liberty is weakened because it is the result of education in fraternity, in dialogue, in the discovery of reciprocity and mutual enrichment as values.[44] This is why "fraternity necessarily calls for something greater, which in turn enhances freedom and equality".[45] The value of fraternity is therefore a cardinal political principle that must guide institutions from within. It is the source of democratic institutional and political culture, which has been secularised in terms of social justice.

Fraternity must therefore be cultivated consciously, through a political will. Democratic societies shouldn't take the practice of fraternity for granted; on the contrary, aware of the effort it represents, it encourages its practice through a constant movement of openness, from close to close. No one immediately becomes everyone's brother, recalls the Pope. Through experience, those close to us are discovered as brothers and sisters, until we become capable of widening our outlook and bringing newcomers into the fraternal field of vision. This process presupposes in particular the promotion of conditions for dialogue and encounter.

The Pope exhorts building a specific environment to develop an ethic of dialogue that embraces the plurality of people. Dialogue is not a threat to the identity of those engaged in it. On the contrary, it presupposes a deeply rooted identity. Taking up the theme of 'roots' used by populist leaders, Francis seems to want to reclaim the term and take it in a different direction. The Pope's approach is therefore to instil what is all too often lacking in the political class: a new political horizon of social friendship with those near and far. The encyclical outlines what is meant by "a way of life marked by the flavour of the Gospel" and urges its readers, whether religious or not, to be partners in dialogue, inviting them to take a fruitful approach to anchoring justice and peace in contemporary societies.

---

43   Pope Francis, *Fratelli Tutti*, 104.
44   Pope Francis, *Fratelli Tutti*, 103.
45   Pope Francis, *Fratelli Tutti*, 103.

3 A Failed Attempt? The Risk of a Repoliticised Theology of Religion

The Pope's proposition is powerful. He delineates a reflection that manages to overcome the binary alternative that opposes the communitarian civilization to the individualist civilization. He proposes a way of reinventing brotherhood and the human need of roots in the face of nationalist's anti-universalist tradition as well as of liberal's cosmopolitan projects. He rejects the idea of a social ethics of its own territory. According to him, there is no substantial community shaped around a religious core that pre-exists the individuals.

The encyclical is therefore one of those with a strong political charge. The word 'political' appears almost a hundred times in the text, in different contexts, and that is significant. This piece of doctrine comes from the necessity for the Pope to clarify the confusion that reigns within the Catholic Church on what should be the public role of religion. Positively, the religious plays as a principle of gathering. Negatively, it plays as a principle of exclusion and discrimination, delimiting the borders of 'the sanctuary', setting apart some and designating others as intruders. Since the crisis caused by the war in Syria in 2011, the migration issue in Europe, which presupposes the question of borders and national identity, has reactivated intense political divisions within the Catholic community. It is in response to these divisions and the confusion that reigns in the Church that the encyclical seeks to clarify its political positioning. But even if the necessity of condemning this phenomenon is crucial, the Pope's mode of arguing replicates a type of political theology that does not serve its purpose.

Within the Catholic Church in Europe, some Catholics want "the old world to come back", affirming the culture of the majority in the face of the "tyranny of minorities" whether sexual, racial, or religious.[46] They nostalgically nurture the political imagination of a close alliance between religion and politics, making the Church the guarantor of the social and political order. They claim to be inspired by Carl Schmitt and his conception of politics on an ideal model that he grounded in the visible and transcendent Church: the absolute sovereign. Carl Schmitt's source of inspiration "has been relayed, from the Russian intellectuals of Izborsk to those of *Nouvelle École*, a journal edited by Alain de Benoist, leader of the 'New Right', and by many networks of influence".[47] He drew on Roman Catholicism to elaborate a restorative power of politics. Papal

---

46 Pascale Tournier, *Le vieux monde est de retour. Enquête sur les nouveaux conservateurs* (Paris: Stock, 2018).

47 Dieckhoff and Portier, "Populist movements and the Religious", 122.

infallibility, for example, served as a model for his theory of decisionism, the idea that "the one who decides on the exceptional situation is sovereign".[48]

In the face of the Antichrist, in the face of the Enemy, a decision-making state is required which does not bother with humanist prejudices.[49] The designation of the political enemy is based on "the vital need to maintain one's own existence in the face of an equally vital negation".[50] The Schmittian interpretation of the Christian narrative stresses its agonistic dimension, underlining how the Roman church led, during its medieval climax, a great fight against the forces of evil. It is easy to see how these thinkers use Schmitt to insist on the nation's need of an enemy to ensure its survival. Reactivating the principle of the scapegoat, they designate an enemy to create political unity. And the enemy is not only outside the nation, but also within it. Their interpretation of Schmittian thought renews an erroneous interpretation of the Gospels to draw a distinction between the public, political enemy and the private enemy, and, in so doing, confines love of enemies to the private sphere.[51] This is how Carl Schmitt's political theology is being used today by Catholic thinkers to legitimise authoritarian regimes or to praise the nation state, with the gospels left as a purely private source of interpersonal fraternity.[52]

But more interestingly, this invocation of Carl Schmitt raises the question of the type of political theology some Catholic thinkers mobilize. An important distinction needs to be made here, that was only implicitly outlined above. The type of political theology used by these Catholics is very different from that forged by Carl Schmitt. For Schmitt, on one hand, political theology is understood as the excavation and recognition of "the historical weight of concepts".[53] Schmitt's concept sets out a programme of scholarly research into the history of the secularisation of the main Catholic theological concepts. Carl Schmitt's concept of political theology refers to the search and analysis of certain structural analogies, formulated analytically and explained historically, between theological concepts and legal concepts. Carl Schmitt's work is to demonstrate that all the prominent concepts of modern state theory are indeed secularised theological concepts. Carl Schmitt gives the name political

---

48   Carl Schmitt, *Political Theology* (Chicago: University of Chicago Press, 2021 (1922)). Translation mine.
49   Carl Schmitt, "The Visibility of the Church: A Scholastic Consideration", in *Roman Catholicism and Political Form*, trans. G.L. Ulmen (Westport: Greenwood, 1996 (1917)), 45–61.
50   Carl Schmitt, *The Concept of the Political* (Chicago: University of Chicago Press, 1996 (1932)). Translation mine.
51   See in particular his interpretation of Mt. 5.44 and Lk. 6.27 in *The Concept of the Political*.
52   In France, this is the case of Rémi Brague, Pierre Manent and Chantal Delsol, for example.
53   Hans Maier, *Kritik der politischen Theologie* (Einsiedeln: Johannes Verlag, 1970), 14.

theology to what is in reality a theory of sovereignty and not a justification of the political role of religion. In other words, he doesn't try to justify the capacity of religion to generate political affirmations that are taken up publicly. One might even say, as Hermann Lübbe does, that Carl Schmitt's concept of political theology is in fact politically inoffensive: it is a search for analogies between theological concepts and their secularised legal product.[54]

For these Catholics, on the other hand, the political theology they elaborate is a repoliticised version of religion. It is a theology that regrets that the Catholic religion no longer has the constitutive power over politics that it had in the past. It is therefore a completely different programme from that of Carl Schmitt, which is above all an academic research programme, even if it is mistakenly used to justify the repoliticisation of the Catholic religion. The agenda for this new political theology is not to broaden scholarly perspectives on the analogies between theological and legal concepts. Lübbe warns that political theology as the theology of a repoliticised religion and political theology as the history of the secularisation of theological concepts and their relationship to legal concepts are two things that shouldn't be confused.[55]

However, on this reading of *Fratelli Tutti*, the Pope's encyclical leaves room for a political theology conceived as a theology of a political religion. Although the political theology forged by Francis in his encyclical is different in terms of political positioning, this type of political theology is nonetheless part of the same scope of repoliticising religion, as the Catholic thinkers he is responding to. What I am interested in here is questioning this type of political theology, which is trying to turn the Christian religion into a political force and to mobilise Christians for this project. If the Pope is seeking to counter the effects of this political theology which feeds a dangerous Christian nationalism, his ambition fails in part because he responds with a proposal that is of the same order, even though it is on the opposite end of the political spectrum.

But what does the term 'political theology' refer to? What distinguishes a theology that maintains that "Marxism" has "reminded Christians of the topicality of the proclamation of the reign of God" and urged them to "carry out at least approximately the revolutionary programme and the relative utopia of transforming the existing situation and abolishing, on the greatest possible

---

54   Herman Lübbe, "Politische Theologie als Theologie repolisierter Religion?", in *Der Fürst dieser Welt. Carl Schmitt und die Folgen*, ed. Jacob Taubes (Munich: Paderborn, Wilhelm Fink Verlag, 1983), 7.
55   Lübbe, "Politische Theologie als Theologie repolisierter Religion?", 45–56.

scale, all injustice and oppression",[56] from a theology like *Fratelli Tutti*, which invites Christians to savour fraternity as a way of living politics with the flavour of the Gospel, or a theology that remobilises Carl Schmitt to defend national particularism? These three political theologies work on the basis of the same axiom, namely that of wanting to mobilise Christians politically by appealing to their religious conscience. At the end, this type of political theology is a theology that seeks to reassert the critical potential of religion.

Consequently, it raises the question of the political status of these theological statements on issues that affect the entire political community. The controversy that *Fratelli Tutti* has stirred up in Catholic circles, between those who welcome its call for universal fraternity and those who question it, poses a problem: what is the status of a theological statement on a political issue? Is it for the personal discernment of each Catholic citizen? Does it have a normative aim for Catholic communities in terms of the direction they should give to their political commitment? All these questions point out that a political theology of a repoliticized religion as informed by Francis or by conservative Catholic thinkers generates a reworking of the liberal dualism between private morality and the political sphere.

Essentially, it's a question of asking what these theological-political discourses really add to a political issue when, on all sides, they claim to "root this aspiration in the Gospel".[57] The risk for this type of theology is that it renders the Gospel meaningless when it is used to say what can be said every day in political discussions, without the help of religion.[58] Theologies that postulate that "every religious statement must also be a political statement" in fact signal the disappearance of religion in its most singular form: the possibility of an address to God.[59] In this sense, the attempt to develop a theology that is also a political theory presents dangers for both politics and religion. It is not a question of preferring to marginalise the religious question, but of ensuring that it does not become the main axis of political positioning.

Fratelli Tutti testifies a mutation of politics in Europe. With the long process of secularization, it was expected that religion would be reduced to its sole private function. However, nationalism and populism break with this trend,

---

56   Helmut Gollwitzer, "La révolution du règne de Dieu et la société", in Jürgen Moltmann et al., *Discussion sur la "Théologie de la révolution"* (Paris: Cerf-Mame, 1972).

57   Dorothee Sölle, *Politische Theologie* (Stuttgart, Berlin: Kreuz Verlag, 1971), 97.

58   Robert Spaemann, "Theologie, Prophetie, Politik. Zur Kritik der Politischen Theologie", in *Zur Kritik der politischen Utopie. Zehn Kapitel politischer Philosophie* (Stuttgart: Ernst Klett Verlag, 1977), 57–76.

59   Dorothee Sölle and Fulbert Steffensky, eds., *Nachgebet in Köln* (Stuttgart: Kreuz Verlag, 1969), 21.

incorporating the Christian religious narrative into its core discourses. Far from being simply an aestheticization of the discourse for political purposes, it seems to be backed by some religious thinkers and associations to whom Francis responds with his encyclical. He urges a swift reaction to fight against the infiltration of nationalist rhetoric within religious circles. To a corrosive political situation of endless dualism between 'us' and 'them', the Pope calls upon a political friendship that sees differences as a God-given plurality. But in this pluralism, opinions that incite violence, hostility or the building of walls are certainly wrong and need to be disqualified: "still", he writes, "there are those who appear to feel encouraged or at least permitted by their faith to support varieties of narrow and violent nationalism, xenophobia and contempt, and even the mistreatment of those who are different".[60]

Yet it is here, for him, in the test of otherness represented by the practice of fraternity, that not only the gospel message is fulfilled, but also the promise of a democratic pact that needs to be constantly refounded. This is so crucial that the Pope calls on the Catholic Church and her officials to become more political in their catechesis and preaching, so that they "speak more directly and clearly about the social meaning of existence, the fraternal dimension of spirituality, our conviction of the inalienable dignity of each person, and our reasons for loving and accepting all our brothers and sisters".[61] However, this kind of exhortation as a response to Catholic support of nationalism can be risky; both narratives are locked into a kind of theo-political enunciation that have a performative value, configuring a space of meaning that normatively determines the politics and the religious.

Bibliography

Brubaker, R. (2017). "Between Nationalism and Civilizationism: The European Populist Moment in Comparative Perspective". *Ethnic and Racial Studies* 40, no. 8: 1191–1226.

Cardinal R.S. Henríquez. (1974). "Homily at the Te deum in Santiago de Chile". 18 September 1974.

Dieckhoff, A., and P. Portier. (2023). "Populist movements and the Religious. Toward a Return of the Theo-Political?". *Journal of Religion in Europe* 16: 113–124.

Dieckhoff, A., C. Jaffrelot, and E. Massicard, eds. (2022). *Contemporary Populists in Power*. Cham: Palgrave Macmillan.

---

60   Pope Francis, *Fratelli Tutti*, 86.
61   Pope Francis, *Fratelli Tutti*, 86.

Faggioli, M. (2020). *The Liminal Papacy of Pope Francis: Moving toward Global Catholicity*. New-York: Orbis.

Gollwitzer, H. (1972). "La révolution du règne de Dieu et la société". In Jürgen Moltmann et al., *Discussion sur la "Théologie de la révolution"*. Paris: Cerf-Mame.

Hastings, A. (1997). *The Construction of Nationhood: Ethnicity, Religion and Nationalism*. Cambridge: Cambridge University Press.

Koch, T. (2024). "Family Ties and Ethnic Lines: Ethnopluralism in the Far Right's Mobilization in Europe". *Ethnic and Racial Studies*: 1–21.

Kuhar, R., and D. Paternotte, eds. (2018). *Anti-Gender Campaigns in Europe*. London: Rowman & Littlefield International.

Kwasniewski, P.A., ed. (2021). *From Benedict's Peace to Francis's War. Catholics Respond to the Motu Proprio "Traditionis Custodes" on the Latin Mass*. New-York: Angelico Press.

Lübbe, H. (1983). "Politische Theologie als Theologie repolisierter Religion?". In: J. Taubes (ed.), *Der Fürst dieser Welt. Carl Schmitt und die Folgen*. Munich, Paderborn, Wilhelm Fink Verlag.

Maier, H. (1970). *Kritik der politischen Theologie*. Einsiedeln: Johannes Verlag.

Marchetti, R., N. Righetti, S. Pagiotti, and A. Stanziano. (2023). "Right-Wing Populism and Political Instrumentalization of Religion. The Italian Debate on Matteo Salvini's Use of Religious Symbols on Facebook". *Journal of Religion in Europe* 16: 144–171.

Pope Benedict XVI. (2008). "Meeting with French Episcopal Conference. Address of His Holiness Benedict XVI" [Speech]. The Holy See, 14 September 2008. https://www.vatican.va/content/benedict-xvi/en/speeches/2008/september/documents/hf_ben-xvi_spe_20080914_lourdes-vescovi.html.

Pope Francis and Grand Imam of Al-Azhar Ahmad Al-Tayyeb. (2019). *A Document on Human Fraternity for World Peace and Living Together*. Abu Dhabi, 3–5 February 2019. https://www.vatican.va/content/francesco/en/travels/2019/outside/documents/papa-francesco_20190204_documento-fratellanza-umana.html.

Pope Francis. (2020). *Fratelli Tutti* [Encyclical Letter on Fraternity and Social Friendship]. The Holy See, 3 October 2020. https://www.vatican.va/content/francesco/en/encyclicals/documents/papa-francesco_20201003_enciclica-fratelli-tutti.html.

Pope John Paul II. (1979). *Redemptor Hominis* [Encyclical]. The Holy See, 4 March 1979. https://www.vatican.va/content/john-paul-ii/en/encyclicals/documents/hf_jp-ii_enc_04031979_redemptor-hominis.html.

Pope John Paul II. (1994). "Address of His Holiness John Paul II to the Diplomatic Corps Accredited to the Holy See" [Speech]. The Holy See, 15 January 1994. https://www.vatican.va/content/john-paul-ii/en/speeches/1994/january/documents/hf_jp-ii_spe_19940115_corpo-diplomatico.html.

Portier, P., and J.P. Willaime. (2021). *La Religion dans la France contemporaine: entre sécularisation et recomposition*. Paris : Armand Colin.

Raison Du Cleuziou, Y. (2019). *Une Contre-révolution catholique : aux origines de la Manif pour tous.* Paris: Le Seuil.

Ricoeur, P. (1954). "Le socius et le prochain". In: *Histoire et vérité.* Paris: Seuil.

Rousselet, K. (2023). "Russian Orthodox Imaginaries and Their Family Resemblance to Populism". *Journal of Religion in Europe* 16: 172–198.

Roy, O. (2016). "Beyond Populism". In Nadia Marzouki, Duncan McDonnell, and Olivier Roy (eds.), *Saving the People: How Populists Hijack Religion.* London: Hurst.

Schmitt, C. (1996a (1917)). "The Visibility of the Church: A Scholastic Consideration". In *Roman Catholicism and Political Form.* Translated by G.L. Ulmen. Westport: Greenwood. Pp. 45–61.

Schmitt, C. (1996b (1932)). *The Concept of the Political.* Chicago: University of Chicago Press.

Schmitt, C.. (2021 (1922)). *Political Theology.* Chicago: University of Chicago Press.

Sölle, D. (1971). *Politische Theologie.* Stuttgart, Berlin: Kreuz Verlag.

Sölle, D., and F. Steffensky, eds. (1969). *Nachgebet in Köln.* Stuttgart: Kreuz Verlag.

Spaemann, R. (1977). "Theologie, Prophetie, Politik. Zur Kritik der Politischen Theologie". In *Zur Kritik der politischen Utopie. Zehn Kapitel politischer Philosophie.* Stuttgart: Ernst Klett Verlag.

Suslov, M. (2014). "Holy Rus: The Geopolitical Imagination in the Contemporary Russian Orthodox Church". *Russian Politics & Law* 52, No. 3.

Tournier, P. (2018). *Le vieux monde est de retour. Enquête sur les nouveaux conservateurs.* Paris: Stock.

CHAPTER 5

The Russian World, The Hungarian World, and Make America Great Again: Political Imaginaries and Their Spaces

Marietta van der Tol

1   Introduction

This chapter explores the role of space in three current political imaginaries: the Kremlin's use of the Russian World, Viktor Orbán's notion of the Hungarian World, and Donald Trump's Make America Great Again campaign.[1] These political imaginaries sustain pseudo-historical claims to specific spaces which are reinforced through attempts at establishing political dominance within those spaces and are sanctioned through the sacralisation of the triangle of people, space, and 'traditional values'. The function of these political imaginaries is not necessarily descriptive or indeed historical: they contest the political order as it was settled after the world wars of the twentieth century. These political imaginaries are reflections of loss and anger, or of the belief that certain states have lost out in recent history.[2] These reflections of loss and anger might refer to the demise of the Russian Empire, the loss of territories that were previously associated with the Kingdom of Hungary, and Latino migration to the United States of America. Imaginaries such as Russian World, the Hungarian World, and the MAGA-campaign might be understood as contestations of what is more than as an imagination of what can be.

This chapter is not invested in proving either of these political imaginaries wrong. Since they do not rely on historical accuracy, they cannot be rebutted by mere historical facts. Instead, this chapter analyses the significance of the sacred and of sacred space in these imaginaries, building on the idea

---

1   Benedict Anderson, *Imagined Communities: Reflections on the Origin and Spread of Nationalism* (London: Verso, 1983).
2   Alexandra Homolar and Georg Löfflmann, "Populism and the Affective Politics of Humiliation Narratives", *Global Studies Quarterly* 1, no. 1 (2021): 1–11; Vincent Lloyd, "Anger: A Secularized Theological Concept", in *The Spirit of Populism*, eds. Ulrich Schmiedel and Joshua Ralston (Leiden: Brill, 2021), 25–39.

of "secularisation as the fragmentation of the sacred and of sacred space".[3] Whereas the engagement of the sacred has been important for attracting the support of (some) religious conservatives, this chapter argues that the Russian World, the Hungarian World, and the MAGA-campaign are stories of the sacred that fundamentally serve (secular) political interests. Whereas they may court both secular and religious cultural and intellectual repertoires, their contestation of the secular-liberal order should not be merely understood within the 'return of religion' frame. Instead, these political imaginaries contest what has been understood as the secular as well as the sacred, offering an alternative cultural Christianity that is more or less distanced from scripture, tradition, and reason.[4] What remains of the religious moorings of Christian identity is at best ancillary to, and potentially at odds with, them.

2 Typologies of Space as Mediators of the Spiritual and the Material

Much like time, material space is capacious to a variety of ascriptions of meaning.[5] In the Western tradition, space is primarily conceived of as sacred or profane and is mediated through the notions of religious freedom and theoretical distinctions between religious and public spaces. Sacred spaces are bounded through symbolic presence, for example, the location of churches, the height of the tower, parish boundaries, and the location of cemeteries. Space is also understood along the typologies of the public and the private, while private spaces may or may not be bounded by material frames of reference, such as fences, gates, and walls.[6] They signal ownership and authority over space and are designed to keep others out. State borders carry this material and symbolic meaning too, and it matters who can gain access and who is denied it. The political imaginary of the nation state appends further layers of meaning to state boundaries: it signals ownership and authority over a specific territory and ascribes this to the imagined communities of nations.

---

3   M.D.C. Van der Tol and P.S. Gorski, "Secularisation as the fragmentation of the sacred and of sacred space", *Religion, State and Society* 50, no. 5 (2022): 495–512.
4   M. Balkenhol, E. van den Hemel, and I. Stengs, "Introduction: Emotional Entanglements of Sacrality and Secularity—Engaging the Paradox" in *The Secular Sacred*, eds. M. Balkenhol, E. van den Hemel, and I. Stengs (Cham: Palgrave Macmillan, 2020), 1–18.
5   M.D.C. Van der Tol, *Constitutional Intolerance: The Fashioning of the Other in Europe's Constitutional Repertoires* (Cambridge: Cambridge University Press, 2025); R. Koselleck, *Futures Past: On the Semantics of Historical Time*, trans. K. Tribe (New York: Columbia University Press, 2004).
6   Chris C. Clark, *Sacred Worlds: An Introduction to Geography and Religion* (London: Routledge, 1994).

Post-war amalgamations of states and state borders have created these material frames of reference on the world map. Sometimes they are intricately drawn, while others originate on the political drawing tables of the great powers. State borders, like history, tend to be determined by those who are powerful. While they might settle the aspirations of some political communities, they may well alienate others. For example, Hungarian nationalists have successfully appropriated the Treaty of Trianon as a national trauma: contemporary Hungary is significantly smaller than the Kingdom of Hungary was as part of the Austro-Hungarian Empire before 1918.[7] The unification of Romania meant that a sizable ethnic Hungarian minority living in the multi-ethnic region of Transylvania became part of Romania, which continue to fuel powerful sentiments of loss among Hungarian nationalists. While the state borders are not subject to negotiation, these sentiments of loss can be played up on a perennial basis. The notion of the Russian World, however, reaches back to the spatial significance of the Russian Empire, constructing the establishment of post-Soviet states as independent states as a challenge to the civilisational self-consciousness that it supports. The MAGA-campaign oriented a sense of loss at both external and internal others, signalled through hostility towards Latino migrants, the notion of 'Take America Back', and the current attack on its own state institutions.

Political imaginaries provide typologies of space. They claim space for a certain narrative of belonging, in the context of this chapter, for the Russian Federation, Hungary, and the United States of America. The significance of political imaginaries does not necessarily rest on the content of specific typologies: that there is a space that they consider as Russian, Hungarian, or American. Rather, its significance relies on its capacity to contest the material delineations of space. As is discussed in greater detail below, the Russian World ideology contests the sphere of liberal influence in post-Soviet states, most notably in Ukraine and Georgia. Similarly, the Hungarian World relies on its contestation of liberalism in Hungary and collapses this contestation in constructed memories of the loss of land and people. The MAGA-campaign is different in that its outlook is primarily protectionist, signified through the trope of 'America First' – echoing the idea of 'Russia First'.[8] The political

---

7 László Levente Balogh and Christoph Leitgeb, eds., *Opfermythen in Zentraleuropa* (Munich: Praesens Verlag, 2021).
8 Anna Matveeva, cited in Igor Torbakov, "'Middle Continent' or 'Island Russia': Eurasianist Legacy and Vadi Tsymburskii's Revisionist Geopolitics", in *Cultural and Political Imaginaries in Putin's Russia*, eds. Niklas Bernsand and Barbara Törnquist-Plewa (Leiden: Brill, 2019), 37–62.

significance lies in threats to democracy, whether through the violence of the Capitol Insurrection and the current authoritarian turn, Orbán's illiberal politics and repeated clashes with the European Commission, as well as Russia's contestation of the international order.

In other words, the assertion of these narratives of dominance occur where belonging (and borders) are contested. This spiritualisation is not a new phenomenon: it is often a response to pressure, whether real, perceived, or projected.[9] Histories of toleration narrate how minorities often relied on the spiritualisation of their lives, so as to make sense of incongruities between theology and their political reality. This is not to say that the political imaginaries at hand can legitimately claim to be in the position of the marginalised. Rather, what is interesting is how these political imaginaries mediate tensions between the 'subjective ought' and the 'political is'. This is clearly demonstrated in Putin's references to a 'special military operation' in Ukraine. To those who affirm the territorial integrity of Ukraine, this invasion is clearly a war between two sovereign states. But in the spiritualised mode of the Russian World, Putin projects the spiritual unity of Russia and Ukraine, asserting that the war is essentially a domestic matter, contrasting the 'subjective ought' with the 'political is'.[10] Beyond the immediate interest of the war, lies another question, namely how the war in Ukraine and Russia's investment in the rise of right-wing populism across Europe and in the USA are part of the same economy of ideas.[11]

3 Spirituality and Religion in the Sacralisation of Space

The political imaginaries of the Russian and Hungarian Worlds as well as the MAGA campaign have in common that they overtly engage religious traditionalists. From Moscow to the Midwest, conservative churches of various kinds are entangled in the proliferation of these political imaginaries, and sometimes benefit from associated political patronage. This raises questions about

---

9   Brent J. Steele and Alexandra Homolar, "Ontological insecurities and the politics of contemporary populism", *Cambridge Review of International Affairs* 32, no. 3 (2019): 214–21.
10 Christopher Marsh, "Putin's Playbook: The Development of Russian Tactics, Operations, and Strategy from Chechnya to Ukraine", in *The Great Power Competition Volume 5: The Russian Invasion of Ukraine and Implications for the Central Region,* eds. Adib Farhadi, Mark Grzegorzewski, Anthony Masys (Cham: Springer, 2023), 161–183, 179.
11 Kristina Stoeckl and Dmitry Uzlaner, *The Moralist International: Russia in the Global Culture Wars* (New York: Fordham University Press, 2022); Gionathan Lo Mascolo, *The Christian Right in Europe: Movements, Networks, and Denominations* (New York: Transcript, 2023).

the nature of the relationship between religion as it has traditionally been understood in scholarship and new forms of spirituality. Whereas the Schmittian approach might be that much of politics fundamentally derives from historical Christian concepts, the question is whether the secular and the sacred exist in a binary or if they exist on a spectrum.[12] Gorski and I have argued elsewhere that secularisation might be understood as the fragmentation of the sacred and of sacred space in a way that facilitates new forms of sacralisation.[13] The sacralisation of nations and civilisations emerges as a phenomenon that defies categories of both the sacred and the secular. Instead, they offer a complex mixture of secular ideas and religious repertoires, and which cannot be reduced to either. On this understanding, political imaginaries may be anchored in both notions of the sacred and the secular, without being conclusively grounded in either.

Imaginaries of the Russian World, the Hungarian World, and the MAGA-campaign are similarly anchored in both the secular and the sacred, further questions must be asked about the nature of the sacred, especially given the involvement of churches in defending such imaginaries. Scholars such as Olivier Roy, Duncan McDonnell, Nadia Marzouki, and Wolfgang Palaver have offered insights into this relationship, as they assert that right-wing populism has an ambivalent relationship with churches: whereas religious repertoires can be convenient, too strong confessional commitments are not.[14] This leads Tobias Cremer to conclude that these movements fundamentally function like "crusades without God", and that churches might need to be careful in their alignment with right-wing politics.[15] Other publications, such as *The Claim to Christianity*, by Hannah Strømmen and Ulrich Schmiedel, show that churches that have spoken out against the Far Right's claim to Christianity can impact how confidently political movements co-opt religious repertoires.[16]

---

12   Ulrich Schmiedel, "Introduction: Political Theology in the Spirit of Populism—Methods and Metaphors", in *The Spirit of Populism*, eds. Ulrich Schmiedel and Joshua Ralston (Leiden: Brill, 2021), 1–22.

13   Van der Tol and Gorski, "Secularisation as the fragmentation of the sacred and of sacred space".

14   Nadia Marzouki, Duncan McDonnell, and Olivier Roy, eds., *Saving the People: How Populists Hijack Religion* (Oxford University Press, 2016); Wolfgang Palaver, "Fraternity versus Parochialism: On Religion and Populism", *Religions* 11, no. 7 (2020): 319.

15   Tobias Cremer, "Defenders of the Faith? How shifting social cleavages and the rise of identity politics are reshaping right-wing populists' attitudes towards religion in the West", *Religion, State and Society* 50, no. 5 (2022): 532–552.

16   Hannah Strømmen and Ulrich Schmiedel, *The Claim to Christianity: Responding to the Far Right* (London: SCM Press, 2020).

It appears that religious repertoires can be useful tools, but that their usage depends on political expediency, and that a broader confessional content is not necessarily welcome. As Cremer argues, support of the churches for this secular usage of religious repertoires fundamentally contributes to processes of secularisation.[17]

Whereas their conclusions give the impression that political imaginaries are categories of the secular or indeed the secular-sacred, the more interesting transformation occurs on the level of the sacred.[18] It could be argued that these political imaginaries effectively transform the sacred and are in competition with the role of 'the beyond' or the divine. Whereas religious repertoires that stem from Orthodoxy, Evangelicalism, and Latin Christianity would speak about God as a source of being, these political imaginaries ascribe that being onto themselves: as a being that is at once immanent and metaphysical, temporal and eternal. They clearly spring from a particular immanent context— the political entities of the Russian Federation, Hungary, the United States of America—but they claim a transcendence that hovers over their political realities, as the Spirit of God that hovered over the yet unordered waters in Genesis. As if in an imminent moment of creation, the authority to transform space resides in the voice of the people (*vox populi*), represented by Messiah-esque figures like Putin, Orbán, and Trump.[19] Despite the forceful allusions to the creation story from Genesis, they do not transform disorder into order, but instead, are willing to create chaos in the political institutions which order political life.

Political imaginaries play an important role in mediating between political realities and spiritual ascriptions of what that reality 'ought' to be. The spiritual content contributes to the legitimation of claims to certain territories, regardless of whether or how borders are challenged. What is more, such spiritual content comes with the assertion of an authority that transcends the political reality as well as the political authority of one's opponents. This assertion of

---

17   Cremer, "Defenders of the Faith?".
18   Elizabeth Shakman Hurd, "America Transcendent", in *The Spirit of Populism*, eds. Ulrich Schmiedel and Joshua Ralston (Leiden: Brill 2021), 70–81; John Heathershaw, *Security After Christendom* (Wipf & Stock: 2023); Natalia Majsova, "The Cosmic Subject in Post-Soviet Russia: Noocosmology, Space-Oriented Spiritualism, and the Problem of Securitization of the Soul", in *Cultural and Political Imaginaries in Putin's Russia*, eds. Niklas Bernsand and Barbara Törnquist-Plewa (Leiden: Brill 2019), 232–58.
19   Minhea S. Stoica, "Conceptualising vulnerability to populist narratives: the Messianic claim of populist leaders", *Journal for the Study of Religions and Ideologies* 22, no. 64 (2023): 3–19.

authority underpins the claim to political legitimacy, even the legitimacy to use political power to change that political reality, removing responsibility for intent, action, and consequence. Thus, it creates an ethical vacuum that is not sanctioned by (or in a spiritual sense sanctionable by) other means, whether through religious dogma, the rule of law, or international treaties. But it does not mean that political actions are unguided or by definition unethical: this is where political realism comes into play.

The school of political realism holds that decisions are guided by the brute pursuit of one's own interests: economic, social, political, geopolitical. These interests are pursued without particular ethical restraints. Within the Christian tradition, such as that of Reinhold Niebuhr, the ethical vacuum of realism is mitigated with reference to the Christian tradition, in which churches play an important role in preserving the ethical capital of a state – while remaining technically separated from the state.[20] What makes Christian realism different from the political imaginaries at hand is that some ethical restraints emanate from the transcendent being of God, whereas Putin, Orbán, and Trump seemingly assert themselves as an immanent personification of the transcendent, albeit in varying degrees. This means that they re-insert an ethic into political realism, but an ethic of a specific and largely self-referential kind. An ethic that emanate from other sources, including religious ethics, may be subservient to this political spiritualism. While some churches might play an important role in shoring up political figures through their religious repertoires and might even think of themselves as important to them, they may in fact be altar boys of a different religion.

4   The Russian World

The notion of the Russian World is increasingly developing as a competitor to the *Pax Americana,* signifying a cultural, political, and military space of influence, with Moscow – the 'Third Rome' – at its centre.[21] While this space chiefly concerns contemporary Russia, Belarus and Ukraine, other territories are

---

20 Simon Polinder, "Towards a New Christian Political Realism? The Amsterdam School of Philosophy and the Role of Religion in International Relations" (PhD diss., Vrije University, 2021).

21 Elizaveta Gaufman, "Come all ye faithful to the Russian World: Governmental and grassroots spiritual discourse in the battle over Ukraine", in *Religion during the Russian-Ukrainian Conflict,* eds. Elizabeth Clark and Dmytro Vovk (Abingdon: Routledge, 2020), 54–68.

sometimes included as well, such as Moldova (Transnistria), Georgia, Poland, or the Baltic States. The geopolitical angle to the Russian World builds on diffuse discourses in political and religious institutions as well as in civil society, which may come dressed as Russkii Mir, Holy Rus', Ancient Rus' as is explained by Veronica Cibotaru and Dmytro Bintsarovskyi in this volume.[22] Although both the Kremlin and Patriarch Kirill might opt for either of these notions depending on the audience, the significance of the Russian World lies in its capacity to attract support from a wide range of political, religious, and social actors for the war in Ukraine.[23]

On the eve of the Russian invasion of Ukraine, Putin delivered a lengthy speech about the historic claim of the Russian World to Ukraine, and especially the city of Kyiv:

> Any further expansion of the North Atlantic alliance's infrastructure or the ongoing efforts to gain a military foothold of the Ukrainian territory are unacceptable for us. Of course, the question is not about NATO itself. It merely serves as a tool of US foreign policy. The problem is that in territories adjacent to Russia, which I have to note is our historical land, a hostile 'anti-Russia' is taking shape. Fully controlled from the outside, it is doing everything to attract NATO armed forces and obtain cutting-edge weapons.
>
> For the United States and its allies, it is a policy of containing Russia, with obvious geopolitical dividends. For our country, it is a matter of life and death, a matter of our historical future as a nation. This is not an exaggeration; this is a fact. It is not only a very real threat to our interests but to the very existence of our state and to its sovereignty. It is the red line which we have spoken about on numerous occasions. They have crossed it.[24]

Putin's references to historical land and the historical future need to be read in conjunction with his essay 'On the Historical Unity of Russians and Ukrainians'

---

22   Thomas Bremer, "Diffuses Konzept: Die Russische Orthodoxe Kirche und die 'Russische Welt'", *Osteuropa* 66, No. 3 (2016):3–18.
23   Mikhail Suslov, "Russian World Concept: Post-Soviet Geopolitical Ideology and the Logic of Spheres of Influence", *Geopolitics* 23, No. 2 (2018): 330–353, 344; Mikhail Suslov, "Holy Rus: The Geopolitical Imagination in the Contemporary Russian Orthodox Church", *Russian Politics & Law* 52, No. 3 (2014):67–86, 69.
24   Address by the President of the Russian Federation, the Kremlin, 24 February 2022, accessed 9 April 2024, http://en.kremlin.ru/events/president/news/67843.

(2021). This essay emphasised the 'sacred' commonality of land and people, based on the idea of 'Rus' as a 'common territory or homeland':

> First of all, I would like to emphasize that the wall that has emerged in recent years between Russia and Ukraine, between the parts of what is essentially the same historical and spiritual space, to my mind is our great common misfortune and tragedy.
>
> When the USSR collapsed, many people in Russia and Ukraine sincerely believed and assumed that our close cultural, spiritual and economic ties would certainly last, as would the commonality of our people, who had always had a sense of unity at their core.[25]

His allusions to the sacred and to sacred space, mediated through the idea of the Ancient Rus' seemed peculiar, turned cynical as words were followed by missiles, forced displacement, and credible allegations of war crimes in the weeks that followed. His disregard for the territorial integrity of the state of Ukraine could be understood as merely geopolitical and even secular, inspired by a desire to secure a tsarist legacy, to gain dominance over Ukraine's natural resources, or to counter the political significance of the NATO alliance. In all of this, the spatial element is crucial to the sacralisation of the Russian World: without Ukraine, this triunity of peoples and spaces can no longer reflect its supposed divine mandate, making Ukraine the scene of a supposed clash of cosmic proportions.[26]

Putin projects a Manichaean binary of good and evil on the competition between the Pax Americana and the Russian World, in which Russia is the source of all that is good and the West all that is corrupted.[27] Stanislav Panin shows this evil is projected on the West through the language of satanism or sectarianism, Westernisation, NATO, and LGBT+ identities, for example in the movie *Children versus Magicians* that was funded by the Ministry of Culture.[28] From a theological perspective, communications such as these make a loose

---

25 Vladimir Putin, "On the Historical Unity of Russians and Ukrainians", the Kremlin, 12 July 2021, accessed 9 April 2024, http://en.kremlin.ru/events/president/news/66181.
26 Gaufman, "Come all ye faithful to the Russian World"; Samuel P. Huntington, "The Clash of Civilisations?" *Foreign Affairs* 72, no. 3 (1993): 22–49.
27 Cyril Hovorun, "Orthodoxy political theology between national identity and empire" (conference keynote lecture, Christian identity in national, transnational, and local space, University of Oxford, 4–5 April 2022); Torbakov, "Middle Continent or Island Russia".
28 Stanislav Panin, "Alternative spiritualities in Russia during the conflict in Ukraine", in *Religion during the Russian-Ukrainian Conflict,* eds. Elizabeth Clark and Dmytro Vovk (Abingdon: Routledge, 2020), 69–85.

suggestion that Russia's own survival would be eschatologically necessary, and that through divine power, it will eventually triumph over all its enemies, as is further explored by Dustin Byrd in this volume. Similar themes arise in the sermons of Patriarch Kirill on the war in Ukraine, the West, NATO and LGBT+ identities when he spoke of a "battle that holds not a physical, but metaphysical significance" weeks after the start of the invasion.[29] He says that "our country has a special mission today", echoing the language of the 'special military operation':

> In this sense, our country has a special mission today. We are among the few who call evil evil and good good, who do not give the powerful propaganda forces the opportunity to muddle these concepts so that man does not discern between good and evil. … Therefore, what is happening today is indeed part of a very important battle, a cosmic struggle between good and evil. And God grant that through the prayers of the holy saints who shone in our land, our people, in spite of any seductions, temptations, and influences, will preserve the Orthodox faith, faith in the Lord and Saviour, in the Protection of His Most Blessed Mother, and thus the ability to distinguish good from evil, the ability to be truly free people. For *ye are called unto liberty, brethren*, saith the apostle, Galatians 5:13.[30]

Putin's idea of the Russian World was partially developed in the political theology of the Orthodox Church and its emphasis on Holy Rus' as well as *symphonia,* or the interdependence of church and state.[31] Cyril Hovorun, in his keynote lecture at the University Church in Oxford in 2022, underlined that this political theology reproduces the spirit of the theology of the 1930s, which turned inward as opposed to the ecumenically minded political theologies

---

29   Patriarch Kirill, "Sermon of 6 March 2022", the Moscow Patriarchate, accessed 9 April 2024, http://www.patriarchia.ru/db/text/5906442.html. For more elaborate analysis, see Natalia Dubtsova, *The Role of the Orthodox Church in advancing Putin's war messaging* (Journalist Fellowship Paper, University of Oxford, 2023), accessed 9 April 2024, https://reutersinstitute.politics.ox.ac.uk/sites/default/files/2024-02/RISJ%20Fellows%20Paper_Natalia_Trinity2023_Final.pdf.

30   Patriarch Kirill, "Sermon of 1 September 2022", the Moscow Patriarchate, accessed 9 April 2024, http://www.patriarchia.ru/db/text/5955921.html. Translation by Yelizaveta Raichynets.

31   Lena Jonson, "Russia: Culture, Cultural Policy, and the Swinging Pendulum of Politics", in *Cultural and Political Imaginaries in Putin's Russia*, eds. Niklas Bernsand and Barbara Törnquist-Plewa (Leiden: Brill 2019), 13–36; Pantelis Kalaitzidis, *Orthodoxy and Political Theology* (Geneva: WCC Publications, 2015).

of the 1920s.[32] Putin's reliance on Orthodoxy is not a coincidence. His investment in the restoration of Orthodox churches in the post-Soviet context was carefully exchanged for the loyalty of the church, and especially that of the current patriarch Kirill, whose personal wealth and financial interests are not insignificant.[33] A source of frustration for both state and church was perhaps its declining sphere of influence of Russia in post-Soviet states.[34] In the case of Ukraine, concerns over the jurisdiction of the Moscow Patriarchy intersect with the idea that Ukraine would be part of the Russian World, whereas the state of Ukraine is invested in its spiritual independence from Moscow.[35]

The language of good and evil is certainly reproduced in transnational conservative and right-wing nationalist movements outside of Russia, mediated through discourses on traditional values, LGBT+ identities, and illiberalism. Other commonalities with the Far Right elsewhere include an openness to conspiracy theories and violence, and a willingness to promote the same content across 'the West', especially during election seasons.[36] Though their underlying anti-liberal attitudes might appear to be normatively thick on conflicts over gender, sexuality, and reproduction, the political significance lies elsewhere, namely in the contestation of accountability and responsibility stemming from the rule of law and democracy. However, Putin's notion of the Russian World cannot be characterised as simply one among these far-right movements.[37]

Principally, the notion of the Russian World is civilisationalist and neo-imperialist, and finds both support and opposition from Russian ethnonationalists,[38] as well as other nations that assert their independence from it. The notion of the Russian World has significant spiritual capital, as transcending the peoples and spaces it assumes, and as a civilisation which would play an extraordinary role (*Sonderweg*) among the world's nations.[39] What it means to be Russian thus is not simply about ethnicity, language, or even Orthodoxy, but about an

---

32 Hovorun, "Orthodoxy political theology".
33 Mikhail Suslov, "Holy Rus", 80.
34 Heathershaw, *Security After Christendom*.
35 Tornike Metreveli, *Orthodox Christianity and the Politics of Transition: Ukraine, Serbia and Georgia* (London: Routledge, 2021).
36 Lo Mascolo, *The Christian Right in Europe*.
37 Mikhail Suslov, *Putinism: Post-Soviet Russian Regime Ideology* (Abingdon: Routledge, 2024).
38 Andrei Rogatchevski, "Eduard Limonov's National Bolshevik Party and the Nazi Legacy: Titular Nations vs Ethnic Minorities", in *Cultural and Political Imaginaries in Putin's Russia*, eds. Niklas Bernsand and Barbara Törnquist-Plewa (Leiden: Brill 2019), 63–82.
39 Jonson, "Russia".

amalgamation of anchors of belonging, which include but are not limited to ethnicity, language, and (nominal) religion. This loose, broader base of 'Russianness' is what bears the state and the cultural consciousness of the state of Russia.[40] This immanent-transcendent character is held together by the temporalities of the Russian World, which include the idea of a thousand-year state.[41] The imaginaries of the Hungarian World and the MAGA-campaign are indebted to the notion of the Russian World, even if in slightly different ways, as shown below.

5   The Hungarian World

In the summer of 2022, the Hungarian prime minister Orbán delivered his annual speech at the 'Summer University' Tusványos, organised in the Transylvanian village of *Băile Tuşnad* in Romania, which I attended. The choice for *Tusnádfürdő*, as it is called in Hungarian, is significant, as Transylvania today is home to a significant minority of ethnic Hungarians, in whom the Orbán administration takes a cultural and electoral interest.[42] Budapest usually sends a high-level delegation, including various cabinet ministers and other senior officials, to mingle with political and religious elites, and to participate in a range of panels on politics, culture, international relations, and religion. The slogan of the festival in 2022 was "*ami, van örök*", translated as "there are things which are eternal".[43] This slogan alluded to a sacralisation of Hungarian national consciousness along with the sacralisation of contemporary Hungarian politics. In his speech, which is referenced across this section,[44] Orbán referenced the idea of the 'Hungarian World', explicitly echoing Putin's references to the Russian World: "The ninth key to a successful strategy of local exceptionalism is our intellectual and spiritual foundations. Hungary still has

---

40   Torbakov, "'Middle Continent' or Island Russia".
41   Olga Malinova, "Constructing the 'Usable Past': The Evolution of the Official Historical Narrative in Post-Soviet Russia", in *Cultural and Political Imaginaries in Putin's Russia*, eds. Niklas Bernsand and Barbara Törnquist-Plewa (Leiden: Brill 2019), 85–104.
42   Gábor Scheiring, "Dependent development and authoritarian state capitalism: Democratic backsliding and the rise of the accumulative state in Hungary", *Geoforum* 124 (2021): 267–78.
43   Details of the Tusványos programme can be found online at https://www.tusvanyos.ro/en/ and https://www.tusvanyos.ro/Download/Program-Tusvanyos31-ENG.pdf (accessed 7 November 2022).
44   Viktor Orbán, "Some things last forever!" (Speech at Tusványos Summer University, 23 July 2022), accessed 9 April 2024, https://2015-2022.miniszterelnok.hu/speech-by-prime-minister-viktor-orban-at-the-31st-balvanyos-summer-free-university-and-student-camp/.

its national conception, its sphere of national sentiment, its culture, and a language capable of describing a complete Hungarian World".

Orbán asserted that entire regions in the Carpathian Basin historically and ontologically belong to the Hungarian nation, some of which were lost in the Treaty of Trianon in 1920. One of the tropes is that Germany was allowed to reunite after the decline of the Soviet regime, but that Hungary remains divided, and that this is an historical injustice inflicted upon the Hungarian people. A handful of ultranationalist Romanian protesters brought a provocative banner stating, "There are things which are eternal: Transylvania belongs to Romania", which they held up at the beginning of Orbán's speech. They were quickly led out by security staff, not least because of the rising temperature in the audience surrounding them. Orbán, however, was careful to emphasise he would not contest Hungary's current state borders. Rather, his narrative was that the preservation of the Hungarian consciousness was necessary to protect Christian values in Europe, and that the entire European civilisation depended on the purity of the Hungarian nation. He employed the category of race twice in relation to national purity, but in relation to Western Europe, which in his estimation had become racially mixed because of migration.[45]

Orbán's interest here entwines concerns over Hungarian space with European space, which he divides in different worlds.[46] On the one hand, there would be the world that has become racially mixed because of liberal migration policies, and the world that has not:

> In such a multi-ethnic context, there is an ideological feint here that is worth talking about and focusing on. The internationalist left employs a feint, an ideological ruse: the claim—their claim—that Europe by its very nature is populated by peoples of mixed race. This is a historical and semantic sleight of hand, because it conflates two different things. There is a world in which European peoples are mixed together with those arriving from outside Europe. Now that is a mixed-race world. And there is our world, where people from within Europe mix with one another, move around, work, and relocate. So, for example, in the Carpathian Basin we

---

45   Viktória Kóczián, "'This nest is for all kinds of birds'? National identity questions in the refugee reception of the Reformed Church in Hungary", *Religion, State and Society* 50, no. 5 (2022): 553–68; Alexander Faludy, "The troubling Christian roots of Orbán's rhetoric", *Church Times*, 19 August 2022, accessed 9 April 2024, https://www.churchtimes.co.uk/articles/2022/19-august/comment/opinion/the-troubling-christian-roots-of-orbans-rhetoric.

46   András László Pap, "Illiberalism as Constitutional Identity—The Case of Hungary" *Hungarian Journal of Legal Studies* 59, no. 4 (2018): 378–402.

are not mixed-race: we are simply a mixture of peoples living in our own European homeland.

Orbán's reference to 'worlds' echoes Putin's references to civilisation through the binary of the 'Russian World' and 'the West'. Orbán plays with a very similar binary of good and evil, expressed through the language of liberalism and illiberalism, as well as traditional values and cultural Christianity. To this end, Orbán too employs clientelist relationships with Hungarian churches, formally as part of a "National System of Cooperation".[47] His claim reads very similar to Putin's, but with the boundary between these worlds "moved slightly further to the west" from Moscow.[48] In Orbán's estimation, however, it is Hungary that will save Europe from a descent into moral decay, and as such would play an exceptional role in world history (*Sonderweg*). However, contrary to the United States of America and Russia, the Hungarian *Sonderweg* would necessarily be less violent, because the country is small and relies on bargaining with other states. Contrary to the claims of the Russian World, to Orbán, Ukraine is not the scene of a supposed clash of civilisations. Rather, he claimed it is "a Slavic war", and told his audience he was bargaining with President Volodymyr Zelensky to avoid the conscription of ethnic Hungarians who reside in Transcarpathia; or "no Hungarian blood should flow", as per the festival's official translators.

Instead, the site of contestation is the European Commission and its decision to attach conditions to approximately 28 billion in European funding. These conditions relate to the rise of hybrid authoritarianism under Orbán and the thoroughly legitimate concerns over the rule of law in Hungary. Much has been written about the technicalities of the illiberal toolkit.[49] What is interesting here is Orbán's connection between his bargaining politics and ideas of

---

47　Júlia Mink, "Human Rights Protection and Traditional Churches in the System of National Cooperation in Hungary", *Religion and Human Rights* 13 (2018): 245–69; János Mátyás Kovács and Balász Trencsényi, eds., *Brave New Hungary: Mapping the System of National Cooperation* (Lanham MD: Lexington Books, 2019); Milada Anna Vachudova, "Ethnopopulism and democratic backsliding in Central Europe", *East European Politics* 36, no. 3 (2020): 318–40.

48　Discussions at Religionspolitologische Forum zum Thema Nationalismus und Christentum, University of Debrecen, 12 May 2023.

49　András Sajó, Renáta Uitz, and Stephen Holmes, eds., *Routledge Handbook of Illiberalism* (New York: Routledge, 2022); Gábor Halmai, "Illiberal Constitutionalism in East-Central Europe", in *Rule of Law in the European Union: 30 Years after the Fall of the Berlin Wall*, eds. Antonina Bakardjieva Engelbrekt, Andreas Morberg and Joakim Nergelius (Oxford: Hart Publishing, 2021), 51–74; Andrea Pirro and Ben Stanley, "Forging, Bending, and Breaking: Enacting the 'Illiberal Playbook' in Hungary and Poland", *Perspectives on Politics* 20, no. 1 (2022): 88–101.

illiberalism and Hungarian autonomy. Much like his copying of the Russian World, he previously borrowed the notion of 'illiberalism' from Putin. In his speech at Tusványos in 2014, he introduced this notion:

> (M)eaning, that Hungarian nation is not a simple sum of individuals, but a community that needs to be organized, strengthened and developed, and in this sense, the new state that we are building is an illiberal state, a non-liberal state. It does not deny foundational values of liberalism, as freedom, etc. But it does not make this ideology a central element of state organization, but applies a specific, national, particular approach in its stead.[50]

The authority of this community, or nation, of which ethnic Hungarians are the bearer among many ethnic minorities, is sacralised by means of 'the Holy Crown', which once belonged to one of its historic kings, St. Stephen (c. 975–1038). The Preamble of the Hungarian Constitution of 2011 references the crown and its illustrious king as the thousand-year anchor point of the Hungarian consciousness:

> We are proud that our king Saint Stephen built the Hungarian State on solid ground and made our country a part of Christian Europe one thousand years ago ...
>
> We honour the achievements of our historic constitution and we honour the Holy Crown, which embodies the constitutional continuity of Hungary's statehood and the unity of the nation.[51]

The crown is housed in the central dome of the Hungarian Parliament and allegedly embodies the political legitimacy of 'the people' and the idea that the will of the people can only be bound by itself. The popularisation of these ideas through museums, such as the renovated St Stephen's Hall, education,

---

50 Viktor Orban, "Prime Minister Viktor Orbán's Speech at the 25th Bálványos Summer Free University and Student Camp", 30 July 2014, accessed 16 August 2023, https://2015-2019.kormany.hu/en/the-prime-minister/the-prime-minister-s-speeches/prime-minister-viktor-orban-s-speech-at-the-25th-balvanyos-summer-free-university-and-student-camp.

51 The Fundamental Law of Hungary as in force on 23 December 2020, accessed 16 August 2024, https://www.google.com/url?sa=t&rct=j&q=&esrc=s&source=web&cd=&ved=2ahUKEwjp4oqQoJz7AhUg8LsIHaXwARIQFnoECA4QAQ&url=https%3A%2F%2Fwww.parlament.hu%2Fdocuments%2F125505%2F138409%2FFundamental%2Blaw%2F73811993-c377-428d-9808-ee03d6fb8178&usg=AOvVaw2RuJeOcYc2BwDu5bTFF8S8.

and other cultural institutions assists in shoring up popular support for Orbán's 'resistance' to European oversight, even to the detriment of the interests of ordinary citizens of Hungary.[52]

6   The MAGA Campaign

The Make America Great Again campaign exists on the same ideological spectrum as the Russian and Hungarian Worlds, in that it positions itself in opposition to liberalism and draws on populist repertoires. However, whereas the Russian and Hungarian authorities have projected the 'evil' of liberalism on 'the West', for the MAGA campaign America exemplifies much of the 'evil' itself. The sentiments of raising up a wall against a 'flood' of Mexican migrants echoed Orbán's pushing back of millions of refugees into Serbia. However, greater than the supposed external enemy was the supposed internal one: the MAGA campaign has made its own space the scene of a clash of civilisations.[53] Through a sustained focus on gender, sexuality, and reproductive rights, investments in the so-called culture wars paid off in the presidential elections of 2016 and 2024. These anti-liberal flexes originate partially in American Evangelical movements, even as they have been encouraged by organisations like the World Congress of Families and other transnational pro-life initiatives.[54] The language of good and evil is as present as elsewhere in the populist family tree, and when Trump lost the election despite 'prophecies' promising otherwise, it served to justify the violence of January 6th.[55]

The MAGA campaign was particularly strong at creating parallel realities, often conflating its political imaginary and even conspiracy theories with reality, not unlike what can be seen with Putin's reference to the 'special military operation' today. This was clear from Trump's assertions, then relayed

---

[52] Miklós Könczöl and István Kevevári, "History and Interpretation in the Fundamental Law of Hungary", *European Papers* 5, no. 1 (2020): 161–74; Van der Tol, *Constitutional Intolerance*.

[53] Jeffrey Haynes, *From Huntington to Trump: Thirty Years of the Clash of Civilisations* (Rowman & Littlefield, 2019); P.S. Gorski and S.L. Perry, *The Flag and the Cross: White Christian Nationalism and the Threat to American Democracy* (Oxford: Oxford University Press, 2022).

[54] Lo Mascolo, *The Christian Right in Europe*; Stoeckl and Uzlaner, *The Moralist International*.

[55] M.P. Rowley, "Prophetic Populism and the Violent Rejection of Joe Biden's Election: Mapping the Theology of the Capitol Insurrection", *International Journal of Religion* 2, no.2 (2011): 145–64.

by White House Press Secretary Sean Spicer, about the size of the inauguration crowd in 2017, which stood in sharp contrast with footage of the event.[56] Former counsellor to then President Trump, Kellyanne Conway, would soon introduce the idea of "alternative facts" in a news interview on the inauguration.[57] This was a pivotal moment, paving the way for institutionalised misinformation during and after the Trump presidency, and not just during the election campaign itself.[58] This alternative reality, as a 'subjective ought' rather than a 'political is', is perhaps bookmarked by the political realities of January 6th, when radicalised supporters stormed the U.S. Capitol in a bid to thwart the confirmation of the election results by then Vice-President Mike Pence.

Much of MAGA's alternative reality was sacralised, not only through religious legitimation offered by Evangelicals, but also through Trump's conscription of alternative 'prophets',[59] his portrayal of biblical figures, such as Moses (who led Israel from Egypt), Cyrus (who ended the Babylonian captivity), and Jesus (as saviour of the world).[60] These images derive from a long tradition of covenantal thinking in America.[61] These images shore up the binary of good and evil, as well as the figure of Trump as a contemporary saviour to what is projected to be evil: the political left and the elites, as is custom in the populist playbook, and especially his rival Hilary Clinton, who had won the popular vote at his election. As Matthew Rowley and I have written elsewhere, the MAGA campaign appropriated what is known in the Christian tradition as the apocalypse, or the end times, but in a predominantly secular moment.[62] While this appropriation was certainly met with criticism from within some religious

---

56 White House Press Secretary Sean Spicer, 21 January 2017, "Spicer: Inauguration had largest audience ever", *CNN*, accessed 9 April 2024, https://www.youtube.com/watch?v=PKzHXelQi_A.

57 "Kellyanne Conway: Press Secretary Sean Spicer Gave 'Alternative Facts'", *NBC News*, accessed 9 April 2024, https://www.youtube.com/watch?v=VSrEEDQgFc8.

58 W. Bradley Wendel, "Truthfulness as an Ethical Form of Life", *Duquesne Law Review* 56, no.2 (2018): 141–67.

59 Rowley, "Prophetic Populism"; Shakman Hurd, "America Transcendent".

60 Judd Birdsall and Matthew Rowley, "Stop weaponizing the Bible for Trump: No politician is a Cyrus, David or Caesar", *The Washington Post*, 19 June 2019, accessed 9 April 2024, https://www.washingtonpost.com/religion/2019/06/19/stop-weaponizing-bible-trump-no-politician-is-cyrus-david-or-caesar/.

61 P.S. Gorski, *American Covenant: A History of Civil Religion from the Puritans to the Present* (Princeton University Press, 2017); Sophia R.C. Johnson, "'We the People of Israel': Covenant, Constitution, and the Supposed Biblical Origins of Modern Democratic Political Thought", *Journal of the Bible and its Reception* 8, no. 2 (2021): 247–68.

62 M.D.C. Van der Tol and M. Rowley, "A Posture of Protest? The Search for Christian Identity in A Post-Secular Society: Between Secularised Eschatology and A Sacralisation of History", *International Journal of Religion* 2, no.2 (2021): 101–13.

communities, the absence of a somewhat unified Christian voice or a clearly defined religious authority contributed to the proliferation of quasi-Christian overtones in the MAGA campaign.[63]

The MAGA campaign also sacralised space, but with a greater emphasis on domestic issues than in Russia or Hungary. The boundaries of American space were policed through limitations on travel from several 'Muslim states'. A series of executive orders and presidential proclamations aimed at travel, immigration, and refugee resettlement, many of which were challenged before the courts.[64] The Trump administration took a hard line on Latino migration through its endeavour at building a wall, together with its much-criticised family separation policy. The association of the first group of Muslim migrants with terrorism signals a projection of evil, but so did his comments on Mexican migrants in his speech announcing his candidacy in 2015:

> When do we beat Mexico at the border? They're laughing at us, at our stupidity. And now they are beating us economically. They are not our friend, believe me. But they're killing us economically.
>
> When Mexico sends its people, they're not sending their best. They're not sending you. They're not sending you. They're sending people that have lots of problems, and they're bringing those problems with us. They're bringing drugs. They're bringing crime. They're rapists. And some, I assume, are good people.[65]

The final days of the Trump Presidency will be remembered for the violent storming of the U.S. Capitol. Since much has already been written on the subject, this section highlights three particular moments on the Senate floor as documented by Luke Mogelson for *The New Yorker*.[66] The first entails the moment insurrectionists entered the Senate floor. Some people took to the seats and desks of the Senators and rummaged through their files. One man walks up to the chair of the Vice-President, sits down, and gets called out by another insurrectionist.

---

63   Cremer, "Defenders of the Faith?"
64   Anthony S. Winer, "Action and reaction: The Trump executive orders and their reception by the federal courts", *Mitchell Hamline L. Rev.* 44 (2018): 907–934.
65   "Here's Donald Trump's Presidential Announcement Speech", *Time*, 16 June 2015, accessed 16 August 2023, https://time.com/3923128/donald-trump-announcement-speech/.
66   "Watch a Reporter's Video from Inside the Capitol Siege", *The New Yorker*, 17 January 2021, accessed 16 August 2023, https://www.newyorker.com/news/video-dept/a-reporters-footage-from-inside-the-capitol-siege.

> "Hey, get outta that chair"
> "No this is our chair"
> "I agree with you brother, but the chair is not ours"
> "We're a democracy"
> "It belongs to the Vice-President of the United States. But he isn't here. It's not our chair. Look, I love you guys, you're brothers, but we can't be disrespectful".

The exchange is then followed by comments about the need to win "the IO war" (information operation) and "the PR war" (public relations), and several men curiously rummaging through desks and files.

Secondly, Jason Chansley, also known as the QAnon Shaman, enters the Senate floor and takes position at the desk of the Vice-President, while a police officer tells them they need to leave. As Chansley assures the police officer that they will and he has "been makin' sure they ain't disrespectin' the place", the police officer responds: "Okay, just wanna let you guys know, this is like the sacredest [sic] place". Chansley responds "I know" and then sits down in the chair of the Vice-President "cause Mike Pence is a fucking traitor".

The third moment is when Chansley says a prayer while standing at the same desk with three other men: "Hold on, let's say a prayer. Let's all say a prayer in this sacred space", and then speaks through an amplifier:

> Thank you heavenly father for gracing us with this opportunity [He takes his horns off] Thanks to our heavenly father for this opportunity to stand up for our God-given unalienable rights. Thank you heavenly father for being the inspiration needed to these police officers to allow us into the building, to allow us to exercise our rights, to allow us to send a message to all the tyrants, the communists, and the globalists, that this is our nation, not theirs, that we will not allow the America, the American way of the United States of America to go down. Thank you divine, omniscient, omnipotent, and omnipresent creator God for filling this chamber with your white light of love, with your white light of harmony. Thank you for filling this chamber with patriots that love you. And that love Christ. Thank you divine, omniscient, omnipotent, and omnipresent creator God for blessing each and every one of us here and now. Thank you divine creator God for surrounding and strengthening us with divine omnipresent white light of love and protection, peace and harmony. Thank you for allowing the United States of America to be reborn. Thank you for allowing us to get rid of the communists, the globalists, and the

traitors within our government. We love you and we thank you, in Christ's holy name we pray [to which the crowd shouts 'Amen!']

Taken together, these three moments show the discrepancy between spiritual and political understandings of what the Senate floor means. On the one hand, there is a recognition that this space is set apart. After all, the insurrectionists turned up here 'to defend' democracy as they imagined it, by interfering with the certification of the election results. In 'their world', Trump was the rightful President of the United States, the elections would have been 'rigged', and they supposedly were the true loyalists of American democracy. The police officer, too, understands the Senate floor as sacred, but to him, this means that the insurrectionists are trespassing sacred space, and especially Chansley as he sits down in the Vice-Presidents' chair. For Chansley, this radicalised spirituality made sense (or at least at the time), pointing to a certain rationality that can be found among radicalised persons.[67] The crux of the matter is that for the insurrectionists, their engagement in violence was in some register 'rational', namely, the spiritual register, even as spectators could see it for what it was: open violence.

Despite repeated calls for President Trump to use his influence to end the violence, he remained quiet until later in the day, when he issued two rather different responses during the siege, and the day after. On January 6th, he said:

> I know your pain. I know you're hurt. I know you're hurt, I know your pain. I know you're hurt. We had an election that was stolen from us. It was a landslide election and everyone knows it, especially the other side. But you have to go home now. We have to have peace. We have to have law and order. We have to respect our great people in law and order. We don't want anybody hurt. It's a very tough period of time. There's never been a time like this where such a thing happened where they could take it away from all of us, from me, from you, from our country. This was a fraudulent election. But we can't play into the hands of these people. We have to have peace. So go home, we love you. You're very special. You've seen what happens. You see the way others are treated that are so bad and so evil. I know how you feel, but go home and go home at peace.[68]

---

67 Rik Peels, *De Extremist en de Wetenschapper. Hoe we radicalisering beter kunnen begrijpen* (Amsterdam: Balans, 2024).
68 "Trump tells rioters to 'go home' while repeating election lies", CNN, 6 January 2021, accessed 16 August 2023, https://www.youtube.com/watch?v=3_JxN9CwIMU.

On January 7th, however, he said:

> I like to begin by addressing the heinous attack on the United States Capitol. Like all Americans, I am outraged by the violence, lawlessness, and mayhem …
>
> To demonstrators who infiltrated the Capitol: you have defiled the seat of American democracy. To those who engaged in the acts of violence and destruction: you do not represent our country. And to those who broke the law: you will pay.[69]

The contrast between "good people" on January 6th and "you have defiled" on January 7th is striking. First, the language of defiling is deeply religious, echoing the language of Old Testament prophets. Second, the language of defiling refers to a certain space, namely Capitol Hill, and ironically mirrors the understanding that both the police officer and Chansley seem to have had, namely that this space was "the sacredest". Third, by January 7th it was clear that the insurrection had failed and that the political reality had changed to his disadvantage. From here, Trump would focus on exonerating himself from accusations that he had instigated or otherwise encouraged the insurrection, but without departing from the rhetoric that the election would have been rigged. Striking is the alternative spirituality of the 'rigged elections', which is not supported by evidence or facts, but a spiritualised interpretation of political events that unfolded contrary to Trump's own interests. It is an alternative spirituality that at once sounds approving of the insurrection and yet denounces it when political reality comes around, a contradiction on the level of the 'political is' that can easily coexist in the MAGA-imagination.

Juxtaposing these different forms of speech is instructive for a deeper understanding of the sacralisation of space. Unlike the Russian and Hungarian World ideologies, the MAGA campaign did not look to external territory to validate its claims to sacred space. The MAGA campaign looked inward, and specifically at the state of democracy, such as represented at the U.S. Capitol, "the sacredest space". Having tried every sort of legal procedure to contest the election results in vain, Trump continued to speak of election fraud, but was also compelled to hand the presidency over to Joe Biden. This highlights again the contrast between the spiritualised 'realities' of the MAGA campaign and the political reality of having to concede power. But it also shows a willingness to

---

69 "President Trump on Election and Breach of the U.S. Capitol", *C-SPAN*, 7 January 2021, accessed 16 August 2023, https://www.c-span.org/video/?507829-1/president-trump-election-breach-us-capitol.

test the boundaries of law and order, and a willingness to threaten the stability of American democracy. Since January 2025, illiberal practices have indeed proliferated in a cascade of executive orders, the chaos around the Department of Government Efficiency, the particularly harsh practices of the U.S. Immigration and Customs Enforcement, and reckless economic and foreign policies – effectively creating parallel legal and political 'realities'.

7 Conclusion

The political imaginaries of the Russian World, the Hungarian World, and the MAGA-campaign share multiple characteristics. They share the exploitation of a sharp binary between good and evil. Each projects evil on liberalism, whether represented by 'the West', 'liberal elites', 'globalists', and do so with reference to different geographical and political contexts. Each claims a form of exceptionalism, embodying what is good against all that is conceived of as evil. Anti-liberal sentiments coexist with an openness to the Extreme Right and to conspiracist thinking. Anti-liberal sentiments also seem to coexist with religious anti-liberalism emanating from conservative religious institutions and organisations, and make an effort to maintain their political support, whether they be the Russian Orthodox Church, a range of churches and religious organisations in Hungary, or Evangelical churches and organisations in the USA. Despite such religious support, the political imaginaries of the Russian World, the Hungarian World, and the MAGA campaign cannot be seen as primarily religious imaginaries: the centre of power is not with the churches or religious organisations, the political aims attached to these imaginaries are not primarily religious, and the political methods are predominantly secular. Instead, these political imaginaries comprise hybrid forms of sacralisation, which are broad and fluid enough to contract support from a variety of constituencies, including a significant number of churches.

The Russian World, Hungarian World, and MAGA campaign also have notable differences. For example, the Hungarian and American variants have strong support among nationalists, whereas the Russian World as an imperial project is a civilisationalist alternative to the nationalist right. Another difference is that both Russia and Hungary claim a thousand-year history that in the MAGA imagination simply does not exist. They also have a different relationship to space as a result of it. Whereas Russia actively tries to seize parts of its former empire through war and war crimes, the Hungarian government remains quiet on Transcarpathia, while Trump's references to the Panama Canal, Canada and Greenland suggest a worrisome openness to the redrawing of state borders. The events of January 6th in the USA show that a willingness to overthrow political order was present in the MAGA-movement, which was at the time contained by American institutions. Since January 2025, Trump has fast-tracked the process of power consolidation, something that Orbán and Putin have both already achieved. Perhaps the most decisive difference is that the MAGA campaign can be understood as a movement, whereas the Russian and Hungarian World imaginaries lack a large movement but rather rely on domestically consolidated political and economic power.

Overarching these similarities and differences is the location of the sacred and the forms of sacralisation that inhere in the imaginaries of the Russian World, the Hungarian World, and the MAGA campaign. Whereas sacralisation has usually been located in the use and abuse of religion, the concept of the secular-sacred sheds a different light on the matter: namely, that attempts at sacralisation can also be located in an understanding of time, space, or saviour-like political figures. Perhaps the most important aspect of this sacralisation is the successful creation of an imagination that both contests and co-exists with reality. As a form of political gaslighting, the differences between the 'subjective ought' and the 'political is' are constantly played with, in ways that seem largely unreceptive to evidence or argument. This contemporaneity of the spatially or temporally irreconcilable poses a real challenge to the status-quo of political communication. The question is at which point the costs of political polarisation, and, in the case of Russia, an open war, will outweigh the benefit to the current political protagonists.

Bibliography

Anderson, B. (1983). *Imagined Communities. Reflections on the Origin and Spread of Nationalism.* London: Verso.

Balkenhol, M., E. van den Hemel, and I. Stengs. (2020). "Introduction: Emotional Entanglements of Sacrality and Secularity—Engaging the Paradox". In: M. Balkenhol, E. van den Hemel, and I. Stengs (eds.). *The Secular Sacred.* Cham: Palgrave Macmillan. Pp. 1–18.

Bernsand, N., and B. Törnquist-Plewa, eds. (2019). *Cultural and Political Imaginaries in Putin's Russia.* Leiden: Brill.

Bremer, T. (2016). "Diffuses Konzept: Die Russische Orthodoxe Kirche und die 'Russische Welt'", *Osteuropa* 66, No. 3:3–18.

Clark, C.C. (1994). *Sacred Worlds: An Introduction to Geography and Religion* London: Routledge.

Cremer, T. (2022). "Defenders of the Faith? How shifting social cleavages and the rise of identity politics are reshaping right-wing populists' attitudes towards religion in the West". *Religion, State and Society* 50, no. 5: 532–52.

Dubtsova, N. (2023). *The Role of the Orthodox Church in advancing Putin's war messaging*. Journalist Fellowship Paper. University of Oxford. Accessed 9 April 2024. https://reutersinstitute.politics.ox.ac.uk/sites/default/files/2024-02/RISJ%20 Fellows%20Paper_Natalia_Trinity2023_Final.pdf.

Gaufman, E. (2020). "Come all ye faithful to the Russian World: Governmental and grass-roots spiritual discourse in the battle over Ukraine". In: E. Clark and D. Vovk, (eds.). *Religion during the Russian-Ukrainian Conflict*. Abingdon: Routledge. Pp. 54–68.

Gorski, P.S. (2017). *American Covenant: A History of Civil Religion from the Puritans to the Present*. Princeton, NJ: Princeton University Press.

Gorski, P.S., and S.L. Perry. (2022). *The Flag and the Cross: White Christian Nationalism and the Threat to American Democracy*. Oxford: Oxford University Press.

Halmai, G. (2021). "Illiberal Constitutionalism in East-Central Europe". In: A.B. Engelbrekt, A. Morberg, and J. Nergelius (eds.). *Rule of Law in the European Union: 30 Years after the Fall of the Berlin Wall*. Oxford: Hart Publishing. Pp. 51–74.

Haynes, J. (2019). *From Huntington to Trump: Thirty Years of the Clash of Civilisations*. Rowman & Littlefield.

Heathershaw, J. (2023). *Security After Christendom*. Wipf & Stock.

Homolar, A., and G. Löfflmann. (2021). "Populism and the Affective Politics of Humiliation Narratives". *Global Studies Quarterly* 1, no. 1: 1–11.

Hovorun, C. (2022). "Orthodoxy political theology between national identity and empire". Christian identity in national, transnational and local space. Conference keynote lecture, University of Oxford, 4–5 April.

Huntington, S.P. (1993). "The Clash of Civilisations?" *Foreign Affairs* 72, no. 3: 22–49.

Johnson, S.R.C. (2021). "'We the People of Israel': Covenant, Constitution, and the Supposed Biblical Origins of Modern Democratic Political Thought". *Journal of the Bible and I Reception* 8, no. 2: 247–68.

Jonson, L. (2019). "Russia: Culture, Cultural Policy, and the Swinging Pendulum of Politics". In: N. Bernsand and B. Törnquist-Plewa (eds.). *Cultural and Political Imaginaries in Putin's Russia*. Leiden: Brill. Pp. 13–36.

Kalaitzidis, P. (2015). *Orthodoxy and Political Theology*. Geneva: WCC Publications.

Kóczián, V. (2022). "'This nest is for all kinds of birds'? National identity questions in the refugee reception of the Reformed Church in Hungary". *Religion, State and Society* 50, no. 5: 553–68.

Könczöl, M., and I. Kevevári. (2020). "History and Interpretation in the Fundamental Law of Hungary". *European Papers* 5, no. 1: 161–74.

Koselleck, R. (2004). *Futures Past: On the Semantics of Historical Time*. Translated by K. Tribe. New York: Columbia University Press.

Kovács, J.M., and B. Trencsényi, eds. (2019). *Brave New Hungary: Mapping the System of National Cooperation*. Lanham MD, Lexington Books.

Levente Balogh, L., and C. Leitgeb, eds. (2021). *Opfermythen in Zentraleuropa*. Munich: Praesens Verlag.

Lloyd, V. (2021). "Anger: A Secularized Theological Concept". In: U. Schmiedel and J. Ralston (eds.). *The Spirit of Populism*. Leiden: Brill. Pp. 25–39.

Lo Mascolo, G. (2023). *The Christian Right in Europe: Movements, Networks, and Denominations*. New York: Transcript.

Majsova, N. (2019). "The Cosmic Subject in Post-Soviet Russia: Noocosmology, Space-Oriented Spiritualism, and the Problem of Securitization of the Soul". In: N. Bernsand and B. Törnquist-Plewa (eds.). *Cultural and Political Imaginaries in Putin's Russia*. Leiden: Brill. Pp. 232–58.

Malinova, O. (2019). "Constructing the 'Usable Past': The Evolution of the Official Historical Narrative in Post-Soviet Russia". In: N. Bernsand and B. Törnquist-Plewa (eds.). *Cultural and Political Imaginaries in Putin's Russia*. Leiden: Brill. Pp. 85–104.

Marsh, C. (2023) "Putin's Playbook: The Development of Russian Tactics, Operations, and Strategy from Chechnya to Ukraine", In: A. Farhadi, M. Grzegorzewski, A. Masys (eds.). *The Great Power Competition Volume 5: The Russian Invasion of Ukraine and Implications for the Central Region*. Cham: Springer. Pp 161–183.

Marzouki, N., D. McDonnell, and O. Roy, eds. (2016). *Saving the People: How Populists Hijack Religion*. Oxford University Press.

Metreveli, T. (2021). *Orthodoxy Christianity and the Politics of Transition: Ukraine, Serbia and Georgia*. London: Routledge.

Mink, J. (2018). "Human Rights Protection and Traditional Churches in the System of National Cooperation in Hungary". *Religion and Human Rights* 13. Pp. 245–69.

Palaver, W. (2020). "Fraternity versus Parochialism: On Religion and Populism". *Religions* 11, no. 7: 319.

Panin, S. (2020). "Alternative spiritualities in Russia during the conflict in Ukraine". In: E. Clark and D. Vovk (eds.). *Religion during the Russian-Ukrainian Conflict*. Abingdon: Routledge. Pp. 69–85.

Pap, A.L.. (2018). "Illiberalism as Constitutional Identity—The Case of Hungary". *Hungarian Journal of Legal Studies* 59, no. 4: 378–204.

Peels, R.. (2014) *De Extremist en de Wetenschapper. Hoe we radicalisering beter kunnen begrijpen*. Amsterdam: Balans.

Pirro, A., and B. Stanley. (2022). "Forging, Bending, and Breaking: Enacting the 'Illiberal Playbook' in Hungary and Poland". *Perspectives on Politics* 20, no. 1: 88–101.

Polinder, S. (2021). "Towards a New Christian Political Realism? The Amsterdam School of Philosophy and the Role of Religion in International Relations". PhD diss. Vrije University.

Rogatchevski, A. (2019). "Eduard Limonov's National Bolshevik Party and the Nazi Legacy: Titular Nations vs Ethnic Minorities". In: N. Bernsand and B. Törnquist-Plewa (eds.). *Cultural and Political Imaginaries in Putin's Russia.* Leiden: Brill. Pp. 63–82.

Rowley, M.P. (2021). "Prophetic Populism and the Violent Rejection of Joe Biden's Election: Mapping the Theology of the Capitol Insurrection". *International Journal of Religion* 2, no. 2: 145–64.

Sajó, A., R. Uitz, and S. Holmes, eds. (2022). *Routledge Handbook of Illiberalism.* New York: Routledge.

Scheiring, G. (2021) "Dependent development and authoritarian state capitalism: Democratic backsliding and the rise of the accumulative state in Hungary". *Geoforum* 124: 267–78.

Schmiedel, U. (2021). "Introduction: Political Theology in the Spirit of Populism—Methods and Metaphors". In: Ulrich Schmiedel and Joshua Ralston (eds.). *The Spirit of Populism.* Leiden: Brill. Pp. 1–22.

Shakman Hurd, E. (2021). "America Transcendent". In: U. Schmiedel and J. Ralston (eds.). *The Spirit of Populism.* Leiden: Brill. Pp. 70–81.

Steele, B.J., and A. Homolar. (2019). "Ontological insecurities and the politics of contemporary populism". *Cambridge Review of International Affairs* 32, no. 3: 214–21.

Stoeckl, K., and D. Uzlaner. (2022). *The Moralist International: Russia in the Global Culture Wars.* New York: Fordham University Press.

Stoica, M.S. (2023). "Conceptualising vulnerability to populist narratives: the Messianic claim of populist leaders". *Journal for the Study of Religions and Ideologies* 22, no. 64: 3–19.

Strømmen, H., and U. Schmiedel. (2020). *The Claim to Christianity: Responding to the Far Right.* London: SCM Press.

Suslov, M. (2014). "Holy Rus: The Geopolitical Imagination in the Contemporary Russian Orthodox Church". *Russian Politics & Law* 52, no. 3:67–86.

Suslov, M. (2018). "Russian World Concept: Post-Soviet Geopolitical Ideology and the Logic of Spheres of Influence", *Geopolitics* 23, No. 2: 330–353.

Suslov, M. (2024) *Putinism: Post-Soviet Russian Regime Ideology.* Abingdon: Routledge.

Torbakov, I. (2018). "'Middle Continent' or 'Island Russia': Eurasianist Legacy and Vadi Tsymburskii's Revisionist Geopolitics". In: N. Bernsand and B. Törnquist-Plewa (eds.). *Cultural and Political Imaginaries in Putin's Russia.* Leiden: Brill. Pp. 37–62.

Vachudova, M.A. (2020). "Ethnopopulism and democratic backsliding in Central Europe" *East European Politics* 36, no. 3: 318–40.

Van der Tol, M.D.C. (2025). *Constitutional Intolerance.* Cambridge University Press.

Van der Tol, M.D.C., and M. Rowley (2021). "A Posture of Protest? The Search for Christian Identity in A Post-Secular Society: Between Secularised Eschatology and A Sacralisation of History". *International Journal of Religion* 2, no. 2: 101–13.

Van der Tol, M.D.C., and P.S. Gorski. (2022). "Secularisation as the fragmentation of the sacred and of sacred space", *Religion, State and Society* 50, no. 5: 495–512.

Wendel, W.B. (2018). "Truthfulness as an Ethical Form of Life". *Duquesne Law Review* 56, no. 2: 141–67.

Winer, A.S. (2018). "Action and reaction: The Trump executive orders and their reception by the federal courts". *Mitchell Hamline L. Rev.* 44: 907–934.

CHAPTER 6

Russian World, Holy Russia: Towards a New Ideology?

Veronica Cibotaru

1   Introduction

This chapter analyses the specific features of the relationship between the Russian Orthodox Church and the Russian government in the post-Soviet era on a theological and ideological level. More particularly, this chapter illuminates the way in which the Russian Orthodox Church conceives of its relationship to the government and to political authority theologically as a symphonic relationship, by referring to a document adopted by the Russian Church in 2000, *The Basis of the Social Concept of the Russian Orthodox Church*. This chapter argues that the close relationship between Russian Orthodox Church and the Russian government is, however, not a mere symphony that would entail the mere necessity of harmonious relationships between state and church, but most of all a theological-political correlation that manifests itself ideologically. Indeed, one can find a common ideological discourse that features two essential characteristics: (1) an anti-Western narrative, and (2) the idea of a common spiritual and religious heritage, which would unite several former Soviet republics, particularly Russia, Ukraine and Belarus.

The ideological idea of a common spiritual and religious heritage has been identified and denounced by contemporary scholars under the notion of 'Russian World'. This chapter argues that this notion must be understood in conjunction with 'Holy Russia', as it bears a specific mythical reading of the history of contemporary nations, which contributes to the justification of the war in Ukraine. One of the aims of this paper is hence to nuance the present scholarly critique against the ideology of the Russian Orthodox Church, proposed for instance by Pantelis Kalaitzidis and Cyril Hovorun, which is focused primarily on the concept of Russian World. It is crucial to take Holy Rus' into account in order to grasp the deeper conceptual fabric of this ideology, as well as its deeper social impact. The concept of Holy Rus' adds to the concept of Russian World a spiritual dimension that can be used as a secondary argument for the war in Ukraine, besides the argument from the linguistic and the cultural unity that is already entailed in the concept of Russian World. The

© VERONICA CIBOTARU, 2025 | DOI:10.1163/9789004731899_007
This is an open access chapter distributed under the terms of the CC BY-NC 4.0 license.

spiritual and mythical, and hence the ahistorical dimension of the concept of Holy Rus' makes it also easier to dismiss possible historical arguments against the unity between Russia and Ukraine as irrelevant.

A second aim of this paper is to show that the relationship between the Russian Orthodox Church and the Russian government features a theological-political correlation that is essentially based on a shared ideological discourse. For this purpose, this chapter approaches the contemporary relationship between the Russian Orthodox Church and the Russian government from a juridical point of view, from a theological and ecclesiological point of view, and finally from the point of view of their respective public discourse. The broader scope of this analysis is to sound the specificity of the ideological dimension of this correlation.

2 The Relationship between the Russian Orthodox Church and the Russian Government from a Juridical Point of View

Since the election of Patriarch Kirill in 2009, a close relationship has developed between the Russian Orthodox Church and the Russian State, while Orthodox Christian religion plays an important role in the public sphere. At the same time, according to the constitution that has been in force since 1993, Russia is a secular state within which "no religion may establish itself as a state religion".[1] Although Vladimir Putin's regime insists on the multi-religious character of Russia, public space is not neutral, since it displays its privileged support for the Russian Orthodox Church. At the same time, one might say that religion today remains an option in Russia and is not imposed in the public space. Contemporary Russia corresponds therefore at least to a certain extent to one of the criteria of secularity proposed by Charles Taylor, according to which a secular society is a society in which religious affiliation or belief is one option among others, such as atheism.[2] As we can see, the secular model that characterises contemporary Russia is steeped in ambiguities, even certain contradictions.

One of the first features that can be observed, is the public image which shows the hierarchs of the Russian Orthodox Church often in the company of state officials, whether to participate in religious or non-religious celebrations,

---

1   The Constitution of the Russian Federation (with amendments dated March 14, 2020), Article 14, accessed 17 September 2023, https://www.wipo.int/wipolex/en/legislation/details/21035.
2   Charles Taylor, *A Secular Age* (Cambridge, MA: Belknap Press of Harvard University Press, 2007).

such as Victory Day on May 9th, or to receive state medals from them. In general, the Patriarch regularly appears in public alongside Putin during national and religious celebrations, while Putin also attends Orthodox religious celebrations, such as Christmas liturgy. Furthermore, the Russian Orthodox Church has an important representation in the public space, for example through religious TV or internet broadcasts that reach a large audience.[3]

3 The Relationship between the Russian Orthodox Church and the Russian Government from a Theological Point of View

On a theological, ecclesiological level, the Russian Orthodox Church conceives its relationship to political power and authority as having to be harmonious and even obedient. This relationship is theorised in a text that was adopted at the Council of the Russian Orthodox Church in 2000, entitled *The Basis of the Social Concept of the Russian Orthodox Church*. This text devotes an entire section to the question of the relationship between church and state. It clearly stipulates that the Church must obey the governmental power. More interestingly however, the text also mentions that the Byzantine Empire constitutes the Orthodox ideal of relations between the church and the state, since it was characterised, according to the authors of this text, by a symphony between church and state, at least in its principles. Here is how the text defines this symphony:

> Its essence is mutual cooperation, mutual support and mutual accountability, without one side intruding into the exclusive sphere of the other. The bishop submits to the authority of the state as a subject, and not because his episcopal authority comes from the representative of the authority of the state. In the same way, a representative of state authority obeys the bishop as a member of the Church seeking salvation in it, and not because his authority comes from the authority of the bishop.[4]

---

3 Until June 2022, a hebdomadal TV programme called "The Church and the World" was broadcasted on one of the most viewed governmental channels, *Rossia-24*. This programme was led by the former chairman of the Department for External Church Relations of the Moscow Patriarchate Hilarion Alfeyev, who was dismissed from this duty in June 2022. This TV programme had a wide audience, not only among Orthodox believers, and was translated into other languages, such as English and French, due to which it could reach an international audience.
4 The Russian Orthodox Church, "The Basis of the Social Concept of the Russian Orthodox Church", the Moscow Patriarchate, 13–16 August 2000, accessed 22 March 2022, http://www.patriarchia.ru/db/text/419128.html.

It is important to note that according to this definition, there is a mutual submission of church and state, a submission that does not take place because they would grant each other their respective authority (thus the bishop does not derive his authority from the state, just as the representative of the state does not derive his authority from the bishop). By this very fact, church and state are autonomous, yet submit to each other, meaning there would be no intrusion from one sphere into another. What legitimises their mutual submission is not the intrusion, but rather reciprocity between these two spheres. Thus, the bishop submits to the state because he is not only bishop but also subject of the state. Conversely, the representative of the state submits to the bishop because he is not only a statesman but also a member of the Church.

For this definition of the symphony between church and state, this text refers to a Byzantine law book dating from the nineth century, called *Epanagogue* or *Eisagogue*, which covers a wide range of domains of law, among which also the relationship between the temporal power (incarnated by the Byzantine emperor) and the spiritual power (incarnated by the patriarch). Nevertheless, while acknowledging the Byzantine roots of this definition, the text also considers that such a symphony has been better embodied throughout Russian rather than Byzantine history. We can see that the contemporary Russian Orthodox Church justifies the close ties that unite it to political power in a doubly historical way, since it refers both to Byzantine and to Russian history, the latter of which is thought to ultimately complete the history of the Byzantine Empire.

It is nevertheless necessary to nuance the scope of this symphony, at least as it is defined in this text, since at the same time it is also written "that above the requirement of loyalty on the part of the Church to the state is that of divine command" and, that "the Church must refuse obedience to the power of the state when the power compels Orthodox believers to renounce the Christ and his Church".[5] This nuance is highly important, especially in the actual political context, since it entails that the Russian Orthodox Church has *de jure* a theological, ecclesiological ground for resisting giving its approval to the war in Ukraine, through an act of civil disobedience, although we observe the opposite fact.

Interestingly, we find a similar vision of the relationship between church and state in Putin's speeches. For example, he declared in 2013 the following:

---

5 The Russian Orthodox Church, "The Basis of the Social Concept of the Russian Orthodox Church".

> The Russian Orthodox Church has been with its people throughout its history, it has shared its joys and its sorrows ... We hope to continue this positive and versatile partnership with the Russian Orthodox Church ... We must continue our cooperation and our common work in order to strengthen the harmony of our society, with high moral values.[6]

This notion of cooperation projects the Russian Orthodox Church as a privileged partner of the state, with a view to "our common work", namely that of strengthening the harmony of Russian society, thanks to the preservation and promotion of moral values, which are also called traditional values.

It is nevertheless necessary to mention that these close relations between the Russian Orthodox Church and the state are not only a matter of a simple partnership but that they can also take on an apologetic tone, which could suggest that the Russian State instrumentalises the Church for the promotion of its actions and its political goals.[7] Thus, it is not uncommon to hear the high clergy of the Russian Orthodox Church directly praise Putin's policy, for example by affirming that his presidency is a miracle,[8] by praising his management of the Nagorno-Karabakh conflict,[9] or by highlighting the feelings of gratitude of the people of African countries towards Putin.[10]

---

6   A. Dolya, "L'Église orthodoxe russe au service du Kremlin", *Revue Défense Nationale* 5, no. 780 (2015): 74–8.

7   In this sense, Cyril Hovorun mentions an "utilitarian symphony" that would exist between the Russian Orthodox Church and the Russian government (see Cyril Hovorun, "Utilitarnaya Simfonia" ["Utilitarian Symphony"], *Vera+*, 25 March 2023, accessed 27 March 2023, https://veraplus.org/2023/03/25/utilitarian-symphony/).

8   Patriarch Kirill declared this in 2012, during Putin's third term campaign in a March 4 election (cf. G. Bryanski, "Russian patriarch calls Putin era 'miracle of God'", *Reuters*, 8 February 2012, accessed 13 March 2023 https://www.reuters.com/article/uk-russia-putin-religion-idUKTRE81722Y20120208). We have also seen this apologetic strategy in 2022, when Patriarch Kirill called Orthodox believers to vote for the modification of the constitution and voted himself publicly for this new constitution (June 25) that would allow Putin to run once again for two presidential terms.

9   Metropolitan Hilarion Alfeyev expressed the following words of praise in his TV programme "The Church and the World" of 14 November 2020: "First of all, I would like to state that the restoration of peace in Nagorny Karabakh is an undoubted political achievement and great foreign policy victory for the Russian State and personally for President Putin" (see Metropolitan Hilarion Alfeyev, interview by Yekaterina Gracheva, *Communications Service of the DECR*, The Russian Orthodox Church, accessed 13 March 2023, https://mospat.ru/en/news/61099/).

10 In his TV programme "The Church and the World" of 5 February 2022, metropolitan Hilarion Alfeyev mentioned the fact that some Ethiopian Christians carried a placard with the words "Thanks to Putin". ("Metropolitan Hilarion: propaganda for an unnatural lifestyle

Hence, one can observe a discrepancy between the way in which the Russian Orthodox Church conceives its relationship to temporal power from a theological point of view, and the real form this relationship takes: while the theological level grants a form of autonomy to the spiritual power of the Russian Orthodox Church, the autonomous voice of the Russian Orthodox Church is often hardly heard.

4 The Relationship between the Russian Orthodox Church and the Russian Government from an Ideological Point of View

Another important characteristic of the way in which the Russian Orthodox Church positions itself in relation to the state and to political power lies in the sharing of a discourse, which, if not identical to, at least has much in common with that of political power, and which indicates the fact that the Russian Orthodox Church shares a common ideology. Two essential features distinguish this common discourse. First, an anti-Western narrative framework and secondly, the idea of a common Russian cultural and spiritual heritage that would unite at least three countries, namely Russia, Belarus and Ukraine. Sometimes other countries are included in this unity, such as Moldova, Kazakhstan, and even the Baltic states, parts of the Caucasus and Central Asia, that is, countries from the former Soviet Union.[11]

The Russian Orthodox Church positions itself as a defender of Christian moral values, the so-called 'traditional values', not only within present-day Russia, but also across the world, and more particularly in relation to the West, which it likes to present as a place where moral and Christian values have been lost. It is in this context that the sermon of the Patriarch Kirill from 6 March 2022, in which he presented the war in Ukraine as a metaphysical fight against evil, embodied by consumerism, illusory freedom and the gay pride characteristic of Western societies, takes on its full meaning.

The image of a Russian state defending Christian values and religious freedom (elsewhere) is, all in all, a non-negligible instrument of soft power. It allows the Russian Orthodox Church and the Kremlin to assert moral leadership that

---

is a great tragedy of Western society", *Communications Service of the DECR*, The Russian Orthodox Church, accessed 14 March 2023, https://mospat.ru/ru/news/88950/).

11   See the message of Patriarch Kirill from December 22, 2022: Patriarch Kirill, "Primate of the Russian Church: The current strife is fratricidal, the fault lies primarily with those who set as their goal the destruction of the unity of Holy Rus'", the Moscow Patriarchate, 22 December 2022, accessed 25 February 2024, http://www.patriarchia.ru/db/text/5986140.html.

sometimes appeals to traditionalist groups in Western societies, who might regret dechristianisation and the loss of traditional values, while conversely having a real admiration and even fascination for the so-called missionary work of Russia. For example, the French newspaper *La Croix* published an article on the war in Ukraine in March 2022, which included a controversial statement: "We regret that people are dying, but with its efforts to recover family policy and Christianization, Russia remains on an interesting path".[12] Expressions such as these reflect the existence of a transnational, transcultural and even transreligious global network that promotes, with international cooperation, a "conservative agenda",[13] both in Europe and the United States.

Anti-Western ideas are echoed in Putin's comments on what genuine Christian values mean, as his message to the Federal Assembly of 21 February 2023 attests:

> Look at what they [Western leaders] are doing with their own peoples: the destruction of the family, cultural and national identity, perversion, abuse of children, up to paedophilia, are declared the norm, the norm of their life, and clergy, priests are forced to bless same-sex marriages. ... [L]ook at the scriptures, the main books of all other world religions. Everything is said there, including that the family is the union of a man and a woman, but these sacred texts are now being questioned. ... [G]od forgive me, "they do not know what they are doing". Millions of people in the West understand that they are being led to a real spiritual catastrophe. ... [W]e have the obligation to protect our children, and we will do it: we will protect our children from degradation and degeneration.[14]

---

12 Mikael Corre and Héloïse de Neuville, "Guerre en Ukraine: ce qu'en disent les amis de la Russie en France", *La Croix*, 31 March 2022, accessed on 31 March 2022, https://www.la-croix.com/France/Guerre-Ukraine-quen-disent-amis-Russie-France-2022-03-31-1201207940.

13 J. Mourão Permoser and K. Stoeckl, "Reframing human rights: the global network of moral conservative homeschooling activists", *Global Networks* 21, no. 4 (2021): 627–702. For a more detailed and specific analysis of the manner in which the Russian Orthodox Church fits into this global conservative agenda and how it has appropriated the strategies of the right-wing Christian groups see Kristina Stoeckl and Dmitry Uzlaner, *The Moralist International, Russia in the Global Culture Wars* (New York: Fordham University Press, 2022). See also Timo Koch, "Family Ties and Ethnic Lines: Ethnopluralism in the Far-Right's Mobilization in Europe", *Ethnic and Racial Studies* 47, No. 9: 1791-1811, for the relationship between this conservative agenda and Far-Right networks, especially from the point of view of the question of gender.

14 The Message of the President of the Russian Federation to the Federal Assembly, 21 February 2023, accessed 25 February 2023. http://kremlin.ru/events/president/news/70565/videos.

This type of discourse is indicative of a characteristic symptom of the contemporary Russian Orthodox Church but also of the Russian government, which is sometimes called the "besieged fortress" symptom,[15] whereby Russia is seen, or is at least presented as being in a spiritually, socially, and politically hostile environment, from which it must defend itself. A few days before the full-scale invasion of Ukraine, metropolitan Hilarion Alfeyev used his TV programme *The Church and the World* to declare that Russians should be protected from the propaganda of Western values, expressing the idea that Western values are not genuine values.[16] Categorised under these values are supposed first of all those values that promote non-traditional sexual practices and ways of living. We find the same type of defensive symptom in Putin's speeches when he insists on the threat that NATO presents to the security of Russia, even going so far as to justify a war by invoking this threat.

This symptom is accompanied, as the Russian researchers Boris Knorre and Aleksei Zygmont show, by a "warrior register" and a "theology of war" in the circles of the Russian Orthodox Church, leading to the development of militant religiosity, called "militant piety".[17] This religious rehabilitation of the war infuses the collective imagination of Russian society with religious symbolism, such as the victory of the USSR in the Second World War. For example, the victory in the Second World War is presented as a manifestation of Easter (resurrection) in Russian history, even of a second Easter relative to the New Testament.[18] At the same time, we also see the use of the notion of holy war in the speeches of the clergy of the Russian Orthodox Church, including in the speeches of Patriarch Kirill himself, for example in 2016, when he designated the war that Russia led in Syria against terrorism as a holy war.[19] Again we find a parallel in the speeches of Vladimir Putin, for instance in his speech dated 18 March 2022, which refers to the gospel in order to greet and ultimately also to

---

15   Maria Lipman, "Putin's 'Besieged Fortress' and its Ideological Arms", in *The State of Russia: What Comes Next?*, eds. Maria Lipman and Nikolay Petrov (London: Palgrave Pivot, 2015), 110–136; Gregory Carleton, *Russia: The Story of War* (Cambridge, MA: Belknap Press of Harvard University Press, 2017).
16   Metropolitan Hilarion, "Metropolitan Hilarion of Volokolamsk: The Russian Church values worship as it inherited it from its ancestors", the Moscow Patriarchate, 19 February 2022, accessed 13 March 2023, http://www.patriarchia.ru/db/text/5903301.html.
17   Boris Knorre and Alexei Zygmont, "'Militant Piety' in 21st-Century Orthodox Christianity: Return to Classical Traditions or Formation of a New Theology of War?" *Religions* 11, no. 1 (2020): 2.
18   Boris Knorre, "Great Patriotic War Narratives in the Russian Orthodox Church", *Russia. Post*, 7 May 2023, https://russiapost.info/politics/war_church.
19   Knorre, "Great Patriotic War Narratives in the Russian Orthodox Church".

justify the military commitment of Russian soldiers in Ukraine, maintaining that "there is no greater love than to lay down your life for your friends".[20]

A second essential feature of this common discourse shared by the high clergy of the Russian Orthodox Church and by the political leadership is the idea of a common heritage, above all spiritual and religious, that would unite at least some if not all former Soviet countries, including Russia, Ukraine, and Belarus. This imagined common space, which corresponds to the canonical territory asserted by the Russian Orthodox Church, is often criticised under the umbrella of the Russian World in the scholarly literature.[21] It is also this concept that often used to criticise the current ideology of the Russian Orthodox Church, as the "Declaration on the 'Russian World' (*Russkii Mir*) Teaching" attests, and which contends that the Russian World ideology is a heresy.[22] The discourse of the hierarchs of the Russian Orthodox Church cannot however be reduced to one single key concept, such as the Russian World, but is instead characterised by diffuse concepts, which bring in different nuances, chiefly among them Holy Russia or Holy Rus'.

It is crucial to analyse this concept in conjunction with the notion of the Russian World. The concept of Holy Russia justifies the pretention to a common heritage that would unite Russia, Ukraine, and Belarus through the idea that these three countries are historically descended from the Principality of Kiev, as the cradle of Russian Orthodoxy.[23] The Russian Orthodox Church therefore does not consider the state borders that exist today between these countries as

---

20   "Russie: Vladimir Poutine déroule sa propagande lors d'une grand-messe patriotique", *Euronews*, 18 March 2022, accessed 29 March 2022, https://fr.euronews.com/2022/03/18/russie-vladimir-poutine-deroule-sa-propagande-lors-d-une-grand-messe-patriotique.

21   See for instance Michael Suslov, "'Russian World' Concept: Post-Soviet Geopolitical Ideology and the Logic of 'Spheres of Influence'", *Geopolitics* 23(2) (2018): 330–353; Thomas Bremer, "Diffuses Konzept: Die Russische Orthodoxe Kirche und die 'Russische Welt'", *Osteuropa* 66(3) (2016): 3–18; Sean Griffin, "Russian World or Holy World War? The Real Ideology of the Invasion of Ukraine", *Public Orthodoxy*, Fordham University, 12 April 2022, https://publicorthodoxy.org/2022/04/12/russian-world-or-holy-world-war/.

22   Public Orthodoxy and the Volos Academy of Religious Studies, "A Declaration on the 'Russian World' (*Russkii Mir*) Teaching", *Public Orthodoxy*, 13 March 2022, accessed on 20 March 2022, https://publicorthodoxy.org/2022/03/13/a-declaration-on-the-russian-world-russkii-mir-teaching/. See also Pantelis Kalaitzidis, "Orthodox Theology Challenged by Balkan and East European Ethnotheologies", in *Politics, Society and Culture in Orthodox Theology in a Global Age*, eds. Hans-Peter Grosshans and Pantelis Kalaitzidis (Paderborn: Brill Schöningh, 2023), 108–159.

23   For the history of the notion of Holy Rus', which appears in Russia already in the 16th century, see Oleksandr Zabirko, "The Concept of 'Holy Rus' in Russian Literary and Cultural Tradition: Between the Third Rome and the City of Kitezh", *Entangled Religions* 13, no. 8 (2022).

spiritual borders, but on the contrary as spaces belonging to a common spiritual space, which is sacred. Thus, Patriarch Kirill declared in March 2022 that the Russian and the Ukrainian people are "one people, descended from the same baptism", namely the baptism of Prince Vladimir I, who reigned over the Principality of Kiev in the tenth century.[24] This speech notably echoed Putin's statements denying the existence of a Ukrainian national identity, especially his speech of 21 February 2022, just before full-scale invasion.

The Russian Orthodox Church mobilises the idea of a spiritual and religious unity which, as the theologian Thomas Bremer rightly argues, neglects the social and historical dimension of nation-building.[25] Because of this oblivion of the social and historical dimensions of national identity, the Russian Orthodox Church refers to a common identity that is mythical[26] and appears to be the result of a "geopolitical imagination".[27] This common identity is not merely cultural or linguistic, an idea that is entailed by the concept of the Russian World, but first of all spiritual and religious, since it is consecrated by a mythical founding event, namely the baptism into the Orthodox faith of various future nations, and leads to a "sacralization of real geographic space".[28] In this way, the unity of the different peoples belonging or having belonged to the canonical territory of the Russian Orthodox Church appears as being above historical and social contingencies, and at the same time able to serve political and colonial interests, by justifying a war in name of the preservation of this unity.[29]

Since this unity is not merely linguistic or cultural, as this is entailed already in the concept of Russian World, but above all spiritual, one can expect that the concept of Holy Rus' augments the social impact of the joint ideology of

---

24 This statement is made in the recording of the opening of the 18 March 2022 session of the Supreme Council of the Russian Church, accessed 18 March 2022, http://www.patriarchia.ru/db/text/5909582.html.

25 Thomas Bremer, "Ukrainian Nationhood, '*Russkii Mir*', and the Abuse of History", *Public Orthodoxy*, 13 March 2022, accessed 31 March 2022, https://publicorthodoxy.org/2022/03/22/ukrainian-nationhood-russkii-mir/.

26 Sergey Filatov, "Patriarch Kirill—dva goda planov, mechtanii i neudobnoi real'nosti" ["Patriarch Kirill-Two Years of Plans, Dreams and Uncomfortable Reality"], in *Provaslavnaya Tserkov' pri Novom Patriarhe*, eds. Alexey Malashenko and Sergey Filatov (Moscow: Rosiiskaya politicheskaya izdania, 2012), 9–68.

27 Mikhail D. Suslov, "'Holy Rus': The Geopolitical Imagination in the Contemporary Russian Orthodox Church", *Russian Politics and Law* 52, no. 3 (2014): 67–86.

28 Zabirko, "The Concept of 'Holy Rus' in Russian Literary and Cultural Tradition". For the colonial implications of this notion see Mirja Lecke, "Early Twenty-First-Century Literary Images from the Margins of the Russian (Orthodox) World", *Entangled Religions* 13, no. 8 (2022).

29 Zabirko, "The Concept of 'Holy Rus' in Russian Literary and Cultural Tradition".

the Russian Orthodox Church and the Russian government, for instance on the Russian collective perception of the war in Ukraine, but more broadly on the perception of the relationship between Russia and its neighbouring countries such as Belarus and Moldova. The concept of Ancient Rus' is present in Putin's discourses as well, although in modified form. This reference to Ancient Rus' (although not Holy Rus', thus introducing an element of asymmetry in the discourses of the clergy of the Russian Orthodox Church and Putin's regime) allows Putin to justify the unity of the Ukrainian and Russian, but also Belarusian peoples, as this quotation from his article "On the Historical Unity of Russians and Ukrainians" attests:

> Both Russians, Ukrainians, and Belarusians are the heirs of Ancient Rus', which was the largest state in Europe. Slavic and other tribes in a vast area—from Ladoga, Novgorod, Pskov to Kiev and Chernigov—were united by one language (now we call it Old Russian), economic ties, the power of the princes of the Rurik dynasty. And after the baptism of Rus'—also by one Orthodox faith. The spiritual choice of St. Vladimir, who was both the prince of Novgorod and the great Kyiv prince largely determines our kinship even today.[30]

Although this text does not explicitly mention the sacred dimension of the historical unity of the Russian and Ukrainian nations, one can nevertheless find an implicit reference to this dimension through the mention of the baptism of Rus' into the Orthodox faith, due to which the "historical unity" of Russians and Ukrainians has not been merely linguistic, economic, or political, but also religious and spiritual.

The anti-Western narrative and the concept of Holy or Ancient Rus' are correlated with each other. It is precisely because Putin considers Ukrainians to be one people with the Russians that every aspect of the Western orientation of Ukraine is perceived as being anti-Russian, fomented by Western powers (the USA and the European Union) who aim at destroying this unity. Precisely because Ukraine and Russia form one unity, Ukraine cannot take an independent political and cultural orientation without becoming "anti-Russia".[31] Ultimately, the Ukrainian nation cannot find an endogenous centrifugal force to extract itself from this unity with Russia. Hence, this centrifugal force can only arise from the outside, namely the West. The West is conceived thus as an

---

30   Vladimir Putin, "On the Historical Unity of Russian and Ukrainians", the Kremlin, 12 July 2021, accessed on 7 March 2023. http://kremlin.ru/events/president/news/66181.
31   Putin, "On the Historical Unity of Russian and Ukrainians".

existential threat to the unity of the Ukrainian and Russian peoples, which is grounded on the concept of Holy or Ancient Rus'.[32]

Hence, the official discourse of the high clergy of the Russian Orthodox Church, articulated both around an anti-Western narrative and the concept of Holy Rus', resonates in a political register. The relationship between the Russian Orthodox Church and the Russian government cannot be reduced to a mere partnership or symphony, but rather entails a shared discourse, which, although not entirely identical, resonates in a double register: a theological-religious, and a political register. This shared discourse can be conceived of as a shared ideology, following the definition of ideology of Hannah Arendt, which is given in this fragment:

> An ideology is quite literally what its name indicates: it is the logic of an idea. Its subject matter is history, to which the "idea" is applied; the result of this application is not a body of statements about something that is, but the unfolding of a process which is in constant change. The ideology treats the course of events as though it followed the same "law" as the logical exposition of its "idea". Ideologies pretend to know the mysteries of the whole historical process-the secrets of the past, the intricacies of the present, the uncertainties of the future-because of the logic inherent in their respective ideas.[33]

In this sense, ideology functions as a rigid system centred around one idea, which does not allow any other comprehension or explanation of reality, particularly of history, outside of the totalitarian logical framework of this idea. Ideology is insensitive to reality and its fluid complexity, on the contrary, it does violence to reality by attempting to make it fit into one single idea and its logical consequences. The shared discourse of the Russian Orthodox Church and the Russian government conforms partly to this definition of ideology, since it denies the contemporary reality of Ukraine which aspires at being an independent nation, with a unique culture and language, in the name of the idea of a mythical unity, Holy/Ancient Russia. This unity is mythical in a double way: (1) it interprets the present through a grounding event that is supposed to

---

32 Interestingly, the concept of Rus' (declinated as Great Rus') is already present in the 1977 version of the state anthem of the Soviet Union, and also in the idea of an indestructible unity: "Unbreakable union of freeborn republics / Great Rus' is welded forever to stand. / Great in struggle by the will of the people / United and mighty, our Soviet land!". This concept is absent in the anthem of the Russian Federation.

33 Hannah Arendt, *The Origins of Totalitarianism* (San Diego: Harcourt Brace Jovanovich, 1973), 469.

have happened in a remote past, namely the baptism into the Orthodox faith of Holy Rus'; (2) it negates the historical complexity of a past reality, in this case the state of Kievan Rus', which included a variety of peoples, through the idea of an idealised unity.

Hence, this common ideological discourse has the particularity of being grounded on a mythical idea, and thus of interpreting the present in the light of a mythical past. This orientation towards the past exemplifies the traditionalist and nostalgic tendency that, as Pantelis Kalaitzidis shows, characterises modern Orthodoxy. As a result,

> The church is transformed from a community that is open to the future and its challenges into one that yearns for the past and its political forms. It no longer yearns for the *eschaton*, the kingdom of God, and the Coming Lord, but instead for a return to a 'Christian' empire and Byzantine theocracy.[34]

This type of orientation leaves aside the eschatological vocation of the Church, apart from which "Christianity is inconceivable",[35] and loses its meaning, since the remembrance and maintenance of the past "is the only way to meet the future, to become ready for it".[36] A focus on tradition that is not linked to eschatology becomes dead traditionalism that cannot carry on the call of Pentecost and is not able to preserve a dialectical distance with the world, thus "blur[ring] the line between the worldly and the religious spheres, between the realms of Caesar and God",[37] and one could say, between theology and politics.[38] Eventually, this traditionalist tendency is associated with a conflictual relationship with modernity, which brings forth an anti-Western attitude, since modernity is considered to be a result of the historical development of the Western world.

---

34 Pantelis Kalaitzidis, *Orthodoxy and Political Theology*, trans. Fr. G. Edwards (Geneva: World Council of Churches Publications, 2012), 131.
35 Kalaitzidis, *Orthodoxy and Political Theology*, 141.
36 John Meyendorff, "Does Christian tradition have a future?", *St Vladimir's Theological Quarterly*, 54 (2010), quoted in Kalaitzidis, *Orthodoxy and Political Theology*, 89.
37 Kalaitzidis, *Orthodoxy and Political Theology*, 131–32.
38 Conversely, "the true traditionalist is not the integrist or the reactionary, but the one who discerns the 'signs of time' (Matt. 16:3)—who is prepared to discover the leaven of the gospel at work even within such a seemingly secular movement as modern feminism" (Kallistos Ware, "Man, Woman and the Priesthood of Christ", in *The Ordination of Women in the Orthodox Church*, ed. Elisabeth Behr-Sigle and Kallistos Ware (Geneva: WCC Publications, 2000), 49–96, 66). Tradition appears thus to be a source of inspiration for the discernment of a deeper meaning in the developments of modernity, which does not justify the rejection of modernity.

This again echoes that the correlation between an anti-Western narrative and an idealisation of the past is ideological.

At the same time, the discourse of the Russian Orthodox Church conforms only partially to the definition proposed by Hannah Arendt, since it entails a conceptual plasticity, by alternating various concepts (Russian World, Holy Rus') that are again slightly modified in the discourse of the Russian government (Ancient Rus'). Such a conceptual plasticity is at odds with Arendt's conception of ideology as a rigid logical system built around one idea as the "logic of an idea".[39] The nature of this peculiar form of ideology remains still to be investigated, but one can already suppose that due to its plasticity it is more difficult to criticise it than a classical form of ideology, such as communism or Nazism, because it is more difficult to clearly identify its main concepts and principles. This was particularly evident when the protodeacon Andrey Kuraev, who is known for his critical stances within the Russian Orthodox Church, was asked his opinion about the "Declaration on the 'Russian World' (*Russkii Mir*) Teaching". His answer consisted partly in the idea that "the doctrine of the Russian world has not been officially formulated and approved".[40] As we can see, the doctrine of the Russian World cannot be easily criticised simply because there is no such doctrine. The discourse of the Russian Orthodox Church is not even built around one key concept—the Russian World—but is characterised, as we have seen, by at least two concepts, Russian World and Holy Russia, which are not developed into a coherent doctrine.

Nevertheless, as Cyril Hovorun argues, it is possible to identify some essential features of this ideological shared discourse. According to Hovorun, Putin took up the essential features of the discourse of the Russian Orthodox Church, developed over many years, in order to fill an ideological gap in legitimising his power.[41] Hovorun understands the political intersections of Holy Russia and the Russian World as the ideology of "Putinism". He argues that this

---

39   Arendt, *The Origins of Totalitarianism*, 469.
40   Andrey Kuraev, "Entretien avec André Kuraev (3/3)—'Les défis contemporains de l'orthodoxie: une perspective historique", interview by Veronica Cibotaru and Fr. Jivko Panev, *Orthodoxie.com*, 3 June 2022, accessed on 10 March 2023, https://orthodoxie.com/entretien-avec-andre-kuraev-3-3/.
41   Cyril Hovorun, "Orthodox theology must be de-Putinized", *La Croix*, 11 March 2023, accessed on 15 March 2022, https://international.la-croix.com/news/religion/orthodox-theology-must-be-de-putinized-says-leading-church-scholar/15772. See also Sarah Riccardi-Schwartz and Robert Saler, "*Einai ho Poutin pragmatika hristianos*" ["Is Putin a true Christian?"] Volos Academy for Theological Studies, 31 March 2023, accessed on 1 April 2022, https://www.polymerwsvolos.org/2022/03/31/einai_o_poutin_pragmatika_xristianos/?fbclid=IwAR1Ocj3MnV8rB2JXMaWoI2dJe4oXLF_XklE3wybh6bDia4JHD1vrOu6FsVo.

Putinism needs to be deconstructed on a theological level, by unveiling its fallacious pseudo-Christian principles, especially Manichaeism, that is, the opposition between two moral and spiritual forces, a good one, incarnated in Russia (hence the idea of a Holy Russia), and a bad one, incarnated in the Western world. It is precisely this Manichaeist framework that gives its full meaning to the idea, defended by Patriarch Kirill, that the war in Ukraine is a metaphysical fight: following the logic of this idea, Russia is indeed not merely a geopolitical but a spiritual force that fights against an evil force.

It is however not entirely clear, if we analyse the discourses of Patriarch Kirill, whether this Manichaeist framework[42] is also associated, as Hovorun argues,[43] with a messianic vocation, in the sense that Russia would have the vocation to save humanity by instituting the Kingdom of God on earth,[44] whether this Manichaeist framework is primarily defensive in character, or whether both dimensions characterize to an equal extent the public discourse of the Russian Orthodox Church. According to this second perspective, Russia should primarily defend itself (which also means Ukraine, since Ukraine would form a spiritual unity with Russia) from this evil force. The discourses of Patriarch Kirill and of the higher clergy of the Russian Orthodox Church tend toward this second option, as we have seen above, and appear to exemplify the spiritual security doctrine that has been promoted by the Russian Orthodox Church from 2000, which eventually "leads to repression of the inside, and to war with the outside world".[45]

---

42   Cyril Hovorun, "Russian World 2.0 and Putin's Spirituality", *Religion in Praxis*, 26 February 2022, accessed on 13 March 2023, https://religioninpraxis.com/russian-world-2-0-and-putins-spirituality/.

43   Cyril Hovorun, *Political Orthodoxies: The Unorthodoxies of the Church Coerced* (Minneapolis: Fortress Press, 2018).

44   It is possible however to find such messianic tendencies among the lower clergy of the Russian Orthodox Church, as reports Boris Knorre, who quotes a declaration of the priest Ivan Okhlobystin dated 13 September 2011: "Then we will have no choice but to destroy the rest of the world, rotten at the core with vices and indifference, and commit suicide in hope that a new, better humanity will emerge from the miraculously survived human individuals. This is the only way God will forgive us" (quoted in Knorre, "Great Patriotic War Narratives in the Russian Orthodox Church"). However, such tendencies are less obvious in the discourse of the higher clergy of the Russian Orthodox Church, particularly in the discourses of the Patriarch.

45   Kristina Stoeckl, "Russia's spiritual security doctrine as a challenge to European comprehensive security approaches", *The Review of Faith & International Affairs* 20, no. 4 (2022): 37–44.

5 Conclusion

The contemporary relationship between the Russian Orthodox Church and the Russian government is characterised by a theological-political correlation, which is based not merely on a specific theological or ecclesiological conception of the relationship between the Church and the temporal power, but on intersecting ideological discourses on the Russian World, Holy Russia, Holy Rus' and Ancient Rus'. These discourses demonstrate a conceptual plasticity due to which it cannot be fully conceived of through the classical categories of ideology, such as they are formulated by Hannah Arendt. Instead, these discourses signal a new type of phenomenon that cannot be analysed by means of classical political theory or by means of classical theological-political categories. It seems difficult to distil one rigid or coherent political or theological doctrine, or indeed discern sufficiently strict parallels between the political and theological dimensions of the discourse. Nevertheless, the powerful intersections of these theological and political imaginaries, however diffuse, shape the predicaments of a changing world order, and it will be important for scholarship to find new tools to fully grasp it.

Bibliography

(2022). "Russie: Vladimir Poutine déroule sa propagande lors d'une grand-messe patriotique". *Euronews*, 18 March 2022. https://fr.euronews.com/2022/03/18/russie-vladimir-poutine-deroule-sa-propagande-lors-d-une-grand-messe-patriotique.

Arendt, H. (1973). *The Origins of Totalitarianism*. San Diego: Harcourt Brace Jovanovich.

Bremer, T. (2016). "Diffuses Konzept: Die Russische Orthodoxe Kirche und die 'Russische Welt'". *Osteuropa* 66(3): 3–18.

Bremer, T. (2022). "Ukrainian Nationhood, *'Russkii Mir'*, and the Abuse of History". *Public Orthodoxy*, 13 April 2022. https://publicorthodoxy.org/2022/03/22/ukrainian-nationhood-russkii-mir/.

Bryanski, G. (2012). "Russian patriarch calls Putin era 'miracle of God'". *Reuters*, 8 February 2012. https://www.reuters.com/article/uk-russia-putin-religion-idUKTRE81722Y20120208.

Carleton, G. (2017). *Russia: The Story of War*. Cambridge, MA: Belknap Press of Harvard University Press.

Corre, M., and H. de Neuville. (2022). "Guerre en Ukraine: ce qu'en disent les amis de la Russie en France". *La Croix*, 31 March 2022. https://www.la-croix.com/France/Guerre-Ukraine-quen-disent-amis-Russie-France-2022-03-31-1201207940.

Dolya, A. (2015). "L'Église orthodoxe russe au service du Kremlin". *Revue Défense Nationale* 5, no. 780: 74–8.

Filatov, S. (2012). "Patriarch Kirill—dva goda planov, mechtanii i neudobnoi real'nosti" ["Patriarch Kirill—Two Years of Plans, Dreams and Uncomfortable Reality"]. In: A. Malashenko and S. Filatov (eds.). *Provaslavnaya Tserkov' pri Novom Patriarhe*. Moscow: Rosiiskaya politicheskaya izdania. Pp. 9–68.

Griffin, S. (2022). "Russian World or Holy World War? The Real Ideology of the Invasion of Ukraine". *Public Orthodoxy*. Fordham University, 12 April 2022. https://publicorthodoxy.org/2022/04/12/russian-world-or-holy-world-war/.

Hovorun, C. (2018). *Political Orthodoxies: The Unorthodoxies of the Church Coerced*. Minneapolis: Fortress Press.

Hovorun, C. (2022). "Orthodox theology must be de-Putinized". *La Croix*, 11 March 2022. https://international.la-croix.com/news/religion/orthodox-theology-must-be-de-putinized-says-leading-church-scholar/15772.

Hovorun, C. (2022). "Russian World 2.0 and Putin's Spirituality". *Religion in Praxis*, 26 February 2022. https://religioninpraxis.com/russian-world-2-0-and-putins-spirituality/.

Hovorun, C. (2023). "Utilitarnaya Simfonia" ["Ultimate Symphony"]. *Vera+*, 25 March 2023. Accessed 27 March 2023. https://veraplus.org/2023/03/25/utilitarian-symphony/.

Kalaitzidis, P. (2012). *Orthodoxy and Political Theology*. Trans. Fr. G. Edwards. Geneva: World Council of Churches Publications.

Kalaitzidis, P. (2023). "Orthodox Theology Challenged by Balkan and East European Ethnotheologies". In: H.-P. Grosshans and P. Kalaitzidis (eds.). *Politics, Society and Culture in Orthodox Theology in a Global Age*. Paderborn: Brill Schöningh. Pp. 108–59.

Knorre, B. (2023). "Great Patriotic War Narratives in the Russian Orthodox Church", *Russia.Post,* 7 May 2023, https://russiapost.info/politics/war_church.

Knorre, B., and A Zygmont. (2020). "'Militant Piety' in 21st-Century Orthodox Christianity: Return to Classical Traditions or Formation of a New Theology of War?" *Religions* 11, no. 1: 2.

Koch, T. (2024) "Family Ties and Ethnic Lines: Ethnopluralism in the Far-Right's Mobilization in Europe". *Ethnic and Racial Studies* 47, No. 9: 1791-1811.

Kuraev, A. "Entretien avec André Kuraev (3/3)—'Les défis contemporains de l'orthodoxie: une perspective historique". Interview by Veronica Cibotaru and Fr. Jivko Panev. *Orthodoxie.com, 3 June 2022.* https://orthodoxie.com/entretien-avec-andre-kuraev-3-3/.

Lecke, M. (2022). *Early Twenty-First-Century Literary Images from the Margins of the Russian (Orthodox) World. Entangled Religions* 13, no. 8. https://doi.org/10.46586/er.13.2022.10221.

Lipman, M. (2015). "Putin's 'Besieged Fortress' and it's Ideological Arms". In: M. Lipman and N. Petrov (eds.). *The State of Russia: What Comes Next?* London: Palgrave Pivot. Pp. 110–36.

Metropolitan Hilarion. (2022). "Metropolitan Hilarion of Volokolamsk: The Russian Church values worship as it inherited it from its ancestors". The Moscow Patriarchate, 19 February 2022. http://www.patriarchia.ru/db/text/5903301.html.

Mourão Permoser, J., and K. Stoeckl. (2021). "Reframing human rights: the global network of moral conservative homeschooling activists". *Global Networks* 21, no. 4: 627–702.

Patriarch Kirill. (2022). "Primate of the Russian Church: The current strife is fratricidal, the fault lies primarily with those who set as their goal the destruction of the unity of Holy Rus'". The Moscow Patriarchate, 22 December 2022. http://www.patriarchia.ru/db/text/5986140.html.

Public Orthodoxy and the Volos Academy of Religious Studies. (2022). "A Declaration on the 'Russian World' (*Russkii Mir*) Teaching". *Public Orthodoxy*, 13 March 2022. https://publicorthodoxy.org/2022/03/13/a-declaration-on-the-russian-world-russkii-mir-teaching/.

Putin, Vladimir. (2021). "On the Historical Unity of Russian and Ukrainians". The Kremlin, 12 July 2021. http://kremlin.ru/events/president/news/66181.

Riccardi-Schwartz, S., and R. Saler. (2022). "Einai ho Poutin pragmatika hristianos," ["Is Putin a true Christian?"] *Volos Academy for Theological Studies*, 31 March 2023. https://www.polymerwsvolos.org/2022/03/31/einai_o_poutin_pragmatika_xristianos/?fbclid=IwAR1Ocj3MnV8rB2JXMaWoI2dJe4oXLF_XklE3wybh6bDia4JHD1vrOu6FsVo.

Stoeckl, K. (2022). "Russia's spiritual security doctrine as a challenge to European comprehensive security approaches". *The Review of Faith & International Affairs* 20, no. 4: 37–44. https://www.tandfonline.com/doi/full/10.1080/15570274.2022.2139536.

Stoeckl, K., and D. Uzlaner. (2022). *The Moralist International, Russia in the Global Culture Wars*. New York: Fordham University Press.

Suslov, M. (2014). "'Holy Rus': The Geopolitical Imagination in the Contemporary Russian Orthodox Church". *Russian Politics and Law* 52, no. 3: 67–86.

Suslov, M. (2018). "'Russian World' Concept: Post-Soviet Geopolitical Ideology and the Logic of 'Spheres of Influence'". *Geopolitics* 23, no. 2: 330–353.

Taylor, C. (2007). *A Secular Age*. Cambridge, MA: Belknap Press of Harvard University Press.

The Russian Orthodox Church. (2000). "The Basis of the Social Concept of the Russian Orthodox Church". The Moscow Patriarchate, 13–16 August 2000. http://www.patriarchia.ru/db/text/419128.html.

Ware, K. (2000). "Man, Woman and the Priesthood of Christ". In: E. Behr-Sigel and K. Ware (eds.). *The Ordination of Women in the Orthodox Church*. Geneva: WCC Publications. Pp. 49–96.

Zabirko, O. (2022). The Concept of Holy Rus' in Russian Literary and Cultural Tradition: Between the Third Rome and the City of Kitezh. *Entangled Religions* 13(8). https://doi.org/10.46586/er.13.2022.9964.

CHAPTER 7

Putinism and Alexander Solzhenitsyn's Religious Motifs

Dmytro Bintsarovskyi

1   Introduction

While the increase in the Kremlin's use of religious rhetoric and imagery has been observable for at least a decade,[1] it became the subject of scholarly debate and widespread public attention after the full-scale invasion of Ukraine. It has been speculated to what extent Vladimir Putin's worldview was influenced by his reading of religious philosophers such as Ivan Ilyin or Vasily Rozanov,[2] the apocalyptical vision of the neo-Eurasianist ideologue Aleksandr Dugin,[3] or the close contacts of his advisor Yuri Kovalchuk,[4] or Metropolitan Tikhon (Shevkunov).[5] More broadly, scholars have discussed how the Russian Orthodox Church, particularly by developing and popularising the notion of

---

1   Marcin Składanowski and Cezary Smuniewski, "From Desecularization to Sacralization of the Political Language: Religion and Historiosophy in Vladimir Putin's Preparations for War", *Verbum Vitae* 40, no. 4 (2022): 869–91.
2   Ilya Zhegulev, "Kak Putin voznenavidel Ukrainu" ["How Putin Came to Hate Ukraine"], *Verstka*, 25 April 2023, accessed 12 September 2023, https://verstka.media/kak-putin-pridumal-voynu.
3   Regularly cited in Western media as "Putin's spiritual guide" and "Putin's brain", in Russia Dugin is usually dismissed as a peripheral figure. A helpful overview of debates about his actual influence on Russian politics can be found in David G. Lewis, *Russia's New Authoritarianism: Putin And The Politics Of Order* (Edinburgh: Edinburgh University Press, 2020), 36. See also Dmitry Shlapentokh, *Ideological Seduction and Intellectuals in Putin's Russia* (Cham: Palgrave Macmillan, 2021), 187–278. On Russian nationalism, see Charles Clover, *Black Wind, White Snow: The Rise of Russia's New Nationalism* (New Haven, CT: Yale University Press, 2016).
4   A longtime friend of Putin, Kovalchuk reportedly became particularly close to him during the coronavirus pandemic. Mikhail Zygar ascribes to him "a worldview that combines Orthodox Christian mysticism, anti-American conspiracy theories and hedonism" ("How Vladimir Putin Lost Interest in the Present", *New York Times*, 10 March 2022, accessed 11 April 2023, https://www.nytimes.com/2022/03/10/opinion/putin-russia-ukraine.html).
5   See Cyril Hovorun, *Political Orthodoxies: The Unorthodoxies of the Church Coerced* (Minneapolis, MN: Fortress Press, 2018), 83–4, 143.

the 'Russian World', has strengthened anti-Western and revanchist attitudes in Russia.[6]

By invoking religious motifs, the Kremlin, supported by the Russian Orthodox Church, seeks to achieve four main purposes. First, such appeals allow them to depict Russia as a unique civilisation and challenge the universal validity of liberal values. Depending on the circumstances, Russia is presented either as a unique civilisation, having Orthodoxy as its spiritual foundation, or as the leader of a more global Orthodox world. Second, while Putin's Russia became increasingly anti-Western, it was not nearly as clear what it stands for. This is where quasi-religious motifs filled the ideological vacuum. It was proclaimed that Russia has a historical mission to stand up for the "traditional values" eroded in the "decadent" West. The Church fully supported this conservative turn: in his 2022 Easter sermon, Patriarch Kirill repeated the old idea of Russians as unique "God-bearers" with an exclusive calling in the world. This way of thinking transforms the negative anti-Western stance into a positive program.

Third, religious rhetoric imparts a metaphysical or cosmic dimension to Russia's cause. Especially after the beginning of the full-scale war, Russia was often described as the last bastion against global evil. According to Putin, Russia is fighting a system of values that represents "pure satanism".[7] Patriarch Kirill contributed to this idea by identifying the "*katechon*" that restrains the Antichrist (2 Thess. 2.6–7) with the (Russian) Orthodox Church and the Russian state.[8] Fourth, religion is employed to emphasise historical and cultural unity between Russia and Ukraine and to downplay the otherness of Ukrainians. In his programmatic article, Putin argued that Russians and Ukrainians are essentially one people united primarily by spiritual ties in the Orthodox faith.[9] Just as ecclesiologically Ukraine is seen in Russia as part of the canonical territory

---

6 On the development of the doctrine of the 'Russian World', see Cyril Hovorun, "Russian Church and Ukrainian War", *The Expository Times* 134, no. 1 (2022): 1–10.
7 Vladimir Putin, "Presidential Address on the Occasion of Signing the Treaties on the Accession of the DPR, LPR, Zaporozhye and Kherson Regions to Russia", the Kremlin, 30 September 2022, accessed 16 March 2023, http://en.kremlin.ru/events/president/news/69465.
8 For more on the concept of the "*katechon*", see Dustin Byrd's chapter in the present volume.
9 Patriarch Kirill, "Svjatejshij Patriarch Kirill: Ot budushhego nashego Otechestva i nashej Cerkvi zavisit, v polnom smysle slova, budushhee mira" ["His Holiness Patriarch Kirill: The Future of the World Depends, in the Full Sense of the Word, on the Future of our Fatherland and our Church"], the Moscow Patriarchate, 5 April 2022, accessed 3 April 2023, http://www.patriarchia.ru/db/text/5978803.html; Vladimir Putin, "On the Historical Unity of Russians and Ukrainians", the Kremlin, 12 July 2021, accessed 26 March 2023, http://en.kremlin.ru/events/president/news/66181.

of the Russian Orthodox Church, so geopolitically and culturally it is perceived as belonging to the Russian orbit.

Given the dominance of such instrumental approaches to religion in Russian politics today, special attention should be paid to alternative uses of religious themes, particularly in Russian thought. As this chapter argues, one of the examples of a more nuanced use of religious motifs in political discourse and public life can be found in the works of Alexander Solzhenitsyn (1918–2008), a famous Russian novelist and dissident. While Solzhenitsyn largely shared the anti-Western and conservative sentiments prevalent in Russia today, his appeals to religion differed from the prevailing patterns. To demonstrate the affinity between Putinism and Solzhenitsyn's *general* worldview, the chapter first briefly discusses two recent instances when Putin referred to Solzhenitsyn, implicitly or explicitly, for vindicating his aggression against Ukraine and his cultural crusade against the West. The following sections will show that, despite this affinity, Solzhenitsyn did not use religion to promote aggressive policies but rather to challenge Russia's expansionism, develop a civic spirit in Russian society, and bring his compatriots to critical self-reflection.

2   Putin's Allusions to Solzhenitsyn

On 21 February 2022, three days before the full-scale invasion of Ukraine, Putin made a long address concerning the events in Ukraine. His main claim was that modern Ukraine was a creation of Vladimir Lenin, who organised the Soviet Union as a confederation of republics with arbitrary borders and the right to self-determination. Although Putin did not refer to any historian in this address, his argument followed the line of thought suggested by Solzhenitsyn.

According to Solzhenitsyn, the communists "charted out arbitrary, ethnically nonsensical and historically unjustifiable internal administrative boundaries".[10] Before 1991, it made no difference because the internal boundaries in the Soviet Union were irrelevant. But as soon as it collapsed, 25 million Russians found themselves outside these "false Leninist borders"[11]—especially

---

10   Alexander Solzhenitsyn, "Interv'ju zhurnalu Forbs" ["Forbes Interview"], in *Publicistika v treh tomah* [*Essays in Three Volumes*], 3 vols (Yaroslavl: Verhne-Volzhskoe knizhnoe izdatel'stvo, 1995–7), 3:477.
11   Solzhenitsyn often repeated this phrase in his interviews and other publications: "Rech' v Mezhdunarodnoj Akademii Filosofii" ["Address at the International Academy of Philosophy"], in *Essays*, 1:610; "'Russkij vopros' k koncu XX veka" ["'The Russian Question' at the End of the Twentieth Century"], in *Essays*, 1:686–7; "Pis'mo Prezidentu El'cinu" ["Letter to President Yeltsin"], in *Essays*, 3:353; "Obrashhenie (K referendumu na Ukraine)" ["Appeal (On

in Eastern Ukraine and Northern Kazakhstan.[12] Solzhenitsyn admitted that Ukrainians have the right to build their own state, "but only within their real ethnic boundaries", that is, without "provinces that never historically belonged to Ukraine ..., the eastern and southern territories of today's Ukraine".[13] These regions are "in fact"[14] or "absolutely" Russian,[15] and must determine for themselves whether they belong to Ukraine.[16] Given the "fanatical suppression and persecution of the Russian language" in Ukraine, the Russian state cannot indifferently observe the sufferings of Russians, Solzhenitsyn warned.[17]

The next major speech of Putin at the Valdai Discussion Club was about the relations between Russia and the West. In this speech, Putin explicitly referred to Solzhenitsyn to reject the belief that all countries should develop along the lines pioneered by the West:

> I would like to quote from Alexander Solzhenitsyn's famous Harvard Commencement Address delivered in 1978. He said that typical of the West is 'a continuous blindness of superiority'—and it continues to this day—which 'upholds the belief that vast regions everywhere on our planet should develop and mature to the level of present-day Western systems'. He said this in 1978. Nothing has changed.[18]

---

the Ukrainian Referendum)"], in *Essays*, 3:358; "Interv'ju shvejcarskomu ezhenedel'niku Vel'tvohe" ["Interview to the Swiss Weekly Weltwoche"], in *Essays*, 3:397. See also "Interv'ju dlja rossijskih telezritelej" [Interview for Russian Television], in *Essays*, 3:469.

12 According to Solzhenitsyn's data, out of these 25 million Russians, 12 million lived in Ukraine and 7 million in Kazakhstan. See Alexander Solzhenitsyn, *Rossija v obvale* [*Russia in Collapse*] (Moscow: Russkij put', 2006), 37–8, 66, 75.

13 Solzhenitsyn, "Forbes Interview", 476. See also Alexander Solzhenitsyn, "Otvet Svjatoslavu Karavanskomu" ["Response to Svyatoslav Karavanskii"], in *Essays*, 3:348–9; "Letter to President Yeltsin", 353.

14 Solzhenitsyn, *Russia in Collapse*, 37.

15 Solzhenitsyn, "Interview to the Swiss Weekly Weltwoche", 397. Elsewhere Solzhenitsyn makes clear which regions he means: Donetsk, Luhansk, the whole Southern region from Melitopol through Kherson to Odesa, and the Crimea (*Russia in Collapse*, 79).

16 Solzhenitsyn, "Appeal (On the Ukrainian Referendum)", 358. Later, Solzhenitsyn sharply criticised the Yeltsin administration that it recognised the 1991 borders and thereby "gave vast Russian regions" to Ukraine and Kazakhstan (*Russia in Collapse*, 45, 81).

17 Alexander Solzhenitsyn, "Interview for Moscow News", *Noblit.ru*, 26 April 2006, accessed 27 March 2023, http://noblit.ru/node/1041. *Cf.* Solzhenitsyn, "Letter to President Yeltsin", 353; *Russia in Collapse*, 79–80.

18 Vladimir Putin, "Valdai International Discussion Club Meeting", the Kremlin, 27 October 2022, accessed 16 March 2023, http://www.en.kremlin.ru/events/president/news/69695.

Indeed, even in Soviet times, Solzhenitsyn admitted that he could not recommend Western patterns as ideal for transforming Russian society. While many Soviet dissenters emphasised the importance of introducing civil liberties and a multi-party system, Solzhenitsyn saw in their aspirations merely a "passive imitation of the West",[19] arguing that Russia must follow its own special path. He had his own version of Russian exceptionalism, believing that Russians, having been purged by sufferings under the communist regime, became spiritually stronger than other nations.

This does not necessarily mean that Solzhenitsyn would have approved the Russian invasion. In 1981, his position was unambiguous: "Under no circumstances and at no time shall I participate in a Russian-Ukrainian clash or allow my sons to do so".[20] In post-Soviet times, he similarly maintained that all tensions between the countries must be solved without "violence and war".[21] It is true that Solzhenitsyn had a cosy personal relationship with Putin and credited him for giving Russians back a sense of dignity and justice. Solzhenitsyn was too sceptical about Russian democratic achievements in the 1990s and party-based parliamentarism in general to feel any sorrow about the definitive elimination of political competition in Russia and the shift to centralised power.[22] When Solzhenitsyn won the 2006 state decoration for outstanding achievements in the cultural and educational spheres, Putin had a personal meeting with him. After it, Putin noted that he drew the writer's attention to "some policies being implemented today that are to a large extent harmonious with Solzhenitsyn's writings".[23] But it is doubtful that Solzhenitsyn would have recognised the war against Ukraine as one of such policies.

This chapter's goal, however, is not to speculate on what Solzhenitsyn's attitude toward the current war would have been but to analyse how his religious views informed his stance. Solzhenitsyn was a devout Orthodox Christian: when living in the United States, he invited an Orthodox priest once a month

---

19 Alexander Solzhenitsyn, "Na vozvrate dyhanija I soznanija" ["As Breathing and Consciousness Return"], in *Essays*, 1:43.
20 Alexander Solzhenitsyn, "Konferencii po russko-ukrainskim otnoshenijam" ["Open Letter to the Conference on Russian-Ukrainian Relations"], in *Essays*, 2:551–2.
21 Solzhenitsyn, "The Russian Question", 690.
22 On the context and reasons of the alliance between Solzhenitsyn and Putin, see Robert Horvat, "Apologist of Putinism? Solzhenitsyn, the Oligarchs, and the Specter of Orange Revolution", *The Russian Review* 70, no. 2 (2011): 300–318.
23 "Vladimir Putin Met with Aleksandr Solzhenitsyn", the Kremlin, 12 June 2007, accessed 18 March 2023, http://www.en.kremlin.ru/events/president/news/40495/print.

to hold a service in the private chapel on the first floor of his house.[24] While it would be an exaggeration to depict him, following his critics, as a zealot calling up a holy war against secularism or as a religious enthusiast believing himself to be in possession of the truth,[25] religious motifs occupy a prominent place in his political and social thought. For many Western Christians on the right, he remains an iconic figure, as evidenced, for example, by Rod Dreher's *Live Not by Lies*, a book titled after Solzhenitsyn's short essay.[26] Solzhenitsyn's works, in general, obviously contributed to the narrative of Russia's victimhood and exceptionalism (and to that extent to the causes of the war). Still, the way he appropriated religious themes hardly strengthened this narrative and—with an eye to the future—can even point to a way out of the situation in which Russian society currently finds itself. To illustrate this, this chapter focuses on three points: the rejection of expansionism, the issue of moralism, and the possibility of repentance.

3 Rejection of Expansionism

First, Solzhenitsyn clearly condemned Russia's aggressive foreign policy and expansive militarism. In his overview of Russia's history,[27] he focuses on its unwarranted interference in the affairs of other countries at the expense of inner development. He was sceptical about Russian campaigns in Europe and opposed pan-Slavism—the belief that Russians must protect and rule the Slavs, particularly in the Balkans—as a "false, arrogant, and useless" idea.[28] According to Solzhenitsyn, the inclusion of Poland and Finland in the Russian Empire became "an unbearable burden on Russian shoulders",[29] while the conquest of Central Asia[30] and the Caucasus (including Dagestan)[31] was a "mistake". Even worse was the Soviet occupation of Eastern Europe after the Second World War

---

24   Donald M. Thomas, *Alexander Solzhenitsyn: A Century in His Life* (New York: St. Martin's Press, 1998), 500.
25   "The Obsession of Solzhenitsyn", editorial, *New York Times*, 13 June 1978, reprinted in *Solzhenitsyn at Harvard*, ed. Roland Berman (Washington, D.C.: Ethics and Public Policy Center, 1980), 23–4.
26   Rod Dreher, *Live Not by Lies: A Manual for Christian Dissidents* (New York: Penguin Publishing Group, 2022).
27   Solzhenitsyn, "The Russian Question".
28   Solzhenitsyn, "The Russian Question", 634, 650; "Teleinterv'ju kompanii Ostankino" ["Interview for Ostankino"], in *Essays*, 3:362; *Russia in Collapse*, 75.
29   Solzhenitsyn, "The Russian Question", 641, 643.
30   Solzhenitsyn, "Forbes Interview", 478.
31   Solzhenitsyn, "Forbes Interview ", 479; "The Russian Question", 643.

and the demagogy about the world revolution.[32] Solzhenitsyn insisted that the Soviet Union must "withdraw from all occupied territories, threaten no one, conquer no one, renounce world claims and any violence against nations near and far".[33]

To be sure, in 1990, when the collapse of the Soviet Union was almost inevitable, Solzhenitsyn hoped for the establishment of a Russian Union including Russia, Ukraine, Belarus, and Kazakhstan.[34] When these hopes did not materialise, he called the Russian authorities to protect the Russian-speaking population, particularly in Ukraine. Still, this does not detract from the validity of his main point that, given its imperial history, Russia must learn to focus on domestic policies rather than on foreign affairs. The fact that ethnic identity was more important for Solzhenitsyn than state borders also makes this point relevant for better management in the event of the possible disintegration of the Russian Federation. His emphasis on inner development would then imply that the Russian state must focus on territories where ethnic Russians form a clear majority and provide more freedom to regions with distinctive ethnic, cultural, and religious identities. Indeed, Solzhenitsyn did not object to recognising Chechen independence or giving the Kuril Islands back to Japan,[35] and admitted that Dagestan and Tuva could be seen as independent states.[36] He also recognised that many other territories were joined to the Russian Empire by force and that large numbers of local inhabitants were wiped out.[37]

What is important for our purposes is that Solzhenitsyn's anti-imperial stance stemmed from his *spiritual* concerns. In his observation, "the peoples who created empires have always suffered spiritually as a result".[38] Beginning with Peter the Great, the Russian state transformed into an empire and later reached its geopolitical and geographical zenith, but for Solzhenitsyn, it was

---

32   Alexander Solzhenitsyn, *Letter to the Soviet Leaders*, trans. Hilary Sternberg (New York: Harper and Row, 1974), 75.
33   Alexander Solzhenitsyn, "Press-konferencija v Cjurihe" ["Press-conference in Zurich"], in *Essays*, 2:162–3.
34   Solzhenitsyn, "The Russian Question", 689; "Forbes Interview", 478; "Interview for Ostankino", 370–71; *Russia in Collapse*, 39. By 1993, however, Solzhenitsyn did not believe in this project in view of the fact that "Ukraine is separating from us with short-sighted hatred". The only promising union was between Russia, Belarus, and Kazakhstan, he argued ("Otvet V. P. Lukinu, poslu Rossii v SShA" ["Response to V. Lukin, Russia's Ambassador to the United States"], in *Essays*, 3:392).
35   Solzhenitsyn, *Russia in Collapse*, 45, 84–5.
36   Solzhenitsyn, "Interview for Russian Television", 466.
37   Solzhenitsyn, *Russia in Collapse*, 111; *Letter to the Soviet Leaders*, 39.
38   Solzhenitsyn, *Letter to the Soviet Leaders*, 75; cf. *Russia in Collapse*, 113.

a period of spiritual and national decline.[39] He insisted that the nation must focus on its spiritual health and moral integrity rather than conquests and prestige abroad. Opposing the traditional understanding of Russia's greatness, Solzhenitsyn argued: "The greatness of a nation is not in its conquests, not in the breadth of its borders, but in the breadth of its soul ... The national spirit must be built on moral purity rather than military formidability".[40] True national greatness is revealed in the unarmed moral steadfastness demonstrated by the Czechs and Slovaks in 1968 rather than in the Soviet Union's ability to crush them.[41]

At the root of this understanding of national priorities was the idea of self-limitation, which, Solzhenitsyn emphasises, has a religious foundation.[42] As Daniel Mahoney observes, Solzhenitsyn understands "the 'turn toward inner development' ... in explicitly Christian terms".[43] Solzhenitsyn believed self-limitation must be "the highest principle of each individual and each nation".[44] To be sure, it is easier to proclaim a principle than to apply it, especially on a national level. The American withdrawal from Vietnam could be seen as a proper application of self-limitation, but Solzhenitsyn condemned it as cowardice and a failure to comply with America's world commitments. The largely peaceful disintegration of the Soviet Union along the existing 1991 boundaries could also be seen as an example of non-aggressive politics, but Solzhenitsyn criticised the weakness of Russian diplomacy that gave up Crimea and other regions "without any complaints".[45] On the other hand, Solzhenitsyn rebuked Ukrainians for not practising self-limitation when they accepted the "false Leninist borders" and thereby "conquered"(!) regions that he claimed

---

39 Such estimation has to do, of course, not only with the condemnation of expansionism, but also with Solzhenitsyn's negative attitude to the elements of the Enlightenment that Peter the Great brought from the West. See more in Niels C. Neilsen, *Solzhenitsyn's Religion* (London: A. R. Mowbray, 1975), 87.

40 Alexander Solzhenitsyn, "Tri uzlovye tochki japonskoj novoj istorii" ["Three Nodal Points of Japanese Modern History"], in *Essays*, 3:61; cf. *Russia in Collapse*, 202.

41 Alexander Solzhenitsyn, "Repentance and Self-limitation in the Life of Nations", in *From Under the Rubble*, trans. Michael Scammel (Paris: YMCA-Press, 1974), 119.

42 Alexander Solzhenitsyn, "Interv'ju nemeckomu ezhenedel'niku Di Cajt" ["Interview to the German weekly Die Zeit"], in *Essays*, 3:458.

43 Daniel J. Mahoney, *Aleksandr Solzhenitsyn: The Ascent from Ideology* (London: Rowman and Littlefield, 2001), 129.

44 Solzhenitsyn, "Three Nodal Points", 62.

45 Solzhenitsyn, *Russia in Collapse*, 81. Solzhenitsyn believed that history does not know examples of such peaceful conduct as demonstrated by Russia in the 1990s ("Forbes Interview", 475).

were "historically and ethnically" alien to Ukraine.[46] Despite these difficulties, elevating self-limitation to the controlling principle of foreign policy seems promising—especially in a context in which personal ascetic rigidity can be coupled with unrestricted geopolitical fantasies.[47]

In this sense, it is worth mentioning that Solzhenitsyn was also sceptical about the global Russian mission to "help and save" Orthodox people in the Caucasus and the Balkans.[48] Solzhenitsyn bitterly notes that even Dostoevsky did not escape this temptation: "It has long been a shame to read Dostoevsky's dreams about conquering Constantinople, about how 'the East will defeat the West', or his contemptuous statements about Europe".[49] At the same time, Solzhenitsyn shared Dostoevsky's belief that it is in Russia that the Spirit of Christ will triumph against all his enemies.[50] While he could not abandon his belief in Russian messianism, Solzhenitsyn tried to disassociate it from expansionist overtones and interpret it in the sense of the unique sufferings of the Russian people.[51]

---

46 Solzhenitsyn, "Address", 610.
47 Solzhenitsyn's plea to focus on internal problems was criticised for the lack of international consciousness. It was argued, for example, that by focusing on Russia Solzhenitsyn's vision "seems oblivious to the real needs of the rest of mankind" and in that sense is less Christian than Marxism (James V. Schall, "Solzhenitsyn's Letter", *Worldview* 17, no. 7 (1974): 29). Indeed, for any country, taking his plea seriously would mean withdrawing from the world arena and slipping into isolationism. But, as his understanding of the Vietnam War shows, Solzhenitsyn realised that his advice should not be followed universally and unreservedly. He constantly emphasised that he wrote for Russians and for the Russian context, and it is hard to deny that following his advice would have favourable consequences for Russia and especially its neighbours.
48 Solzhenitsyn, "The Russian Question", 662.
49 Solzhenitsyn, "The Russian Question", 661. This critical note is especially remarkable given that Solzhenitsyn held Dostoevsky in high esteem.
50 Alexander Solzhenitsyn, "Teleinterv'ju s Malkolmom Magjeridzhem" ["Interview with Malcolm Muggeridge"], in *Essays*, 3:139.
51 Solzhenitsyn's own remarks about Russian messianism were somewhat inconsistent. In his lengthy 1980 article, he categorically denied it: "As for 'historical Russian messianism,' this is contrived nonsense: it has been several centuries since any section of the government or intelligentsia influential in the spiritual life of the country has suffered from the disease of messianism" ("Misconceptions About Russia Are a Threat to America", *Foreign Affairs*, 1 March 1980, accessed 16 March 2023 https://www.foreignaffairs.com/articles/russia-fsu/1980-03-01/misconceptions-about-russia-are-threat-america). In 1994, however, he admitted that "there is some truth in the reproaches leveled at Russian ruling and intellectual elites for their belief in Russian exclusiveness and messianism" (Solzhenitsyn, "The Russian Question", 661).

4 Moralism

Thus, nations must concentrate on their domestic tasks: spiritual health, moral upbringing, and inner development. Here the public role of faith comes to the fore as Solzhenitsyn believed that only Christianity could bring spiritual healing to Russia.[52] To be sure, he did not seek special privileges for Christianity and opposed not only the coercive imposition of religion but also its vigorous promotion.[53] Still, Solzhenitsyn belonged to the tradition that deemed religion necessary for morality. In the Russian context, this tradition was encapsulated in Dostoevsky's famous dictum, "If there is no God, then all is permitted".

Solzhenitsyn himself used similar expressions. On the occasion of his acceptance of the Templeton Prize for Progress in Religion, Solzhenitsyn delivered an address arguing that the great disasters that had befallen Russia could be best explained by the fact that "men have forgotten God".[54] The reason for what he saw as the "catastrophic weakening of the Western world" was the same. According to Solzhenitsyn, after the Renaissance and the Enlightenment, the West lost the sense of a supreme being and fell into a "moral crisis affecting the entire culture".[55] In the humanist worldview, he claimed, human beings became the measure of all things, and their needs and interests determined the supreme imperatives of the universe.[56] Both socialism in the East and humanism in the West are infected by the virus of materialism, which can be cured only by a return to spiritual values: "There is no other way to save the East and the West ... but through a religious and moral revival".[57]

---

52 Solzhenitsyn, *Letter to the Soviet Leaders*, 77–8.
53 Alexander Solzhenitsyn, "Parizhskaja vstrecha v prjamom jefire" ["The Paris Meeting Live"], in *Essays*, 3:429–30.
54 "Acceptance Address by Mr. Aleksandr Solzhenitsyn", Templeton Prize, 10 May 1983, accessed 6 March 2023, https://www.templetonprize.org/laureate-sub/solzhenitsyn-acceptance-speech.
55 Solzhenitsyn, *Letter to the Soviet Leaders*, 8–9; "Interview to the German weekly Die Zeit", 458.
56 Alexander Solzhenitsyn, *Warning to the West*, trans. Harris Coulter and Nataly Martin (New York: Farrar, Straus and Giroux, 1976), 30. While some scholars depicted Solzhenitsyn as a "Christian humanist" (see, for example, Edward E. Ericson Jr., *Solzhenitsyn: The Moral Vision* (Grand Rapids, MI: Eerdmans, 1980), 206), Solzhenitsyn himself rejected such designations and believed that humanism and Christianity are mutually exclusive: "There is no such concept as 'a humanism with God.' Sooner or later, humanism puts man in God's place" (Alexander Solzhenitsyn, "Kruglyj stol v gazete Jomiuri" ["Round Table in the Yomiuri Newspaper"], in *Essays*, 3:88–9).
57 Alexander Solzhenitsyn, "Press-konferencija v Stokgol'me" ["Press-conference in Stockholm"], in *Essays*, 2:198. Cf. Alexander Solzhenitsyn, "Glavnyj urok" ["The Main Lesson"], in *Essays*, 3:10.

Solzhenitsyn was convinced that it is through moral witness that Christianity influences society. He understood the essence of the Christian message, especially in the public sphere, in a moralistic way. Christianity is all about the virtues of temperance, humility, courage, honesty, and integrity. Solzhenitsyn was not deeply interested in Christian dogmas and did not see a significant difference between Orthodoxy and Catholicism.[58] The peculiarities of religious rites concerned him even less, as his defence of the Old Believers shows, and his relationship with the institutional Church was rather complicated. But Christianity as a particular worldview underpinning strong moral convictions was indispensable for him in fighting organised evil in the East and challenging what he saw as liberal relativism in the West.

Solzhenitsyn's assertive morality in dealing with culture surprised those in the West who previously knew him only as a fearless fighter against communism. Some who attended his Harvard speech felt they had witnessed the sermon of a puritanical moralist offering an indictment of Western society. Indeed, in this speech, as well as in other addresses and publications, Solzhenitsyn lamented the dominance of consumerism and hedonism in the West, the superficiality of the press, the mediocrity of mass culture, an excess of legalism, the decline of courage and self-discipline, and other supposed flaws in Western culture.

Even though the Harvard speech was often misunderstood to the point that Solzhenitsyn was depicted as a proponent of theocracy or an opponent of democracy, his criticism of the West was largely misplaced. Solzhenitsyn's conclusion—that "the Western system in its present state of spiritual exhaustion" cannot be a model for Russia's transformation since through deep suffering, Russians achieved a higher spiritual level[59]—is yet another confirmation of his belief in Russian exceptionalism.

In the present *Russian* context, however, a type of religious moralism could be beneficial. Solzhenitsyn's simple Christian prescripts—"Live not by lies" or "Be courageous and do not be frightened"—can help heal a society built on violence and fear, on lies and silence. To be sure, not all aspects of Solzhenitsyn's moral vision are equally relevant and valid. As the current war proves, "the capacity for self-sacrifice" and "the ease of dying", which Solzhenitsyn

---

58   Alexander Solzhenitsyn, "Interv'ju s Danijelem Rondo" ["Interview with Daniel Rondeau"], in *Essays*, 3:200. At the same time, Solzhenitsyn was clearly offended by Roman Catholic missionary activities in the lands which he perceived as historically Eastern Orthodox. He condemned the seventeenth century efforts to convert the Orthodox into Catholicism that resulted in the Union of Brest and disapproved attempts to start Catholic mission in the (post-)Soviet Russia ("Paris Meeting", 430–31).

59   Solzhenitsyn, "A World Split Apart", in *Solzhenitsyn at Harvard*, 12.

appreciates as Christian qualities traditionally peculiar to Russian peasants,[60] can be abused to rationalise participation in a bloody war of aggression. Solzhenitsyn's rejection of "unrestricted freedom" endangers individual liberties, and his attacks on Western legalism vindicate the lack of legal consciousness in Russia. The tendencies that Solzhenitsyn considered examples of Western moral corruption have been emphasised to incite anti-Western attitudes and proclaim Russia's spiritual superiority. Nonetheless, these aspects do not constitute the core of Solzhenitsyn's moral thinking. Instead, that core is based on his call to personal responsibility and social justice against a "comfortable obedience"[61] built on purely materialistic concerns and paralysing fear.

Solzhenitsyn's moralistic, anti-speculative faith compares favourably with the current attempts of the Russian Orthodox leadership to provide metaphysical depth to the aggressive politics of their state, and his strong sense of civic spirit challenges both the militaristic enthusiasm as well as the social passivism characteristic of Orthodox preaching today. For all its mystical or liturgical richness, Russian Orthodoxy has not been as strong in ethics and social thought. This is where the work of Christian public intellectuals could be most fruitful. If Christianity has something to offer the broad circles of present-day Russian society, it is primarily the readiness to take responsibility for everyday life.

5   Repentance

Solzhenitsyn shared the organicist theory that treated nations as organisms and discussed social problems in terms of individual ethics. He insisted that political leaders and entire nations are not exempt from the moral requirements that apply to individual persons. We have already seen this with self-limitation: a principle that initially belonged to personal ascesis is transferred by Solzhenitsyn to the nation as a whole. The same holds true for repentance—"a gift which perhaps more than anything else distinguishes man from the animal world".[62] As organisms, nations are "very vital formations, susceptible to all moral feelings, including … repentance".[63] Solzhenitsyn set out his understanding of national repentance in a separate article, which he called

---

60   Solzhenitsyn, *Russia in Collapse*, 161–2.
61   Solzhenitsyn, *Russia in Collapse*, 171; cf. 162–3.
62   Solzhenitsyn, "Repentance", 106.
63   Solzhenitsyn, "Repentance", 108.

his "major programmatic publication".⁶⁴ In an interview with his biographer Joseph Pearce a quarter of a century later, Solzhenitsyn noted that he still considered it "one of his most important articles, expressing one of his key thoughts".⁶⁵

In the article, Solzhenitsyn admits that there is nothing new in the idea of national guilt—and hence in the possibility of national repentance. He takes it as self-evident, for example, that the British, French, and Dutch peoples as a whole bear the guilt of their colonial policies.⁶⁶ Another example is post-war Germany: Solzhenitsyn appreciated the moral impulse behind German gestures of penitence, even if it resulted in an "unbalanced" and "ill-considered" *Ostpolitik*.⁶⁷

Things become more complicated when it comes to Russian people living under a totalitarian regime (Solzhenitsyn wrote the article about national repentance in the 1970s). He is adamant, however, that "even in the most totalitarian states, whose subjects have no rights at all, we all bear responsibility— for the decisions of our government, for the campaigns of our military leaders, for the deeds of our soldiers".⁶⁸ Totalitarian regimes, after all, rest "on the support of some and the passivity of others".⁶⁹

While Solzhenitsyn argues that Russians must repent primarily for what they did to themselves (he believed that Russians suffered more than any other nation—not only in the Soviet Union but in the whole world),⁷⁰ he also goes further and calls for a confession of "our *external* sins, those against other people".⁷¹ "There is no neighbour toward whom we bear no guilt".⁷² Practically, repentance must be expressed in giving genuine freedom to "all the peoples in and beyond our borders forcibly drawn into our orbit".⁷³

---

64 Alexander Solzhenitsyn, "Interv'ju s Hiltonom Kramerom" ["Interview with Hilton Kramer"], in *Essays*, 2:533.
65 Joseph Pearce, *Solzhenitsyn: A Soul in Exile* (London: Harper Collins, 1999), 209. Indeed, even his *Gulag Archipelago* Solzhenitsyn described as a call to repentance (Lee Congdon, *Solzhenitsyn: The Historical-Spiritual Destinies of Russia and the West* (DeKalb, IL: Northern Illinois University Press, 2017), 68).
66 Solzhenitsyn, "Repentance", 110.
67 Solzhenitsyn, "Repentance", 113.
68 Solzhenitsyn, "Repentance", 113.
69 Solzhenitsyn, "Press-conference in Zurich", 140.
70 Solzhenitsyn, *Letter to the Soviet Leaders*, 37; Alexander Solzhenitsyn, "Vystuplenie po francuzskomu televideniju" ["Interview on French Television"], in *Essays*, 2:396.
71 Solzhenitsyn, "Repentance", 127, author's emphasis.
72 Solzhenitsyn, "Repentance", 128.
73 Solzhenitsyn, "Repentance", 134.

Solzhenitsyn also focused on the guilt and responsibility of the Russian Orthodox Church. First, he lamented that it never proclaimed its repentance for "the monstrous punishment" and "devilish persecution" of the Old Believers.[74] Second, the Church must repent because "it allowed itself to become a spineless appendage of the state, failed to guide the people spiritually and to purify and defend the Russian spirit … And if today the satanic regime is strangling the country and threatens to suffocate the whole world, we, the Russian Orthodox, are among the first to blame".[75] In his open letter to Patriarch Pimen, Solzhenitsyn complained that the Church too quickly submitted to state regulations and effectively gave up its independence.[76] Appalled by the compliance of the Russian Church with communist policies, he contrasted it with the more firm and strong voice of the Polish Church that "possesses the souls of the people despite the oppressive atheistic dictatorship".[77] He emphasises that the Roman Catholic Church in Poland deserved respect for its involvement in the anti-communist resistance and its social activism in general. While Solzhenitsyn believed that the Russian Orthodox Church should be separated from the state, he advocated for more active participation of the Church in public affairs. The problem is not confined to *Russian* Orthodoxy, however: he lamented the centuries-long social passivity of Orthodoxy, especially in comparison with Catholicism, Protestantism, and Islam.[78]

Solzhenitsyn believed that repentance should not be a difficult step for those who remain faithful to the main traits of the Russian character. As Solzhenitsyn understood it, the true Russian spirit is disposed to (public) repentance, self-condemnation, and even some exaggeration of its own weaknesses and mistakes.[79] He adds, however, that this disposition deteriorated under the imperial and communist regimes. Although his works suffered from a certain

74 Solzhenitsyn, "Repentance", 115; Alexander Solzhenitsyn, "Pis'mo iz Ameriki" ["Letter from America"], in *Essays*, 2:303.
75 Solzhenitsyn, "Letter from America", 303.
76 Alexander Solzhenitsyn, "Vserossijskomu Patriarhu Pimenu" ["Lenten Letter to Patriarch Pimen"], in *Essays*, 1:135.
77 Alexander Solzhenitsyn, "Persidskij trjuk" ["Persian trick"], in *Essays*, 2:511. Solzhenitsyn praised the Poles for their love of freedom and emphasised the key role of the Church in their resistance and, more broadly, in the formation and development of the Polish national spirit ("The Main Lesson", 9). He saw Solidarność as based on Christian values, admired its leader Lech Wałęsa, and blamed the West for the lack of support of this movement ("Press-konferencija v Londone" ["Press-conference in London"], in *Essays*, 3:106, 118; "Interv'ju s Bernarom Pivo" ["Interview with Bernard Pivot"], in *Essays*, 3:189; "Interview with Daniel Rondeau", 200).
78 Solzhenitsyn, *Russia in Collapse*, 183.
79 Solzhenitsyn, *Russia in Collapse*, 161.

idealisation of the Russian peasantry, Solzhenitsyn diverged from Dostoevsky again by challenging his "myth of the holy Russian common man". While working on his major novel on the February Revolution, he was struck to find how easily "madness overtakes the masses". It looked as if "this holy 'god-bearer'—as Dostoevsky saw the Russian people—disappeared altogether", Solzhenitsyn observes.[80] The process of moral degradation continued after the Revolution: Solzhenitsyn was painfully aware that in Soviet times Russians were "losing the last traces and signs of a Christian people",[81] even if elsewhere he notes some revitalisation of religious life in the Soviet Union, especially among the youth.[82] The moral squalor of post-Soviet Russia made him even more depressed—but also more convinced of the necessity of national repentance.

For Solzhenitsyn, national repentance is fully compatible with patriotism. He vehemently rejected the idea that denouncing the evils of a country and its political system results in "a sin against patriotism".[83] On the contrary, patriotism properly understood implies a "frank assessment of national vices and sins, and penitence for them", he insisted.[84] Such understanding of patriotism stands in striking contrast to the military patriotism currently being displayed throughout Russia. The current state-led and state-sponsored patriotic campaigns instil the sense of greatness and superiority, celebrate Russia's valiant military history, evoke nostalgia for the Soviet era, rehabilitate Stalin and Stalinism, deplore the West's supposedly unfair treatment of Russia, and advance the vision of Russia as a unique civilization.[85] Even though, as we saw at the beginning of this chapter, Solzhenitsyn shared some of these sentiments (particularly the emphasis on Russia's exclusiveness and victimhood), he did not allow them to prevail over his aversion to aggressive militarism. As Mahoney notes, Solzhenitsyn's "thirty-year effort to root patriotism in repentance and self-limitation is among the least understood and least appreciated intellectual projects in the modern world".[86]

---

80   Alexander Solzhenitsyn, "Interv'ju s Rudol'fom Augshtajnom dlja zhurnala Shpigel'" ["The Spiegel Interview with Rudolf Augstein"], in *Essays*, 3:288.
81   Solzhenitsyn, "Lenten Letter", 135.
82   Solzhenitsyn, "Round Table", 89; *Warning to the West*, 83.
83   Solzhenitsyn, "As Breathing and Consciousness Return", 32.
84   Solzhenitsyn, "Repentance", 119.
85   See an analysis of the Russian state programs on patriotic education in: Petr Kratochvíl and Gaziza Shakhanova, "The Patriotic Turn and Re-Building Russia's Historical Memory: Resisting the West, Leading the Post-Soviet East?" *Problems of Post-Communism* 68, no. 5 (2021): 442–56.
86   Mahoney, *Aleksandr Solzhenitsyn*, 120.

6   Conclusion

It is not without reason that Putin appealed to Solzhenitsyn, implicitly or explicitly, before launching the unprovoked war of aggression against Ukraine and a cultural crusade against the West. After all, Solzhenitsyn's comments on Ukraine and the West reveal a sense of resentment and humiliation. A master of words, Solzhenitsyn overemphasised the importance of language in forming people's identities and might have thought of Russian-speaking Ukrainians as almost an oxymoron. A Russian with a strong sense of national identity, he did not envision the development of Ukraine as a political nation. He could not get rid of anachronistic notions about Ukrainian history and language.[87] Even more profound was his resentment towards the West: first, Solzhenitsyn lamented that the West lacked courage in fighting communism and promoting freedom in the world, and later that the West lacked sensitivity to Russia's uniqueness and security concerns.

Solzhenitsyn's religious motifs, however, prevented him from developing this resentment into revanchism. They could be relevant for the transformation of Russian society today, regardless of the outcome of the current war. His insistence on self-limitation implied that Russia must focus on its inner development and put its own house in order instead of pursuing foreign adventurism and expansionism. The moral imperatives, which he saw as rooted in Christian tradition and indispensable for social and political life, were centred on temperance, self-discipline, civic courage, and responsibility. Finally, his conviction of the necessity of repentance, even for nations under a totalitarian government, may provide a promising basis for stimulating a reconsideration of Russia's imperial, communist, and post-Soviet history.

Bibliography

(2007). "Vladimir Putin Met with Aleksandr Solzhenitsyn". The Kremlin, 12 June 2007. http://www.en.kremlin.ru/events/president/news/40495/print.

Berman, R., ed. (1980). *Solzhenitsyn at Harvard*. Washington, D.C.: Ethics and Public Policy Center.

Clover, C. (2016). *Black Wind, White Snow: The Rise of Russia's New Nationalism*. New Haven, CT: Yale University Press.

---

87   For a detailed analysis, see John-Paul Himka, "Ukrainians, Russians and Alexander Solzhenitsyn", *Cross Currents: A Yearbook of Central European Culture* 11 (1992): 193–204.

Congdon, L. (2017). *Solzhenitsyn: The Historical-Spiritual Destinies of Russia and the West*. DeKalb, IL: Northern Illinois University Press.

Dreher, R. (2022). *Live Not by Lies: A Manual for Christian Dissidents*. New York: Penguin Publishing Group.

Ericson, E.E. Jr. (1980). *Solzhenitsyn: The Moral Vision*. Grand Rapids, MI: Eerdmans.

Himka, J.P. (1922). "Ukrainians, Russians and Alexander Solzhenitsyn". *Cross Currents: A Yearbook of Central European Culture* 11: 193–204.

Horvat, R. (2011). "Apologist of Putinism? Solzhenitsyn, the Oligarchs, and the Specter of Orange Revolution". *The Russian Review* 70, no. 2: 300–18.

Hovorun, C. (2018). *Political Orthodoxies: The Unorthodoxies of the Church Coerced*. Minneapolis, MN: Fortress Press.

Hovorun, C. (2022). "Russian Church and Ukrainian War". *The Expository Times* 134, no. 1: 1–10.

Kratochvíl, P., and G. Shakhanova. (2021). "The Patriotic Turn and Re-Building Russia's Historical Memory: Resisting the West, Leading the Post-Soviet East?" *Problems of Post-Communism* 68, no. 5: 442–56.

Lewis, D.G. (2020). *Russia's New Authoritarianism: Putin And The Politics Of Order*. Edinburgh: Edinburgh University Press.

Mahoney, D. J. (2001). *Aleksandr Solzhenitsyn: The Ascent from Ideology*. London: Rowman and Littlefield.

Neilsen, N.C. (1975). *Solzhenitsyn's Religion*. London: A.R. Mowbray.

Patriarch Kirill. (2022). "Patriarshaja propoved' v Prazdnik Blagoveshhenija Presvjatoj Bogorodicy posle liturgii v hrame Hrista Spasitelja" ["Patriarchal Sermon on the Feast of the Annunciation of the Blessed Virgin Mary after the Liturgy in the Cathedral of Christ the Saviour"]. The Moscow Patriarchate, 5 April 2022. http://www.patriarchia.ru/db/text/5915151.html.

Patriarch Kirill. (2022). "Svjatejshij Patriarh Kirill: Ot budushhego nashego Otechestva i nashej Cerkvi zavisit, v polnom smysle slova, budushhee mira" ["His Holiness Patriarch Kirill: The Future of the World Depends, in the Full Sense of the Word, on the Future of our Fatherland and our Church"]. The Moscow Patriarchate, 20 November 2022. http://www.patriarchia.ru/db/text/5978803.html.

Pearce, J. (1999). *Solzhenitsyn: A Soul in Exile*. London: Harper Collins.

Putin, V. (2021). "On the Historical Unity of Russian and Ukrainians". The Kremlin, 12 July 2021. http://kremlin.ru/events/president/news/66181.

Putin, V. (2022). "Presidential Address on the Occasion of Signing the Treaties on the Accession of the DPR, LPR, Zaporozhye and Kherson Regions to Russia". The Kremlin, 30 September 2022. http://en.kremlin.ru/events/president/news/69465.

Putin, V. (2022). "Valdai International Discussion Club Meeting". The Kremlin. 27 October 2022. http://www.en.kremlin.ru/events/president/news/69695.

Schall, J.V. (1974). "Solzhenitsyn's Letter", *Worldview* 17, no. 7: 26–29.

Shlapentokh, D. (2021). *Ideological Seduction and Intellectuals in Putin's Russia*. Cham: Palgrave Macmillan.

Składanowski, M., and C. Smuniewski. (2022). "From Desecularization to Sacralization of the Political Language: Religion and Historiosophy in Vladimir Putin's Preparations for War". *Verbum Vitae* 40, no. 4: 869–91.

Solzhenitsyn, A. (1974). *Letter to the Soviet Leaders*. Trans. Hilary Sternberg. New York: Harper and Row.

Solzhenitsyn, A. (1976). *From Under the Rubble*. Trans. Michael Scammel. Paris: YMCA-Press.

Solzhenitsyn, A. (1976). *Warning to the West*. Trans. Harris Coulter and Nataly Martin. New York: Farrar, Straus and Giroux.

Solzhenitsyn, A. (1980). "Misconceptions About Russia Are a Threat to America". *Foreign Affairs*, 1 March 1980. https://www.foreignaffairs.com/articles/russia-fsu/1980-03-01/misconceptions-about-russia-are-threat-america.

Solzhenitsyn, A. (1983). "Acceptance Address", Templeton Prize, 10 May 1983. https://www.templetonprize.org/laureate-sub/solzhenitsyn-acceptance-speech.

Solzhenitsyn, A. (1995–7). *Publicistika v treh tomah* [*Essays in Three Volumes*]. 3 vols. Yaroslavl: Verhne-Volzhskoe knizhnoe izdatel'stvo.

Solzhenitsyn, A. (2006). "Interview for Moscow News". *Nobilit.ru, 26 April 2006. http://noblit.ru/node/1041*.

Solzhenitsyn, A. (2006). Rossija v obvale [*Russia in Collapse*]. Moscow: Russkij put'.

Thomas, D.M. (1998). *Alexander Solzhenitsyn: A Century in His Life*. New York: St. Martin's Press.

Zhegulev, I. (2023). "Kak Putin voznenavidel Ukrainu" ["How Putin Came to Hate Ukraine"]. *Verstka*, 25 April 2023. https://verstka.media/kak-putin-pridumal-voynu.

Zygar, M. (2022). "How Vladimir Putin Lost Interest in the Present". *New York Times*, 10 March 2022. https://www.nytimes.com/2022/03/10/opinion/putin-russia-ukraine.html.

CHAPTER 8

From St. Paul and Carl Schmitt to Alexander Dugin: The Katechon as a Political Category in Empire Building

Dustin J. Byrd

1   Introduction

"We Russians don't need Ukraine. Christ needs it. And that is why we are there". This theologically explosive statement was written by the Russian philosopher Alexander Dugin regarding Vladimir Putin's 2022 invasion of Ukraine. Published on the Neo-Eurasianist website katehon.com and entitled "Apocalyptic Realism", Dugin expounds on his political theology, couching the ongoing conflict as an eschatological collision between good and evil, Christ and Satan.[1] Dugin writes, "the main battle from now on unfolds between … the Russian Idea, the Katechon, the Orthodox Civilisation, and the world of the Western Antichrist, coming at us".[2] From the perspective of Dugin, the struggle for Ukraine is not simply a struggle for an independent country to maintain its sovereignty, nor a proxy war between NATO and the Russian Federation, but rather a struggle for the future of the entire world: the very salvation of the

---

1   Alexander Dugin, "Apocalyptic Realism", *Katehon*, 4 April 2022, https://katehon.com/en/article/apocalyptic-realism, no longer available on Katehon.com.
2   Dugin, "Apocalyptic Realism". For the purposes of consistency, I will utilise the generally accepted Latinisation of the Greek word ὁ κατέχων, spelling it as "katechon", as opposed to "catechon" or "katehon". Additionally, the notion of the "Russian World" (*Russkii Mir*) or "Russian Idea", was first introduced into Russian philosophy by Fyodor Dostoevsky (although it had precedence in the Russian Orthodox Church), to denote the sum totality of Russianness, i.e., its culture, history, spiritual matrix, etc. The cultural and political dimensions of the phrase were later developed by the first generation of Eurasianists, such as Nikolay Danilevsky and Yevgeny Trubetskoy, as well as the Russian fascist philosopher, Ivan Ilyin. Post-Soviet Union, the "Russian Idea" is often invoked to express the ideological claim that the Russian "civilisation", seen as a constitutionally differentiated civilisation from the West, has a unique eschatological mission in world history: to protect the world from decay, degeneration, and collapse into nihilism. As we'll see, the notion of the "Russian Idea" compliments Dugin's assertion that Russia today is the new katechon (Restrainer of the Antichrist). See Paul Robinson, *Russian Conservatism* (Cornell, NY: Cornell University Press, 2019), 181–212.

world is at stake. By locating this struggle within an eschatological framework, Dugin imbues spiritual and existential necessity into Russia's war on Ukraine.

In order to lend this religious and eschatological legitimacy to Putin's "special military operation" in Ukraine, Alexander Dugin turns to a concept originally found in the New Testament, specifically in St. Paul's Second Epistle to the Thessalonians: the "katechon", or "that which restrains".[3] In this essay, I will trace the life of this eschatological concept from its origins in St. Paul's letter through its "determinate negation" (*Aufheben*) and secularisation by the Nazi jurist Carl Schmitt, to its theo-political usage by Alexander Dugin. I will argue that as a theo-political concept, it gives those who invoke it expansive justification to engage in a "total war" (*Der totale Krieg*) against a civilian population, all in the name of rescuing the world's population from the oncoming apocalypse. In this sense, the invocation of St. Paul's katechon is an ideological cover for war crimes in the name of universal eschatological benevolence. Through the politicization of the theological notion of the katechon, it is transformed from an eschatological hope to an ideology of conquest in the name of a palingenetic imperial project: the construction of a new 'Holy Russian Empire' (*Russkii Mir*).

2   St. Paul's Restrainer of the Anti-Christ

The concept of the katechon originally appears in two forms in St. Paul's Second Epistle to the Church of Thessalonica, chapter 2, wherein St. Paul writes,

> Concerning the coming of our Lord Jesus Christ and our being gathered to him, we ask you, brothers and sisters, not to become easily unsettled or alarmed by the teaching allegedly from us—whether by a prophecy or by word of mouth or by letter—asserting that the day of the Lord has already come. Don't let anyone deceive you in any way, for that day will not come until the rebellion occurs and the man of lawlessness (*anomia*) is revealed, the man doomed to destruction (*apoleia*). He will oppose and will exalt himself over everything that is called God or is worshiped, so that he sets himself up in God's temple, proclaiming himself to be God.

---

3   The Russian President, Vladimir Putin introduced the phrase "special military operation" in his 24 February 2022 speech, wherein he claimed he would launch an invasion of Ukraine to "demilitarise" and "denazify" Ukraine. Putin would later go on to sign a law that could impose a 15-year prison sentence for those referring to the conflict as a "war" or an "invasion", and not a "special military operation".

> Don't you remember that when I was with you I used to tell you these things? And now you know what is holding him back (τὸ κατέχον, that which restrains), so that he may be revealed at the proper time. For the secret power of lawlessness (*anomia*) is already at work; but the one who now holds it back (ὁ κατέχων, the one who restrains) will continue to do so until he is taken out of the way. And then the lawless one (*anomos*) will be revealed, whom the Lord Jesus will overthrow with the breath of his mouth and destroy by the splendour of his coming. The coming of the lawless one will be in accordance with how Satan works. (2 Thess. 2.2-9, NIV).[4]

Being a polysemantic hapax legomena, the concept of the katechon is multifaceted as well as unique to St. Paul's letter, not found in any extant text before St. Paul. In the context of first century Greece, wherein the early Christian communities were expecting the apocalypse and thus the imminent return of Christ, the function of Paul's katechon is to diminish the eschatological expectations in the overly zealous Thessalonian Church, who were expecting the return of Christ in their lifetimes.[5] Paul explains in his letter that something (τὸ κατέχον) or someone (ὁ κατέχων) referred to as the "restrainer", holds back the forces of evil who bring about the lawlessness and disorder associated with the apocalypse. As such, the Christian community must not act as if the "Day of the Lord" (ἡμέρα κυρίου) was imminent, as the Antichrist, or the "Son of Perdition" (ὁ υἱὸς τῆς ἀπωλείας), must be revealed prior to Christ's return.[6] However, the revealing of the identity of the Antichrist is conditioned on the overcoming of what St. Paul called the "restrainer", the "katechon", who holds back the Antichrist and its lawlessness and disorder. The period of the eschaton (the final days), wherein the believers wait for the parousia (coming/presence) of Christ, must be endured with patience, even though that world is saturated by evil, suffering, mendacity, and persecution. It is out of God's abundance of mercy and compassion for humanity that the katechon is instituted, as it will serve as the agent of order and stability despite the anomic and unjust condition brought by the forces of evil. As such, the eschaton is determined by a struggle between the forces of evil, disorder, confusion, and dysgenic decline against the forces of good, order, law, and stability. When the katechon is "taken out of the way", leaving the Antichrist unrestrained, evil

---

4 The Greek and Latinised Greek terms were included by the author, as well as the italicisation.
5 Ian Almond, *The Antichrist: A New Biography* (Cambridge: Cambridge University Press, 2020), 20; Maarten J.J. Menken, *2 Thessalonians* (London: Routledge, 1994), 96–124.
6 Jn. 7.12; 2 Thess. 2.3.

envelops the world, thus bringing about a chaotic and violent condition that will reign until the second coming of Christ.

There are three pertinent issues that must be understood when examining St. Paul's concept of the katechon: first, St. Paul's notion of the katechon is eschatologically ambiguous. Due to its restraint of the forces of disorder and chaos, it restrains the eschatological conditions that would bring about the triumph of the Antichrist. In doing so, it delays the second coming of Christ that would occur in response to the Antichrist's triumph. Because of the resulting "parousia (Παρουσία) delay" (delay to the coming of the presence of God), the katechon inadvertently prolongs the existential suffering that is inherent within the human condition. Without the second coming of Christ, humanity must continue to suffer its beleaguered fate in this world, including the ravages of aging, sickness, childbirth, and death. In this way, the katechon is both the agent of civilisational stability, a necessary entity for human flourishing, but also the means by which humanity's miserable existence is extended in perpetuity. It is inherently reactionary and conservative. As long as the katechon performs its function and restrains the triumph of evil in the world, humanity will not witness the second coming of Christ nor Christ's ultimate triumph over evil: an evil best personified by the Antichrist.[7]

Secondly, the Second Epistle to the Thessalonians is ambiguous as to the identity of the katechon. Both variations of the term restrainer in Paul's letter to the Thessalonian Church fail to positively identify who the force restraining the Antichrist is. It is possible that St. Paul understood the katechon to be the Roman Empire and/or Roman Emperors, as he implores the Christian community in Rome to "subject themselves to the governing authorities, for there is no authority except that which God has established. The authorities that exist have been established by God" (Rom. 13.1). This view was shared by Tertullian, John Chrysostom, and St. Augustine, who understood the first of the two variations of the katechon (τὸ κατέχον, that which restrains) as the Roman Empire, and the second mention of the katechon (ὁ κατέχων, the one who restrains) as the Roman Emperor. For example, Tertullian, often referred to as the 'father of Latin Christianity', wrote the following in his Apology,

> There is also another need, a greater one, for our praying for the Emperors, as for the whole estate of the empire and the interest of Rome. We know that the great force which threatens the whole world, the end of the age itself with its menace of hideous suffering, is delayed by the respite which

---

7 Almond, *The Antichrist*, 23–5.

the Roman Empire means for us. We do not wish to experience all that; and when we pray for its postponement are helping forward the continuance of Rome.[8]

As for the Eastern Orthodox Church, it has been suggested that the katechon is a Grand Monarch or an Orthodox Emperor, while others believe that the katechon refers to a palingenetic Holy Roman Empire.[9] Additionally, it has been suggested that the katechon is the Holy Spirit, the Archangel Michael, the name of God, or the Institution of the Church itself.[10]

Nevertheless, the inherent ambiguity of St. Paul's usage of the term katechon allows the biblical concept to be utilized by all those who wish to claim divine authority and prerogatives and/or to assign such divine authority and prerogatives to earthly institutions and individuals. To claim that such entities are that which holds back the forces of evil, disorder, and lawlessness, and thus restrains the apocalypse, is to give that them a level of existential power and authority beyond the mere political. Once adorned by the power of the divinely instituted katechon, the individual or institution becomes a necessity for the continual existence of humanity and society. It is that which guarantees that the world does not succumb to the Antichrist – the personification of all things evil and destructive. Thus, the fate of the katechon is likewise the fate of humanity.

Third, the "lawless one" shares the same ambiguous identity as the katechon. Considering that St. Paul does not positively identify who it is, it would be pertinent to explore who the "lawless" were in recent Jewish history, as that may provide insights into how St. Paul was framing his concept.[11] As

---

8 Tertullian, *Apology*, trans. Terrot R. Glover (Cambridge, MA: Harvard University Press, 1977), 154–5.

9 One should bear in mind that traditional Orthodox teachings see Moscow as the 'Third Rome', the inheritor of Roman/Christian authority after the fall of the Roman Empire and later the Byzantine Empire. This is based on the Byzantine concept of *Roma Mobilis*, or the "floating Rome", which justified the idea of Constantinople and later Moscow as having the Christian authority of Rome. As such, an Orthodox Emperor as the katechon is the logical extension of the claim that the Roman Empire was the original katechon, having then passed that mantle on to its successors in Constantinople and Moscow. See Cyril Toumanoff, "Moscow the Third Rome: Genesis and Significance of Politico-Religious Idea", *The Catholic Historical Review* 40, no. 4 (1955): 411–47.

10 Jens Meierhenrich and Olivet Simons, eds., *The Oxford Handbook of Carl Schmitt* (New York: Oxford University Press, 2019), 47; Dennis Eugene Engleman, *Ultimate Things: An Orthodox Christian Perspective on the End Times* (Indiana: Conciliar Press, 1995).

11 Almond, *The Antichrist*, 21–2. Also see Colin R. Nicholl, *From Hope to Despair in Thessalonica: Situating 1 and 2 Thessalonians* (Cambridge: Cambridge University Press, 2004).

such, St. Paul could have had in mind the Hellenistic Seleucid King Antiochus IV Epiphanes (c. 215–164 bce), who scandalously installed an idol of Zeus in the Temple of Jerusalem—the holiest of holies—and performed the blasphemous sacrifice of a pig on the temple altar.[12] Some Jews and Christians believe that the prophet Daniel condemned Antiochus IV Epiphanes' desecration of the Temple in his "prophecy",[13] thus giving this event significance beyond mere history.[14] Nevertheless, this imperial attempt to disturb the divinely instituted order of the Jewish world within which St. Paul lived marks Epiphanes as a potential agent of lawlessness, chaos, and destruction. It is also possible that St. Paul saw himself, prior to his conversion, as an agent of evil and chaos, as he bitterly opposed the emergence of the Jesus movement that he would later lead.

Whatever is the case, these historical figures give us a picture as to what kind of lawlessness, chaos, and evil St. Paul would have been familiar with, and who he could have modelled his "Antichrist" on. Such historical memories of anomic figures in Jewish history appear to have migrated into the Christian tradition with St. Paul's conversion to Christianity, and later Christians amalgamated the image of the "lawless one" with the Gospel of John's notion of the "Antichrist" as well as with the image of the eschatological "beast" that persecutes the faithful and speaks blasphemously about God, found in St. John of Patmos' Book of Revelation.[15] Combined, it produced the familiar image of the Antichrist that spreads evil in the world, which was only "restrained" by the work of the katechon. Just like the katechon, the precise identity of the Antichrist remains up for debate. However, in each epoch of Christian history, someone or something has been identified as being the Antichrist or the agent

---

12   Almond, *The Antichrist,* 22; Bezalel Bar-Kochva, *Judas Maccabaeus: The Jewish Struggle Against the Seleucids* (Cambridge, UK: Cambridge University Press, 1989).

13   Dan. 11.29–35

14   Daniel 11.29–35 reads as follows: "At the appointed time he will invade the South again, but this time the outcome will be different from what it was before. Ships of the western coastlands will oppose him, and he will lose heart. Then he will turn back and vent his fury against the holy covenant. He will return and show favour to those who forsake the holy covenant. His armed forces will rise up to desecrate the temple fortress and will abolish the daily sacrifice. Then they will set up the abomination that causes desolation. With flattery he will corrupt those who have violated the covenant, but the people who know their God will firmly resist him. Those who are wise will instruct many, though for a time they will fall by the sword or be burned or captured or plundered. When they fall, they will receive a little help, and many who are not sincere will join them. Some of the wise will stumble, so that they may be refined, purified and made spotless until the time of the end, for it will still come at the appointed time".

15   Almond, *The Antichrist,* 25–31; Rev. 13.1–10, 16.13–16.

of the Antichrist due to their perceived wickedness. This is true even in the twentieth century, wherein the Nazi jurist, Carl Schmitt, positively identified the Antichrist as well as the katechonic force that opposed it.

3 Carl Schmitt's Transhistorical Katechon

The notion of the katechon in Carl Schmitt's thought is subterranean, although it surfaces often to legitimate his expansive concept of political sovereignty. It first appears in his work in the mid 1940s, during his enthusiastic support for Nazism, and later reappears in the postwar years of 1950–1957, wherein he looks back at the war years and offers what can only be called an 'apology' for his juridic work in service to the Third Reich, and by extension, World War II and the Holocaust.[16] He mentions the katechon for the last time in 1970, when his book, *Political Theology II*, was published.[17] Despite the defeat of German fascism, Schmitt's influence has not ceased to be a potent factor in contemporary political philosophy. Rather, today, especially among Russian intellectuals, Schmitt's geopolitical thought, as well as his political theology, is being rediscovered, adapted, and appropriated into the Neo-Eurasianism that saturates Putin's Kremlin.[18] Most profoundly, Schmitt has influenced Alexander Dugin, whose own version of Neo-Eurasianism, as well as his 'Fourth Political Theory', is partially rooted in Schmitt's geopolitics and political theology. Ironically, the theoretical work that built much of the juridical scaffolding of Nazi ideology and the Nazi state—responsible for the death of 27 million Soviets—is itself given refuge in contemporary Russia, wherein it has found a heartfelt welcome among intellectuals and their counterparts in the Russian military hierarchy and state.[19]

Best known as a 'political theologian', Carl Schmitt "determinately negated" (*Aufheben*) Christian concepts, wherein theological notions migrated from the depth of the religious mythos into secular semantics, thus losing their

---

16 Gopal Balakrishnan, *The Enemy: An Intellectual Portrait of Carl Schmitt* (New York: Verso, 2000). Also see Jan Werner Müller, *A Dangerous Mind: Carl Schmitt in Post-War European Thought* (New Haven, CT: Yale University Press, 2003).
17 Meierhenich and Simons, *The Oxford Handbook of Carl Schmitt*, 47.
18 For a thorough exposition of Schmitt's influence on Putin's regime, see David G. Lewis (1989), *Russia's New Authoritarianism: Putin and the Politics of Order* (Edinburgh: Edinburgh University Press). Also see Stefan Auer, "Carl Schmitt in the Kremlin: The Ukraine Crisis and the Return of Geopolitics", *International Affairs* 91, no. 5 (2015): 953–68.
19 Charles Clover, *Black Wind, White Snow: The Rise of Russia's New Nationalism* (New Haven, CT: Yale University Press, 2016), 178, 180, 239, 283; Lewis, *Russia's New Authoritarianism*.

religious veneer while maintaining their underlying logic as concepts. For Schmitt, St. Paul's notion of the katechon was a concept saturated with political potential, as it was essential for the growth, maintenance, and perpetual meaningfulness of the Christian tradition itself. Testifying to the importance of the katechon in his political theology, he wrote to his friend Hans Blumenberg on October 22, 1974, that "for more than 40 years I have collected materials on the problem of the κατέχων or κατέχον (2 Thess. 2.6); and during these years I have looked for a human ear that would listen to this question and understand it. For me, it is the most important question (*Kernfrage*) of my political theology".[20]

Schmitt first invoked the concept of the katechon in his article of 19 April 1942 entitled "Unintentional Accelerator" (*Beschleuniger wider Willen*), published by the journal *Das Reich,* wherein he identifies the United States as a "delayer of world history" (*Verzögerer der Weltgeschichte*).[21] However, for Schmitt, it was the United States under President Franklin D. Roosevelt who dislodged the "paralyzed" or "spellbound" (*wie Festgebannt*) British Empire from their katechonic imperial state, thus transforming the United States, although reluctantly, into a "restrainer" (*der Aufhalter*) as opposed to an "accelerator" (*Beschleuniger*) of history.[22] Later that year, Schmitt invokes the katechon in his famous essay *Land and Sea,* which will later have a profound effect on Alexander Dugin's own geopolitical thought.[23] In this essay, Schmitt argues that the Byzantine Empire served as a katechon—a "rampart"—against the growing assertiveness of Islam.[24] Likewise, the Holy Roman Emperor Rudolf II (1552–1612) served "not as an active hero, but rather a brake, a delaying factor", since he stalled a divided Europe's historical drive towards the Thirty Years War by decades.[25] Schmitt, writing in agreement with Nietzsche, even identifies Georg W.F. Hegel as being a philosophical instantiation of a katechonic force—restraining Europe's march toward theomachist atheism by his theologically saturated philosophy of history. Schmitt writes, "Nietzsche furiously

---

20   Alexander Schmitz and Marcel Lepper, eds., *Hans Blumenberg, Carl Schmitt: Briefwechsel 1971–1978 und weitere Materialien* (Frankfurt: Suhrkamp Verlag, 2007), 120. My translation.
21   Carl Schmitt, "Beschleuniger wider Willen", *Das Reich*, 19 April 1942.
22   Schmitt, "Beschleuniger wider Willen". Schmitt would come to believe that the United States of America as a Katechon was not an entirely good thing, especially since it opposed the world-historical project of the Third Reich, which held back the chaos and disorder of Bolshevism.
23   Carl Schmitt, *Land and Sea: A World-Historical Meditation,* trans. Simona Draghici (Washington D.C., Plutarch Press, 1997).
24   Schmitt, *Land and Sea*, 8.
25   Schmitt, *Land and Sea*, 43.

identified Hegel as the sixth sense of the Germans, i.e., the historical sense, as the great deferrer on the way to expressed atheism".²⁶ Hegel's World Spirit (*Weltgeist*), working its way towards the realm of absolute freedom, in a sense was a reiteration of God's presence and activity in the world, even in catastrophe. Thus, even in the highly abstract philosophical language of Hegel, a katechonic force is identifiable, as Hegel's theo-philosophical language restrains Western Christendom from collapsing into its own civilisational nihilism via the modern pillars of atheism: instrumental reason, natural science, and positivism.²⁷

Unlike the Christian theologians before him, who understood an individual, institution, or even the Holy Spirit to be the divinely appointed delayer of the apocalypse, Schmitt accelerates the process—already started by John Calvin's own depersonalized interpretation of the katechon—to divorce the concept from a divinely appointed position in the singular, to a "metahistorical" force in the plural, one that structures the dialectic of history within each epoch.²⁸ In Schmitt's *Glossarium,* dated December 17, 1947, he states the following:

> I believe in the Katechon: it is for me the sole possibility as a Christian to understand history and its meaning. ... We must name the Katechon for every epoch for the last 1,948 years. The position [of the Katechon] has never been vacant, if it had, we would not be present anymore. ... There are temporary, transient, splinter-like fragmentary bearers of this task.²⁹

From this passage, we see Schmitt's divorce of the katechon from St. Paul's rendering as a singular divinely-appointed force, to a generalised force—or even individuals—that emerges routinely from the dynamics of history to hold back

---

26 Carl Schmitt, "Drei Stufen historischer Sinngebung", *Universitas* 5, no. 8 (August 1950), 929–30.

27 Reinhard Mehring, *Carl Schmitt: A Biography,* trans. Daniel Steuer (Malden, MA: Polity Press, 2022), 442–3.

28 John Calvin believed that the katechon was not an individual, institution, or the Holy Spirit, but rather thought that it was the process of evangelisation, i.e., the "universal call of the Gentiles". In other words, the eschaton would not come until the whole of the world had heard the Gospel of Christ. Only then would the apocalypse come to fruition. This interpretation detaches the concrete particularity of the katechon, as it seems to have been formulated in St. Paul's Second Epistle to the Thessalonians, to Christian praxis. See John Calvin, *Calvin's Commentaries: The Epistles of Paul the Apostle to the Romans and to the Thessalonians,* trans. Ross Mackenzie (Grand Rapids, MI: Wm B. Eerdmans Publishing Company, 1976).

29 Carl Schmitt, *Glossarium. Aufzeichnungen der Jahre 1947–1951* (Berlin: Duncker & Humblot, 1991), 63. My translation.

the forces of chaos. When Schmitt states that "we must name the katechon for every epoch", he assumes that the katechon is not singular, and thus must be identified within each epoch, for the katechonic force is born of the historical particularities of each epoch, and therefore is also a history-bound force. As such, that which "restrains" the forces of evil, instability, and chaos could not simply be a singular individual, institution, or even the Holy Spirit, somehow traversing throughout time, but rather a historical agent that corresponds to the historical dialectic of the epoch, even if only in a "splinter-like fragment". Thus, St. Paul's singular "restrainer", bound to the Roman Empire, gives way to Schmitt's reformulation: the katechon is an historical force that emerges out of the particularities of each historical epoch in response to each threat to order, stability, and goodness. As such, Schmitt can identify various katechons by examining the world-historical forces that held evil—or what he perceives as evil—in abeyance.

In his book *The Nomos of the Earth*, Schmitt, much like Tertullian, John Chrysostom, and Augustine, identifies the katechon in early Christian history as being the Roman Empire. However, Schmitt includes, and emphasises, the later Christianized Roman Empire, especially as it was substantiated in its *Imperium* (empire), which it inherited from the pagan Roman Empire, and its "priesthood" (*sacerdotium*), in its uniquely Christian form.[30] He writes:

> This Christian empire was not eternal. It always had its own end and that of the present eon in view. Nevertheless, it was capable of being a historical power. The decisive historical concept of this continuity was that of the restrainer: *Katechon*. "Empire" in this sense meant the historical power to restrain the appearance of the Antichrist and the end of the present eon; it was a power that withholds (*qui tenet*), as the Apostle Paul said in his letter to the Thessalonians ... The empire of the Christian Middle Ages lasted only as long as the idea of the Katechon was alive.[31]

Schmitt here admits that that which is at one time a katechonic force can lose such status when it no longer believes in itself as a katechonic force (or believes in the katechon at all). He makes a point to distinguish between empires that maintain their katechonic charge and those that do not; the latter devolve into Caesarism (monarchic absolutism).[32] When such empires foreclose on their

---

30   Carl Schmitt, *The Nomos of the Earth*. trans. G. L. Ulmen (New York: Telos Press Publishing, 2006), 59.
31   Schmitt, *The Nomos of the Earth*, 59–60.
32   Schmitt, *The Nomos of the Earth*, 62–6.

katechonic task, they can no longer "restrain" the Antichrist, and evil pervades the world. Indeed, they may become part or even a source of that pervasive evil. As such, the weakening or absence of the katechon is dysgenic for the world. The more its power to restrain the Antichrist fades away, the more anomie grows; the more anomie grows, the more the world reflects the chaos and lawlessness of the Antichrist.

From a dialectical perspective, the collapse of the katechonic force creates the conditions wherein a new katechonic force is called for and is ultimately brought into existence to restrain the anomie that has become normative amidst the lack of restraints. This new katechonic force will last, according to Schmitt's logic, as long as it understands itself as being the katechon and fulfils that law-giving and order-maintaining function. Additionally, while such a katechonic force substantiates itself within a still-religious context, wherein religion remains determinate in social ethics and morality, such a katechon should appear religious in nature. However, in the modern period, in which ethics and morality have generally migrated from the religious tradition into secular articulations, the katechon(s) may take a secular rendering, for even the secular katechon can hold back the emergence of the Antichrist in the world, as it can be a force of stability, order, and traditional morality. However, within a globalized world that is increasingly secularised, cosmopolitan, and culturally liberal, the return to the concept of the katechon is most likely to be expressed via religious language, especially through a seemingly religious empire that is attempting to stem the tide of postmodernity, which is often identified as the source of today's "evil" in the world. We will return to this point later.

Remembering that Carl Schmitt lent his juridical and theological talents to the Third Reich, which from a historical perspective appears to be a genuine source of disorder, chaos, and outright evil, we must ask why Schmitt is interested in secularising St. Paul's theological concept of the katechon. What did the identification of the katechon in Schmitt's time do for Schmitt and the political order he supported: Hitler's Third Reich?

Considering the various instances wherein Schmitt invokes the katechon, we can first see that Schmitt utilizes it to explain the dialectics of history: the ebb and flow between the forces of order and good against the forces of disorder and evil. This structuring of history between the forces of the Antichrist that bring forth the *eschaton* (ἔσχατον) and the katechon that restrains that anomic force delivers a world historical and apocalyptic importance to that which is identified as the katechon. As such, St. Paul's notion of the katechon, now translated, for Schmitt, into a metahistorical entity materialising within each epoch of history, becomes a way of legitimising Schmitt's concept of sovereignty and the totalitarian state.

For Schmitt, the sovereign is the one who determines the "state of exception" (*Ausnahmezustand*), wherein the will of the ruler is no longer bound to constitutional norms, legal restraints, and other socially recognised restrictions, but rather can act in such a way that would violate all constitutional/legal norms in the name of "suppressing" (*niederhaltend*) the chaos and evil that threatens the order of the status quo.[33] In such a totalitarian state, the authoritarian leader is the new giver of law (*nomos*), which corresponds to their unbridled will. As such, the totalitarian state and its leaders are identified as katechonic forces that restrain the Antichrist, allowing no revolutionary (or counter-revolutionary) movement to disturb or overcome the given order. Since peace and stability are needed for human flourishing, all of humanity becomes dependent on the success of the katechon to hold back the chaos of the Antichrist. Without the authoritarian state, the forces of chaos would reign, and humanity would come to its demise. Whether the world's population knows it or not, that which is designated as the katechon makes their lives possible, as it is the katechon that delivers the possibility of ataraxia (ἀταραξία, stability, calmness, lucidity). In the end, the katechon in Schmitt's analysis is a means of bestowing divine legitimacy and world-historical importance to the totalitarian state ruled by the authoritarian ruler, making their expansive rule the basis of the world's ability to continue without being enveloped by evil. It is the eschatological politics of the present in the cause of maintaining the already established.

It is clear that Schmitt developed this Third-Reich-as-katechon line of thinking in the 1940s as a way of justifying the establishment of the totalitarian fascist state, which wrestled state and social control from the liberal chaos of Weimar democracy, as well as barricading Germany from the growing communist threat emanating from the Soviet Union. The dual forces that threatened world order for Schmitt were culture destroying American-style laissez-faire democratic capitalism, and the overthrow of the aristocratic principle of nature in the name of egalitarianism that animated Marxism.[34] Much like the early Christian writers who interpreted the katechonic forces as being "that which restrains" (τὸ κατέχον) as the Roman Empire, and "the one who restrains" (ὁ κατέχων) as being the Roman Emperors, Schmitt saw the Third Reich as "that which restrains" and Adolf Hitler as "the one who restrains".

---

33 Carl Schmitt, *Political Theology: Four Chapters on the Concept of Sovereignty* (Chicago: University of Chicago Press, 2005), 5–15.
34 Hitler had much to say about the perversion of nature associated with Jewish, Christian, and Marxist forms of egalitarianism. See Adolf Hitler, *Mein Kampf*, trans. Ralph Manheim (Boston: Houghton Mifflin Co., 1999), 65.

Nazism, in Schmitt's view, was the ideology of the "restrainer": a conservative ideology that held back the forces of dysgenic modernity, cultural degeneracy, miscegenation, and racial equality. It was a way of not only winning the "culture war" (*Kulturkampf*) in Germany (and Europe in general), but a means of reversing the dialect of history. Through Nazism, those aspects of German national identity that were waning or had already been determinately negated by cultural modernity could be reinstated, augmented, and turned into an ideology of "authenticity" (*Eigentlichkeit*): a hermetically sealed notion of what it meant to be a German, which was responsible for making the "non-identical" into life-not-worthy-of-life.[35] In the end, an expansive German "Third Reich" (*Imperium*), born from the chaos of the Weimar Republic, pushed itself westward in the name of "living space" (*Lebensraum*) as a means of establishing itself as the dominant power in a Western world, standing alone against the power of the ever-metastasising modern form of anarchy determined by Western nihilism and accompanied by a triumphant Soviet theomachism. Having inherited this soteriological charge from the empires before it, the Third Reich was for Schmitt the new katechonic empire, and it understood itself as such, much like the Christian Empires of old.[36]

4   Alexander Dugin: Putin's Russia as the New Katechon

The Russian philosopher Alexander Dugin has been called many things: "Putin's brain", "Putin's Rasputin", "Putin's special representative", "the Putin Whisperer", "the most dangerous philosopher alive", and even the "St. Cyril and Methodius of Fascism".[37] He is the most influential philosopher in the Neo-Eurasianist movement. However, Alexander Dugin's Fourth Political Theory or Neo-Eurasianism, has older roots, much of which can be found in fascist Italy, Nazi Germany, and the neo-fascist New Right (*Nouvelle Droite*) in post-World War II France, as well as the original anti-Soviet Eurasianist movement in Russia.[38] From Nazi Germany, the writings of Martin Heidegger, Ernst Jünger, Arthur Moeller van den Bruck, Edgar Julius Jung, Oswald Spengler, Othmar Spann, Ernst Niekisch, Karl Haushofer, and Carl Schmitt have all

---

35 Theodor W. Adorno, *The Jargon of Authenticity*, trans. Knut Tarnowski and Frederic Will (New York: Routledge, 2003); Martin Heidegger, *Being and Time,* trans. John MacQuarrie and Edward Robinson (New York: Harper Perennial, 1962).
36 Schmitt, *The Nomos of the Earth*, 59–66.
37 Clover, *Black Wind, White Snow,* 174.
38 Alexander Dugin, *The Fourth Political Theory,* trans. Mark Sleboda and Michael Millerman (London: Arktos Media Ltd, 2012).

been highly influential on Dugin.³⁹ From Fascist Italy, the works of Julius Evola are especially important, and from post-World War II France, the work of the Far Right identitarian thinker, Alain de Benoist, cannot be underestimated. The "traditionalist" strain of Dugin's thought is thoroughly grounded in the anti-modernist work of the French mystic Sufi René Guénon, while the form of ultra-conservative Orthodox Christianity he follows is decidedly the "Old Believers" sect, who rejected the seventeenth century reforms of the official Orthodox Church.⁴⁰

As for the Eurasianist basis upon which Dugin's philosophy stands, he appropriated the works of Nikolai Yakovlevish Danilevsky, especially his book *Russia and Europe,* wherein it is argued that Russia is not Europe, but rather its own unique civilisation, a Eurasian civilisation. This Eurasianist strain of thought is also grounded in the founding generation of anti-European, anti-Bolshevik, and ultra-conservative monarchist thinkers, namely the Russian exiled Prince Nikolai Trubetzkoy and his co-Eurasianists: Petr Savitsky, Petr Suvchinsky, and Georges Florovsky.⁴¹ The latter group of monarchist intellectuals formulated much of their work in response to the Bolshevik Revolution in Russia, as well as against the growing influence of European culture within Russia. The Soviet ethnologist and Neo-Eurasianist, Lev Gumilev, and his concept of "passionarity" (пассионарность), an obscure word akin to "civilisational force", has played a major role in Dugin's ethnological thought.⁴² The Russian philosopher, Ivan Alexandrovich Ilyin, exiled from the Soviet Union due to his fascist philosophy, has also been influential on Dugin.⁴³ However, Ilyin's influence on Vladimir Putin may be even more pronounced, so much so that Putin repatriated Ilyin's

---

39 Clover, *Black Wind, White Snow*, 178.
40 Peter T. De Simone, *The Old Believers in Imperial Russia: Oppression, Opportunism and Religious Identity in Tsarist Moscow* (London: I.B. Tauris, 2018).
41 Nikolai Iakovlevich Danilevskii, *Russia and Europe: The Slavic World's Political and Cultural Relations with the Germanic-Roman West,* trans. Stephen M. Woodburn (Bloomington, IN: Slavica Publishers, 2013); Jafe Arnold and John Stachelski, eds., *Foundations of Eurasianism Vol. I* (Prav Publishing, 2020). For an early critique of Danilevsky and Eurasianist thought, see Robert E. MacMaster, *Danilevsky: A Russian Totalitarian Philosopher* (Cambridge, MA: Harvard University Press, 1967).
42 Mark Bassin, *The Gumilev Mystique: Biopolitics, Eurasianism, and the Construction of Community in Modern Russia* (Ithaca, NY: Cornell University Press, 2016); Alexander Dugin, *Ethnos and Society,* trans. Michael Millerman (London: Arktos Media Ltd, 2018); Alexander Dugin, *Ethnosociology,* trans. Michael Millerman (London: Arktos Media Ltd, 2019).
43 Andrew Stuffaford, "The (Re)birth of Ivan Ilyin", *National Review*, 19 April 2014, https://www.nationalreview.com/corner/rebirth-ivan-ilyin-andrew-stuttaford/.

writings back from the United States in 2006 and frequently quotes him (or his main ideas) in his speeches.[44]

According to Charles Clover, the author of *Black Wind, White Snow: The Rise of Russia's New Nationalism*, which chronicles the development of the Fourth Political Theory and its influence in Putin's Kremlin, it was *Nouvelle Droite* (New Right) author Alain de Benoist who first introduced Dugin to the fascist thinkers that would ultimately define his political philosophy and geopolitics.[45] In Russia's post-Soviet chaos, such fascist thinkers were an intellectual goldmine to Dugin, offering him theological, cultural, and geopolitical analyses that had been officially suppressed in the Soviet Union. While communism stressed egalitarianism and internationalism, these thinkers proposed the opposite: nationalism, anti-modernism, anti-mondialism, and a critique of the West and its perceived nihilism.

Although De Benoist rejected the idea that he introduced Dugin to the work of Karl Haushofer, the "father of Nazi geopolitics", he readily admits he introduced Dugin to the works of Carl Schmitt during one of Dugin's visits to Paris in the 1990s.[46] This encounter between the anti-1968 reactionary intellectual, Alain de Benoist, and the eccentric Russian theorist who would soon have the ear of the Russian military and the Kremlin, was decisive for the twenty-first century, as it married Slavophile thought with European reactionary conservativism. From that point on, Dugin would develop out of these many disparate influences his neo-Eurasianist Fourth Political Philosophy, which animates much of the geopolitical thought of the Kremlin today.[47]

---

44 Ilya Budraitskis, *Dissidents among Dissidents: Ideology, Politics and the Left in Post-Soviet Russia* (New York, Verso, 2022); Michel Eltchaninoff, *Inside the Mind of Vladimir Putin*, trans. James Ferguson (London: Hurst & Co, 2017); "Michigan State University returning papers of late dissident Russian philosopher Ivan Il'in", *MSU Today*, 19 May 2006, https://msutoday.msu.edu/news/2006/michigan-state-university-returning-papers-of-late-dissident-russian-philosopher-ivan-il.

45 Clover, *Black Wind, White Snow*, 180.

46 Clover, *Black Wind, White Snow*; Holger H. Herwig, *The Demon of Geopolitics: How Karl Haushofer "Educated" Hitler and Hess* (Lanham, M.D.: Rowman & Littlefield, 2016). Also see Jan Werner Müller's discussion of Carl Schmitt's influence on the *Nouvelle Droite* in his book, *A Dangerous Mind: Carl Schmitt in Post-War European Thought*, 207–218.

47 Dugin claims that his "Fourth Political Theory" is not liberalism, communism, or fascism, but a new hybrid of these theories, thus creating a *fourth* great political theory. As is often the case with Dugin's eclectic theories, he mistakes a philosophical species for a philosophical genus. While his Fourth Political Theory is a separate species from Italy's fascism and Hitler's National Socialism, it is clearly within the same genus as these two political philosophies. As such, the Fourth Political Theory is merely a Russian form of fascism, cobbled together out of earlier forms of fascism with a smattering of Russian enculturation. In fact, in 1997, Dugin explained his philosophy and referred to it as, "Fascism—Red

While Carl Schmitt's influence on Dugin appears throughout the latter's work in numerous ways, including the binary struggle between "sea power" (*Thalassocracy*) (the West) versus "land-based power" (*Tellurocracy*) (Russia/Eurasia), as well as his "friend/enemy distinction" as the "essence of politics", it is his appropriation of the concept of the katechon that is most poignant.[48] As we shall see, the concept of the katechon has become an integral part of Dugin's ideology justifying Russia's claim to being a resurgent superpower, determined to break the neoliberal hegemony of the West, especially the United States, with the goal of creating a "multipolar world", one in which the U.S. is no longer an international hegemon and nations are free to resist liberalisation and charter their development and politics outside of the current global world order.

In none of Dugin's major books does he deliver an extensive study of the katechon. Rather, it is invoked often, but sporadically, throughout several his books, articles, and social media postings.[49] Despite this, it remains at the core of his political theology. In his writings and speeches, Dugin has returned the notion of the katechon back to St. Paul's religious sphere, and thus away from Schmitt's secularisation. However, Dugin's rendering of the concept is not entirely identical with the anonymous restraining force that St. Paul proposed in his letter to the Thessalonian Church. Rather, Dugin restores the religious nature of the concept but combines it with Carl Schmitt's notion that worldly individuals and institutions can be identified as a katechon well after the historical collapse of the Roman Empire. Thus, the katechon is not merely the Roman Empire or the Emperors, but is a transhistorical force that delays, arrests, and reverses the triumph of the Antichrist (in St. Paul's religious language), or the triumph of chaos (in Schmitt's secular language).

In Dugin's aforementioned article, he discusses Russia's "special military operation", that is, its 2022 war of aggression on Ukraine, by placing the conflict

---

and Borderless". Only later did he name his philosophy the "Fourth Political Theory". See Andreas Umland, "Russia's Creeping Fascism", *Open Democracy*, 15 May 2009, https://www.opendemocracy.net/en/russia-s-creeping-fascism/.

48 Carl Schmitt, *The Concept of the Political*, trans. George Schwab (Chicago: The University of Chicago Press, 1996), 35; Schmitt, *Land and Sea*.

49 Dugin himself did not introduce the concept of the Katechon into the contemporary Russian political sphere. Rather, he radically politicised and amplified the theological concept, which had already returned with the "conservative turn" in post-Soviet Russian politics and national security policy. See Maria Engström, "Contemporary Russian Messianism and New Russian Foreign Policy", *Contemporary Security Policy* 35, no. 3 (2014): 356–379. Also see Alicja Curanović, "Russia's Mission in the World: The Perspective of the Russian Orthodox Church", *Problems of Post-Communism* 66, no. 4 (2019): 253–267.

within the spiritual binary of the Russian katechon versus the Antichrist West. He writes,

> Either this area of the world will come under the omophorion of Christ and His Immaculate Mother, or it will remain under the dominion of Satan, who will immensely strengthen his dominion over what is, in fact, the cradle of our Russian statehood, Church and culture, our people. The fight for Donbass, for Odessa, for Kiev, and even for Lviv is part of the great eschatological battle. Reality precedes dreams – including imperial eschatological dreams. The era of materialism, economics, rational analysis, experts, technocrats, managers is over. Ideas are returning to our world.[50]

He then reminds his reader of the eschatological role Russia is playing in his fight:

> And the main battle from now on unfolds between them [ideas vs. "the era of materialism ..."]. Between the Russia Idea, the *Katechon*, the Orthodox Civilisation, and the world of the Western Antichrist, coming at us. It is not us Russians who need Ukraine. It is Christ who needs it. And that is why we are there. And that is why we are not leaving it.[51]

Dugin's move here is to give the Russian "special military operation" a soteriological meaning and mission: Russia's 24 February 2022 "Blitzkrieg", which quickly transformed into a "totalen Krieg" after Ukraine showed its determination to resist the invasion, was meant to bring the wayward Ukrainian people, who have been spellbound by the Satanic West, back into the fold of God's katechonic empire: Putin's Russia. In this sense, Moscow's war is an attempt to fulfil its eschatological role on earth, bestowed upon it by the privilege of being the "Third Rome"—the rightful inheritor of the Roman Empire's katechonic task, as understood by St. Paul.

In Dugin's book, *Putin vs. Putin: Vladimir Putin Viewed from the Right*, Dugin explains that Moscow "always played a significant eschatological role in Orthodox Russia", because it is the inheritor of Imperial Rome's authority (after the fall of Constantinople to the Muslim Turks in 1453).[52] As such, the "meaning

---

50   Alexander Dugin, "Apocalyptic Realism".
51   Dugin, "Apocalyptic Realism".
52   Alexander Dugin, *Putin vs. Putin: Vladimir Putin viewed from the Right*, trans. Gustaf Nielsen (London: Arktos Media Ltd, 2014), 11. The famous saying by the Russian Orthodox

of the Tsardom was that of a state which recognizes the truth of the Orthodox church in its entirety", including the idea that Orthodox Moscow is "a barrier in the way of the son of perdition, the Antichrist, the Katechon, 'the one who withholds.'"[53] If this designation of Russia as the new katechon is applied to the current war on Ukraine, Russia is transformed from aggressor to Ukraine's eschatological saviour. The logic is as followed: if Ukraine follows the Western/EU/NATO model, with free-market capitalism, democracy, fair elections, political accountability, human rights, including the freedom of speech, expression, and political association, as well as legal rights for LGBTQ+ citizens, it will inevitably lead to the "domination of Satan" in the historic heartland of the Rus'. In other words, Kyiv would succumb to the trappings of the Antichrist, exported by the West, the "civilisation of chaos".[54] If the West prevails, Kyiv, the "mother of all Russian cities", would no longer be distinguishable from London, Paris, Berlin, and Rome, or any other European capitol, wherein secular liberalism, globalism, cosmopolitanism, multiculturalism, individualism, humanistic theomachia, and every other form of "cultural degeneracy" reign supreme. Additionally, a Westernized Kyiv would fall within the military protection of NATO, thus ensuring the "satanization" of the heartland of the Rus'. Such is unthinkable from Dugin's perspective, and thus the God-bearing Russian people must rescue Ukraine for Christ.[55]

monk Hegumen Filofei (Филофей) of Pskov in 1510, was "All Christian kingdoms have come together in you alone: two Romes have fallen, the third stands, and a fourth there will never be; your Christian kingdom will not be replaced by another". This underlies the logic of the supposed Third Rome's historical responsibility to fight the forces of the Antichrist. There will be no fourth Rome if the Third falls to the Antichrist. Thus, the choice is either support the Third Rome or face the apocalypse. See Serhii Plokhy, *Lost Kingdom: A History of Russian Nationalism from Ivan the Great to Vladimir Putin* (New York: Penguin Books, 2017), 24.

53 Dugin, *Putin vs. Putin*, 11–12.
54 Alexander Dugin, "The Order of Katechon", *Katehon*, 22 December 2022, no longer available on Katehon.com.
55 Russian has a long history of seeing itself as having a messianic role in world history. Explaining this phenomenon, the Russian philosopher Nikolai Berdyaev argued that messianism was an integral part of Russia's identity. In his seminal book, *The Russian Idea,* he wrote: "Messianic consciousness is more characteristic of the Russians than of any other people except the Jews. It runs all through Russian history right down to its communist period. In the history of Russian messianic consciousness great importance is attached to a conception which belongs to the philosophy of history, that of Moscow as the Third Rome". See Nikolai Berdyaev, *The Russian Idea,* trans. R.M. French (Hudson, NY: Lindisfarne Press, 1992), 26. Even before Berdyaev, the nineteenth century Russian philosopher Vladimir Solovyov, argued that Russians were among the nations that had "an awakening of their national consciousness" which disclosed a "conviction of the special advantage

For Dugin, if Ukraine will not save itself from the Antichrist, in fraternal solidarity, Russia will rescue it and return it back to the fold of the faithful. As Dugin wrote, "We Russians don't need Ukraine. Christ needs Ukraine. And that is why we're there". It is on behalf of Ukraine's eternal salvation that Russia invades, and it is on behalf of the world that the Russian katechon restrains the Western Antichrist in Ukraine. Being the katechon is, nevertheless, no easy task; Russia suffers due to this inherited burden, as Dugin writes:

> Russia, which today enters the final battle against chaos, is in the position of one who fights against the antichrist himself ... As long as there is a Cross on the throne, it is the Russian Cross, Russia is crucified on it, she bleeds her sons and daughters and all this for a reason ... We are on the right path to the resurrection of the dead. We will play a key role in this world mystery, because we are the guardians of the throne, the inhabitants of Katechon.[56]

For Dugin, Putin's Russia must embody the katechonic responsibility to subdue chaos in its foreign policy, especially in its neighbouring states, most poignantly Georgia and Ukraine, but it also has a responsibility to suppress such chaos within its own borders. Therefore, being the katechon is both a legitimation for external expansion as well as for internal repression. For example, Dugin writes:

> Russia must quickly affirm *internally* the beginnings of the sacred katechetical order, which was established in the 15th century in the continuity of the Byzantine heritage and the proclamation of Moscow as the Third Rome.[57]

With this emphasis on internal transformation, Dugin makes clear that being the katechon is not simply about reintegrating the wayward remnants of the old Russian Empire into Putin's empire, but also about identity production *within* Russia, especially the protection of Russia's Orthodox Christian identity,

---

of the given people, as the chosen bearer and perpetrator (*Sovershitel'*) of the historical fate of mankind". See Peter J.S. Duncan, *Russian Messianism: Third Rome, Revolution, Communism, and After* (London: Routledge, 2014), 7.

56 Dugin, "The Order of the Katechon".
57 Dugin, "The Order of the Katechon". In Orthodox thought, Constantinople was the katechon that held back the anti-Christ forces of Islam, thus denying the Ottoman Turks the ability to threaten Christendom. In 1453, when Mehmet II finally conquered Constantinople, the katechonic force moved northward to Orthodox Russia.

which means the suppression of all forms of culture that are associated with the West, most vividly freedom of the press, free speech, human rights, and the rights of LGBTQ+ citizens.[58]

One should bear in mind that Alexander Dugin blames the post-Soviet Russian state of being a "carbon copy of the secular-European model", which nurtured its own ontology independent of the Russia people, whom he believes have been "chosen by Divine Providence for a special mission".[59] To rectify this historical mistake, the state must engage in an "anagogic" process, wherein it elevates itself to "serve the people and the Church instead of forcing them to serve the state".[60] To attain this, Dugin seeks to "eradicate the state and replace it with the Holy Empire, a *basileus* [king], a comprehensive katechonic tsardom, where the divine rays directly fuse with the great God-bearing people".[61] This removal of the secular-European "carbon copy" state in exchange for an authoritarian Orthodox-infused state, commanded by a Tsarist sovereign, who has the power to determine the "state of exception" both domestically and internationally, has increasingly become the reality of Vladimir Putin's rule over Russia. State power has become more centralised within the office of the President, as substantive opposition is neutralized, no matter what form it comes in: rival politicians, independent media, oligarchs, dissidents, etc.

In a *60 Minutes Overtime* interview with Leslie Stahl, filmed in 2017 but aired in 2022, Dugin reminded Stahl that Putin is in an "absolute position of absolutist power" because Russia is a "monarchist society from below".[62] Thus, from Dugin's perspective, it is not Putin who imposes "monarchism or authoritarian rule" upon the Russian people, but rather he says, "we demand from him to be much more authoritarian than he is. He, a little bit disappoints us, because

---

58 In June 2013, the Russian State Duma unanimously passed federal legislation entitled, "For the Purpose of Protecting Children from Information Advocating a Denial of Traditional Family Values", which was signed into law by Vladimir Putin soon after. This law, commonly called the "gay propaganda law" in the West, criminalized any attempt to normalize homosexuality among minors in the Russian Federation, whether that be through the media or person-to-person communication. The law was extended in November 2022 to cover all age groups, and falsely associated homosexuality with paedophilia. See Human Rights Watch, "Russia: Expanded 'Gay Propaganda' Ban Progresses Toward Law", 25 November 2022, https://www.hrw.org/news/2022/11/25/russia-expanded-gay-propaganda-ban-progresses-toward-law.

59 Dugin, *Putin vs. Putin*, 61–2.

60 Dugin, *Putin vs. Putin*, 63.

61 Dugin, *Putin vs. Putin*, 63.

62 60 Minutes Overtime, "Aleksandr Dugin: The Far Right Theorist Behind Putin's Plan", 12 April 2022, https://www.youtube.com/watch?v=Du7fOoW_euE&t=275s.

it takes too long".63 Thus, to be the katechonic force both *within Russia* and *outside of its internationally recognised borders*, Putin must consolidate governmental, economic, cultural, and religious power into a neo-Tsarist state, one that can dissolve the vestiges of post-Soviet democracy and liberalism, and reject the Westphalian concept of states' sovereignty, especially in former Soviet Republics.

Following Dugin's logic, this consolidation of power is how Putin can most emphatically embody the soteriological role of Russia as the world's present katechon. To democratize or to Westernize Russia is to shirk what Dugin thinks is Russia's God-given eschatological responsibility. To deliver the people "chosen by Divine Providence for a special mission" over to egalitarian liberalism is to abandon the Orthodox world's responsibility to "restrain" the Antichrist – their "special mission", which Russia has had since the fall of the Second Rome, Constantinople. Thus, to not become a neo-Tsar, to not create an authoritarian state, to not reintegrate the post-Soviet Union states back into a Eurasian empire, would be to capitulate to the Antichrist.

That which horrifies Putin's Western critics—his increasing authoritarianism, disregard for international law and international standards, his unprovoked war against Ukraine and Georgia, his assassination of political opponents, his silencing of independent journalists, and so forth—is that which seemingly must be done if his katechonic position is to be realised and maintained. Thus, the more the West pushes back against Russia, the more it impedes Russia's plans for Ukraine and its other post-Soviet neighbours, the more it creates a self-enforcing narrative: the West is the "civilisation of chaos", that is, a liberal "open" society, attempting to undermine and defeat God's traditionalist katechonic force and win the *Russkii Mir* (Russian World) for Satan.64 Following

---

63   60 Minutes Overtime, "Aleksandr Dugin".
64   The notion of the "Russkii Mir" dates to the eleventh century, when first introduced by Iziaslav I of Kyiv to denote the lands of the Russ. The idea continued to exist throughout the Romanov dynasty and even into the Soviet Union, although highly diminished. However, it was resurrected again in the post-Soviet 1990s by conservative scholars, politicians, and clergy rediscovering the historic roots of Russia and forging a new religious identity. In 2009, Orthodox Patriarch Kirill of Moscow gave the concept new life by defining the "Russkii Mir" as a "common civilisational space" situated on three pillars: Eastern Orthodoxy, Russian culture (especially language and historic memory), and a "common vision" for future social development. This definition not only comes strikingly close to what Nazi Germany described as a *Volksgemeinschaft* (ethic people's community), but also has come to serve as a key component to Putin's regime, as it marries Dugin's Neo-Eurasianist ideology and Putin's authoritarianism with the authority of the Orthodox Church. See Patriarch Kirill, "Выступление Святейшего Патриарха Кирилла на торжественном открытии III Ассамблеи Русского мира" ["Speech by His Holiness Patriarch Kirill at

that logic, the more Russian soldiers are killed in Ukraine, the more Putin and Dugin can attest to the ferocity of the Antichrist and the growing need for the katechonic force to do whatever is necessary to defeat the forces of evil, disorder, and chaos that are threatening to unleash the apocalypse.

Dugin's reintegration of Schmitt's formerly secularised katechon back into a religious sphere imbues the "restrainer" with the authority of one appointed by God, thus elevating the force that "restrains" the Antichrist into a cosmic confrontation that takes place within history between the forces of good and evil. It is no longer a matter of an ambiguous force working to delay the apocalypse, as it was with St. Paul; it is no longer a matter of a historical empire or extraordinary individuals working to maintain stability and order in an increasingly chaotic world, as it was with Schmitt's secularisation of the katechon; it is now a combination of both: Russia is the historical empire—the Third Rome—and Vladimir Putin is the new tsar, both of which are active within the earthbound but cosmic struggle between the heavenly forces of good that restrain the Satanic forces of evil.

Putin's Russia, being identified as the new katechon by Alexander Dugin, has been handed a convenient and powerful political theology. In his role as the new tsar, acting as the head-of-state of the holy palingenetic and katechonic empire, Putin assumes the ultimate authority to determine the "state of exception", not only within the borders of his own country, but also within the post-Cold War world order. Utilising Schmitt's political logic wedded to Dugin's Orthodox eschatological framing, Putin has seized the authority to suspend legal norms, to violate international laws (including laws against aggressive warfare), and forcibly reintegrate the former Soviet Republic of Ukraine, which was also a vital piece of the historic Russian Empire, back into the fold of Holy Russia, precisely because he is acting as the divinely legitimated sovereign who unilaterally determines the limits of his earthly power, as the eschatological circumstances require of him.

No constitution, nor domestic law, nor international law, can challenge the authority of this sovereign, if the sovereign is acting in accordance with his katechonic role. Earthly restrictions on the actions of states matter not at all; what matters for Dugin and Putin is that the eschatological confrontation between katechonic Russia and the Antichrist West be won by the former, for the whole world has become dependent on the katechon's success. As such, the Russian forces in Ukraine bear divinely-sanctioned authority to inflict whatever kind of harm deemed necessary to win Ukraine for Christ, for God is on the side of

---

the grand opening of the Third Russian World Assembly"], the Moscow Patriarchate, 3 November 2009, http://www.patriarchia.ru/db/text/928446.html.

the katechonic sovereign.[65] That harm includes: systematic rape of Ukrainian women and girls (and in some cases boys); mutilation and execution of prisoners; the kidnapping of Ukrainian children; torture of captives; the mass execution and deliberate targeting of civilians, including civilian infrastructure (schools, hospitals, energy facilities); and the use of banned weapons, such as cluster munitions and white phosphorus.[66]

5 Conclusion

What Alexander Dugin has created out of the idea of the katechon is an imperial ideology that not only legitimates conquest, but also sanctifies war crimes in the name of St. Paul's "restrainer". While the Apostle Paul's katechon is meant to *restrain* the supposed forces of chaos, destruction, and disorder (*anomos*), Dugin's katechonic ideology paradoxically *unleashes* the forces of chaos, destruction, and disorder, in the name of defeating the Schmittian "enemy", the assumed Antichrist, i.e., the modern West. Dugin's oft-repeated claim, that he seeks a "multipolar" world, wherein other global spheres of influence can determine their own historical trajectory free from the hegemony of the West, is meant to imbue virtue into Putin's acts of aggression against its neighbours, as well as his internal critics and rivals. What Putin seeks, i.e., the reintegration of the former Russian Empire, is what Dugin's Neo-Eurasianist ideology envisions: a reconstructed "Holy Russian Empire", a palingenetic "second chance" inheritor of Christianity, nestled within the boundaries of the former Soviet Union: A Christian empire at war with the Antichrist and Ukrainian "satanism".

Dugin would like to have Russia once again at the forefront of history—a "return to history" that would propel Russia back into being a world-historical force—as opposed to being a mere disruptive force within the neoliberal world order.[67] Marrying the concept of the katechon to that geo-political desire serves to legitimate and sanctify the military actions taken in Ukraine. For Dugin, the God-bearing katechonic Russian Empire will seize the moral, spiritual, and civilisational high ground and fight for all that is good and holy in

---

65 United Nations, "War Crimes have been committed in Ukraine conflict, top UN human rights inquiry reveals", *United Nations News*, 23 September 2022, https://news.un.org/en/story/2022/09/1127691.
66 See Human Rights Watch, "Ukraine: Events of 2022", no date, https://www.hrw.org/world-report/2023/country-chapters/ukraine.
67 Budraitskis, *Dissidents among Dissidents*, 24–27.

the world, while the declared enemy, the West, that which "restrains" Russia's imperial vision, will remain the earthly incarnation of evil in Dugin's ideology.

Bibliography

(2006). "Michigan State University returning papers of late dissident Russian philosopher Ivan Il'in". *MSU Today*, 19 May 2006. https://msutoday.msu.edu/news/2006/michigan-state-university-returning-papers-of-late-dissident-russian-philosopher-ivan-il.

Adorno, T.W. (2003). *The Jargon of Authenticity*. Translated by K. Tarnowski and F. Will. New York: Routledge.

Almond, I. (2020). *The Antichrist: A New Biography*. Cambridge: Cambridge University Press.

Arnold, J., and J. Stachelski, eds. (2020). *Foundations of Eurasianism*. Vol. 1. Prav Publishing.

Auer, S. (2015). "Carl Schmitt in the Kremlin: The Ukraine Crisis and the Return of Geopolitics". *International Affairs* 91, no. 5: 953–68.

Balakrishnan, G. (2000). *The Enemy: An Intellectual Portrait of Carl Schmitt*. New York: Verso.

Bar-Kochva, B. (1989). *Judas Maccabaeus: The Jewish Struggle Against the Seleucids*. Cambridge, UK: Cambridge University Press.

Bassin, M. (2016). *The Gumilev Mystique: Biopolitics, Eurasianism, and the Construction of Community in Modern Russia*. Ithaca, NY: Cornell University Press.

Berdyaev, N. (1992). *The Russian Idea*. Translated by R.M. French. Hudson, NY: Lindisfarne Press.

Blumenberg, H., and C. Schmitt. (2007). *Briefwechsel 1971–1978 und weitere Materialien*. Frankfurt: Suhrkamp Verlag.

Budraitskis, I. (2022). *Dissidents among Dissidents: Ideology, Politics and the Left in Post-Soviet Russia*. New York, Verso.

Calvin, J. (1976). *Calvin's Commentaries: The Epistles of Paul the Apostle to the Romans and to the Thessalonians*. Translated by R. Mackenzie. Grand Rapids, MI: William B. Eerdmans Publishing Company.

Clover, C. (2016). *Black Wind, White Snow: The Rise of Russia's New Nationalism*. New Haven, CT: Yale University Press.

Curanović, A. (2019). "Russia's Mission in the World: The Perspective of the Russian Orthodox Church". *Problems of Post-Communism* 66, no. 4: 253–267.

Danilevskii, N.I. (2013). *Russia and Europe: The Slavic World's Political and Cultural Relations with the Germanic-Roman West*. Translated by S.M. Woodburn. Bloomington, IN: Slavica Publishers.

De Simone, P.T. (2018). *The Old Believers in Imperial Russia: Oppression, Opportunism and Religious Identity in Tsarist Moscow*. London: I.B. Tauris.
Dugin, A. (2012). *The Fourth Political Theory*. Translated by M. Sleboda and M. Millerman. London: Arktos Media Ltd.
Dugin, A. (2014). *Putin vs. Putin: Vladimir Putin viewed from the Right*. Transated by G. Nielsen. London: Arktos Media Ltd.
Dugin, A. (2018). *Ethnos and Society*. Translated by M. Millerman. London: Arktos Media Ltd.
Dugin, A. (2019). *Ethnosociology*. Trans. Michael Millerman. London: Arktos Media Ltd.
Dugin, A. (2022a). "Apocalyptic Realism". *Katehon*, 20 April 2022. https://katehon.com/en/article/apocalyptic-realism. No longer available on Katehon.com.
Dugin, A. (2022b). "The Order of Katechon". *Katehon*, 22 December 2022. No longer available on Katehon.com.
Duncan, P.J.S. (2014). *Russian Messianism: Third Rome, Revolution, Communism, and After*. London: Routledge.
Eltchaninoff, M. (2017). *Inside the Mind of Vladimir Putin*. Trans. James Ferguson. London: Hurst & Co.
Engleman, D.E. (1995). *Ultimate Things: An Orthodox Christian Perspective on the End Times*. Indiana: Conciliar Press.
Engström, M. (2014). "Contemporary Russian Messianism and New Russian Foreign Policy". *Contemporary Security Policy* 35, no. 3: 356–379.
Heidegger, M. (1962). *Being and Time*. Translated by John MacQuarrie and Edward Robinson. New York: Harper Perennial.
Herwig, H.H. (2016). *The Demon of Geopolitics: How Karl Haushofer "Educated" Hitler and Hess*. Lanham, M.D.: Rowman & Littlefield.
Human Rights Watch (2022). "Russia: Expanded 'Gay Propaganda' Ban Progresses Toward Law". 25 November 2022. https://www.hrw.org/news/2022/11/25/russia-expanded-gay-propaganda-ban-progresses-toward-law.
Human Rights Watch. (2023). "Ukraine: Events of 2022". No date. https://www.hrw.org/world-report/2023/country-chapters/ukraine.
Lewis, D.G. (2021). *Russia's New Authoritarianism: Putin and the Politics of Order*. Edinburgh: Edinburgh University Press.
MacMaster, R.E. (1967). *Danilevsky: A Russia Totalitarian Philosopher*. Cambridge, MA: Harvard University Press.
Mehring, R. (2022). *Carl Schmitt: A Biography*. Translated by D. Steuer. Malden, MA: Polity Press.
Meierhenrich, J., and O. Simons, eds. (2019). *The Oxford Handbook of Carl Schmitt*. New York: Oxford University Press.
Menken, M.J.J. (1994). *2 Thessalonians*. London: Routledge.

Patriarch Kirill. (2009). "Выступление Святейшего Патриарха Кирилла на торжественном открытии III Ассамблеи Русского мира" ["Speech by His Holiness Patriarch Kirill at the grand opening of the Third Russian World Assembly"]. The Moscow Patriarchate, 3 November 2009. http://www.patriarchia.ru/db/text/928446.html.

Plokhy, S. (2017). *Lost Kingdom: A History of Russian Nationalism from Ivan the Great to Vladimir Putin*. New York: Penguin Books.

Robinson, P. (2019). *Russian Conservatism*. Cornell, NY: Cornell University Press.

Schmitt, C. (1942). "Beschleuniger wider Willen". *Das Reich*, 19 April 1942.

Schmitt, C. (1950). "Drei Stufen historischer Sinngebung". *Universitas* 5, no. 8: 929–30.

Schmitt, C. (1991). *Glossarium. Aufzeichnungen der Jahre 1947–1951*. Berlin: Duncker & Humblot.

Schmitt, C. (1996). *The Concept of the Political*. Translated by G. Schwab. Chicago: The University of Chicago Press.

Schmitt, C. (1997). *Land and Sea: A World-Historical Meditation*. Transated by S. Draghici. Washington D.C.: Plutarch Press.

Schmitt, C. (2005). *Political Theology: Four Chapters on the Concept of Sovereignty*. Chicago: University of Chicago Press.

Schmitt, C. (2006). *The Nomos of the Earth*. Translated by G. L. Ulmen. New York: Telos Press Publishing.

Stuttaford, A. (2014). "The (Re)birth of Ivan Ilyin". *National Review*, 19 April 2014. https://www.nationalreview.com/corner/rebirth-ivan-ilyin-andrew-stuttaford/.

Tertullian. (1977). *Apology*. Translated by T.R. Glover. Cambridge, MA: Harvard University Press.

Toumanoff, C. (1995). "Moscow the Third Rome: Genesis and Significance of Politico-Religious Idea". *The Catholic Historical Review* 40, no. 4: 411–47.

Umland, A. (2009). "Russia's Creeping Fascism". *Open Democracy*, 15 May 2009. https://www.opendemocracy.net/en/russia-s-creeping-fascism/.

United Nations. (2022). "War Crimes have been committed in Ukraine conflict, top UN human rights inquiry reveals". *United Nations News*, 23 September 2022. https://news.un.org/en/story/2022/09/1127691.

Werner Müller, J. (2003) *A Dangerous Mind: Carl Schmitt in Post-War European Thought*. New Haven, CT: Yale University Press.

CHAPTER 9

Between Religious Nationalism and Universal Familism: Anti-Gender Movement Values in Croatia and Serbia

Ivan Tranfić

1 Introduction and Background

In medieval narratives of Europe, Christianity served as a symbolic fortification against Ottoman incursions. Later nationalist ideologies utilised the *antemurale christianitatis* myth in Croatia and Serbia to imagine the emerging nations as bulwarks of Christendom against Islam. While ethnonationalist actors still use religion similarly, Christianity is also invoked to exclude enemies within— the undeserving, deviant, immoral others. In this chapter, I compare the different ways in which religious social conservatism is utilised by Catholic and Orthodox political actors in Croatia and Serbia, respectively, to oppose gender and sexual equality (GSE). I rely on semi-structured interviews with leaders of illiberal, religiously inspired organisations mobilizing against GSE in both countries, together with content analysis of their organisational documents and statements. Analysing the values and frames of anti-gender actors in both countries allows me to carefully distinguish between their core and peripheral ideological arguments, leading to an identification of two distinct ideal types. Specifically, I argue that a common initial starting point of religious nationalism in both countries gradually diverged into two different ideal types of radical-right mobilisation against GSE. One is a Catholic-inspired universalist familism rooted in lay Catholic mobilisation against 'gender ideology', while the other is an Orthodox-inspired religious nationalism denouncing abortion and sexual minorities as threats to the survival of the Serbian nation. As authors have previously warned, religion should not be ignored: doctrine and political theology can have significant consequences for politics.[1] The effects

---

[1] Anna Grzymala-Busse, "Why Comparative Politics Should Take Religion (More) Seriously", *Annual Review of Political Science* 15, no. 1 (15 June 2012): 421–42, https://doi.org/10.1146/annurev-polisci-033110-130442; Daniel Philpott, "Explaining the Political Ambivalence of Religion", *The American Political Science Review* 101, no. 3 (2007): 505–25.

of ecclesiastical organisation and doctrine are also significant when religious affiliations are politicised for collective mobilisation.[2]

The role of the churches and religion in relation to democracy in Croatia and Serbia was ambivalent during the transition from socialism.[3] On the one hand, organised religion played a democratising role with its anti-authoritarian positioning when championing political pluralism and human rights in relation to the one-party system. On the other hand, the two countries increasingly followed a path of religious nationalism. Religion was deeply imbricated with nationhood as a marker of identity distinguishing the Catholic Croats from Orthodox Serbs, and public homophobia was designed to restrict and regulate sexuality as an important aspect of national self-determination.[4] On the one hand, Serbian Orthodox radicals drew on ethnophyletism and Saint Sava nationalism (*svetosavlje*).[5] On the other hand, Croatian Catholics drew from a theology of the incarnation of Christianity in an ethnically defined people, as well as Polish-inspired practices of celebrating nationhood within a liturgical context.[6] The nationalist regimes and actors in the 1990s tended to treat women primarily as biological and social reproducers of the nation, pushing women to have more children and promoting restrictive reproductive policies.[7] Simultaneously, 'the homosexual' was denounced as a dangerous other, "a dark counterpart of the hypermasculine father/defender/warrior".[8]

The role played by the Roman Catholic Church in Croatia and the Serbian Orthodox Church is not exceptional in the broader regional literature on the populist Radical Right. A specific subset of radical-right actors merges nationalism with religion against liberal pluralism, with religious actors emerging in

---

2 Maciej Potz, *Political Science of Religion: Theorising the Political Role of Religion* (Cham: Palgrave Macmillan, 2020), https://doi.org/10.1007/978-3-030-20169-2.
3 Alex J. Bellamy, "The Catholic Church and Croatia's Two Transitions", *Religion, State and Society* 30, no. 1 (2002): 45–61, https://doi.org/10.1080/09637490220127620; Marko Veković, *Democratization in Christian Orthodox Europe: Comparing Greece, Serbia and Russia*, 1st Ed. (Routledge, 2022).
4 Srđan Sremac and Reinder Ruard Ganzevoort, eds., *Religious and Sexual Nationalisms in Central and Eastern Europe: Gods, Gays, and Governments* (Leiden: Brill, 2015).
5 Branko Sekulić, *Ethnoreligiosity in the Contemporary Societies of the Former Yugoslavia: The Veils of Christian Delusion* (Lanham, MD: Lexington Books/Fortress Academic, 2022).
6 Vjekoslav Perica, *Balkan Idols: Religion and Nationalism in Yugoslav States* (Oxford University Press, 2002).
7 Jeremy Shiffman, Marina Skrabalo, and Jelena Subotic, "Reproductive Rights and the State in Serbia and Croatia", *Social Science and Medicine* 54, no. 4 (2002): 625–42, https://doi.org/10.1016/S0277-9536(01)00134-4.
8 Sabrina P. Ramet, ed., *Gender Politics in the Western Balkans: Women and Society in Yugoslavia and the Yugoslav Successor States* (University Park, PA: Pennsylvania State University Press, 1999).

some Eastern European countries as "torchbearers of radical-right thinking".[9] While social conservatism is only an important predictor of electoral support for the Radical Right in Eastern Europe,[10] family, abortion, and LGBT rights also figure as mobilising issues for Western extreme-right actors.[11] Whether it is against Muslim migrants or sexual minorities, radical-right populists utilise religion to assume "righteousness and purity which places them in a position of superiority towards the 'others'".[12] This feeling of superiority is cultivated by a doctrine of familism, roughly defined as a sociopolitical privileging of the heteronormative family as the nucleus of society. The family is both an "incubator of macro-level sociability",[13] and a political agent mobilised to protect traditional values. As early as the 1980s, the American Christian Right construed 'family values' as a divisive frame, allowing them to denounce their political opponents as "enemies of the family".[14] This 'family values' frame has been brought to the Balkans by a more recent wave of opposition to GSE—the transnational anti-gender movement.

2 The Family and the Nation

Despite the same starting point of religious nationalism in Serbia and Croatia, I argue that parts of the Croatian Radical Right diverged towards a new form of illiberalism. While some actors like Dveri have followed a similar road in the last decade, Serbian opposition to GSE remains rooted in ethnonationalist ideology and framing. Over the last decade, opposition to GSE has been reinvigorated globally by a heterogenous network of religious, conservative, and

---

9   Michael Minkenberg, *The Radical Right in Eastern Europe: Democracy under Siege?* (New York: Palgrave Macmillan, 2017).
10 Jason E Kehrberg, "The Demand Side of Support for Radical Right Parties", *Comparative European Politics* 13, no. 5 (2015): 553–76, https://doi.org/10.1057/cep.2014.6.
11 Manuela Caiani, Donatella Della Porta, and Claudius Wagemann, *Mobilizing on the Extreme Right: Germany, Italy, and the United States* (Oxford: Oxford University Press, 2012).
12 Ov Cristian Norocel and Alberta Giorgi, "Disentangling Radical Right Populism, Gender, and Religion: An Introduction", *Identities* 29, no. 4 (2022): 417–28, https://doi.org/10.1080/1070289X.2022.2079307.
13 Cornelia Möser, Jennifer Ramme, and Judit Takács, eds., *Paradoxical Right-Wing Sexual Politics in Europe*, Global Queer Politics (Cham: Palgrave Macmillan, 2022), https://doi.org/10.1007/978-3-030-81341-3.
14 Seth Dowland, "'Family Values' and the Formation of a Christian Right Agenda", *Church History* 78, 3 (2009): 606–31.

far-right actors mobilising against 'gender ideology'.[15] Anti-gender movements campaign against women's and LGBT activism, sexual and reproductive rights, same-sex marriage and adoption, sexual and civic education, and gender mainstreaming while seeking to reaffirm differences between men and women.[16] The Vatican, Christian clergy of various denominations, and lay activists have played a central role in the movement. In different contexts, they have been creating loose, strategic coalitions with political actors to combat the advances of the transnational feminist movement while championing 'family values'.[17] Anti-gender movements share their ideological core with the Radical Right, including nativism, conservatism, and the defence of a heteronormative gender binary understood as the natural gender order.[18] However, they also utilise secularised frames of human rights and democracy, cooperating transnationally and taking to the streets to collectively engage in peaceful protest, referendums, public vigils, and strategic litigation.[19] While one recent comparison highlighted a common convergence towards Western-style 'family values' in Croatia and Serbia,[20] I contend that a careful unpacking of ideologies, frames, and self-understanding of actors shows, in fact, crucial differences. Based on my analysis of the values and framing of anti-gender movements in Croatia

---

15   Ivan Tranfić and Timo Koch, "From Discourses to Actors: How Analyzing the Christian Right Can Further Our Understanding of Anti-Gender Mobilization", *Engenderings* (Blog), London School of Economics, 12 December 2022, accessed 22 September 2022, https://blogs.lse.ac.uk/gender/2022/12/12/from-discourses-to-actors-how-analyzing-the-christian-right-can-further-our-understanding-of-anti-gender-mobilization/.

16   Roman Kuhar and David Paternotte, *Anti-Gender Campaigns in Europe: Mobilizing Against Equality* (London; New York: Rowman & Littlefield International, 2017).

17   Elizabeth S. Corredor, "Unpacking 'Gender Ideology' and the Global Right's Antigender Countermovement", *Signs: Journal of Women in Culture and Society* 44, no. 3 (2019): 613–38, https://doi.org/10.1086/701171; Elżbieta Korolczuk and Agnieszka Graff, "Gender as 'Ebola from Brussels': The Anticolonial Frame and the Rise of Illiberal Populism", *Signs: Journal of Women in Culture and Society* 43, no. 4 (2018): 797–821, https://doi.org/10.1086/696691; Ivan Tranfić, "Framing 'Gender Ideology': Religious Populism in the Croatian Catholic Church", *Identities* (2022): 1–17, https://doi.org/10.1080/1070289X.2022.2037899.

18   Anja Hennig, "Political Genderphobia in Europe: Accounting for Right-Wing Political-Religious Alliances against Gender-Sensitive Education Reforms since 2012", *Zeitschrift Für Religion, Gesellschaft Und Politik* 2, no. 2 (2018): 193–219, https://doi.org/10.1007/s41682-018-0026-x.

19   David Paternotte and Roman Kuhar, "Disentangling and Locating the 'Global Right': Anti-Gender Campaigns in Europe", *Politics and Governance* 6, no. 3 (2018): 6–19, https://doi.org/10.17645/pag.v6i3.1557.

20   Dragan Šljivić and Martin Mlinarić, "Sexual Othering and Democracy in Post-Yugoslav Societies: A Comparison of Dveri and U Ime Obitelji", in *Minorities under Attack*, eds. Sebastian Goll, Martin Mlinariæ, and Johannes Gold (Harrassowitz Verlag, 2019), 103–28, https://doi.org/10.2307/j.ctvc770t5.9.

and Serbia, I suggest two ideal types of interaction between religious, anti-gender, and nationalist ideologies – universal familism and religious nationalism. We can define religious nationalism as a project seeking to return religion into the public domain by sacralizing the nation state as a collective religious subject whereby state authority and national identity are legitimized by a link to the divine.[21] While emphasis on 'family values' can easily be incorporated into the religious nationalist project, the anti-gender movement emphasizes the family as a central political subject. As one of the founders of the World Congress of Families – the main transnational event of the anti-gender movement – noted: "True sovereignty originates here [in the family]. These homes are the source of ordered liberty, the fountain of real democracy, the seedbed of virtue. ... Even a nation is nothing but the aggregate of the families within its borders".[22]

In contrast to the dominant strand of scholarship defining the anti-gender movement *ex negativo* (as against 'gender' or liberalism), I follow the calls for unpacking positive value systems and ideology of anti-gender actors.[23] On the one hand, the Catholic-dominated anti-gender movement in Croatia uses discursive secularisation and human rights framing in favour of universal family values to combat GSE. On the other hand, the nationalist-Orthodox movement in Serbia primarily opposes GSE in favour of tradition, nation, and Christianity. As ideal types, neither universal familism nor religious nationalism are free of attributes associated with their counterpart. Admittedly, there is an evident increasing tendency among radical-right actors of both countries to appeal to 'family values'.[24] This tendency coincides with the starting point of a global wave of anti-gender mobilisation that also fostered the cooperation of Serbian and Croatian actors with transnational actors such as the World Congress of Families. Having this convergence in mind, universal familism and religious

---

21 Sremac and Ganzevoort, eds., *Religious and Sexual Nationalisms in Central and Eastern Europe*.
22 Allan Carlson, "Universal Declaration on the Family and Marriage", International Organization for the Family, 2016.
23 Elisabeth Holzleithner, "Reactionary Gender Constructions in Illiberal Political Thinking", *Politics and Governance* 10, no. 4 (2022): 6–15, https://doi.org/10.17645/pag.v10i4.5537; Susanna Mancini and Nausica Palazzo, "The Body of the Nation: Illiberalism and Gender", in *Routledge Handbook of Illiberalism*, eds. S. Holmes, A.Sajo, and R. Uitz (Routledge, 2021), https://papers.ssrn.com/abstract=3835305.
24 Šljivić and Mlinarić, "Sexual Othering and Democracy in Post-Yugoslav Societies".

nationalism as concepts make explanatory sense when highlighting the varying degrees and centrality of their specific attributes.[25]

In my comparison, I focus on religiously inspired organisations opposing GSE—including both parties and movement actors—by analysing their guiding values. I start from the initial observation that many major representatives of the Catholic church in Croatia supported the creation of a politicised lay movement *sui generis* to espouse 'evangelical radicalism'.[26] The movement is comprised of religious activists, associations, prayer communities, and NGOs fighting for the 'culture of life' and 'family values' against 'gender ideology'. In contrast, with no systematic organisational support from the Orthodox Church and doctrine,[27] opposition to 'gender ideology' in Serbia has been taken up by the nationalist youth and traditional far-right actors rebranding themselves as pro-family.[28] Anti-gender contention in Serbia could thus be interpreted more as a result of scapegoat-switching, similar to cases like Slovakia and Hungary, where far-right actors change issue focus between the Roma, immigrants, or the LGBTIQ+ minority.[29] Specifically, the nationalist party Dveri became a central node around which the new anti-gender movement crystallised.

Unlike the autocephalous religious nationalism of Serbian Orthodoxy that evades formalised social teaching and doctrines, Catholic actors have at their disposal doctrinally defined appeals to a God-given natural order that does not require references to nationalism. Thus, highly elaborate Catholic doctrines on sexuality, family, and gender, together with a universalist Christian outlook, provided Croatian anti-gender actors with ideological and material resources to reframe their political appeals away from ethnonationalism. As Katja Kahlina demonstrated in her analysis,[30] anti-gender actors in Croatia speak on behalf of citizens—a demos which is not ethnically defined, but a "moral and

---

25   David Collier and James E. Mahon, "Conceptual 'Stretching' Revisited: Adapting Categories in Comparative Analysis", *American Political Science Review* 87, no. 4 (1993): 845–55, https://doi.org/10.2307/2938818.
26   Croatian Episcopal Conference, ed., *Za život svijeta. Pastoralne smjernice za apostolat vjernika laika u Crkvi i društvu u hrvatskoj* (Glas Koncila, 2012).
27   Boris, B2; Rastko, B4; Nikola, B7.
28   Srdan Mladenov Jovanović, "The Dveri Movement through a Discursive Lens. Serbia's Contemporary Right-Wing Nationalism", *Sudosteuropa* 66, no. 4 (2018): 481–502, https://doi.org/10.1515/soeu-2018-0038.
29   Lenka Bustikova and Petra Guasti, "The Illiberal Turn or Swerve in Central Europe?" *Politics and Governance* 5, no. 4 (2017): 166–76, https://doi.org/10.17645/pag.v5i4.1156.
30   Katja Kahlina, "On Behalf of the Family and the People: The Right-Wing Populist Repertoire in Croatia", in *Discursive Approaches to Populism Across Disciplines*, ed. Michael Kranert (Cham: Palgrave Macmillan, 2020), 227–50, https://doi.org/10.1007/978-3-030-55038-7_9.

cultural community supposedly making up the majority of citizens", invoking a kind of "plebiscitarian democracy".[31] In contrast, Serbian opposition to GSE is primarily organised around an ethnonationalist ideological core, with abortion and homosexuality appearing as foreign threats to the nation and its biological survival.

3 Data and Methods

I rely on two types of data to understand which values drive anti-gender movements and explain the diverging paths of opposition to GSE in Croatia and Serbia. Firstly, I analysed qualitative data collected in 2021/22 by conducting 30 semi-structured interviews with leaders, coordinators and board members of anti-gender NGOs, initiatives, and parties in Croatia and Serbia.[32] I asked a series of questions about the values driving their work, including the role of religion. Using convenient sampling and snowballing, I aimed to increase the diversity of respondents and organisations to ensure the representation of different factions within the broader movement (see Appendix).[33] Values are understood here as building blocks of ideology, the moral and ethical commitments defining right and wrong, distinguishing the important from the unimportant.[34] Secondly, I used the actors' websites and online archiving tools to collect organisational documents elaborating missions, values, and principles from different points in time between 2005 and 2020.[35] Corresponding data from national NGO registries was also included. Given the fewer interviews conducted in the Serbian case, organisational texts from two additional anti-gender organizations—the Center for Life and Choose Life—were added. I use

---

31 Tonči Kursar and Ana Matan, "Forms of Politicization in Croatia: A Road to a Consensus Democracy 2.0", in *Democratic Crisis Revisited: The Dialectics of Politicisation and Depoliticisation*, eds. Meike Schmidt-Gleim Ruzha Smilova and Claudia Wiesner (Baden-Baden: Nomos, 2022).

32 The interviews were conducted as party of a broader research project including questions concerning movement values, actions, and relations. In this chapter, I analyse references regarding ideology and framing, as expressed in the respondents' stated values and reflections.

33 Interviewees were contacted as representatives of organisations and initiatives recognised as part of the anti-gender movement in existing scholarship, and through snowballing.

34 Pamela Oliver and Hank Johnston, "What a Good Idea! Ideologies and Frames in Social Movement Research", *Mobilization: An International Quarterly* 5, no. 1 (1 March 2000): 37–54.

35 The period roughly corresponding to the emergence and mobilisation of anti-gender movements.

qualitative content analysis following the causal chain approach[36] to unpack hierarchies of values by identifying central organizing ideas in organisational documents. Since political objectives are always derived from deep-seated value priorities functioning as chains of arguments,[37] it is helpful to distinguish core from peripheral argumentation. Together with interviews, this helps differentiate whether social conservatism is ultimately intertwined with nationalist, or universalist claims against GSE in the documents, thus allowing me to discern between the two ideal types. Combining interviews and organisational documents helps minimise the problem of catching only the movement's more moderate, socially acceptable 'front stage'.[38] This problem also relates to the differences between ideologies as deeply rooted value systems and framing as a strategic process of outward-facing movement 'branding'. I follow Benford and Snow's understanding of ideology as a cultural resource for framing, meaning that frames often work by accentuating pre-existing beliefs and values.[39] In my analysis, I try to flesh out this inherent tension by analysing how a conservative ideology behind the two movements branches out into two different directions; a universalist, secularly framed, but nonetheless illiberal familism in Croatia, and an ethnically centred religious nationalism in Serbia.

4 Movement History and Political Context

After the fall of communism and the Yugoslav wars, Christianity re-emerged as an important cultural and political force in both Croatia and Serbia. Catholicism and Orthodoxy found their way back into public life, the education system, and the media. Although the dominant churches were able to establish formalised relations with the state in both cases through various laws and agreements, their presence in civil society differed significantly. The Catholic church in Croatia established decentralised networks of ecclesial offices and informal associations dedicated to the laity and the family. Conversely, no similar networks were created by the Serbian Orthodox Church. Although Croatia has

---

36   Cas Mudde, *The Ideology of the Extreme Right* (Manchester: Manchester University Press, 2000).
37   Arne Naess, "Ideology and rationality", in *Ideology and Politics,* eds. Maurice W. Cranston and Peter Mair (Alphen aan den Rijn: Sijthoff, 1980).
38   Cas Mudde, *Populist Radical Right Parties in Europe* (Cambridge: Cambridge University Press, 2007).
39   David A. Snow and Robert D. Benford, "Clarifying the Relationship between Framing and Ideology", in *Frames of Protest,* eds. Hank Johnston and John A. Noakes (Rowman & Littlefield Publishers, Inc., 2005).

been an EU member since 2013, while Serbia is still a candidate country, both countries have implemented comprehensive legislative reforms to improve gender and sexual equality.[40] In fact, as the European Union's LGBTIQ+ policies have developed over the years, harmonization requirements around the issue have only increased for Serbia.[41] Nevertheless, unlike the Croatian Life Partnership Act, Serbia still does not legally recognize same-sex partnerships. Finally, we should not assume that EU accession guarantees a consolidation of gender and sexual equality in terms of policies and popular support. In fact, the EU loses its leverage once a country becomes a full member, opening the space for post-accession backsliding.[42]

The first anti-gender social movement organisations (SMOs) in Croatia appeared in the late 2000s in the context of an increasing pace of socio-political liberalisation and Europeanisation. With Spain, Croatia is the earliest case of anti-gender mobilization in Europe.[43] The abstinence-based sexual education program TeenSTAR and the NGO Voice of Parents for Children (GROZD) championing it came first.[44] They formed the core of HRAST[45]—a political platform founded in 2011 by lay Catholics and more traditional radical-right figures. Simultaneously, an Australian Catholic traditionalist of Croatian origins, John Vice Batarelo, founded another influential anti-gender NGO—Vigilare, aligned with the international movement 'Tradition, Family and Property'. Joined by the former head of Zagreb's Caritas, Krešimir Miletić, Vigilare launched 'I Was an Embryo Too'—a campaign against artificial insemination legislation. Claiming it would introduce 'gender ideology' into the Croatian education system, the new movement also prompted the Constitutional Court to suspend a health education reform in 2013, thus winning their first public victory. Their biggest success followed the same year when a church-backed popular referendum successfully changed the Croatian constitution by inserting

---

40   Katja Kahlina, "Local histories, European LGBT Designs: Sexual Citizenship, Nationalism, and "Europeanisation" in Post-Yugoslav Croatia and Serbia", *Women's Studies International Forum* 49 (2015): 73–83.

41   Koen Slootmaeckers, *Coming In: Sexual Politics and EU Accession in Serbia* (Manchester: Manchester University Press, 2022).

42   Milada Anna Vachudova, "Ethnopopulism and democratic backsliding in Central Europe", *East European politics* 36, no.3 (2020): 318–340

43   Maja Gergorić, "Antirodni Pokreti u 21. Stoljeću", *Anali Hrvatskog Politološkog Društva* 17, no. 1 (2020): 149–67, https://doi.org/10.20901/an.17.07.

44   Amir Hodžić et al., "The Politics of Youth Sexuality: Civil Society and School-Based Sex Education in Croatia", *Sexualities* 15, no. 3-4 (2012): 494–514, https://doi.org/10.1177/1363460712439656.

45   Hrast translates to 'oak tree' from Croatian, and is also an acronym for 'Hrvatski rast' (Croatian Growth).

a heteronormative definition of marriage. The referendum was organized by In the Name of Family (INF)—a new citizen's initiative comprised of most of the previously mentioned anti-gender leaders. After 2013, anti-abortion actors sprung after the victory against same-sex marriage to promote a new 'culture of life', including 40 Days for Life, the March for Life, and Students for Life, to name a few. A decade of anti-gender mobilisation translated into fragmented but unmistakably strong electoral support for the anti-gender cause, with close to twenty percent of the total votes cast in the 2020 general elections going to radical-right parties championing family values as the Croatian Sovereigntists, the Bridge and the Homeland Movement.

As in Croatia, anti-gender actors in Serbia started mobilising in a context of gradual liberalisation, particularly after the 2008 victory of the socially liberal Democratic Party. Backed by anti-Western factions within the Serbian Orthodox Church, parts of the Religious Right increasingly turned to grassroots, civil society organizing. Simultaneously, Kosovo's 2008 declaration of independence and the financial crisis further bolstered the religious nationalism of various far-right actors in Serbia. The political system slowly decayed into competitive authoritarianism with the rise of Aleksandar Vučić and his pro-EU populist right-wing party since 2012.[46] Meanwhile, the radical-right party 'Dveri', previously an NGO with an Orthodox and nationalist profile, turned its focus to social issues in the 2010s. It started organizing 'Family Marches' against the Belgrade Pride parade and centring 'family values' in service of the Serbian national reproduction.[47] Dveri sprouted from a nationalist Orthodox movement that built a 'Serbian network' of rar-right civil society groups of students, youth, intellectuals, and the lay-faithful over time. Dveri's electoral successes and international cooperation efforts opened more spaces and resources in Serbian civil society for novel anti-abortion and faith-based associations such as the Center for Life, the Alliance of Orthodox Women, the Alliance for Life, and the Coalition for the Family.

The first publicised use of the GI frame in Serbia was the conservative intellectuals' attack on an educational package problematising gendered violence

---

46 Florian Bieber, "Patterns of Competitive Authoritarianism in the Western Balkans", *East European Politics* 34, no. 3 (2018): 337–54, https://doi.org/10.1080/21599165.2018.1490272; Zoran Stojiljković and Dušan Spasojević, "Populistički Zeitgeist u 'Proevropskoj" Srbiji'", *Politička Misao* 55, no. 3 (2018): 104–28, https://doi.org/10.20901/pm.55.3.04.

47 Tamara Vukov, "Pokret Dveri", in *Nedemokratsko Redizajniranje Političkih Partija u Srbiji*, eds. Zoran Stojiljković, Gordana Pilipović, and Dušan Spasojević (Beograd: Konrad Adenauer Foundation, 2013).

in schools,[48] followed by petitions and protests against proposed same-sex marriage legislation in recent years. Centred around Dveri, the Serbian anti-gender movement primarily mobilizes against 'homosexual' or 'LGBT ideology' and abortion, framed in religious nationalist terms as a "white plague" threatening the survival of Serbs. The historical and organisational paths in the two cases—a lay-Catholic network in the Croatian and a nationalist Orthodox network in the Serbian case—are also reflected in the diverging ideology and framing of the two movements.

5 Values Driving the Anti-Gender Movement

5.1 *Croatia*

To demonstrate this divergence, I interpret the results of thirty interviews—twenty-two from Croatia and ten from Serbia[49]—by analysing anti-gender movement leaders' ideas, values, and self-understanding. Figure 9.1 displays the values the interviewees expressed as central to their organisational efforts, with the N=36 demonstrating coded value utterances. The proportions presented in Figure 9.1 should be understood only as a visual indication of the relevance of the different values, given the limits of quantifying interpretive interview data. Nevertheless, the vast majority of responses are secular values expressed within a human rights master frame, including family values, universal values, justice and human rights.

Organisational documents corroborate the central importance of family, pro-life, and 'universal' values for the SMOs under analysis. The movement platform HRAST and its member, the Family Party, identify the family as a "fundamental form of human community. ... The family precedes any other form of organising of societies. Natural human sociability is found in the family".[50]

---

48   Adriana Zaharijević, "Habemus Gender: The Serbian Case", *Feministiqa*, 2018, accessed 22 September 2022, https://feministiqa.net/wp-content/uploads/2018/05/2018_fem01_zaharijevic.pdf.

49   The asymmetry in the number of interviews reflects the different complexity of the two movements in terms of the number of actors mobilizing against GSE. A full-blown anti-gender movement simply did not exist in Serbia prior to 2018, whereas the Croatian one has been active since at least 2008. This is reflected in the number of organisations in both cases, and, consequently, my interviews.

50   "Izborni program Hrasta", Hrvatsko kulturno vijeće, accessed 12 January 2022, https://www.hkv.hr/vijesti/dokumenti/9306-izborni-program-hrasta.html; "Vrijednosna polazišta", Obiteljska stranka, accessed 12 January 2022, https://web.archive.org/web/20100614141858/http://obiteljskastranka.hr/program/polazista.html.

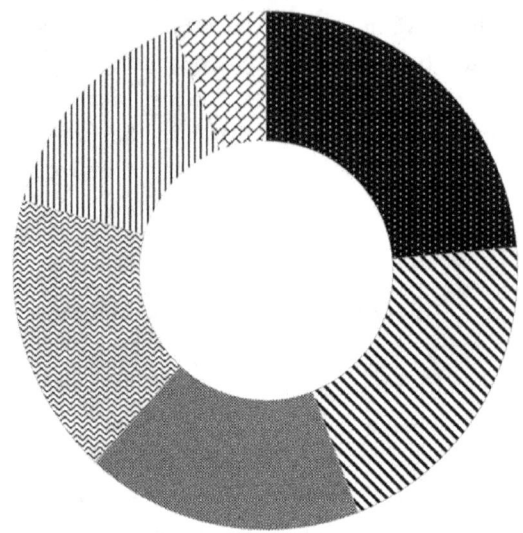

FIGURE 9.1 A donut chart of anti-gender movement values in Croatia. Family Values dominate, followed by Universal Values and Justice & Human Rights. Pro-Life, Christian, Social Rights, and Other hold smaller shares
SOURCE: AUTHOR

Several organisations accentuate the protection of family values and the improvement of the quality of marital and familial life as central goals.[51] More explicitly, INF calls for "empowering families to take on the role of a social subject and … the responsible participation of families in the cultural, social and public life", while the Family Party emphasises a broader goal of preserving "universal", "general", and "human" values.[52] Stemming from the importance of family and human dignity, the protection of "life from conception until natural death" is another common movement goal, particularly for anti-abortion SMOs. In addition, HRAST identifies human life as the highest value from which all other values concerning family policies should be derived. Interestingly, in contrast to religious nationalism, almost no references are made to natality or demography as issues. Among different organisations, only HRAST

---

51 "Statut udruge GROZD", Ministrastvo pravosuđa i uprave; Hrast 2011; "O Nama", Udruga za promicanje obiteljskih vrijednosti – Blaženi Alojzije Stepinac, https://udruga-bas.hr/o-nama/.

52 "Ne može sloboda govora podrazumijevati uvrede i mržnju", In the Name of Family, accessed 12 January 2023, https://projektdomovina.hr/planinic-ne-moze-sloboda-govora-podrazumijevati-uvrede-i-mrznju-kako-bi-neki-zeljeli;"Vrijednosna polazišta", Obiteljska stranka.

recognises the importance of "raising awareness for demographic problems … and increasing natality in Croatia" in a passing note.[53]

While all respondents stated that religion and faith play a vital role personally, most respondents downplay their role in activism. 'Ivan' (A1) notes that religion is only one among many viewpoints that reach the same conclusion about the importance of protecting life, others being anthropology, philosophy, science, and biology. The primary way respondents frame their values as part of a broader set of principles is by insisting on the universality of Christian values as binding for everyone (not just Christians). As 'Ana-Marija' (A16) puts it, "it is a simple question of life, a matter concerning all religions, nations, and humanity as a whole". Similarly, 'Marija' (A3) stated: "I think Christian values are actually good for society, for humans, both individuals and the collective". Finally, 'Gabrijel's' (A5) understanding demonstrates a more explicitly anti-pluralist, illiberal understanding:

> When someone says "conservative values" it is as if there are different worlds of values, but I don't think there are. There is only one spectrum of colours; you can't invent another. One can try to mix colours, but [like colours] there is a hierarchy of values—one can easily destroy it by mixing them.

According to 'Luka' (A12), "all monotheistic religions, at least from a Catholic viewpoint, support the same values that, in their core, are *always valid*". As Enes Kulenović argued, some Catholics are not inclined to accept a pluralism of values in society since they view those disagreeing with them as holding invalid beliefs.[54] Christianity and religion are significantly less present in organisational documents compared to 'universal family values' and appear in three different forms. First, Christianity predominantly figures as a broad source of morality. This is best illustrated by GROZD's definition of family values as "backed by the moral-ethical norms of monotheistic religions rooted in our lands".[55] Second, in a rare instance of political Catholicism, HRAST calls for an explicit "fundamental political stance that Croatia should be rooted in Christian social teaching".[56] Finally, religion appears as a human right. This is best exemplified by Vigilare's appeal to the protection of "the rights of parents to raise their children in accordance with their own philosophical and

---

53   Hrast, 2011, para. 16.
54   Enes Kulenović, "Ratzinger Protiv Rawlsa: Propast Preklapajućeg Konsenzusa", *Politička Misao* 40, no. 1 (2004): 55–61.
55   "Statut udruge", GROZD, Ministarstvo pravosuđa i uprave.
56   Hrast 2011, para. 27.

religious beliefs and values".[57] Interview data further confirms the importance of religious actors' secularisation of discourse and human rights framing when acting in the sociopolitical arena.[58] 'Paula' (A7) describes the challenges their organization faced in approaching supporters:

> We saw that religion is perceived as something very negative in the public. … If you approach them with spiritual rhetoric, they are repelled. We realized we could go with a neutral, affirmative approach while remaining motivated by Catholic values … that are unquestionable.

The secular approach is perceived as more successful not only in addressing a pool of potential supporters but also in the media and the broader public. Perhaps the most interesting finding is that which is not being said, namely, the absence of references to some form of patriotism or nationalism. However, parts of the Croatian anti-gender movement were actively involved in campaigns against Serbian minority rights.[59] In addition, a recent study on ethno-religious attitudes in Croatia found that links between religiosity, nationhood, and right-wing political orientation have grown in the recent decade.[60] Importantly, my argument is not that Croatian anti-gender actors are *not* nationalist but are not *primarily* nationalist. Broader parties and platforms like HRAST are rooted in coalitions with traditional nationalist and war veteran groups. In addition, their appeal to a broader electorate does, in fact, contain nationalist values. For example, HRAST problematises Serbian minority rights, affirms the importance of the Croatian diaspora, and invokes the dignity of the Croatian Homeland War (1991–1995). Similarly, the INF's electoral program refers to "homeland values" and "national pride" in their electoral program.[61] Nonetheless, these values are explicitly elaborated by the party's leadership as inclusive: "The Homeland is not a strictly Croatian national project … It calls for any

---

57 "Statut udruge", Vigilare, Ministarstvo pravosuđa i uprave.
58 José Casanova, *Public Religions in the Modern World* (University of Chicago Press, 1994); Kuhar and Paternotte, *Anti-Gender Campaigns in Europe*; Juan Marco Vaggione, "Reactive Politicization and Religious Dissidence: The Political Mutations of the Religious", *Social Theory and Practice* 31, no. 2 (2005): 233–55, https://doi.org/10.5840/soctheorpract200531210; Tanja Vučković Juroš, "The Rise of the Anti-Gender Movement in Croatia and the 2013 Marriage Referendum", *Europe-Asia Studies* 72, no. 9 (2020): 1523–53, https://doi.org/10.1080/09668136.2020.1820956.
59 Kursar and Matan, "Forms of Politicization in Croatia".
60 Krunoslav Nikodem and Siniša Zrinščak, "Etno-religioznost: Religioznost, nacionalni identitet i političke orijentacije u hrvatskom društvu", in *Uzvjerovah, zato besjedim*, eds. Josip Šimunović, Silvija Migles (Denona, Zagreb, 2019).
61 "Press za 8. Izbornu jedinicu", In the Name of Family, 2015.

type of affirmative communitarianism in *Our Beautiful*. Here, we are building our lives and futures for our children, no matter the nation or religion".[62] In addition, one anti-abortion leader, 'Eva' (A2), critically reflects on one of the movement's slogans:

> I am very sensitive when I see written 'March for Life, Family and Homeland'. … Maybe I don't want to march for the homeland. … I think that the position of someone marching for life is not necessarily a position of marching for 'family and homeland'.

Croatian anti-gender SMOs are, in conclusion, deliberately trying to move beyond ethnonationalist framing by appealing to the universality of Christian morals. Furthermore, Christianity and Catholic values are downplayed due to the strategy of discursive secularisation. Nevertheless, interview data clearly shows that Catholic values are considered the primary source of the movement's morality and appeal to universal values. The Croatian anti-gender movement is thus also an example of the blurring of the sacred and the secular,[63] whereby the number of politicised public prayers and processions in public spaces has risen in parallel to an increasingly secularised anti-gender discourse.

5.2 Serbia

As in the Croatian case, Serbian SMO leaders were asked about the values driving their organisation's work and the role of religion in it. Figure 9.2 displays the values enumerated by respondents. Most importantly, a third of all respondents highlight some form of nationalism or patriotism. The second and third most salient values uttered verbatim in all cases were 'Christian values', followed by 'family values'. Finally, only a few respondents mention 'traditional values', 'life from conception', and the 'culture of life'.

Most interviewees explicitly mention religion and faith as a personal motivating factor in their activist and political work. 'Evgenija' (B1) and 'Dušan' (B6) name the Orthodox Church and Christianity as clear sources of authority for their organisation on issues like abortion and gender roles. Unlike the Croatian case, where scientific argumentation is widespread, only one of my interviewees highlighted the importance of medical sciences in defining life as beginning at conception ('Cvetan', B5). Most importantly, my interviewees elaborate

---

62 "Ne može sloboda govora podrazumijevati uvrede i mržnju", In the Name of Family.
63 M.D.C. Van der Tol and Philip Gorski, "Secularisation as the fragmentation of the sacred and of sacred space", *Religion, State and Society* 50, no. 5 (2022): 508, https://doi.org/10.10 80/09637494.2022.2144662.

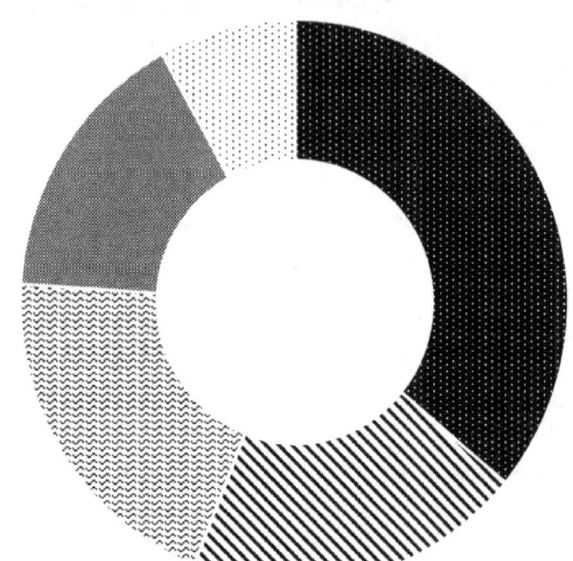

- Nationalist Values
- Christian Values
- Family Values
- Traditional Values
- Pro-life Values

FIGURE 9.2 A donut chart of anti-gender movement values in Serbia. Nationalist Values are the largest, followed by Traditional and Family Values. Smaller sections include Christian, Pro-Life, and Social Values
SOURCE: AUTHOR

on the role of religion in two ways. Firstly, Christianity serves as a source of values and political guidelines for defining the family as heterosexual and the promotion of a 'culture of life'. Secondly, religion and faith are deeply imbricated with nationhood. As 'Boris' (B2) elaborates, "the Church should reassert the position it held in society throughout Serbian history ... the spiritual and national identity are of greatest importance". Clearly, religious nationalism in its Serbian Orthodox form of *svetosavlje* is the central organizing force of Serbian anti-gender efforts. Christian values are intimately tied to national identity: "In Serbian history, we have suffered through grave injustices and extermination—it was our faith that saved us. ... Had we not stuck to Christian values we wouldn't have survived" ('Evgenija', B1).

Half of the interview participants from Serbia mentioned the issue of demography as central, compared to a few passing mentions in the Croatian case. As one leader pointed out, "the first problem of Serbia is the demographic catastrophe known among the people as the white plague" ('Pavle', B8). Another interviewee also emphasises the white plague, the 'demographic winter', and the disappearance of the Serbian people as 'central threats' to family values

('Boris', B2). According to this narrative, Serbs are dying out—the culture of death, which includes non-traditional family models, should be overcome with policies promoting natality and larger families ('Evgenija' B1; 'Rastko' B4; 'Dušan' B6; 'Pavle' B8). While more than a third of all Croatian SMO leaders used human rights framing in the interviews (primarily parents' rights to raise their children according to their values), only one respondent did so vaguely in the Serbian case. The imbrication of demography, nationalism, and pro-family positions is further reflected in the organisational documents and programs of Serbian anti-gender SMOs. All analysed initiatives, NGOs, and parties, no matter their organisational identity and issue focus, strongly link social conservatism and anti-abortion positions to patriotism, nationalism, and demography. This link is perhaps most clearly outlined in Dveri's election program: "all social forces should act to strengthen the family. Without the family, there is neither a healthy individual nor a strong Serbia; without a population, there is no economy nor security".[64]

The importance of family values is thus directly linked to national security. However, Dveri's religious nationalism also changes over time. From an emphasis on the "faith in God and Serbdom" and Serbia's authentic Orthodox culture,[65] a secularised emphasis is put on the family as an "active agent of social life" and the "right of parents to raise their children".[66] Nevertheless, the family model of society, which demonstrates convergence with the Croatian case, remains in the function of preserving the "biological survival of the nation"[67] as a core part of the party's ideology. The issue of Serbian survival is central even for specific policy positions—population decline is listed as the number one (of six) problem of Serbia's education system, for example.[68] Even newer, non-partisan organisations focusing more exclusively on family and abortion issues also firmly integrate social conservatism, religiosity, and nationalism. The Center for Life's values can be summarized in the following threefold formula: a culture of life; backed by a Christian model of the family; to support the survival of the nation.[69]

---

64 "O nama", Dveri Srpske, 2007, accessed 12 January 2023, https://web.archive.org/web/20081207030859/http://www.dverisrpske.com/rubrika/9.

65 "O nama", Dveri Srpske.

66 "Мере породичне политике Двери!" Dveri Srpske, 2011, para. 4, accessed 12 January 2023, https://web.archive.org/web/20081207030859/http://www.dverisrpske.com/rubrika/9.

67 "Мере породичне политике Двери!" Dveri Srpske, para. 3

68 "Просветна политика Двери" Dveri Srpske, 2012, para. 6, accessed 12 January 2023, https://web.archive.org/web/20121018080448/http://www.dverisrpske.com/sr-CS/nasa-politika/izborni-program/prosvetna-politika-dveri.php.

69 "О нама", Centre for Life, accessed 12 January 2023, http://centarzazivot.rs/o-nama/.

Unlike the rest of the anti-gender SMOs, two anti-abortion organisations rooted in Serbia's smaller protestant communities—Choose Life and the Center for Babies—stray from this model by putting less emphasis on nationhood and demography. This might point to the centrality of Orthodoxy and *svetosavlje* as a mediating factor linking social conservatism to nationalism. According to the NGO Choose Life: "the meaning of family, marriage, and children has been devalued—the value of each individual is endangered. The traditional order is disappearing before our eyes".[70] While individuals and families are framed as threatened by the changing social morality, there is no mention of the nation or of Serbia's survival.

6   Conclusions and Discussion

In this chapter, I have argued that Christian denominational differences are relevant to understanding divergence in radical-right ideology and framing against gender and sexual equality in Croatia and Serbia. Croatian anti-gender SMOs are driven by values rooted in conservative ideology and framed primarily in terms of protecting the family, human life, and a set of vaguely defined universal human values. Although Christianity is admittedly an important motivating factor of movement leaders in Croatia, organisations strategically use secular framing for a broader social appeal. References to demography and national identity are mostly avoided, and deliberate attempts are made by some movement leaders and figures to avoid ethnonationalist framing. Nationalism is underemphasised and does not appear as the primary driving force of the movement, possibly since it has figured as a staple of far-right politics in Croatia and would not allow anti-gender organizations to distinguish themselves as new actors. This, however, does not imply that the Croatian anti-gender movement could be classified as having a mainstream conservative profile. On the contrary, its illiberalism and anti-pluralism are visible in its exclusionary politics. Following a more traditional form of religious nationalism, Serbian anti-gender actors are driven by values rooted in the Orthodox-nationalist imbrication of religious morality, nationhood, and reproduction. Despite the post-2011 discursive innovations and the adoption of 'family values', said values are explicitly linked to national survival and prosperity—possible only with a thriving and socio-politically powerful Orthodox Church. Investigating the

---

70   "Dobrodošli u 'Izaberi život'", Choose Life, 2013.

different ideological accents and framing used by actors depending on their religious affiliations should also be undertaken within country-cases. Predominantly Orthodox Bulgaria is an example where minority Evangelical groups have initiated the innovative anti-gender fight for family values,[71] attempting to distinguish themselves from the Orthodox Far Right.

The differences in ideology and strategic framing between the two cases reflect the different profiles of the central actors in each country's movement. While the Croatian anti-gender movement sprouted from Church-backed lay Catholic organisations and initiatives, the Serbian movement was formed around a radical-right party as the dominant actor. Opposition to GSE is linked to ethnonationalism as a core ideological feature in the Serbian case. Conversely, the Croatian anti-gender movement roots its illiberal familism in secularised moral criteria of exclusion of the undeserving others. Both variants reflect different elements of nativist ideology typical for radical-right actors in Eastern Europe.[72] Stronger discursive secularisation in the Croatian case does not align with general levels of religiosity. The Croatian population demonstrates significantly higher levels of religious attendance, practice, and importance attributed to religion in their life compared to the Serbian population.[73] However, only 58% of Croats say being Catholic is very or somewhat important to truly be a national of Croatia, compared to a high 78% of Serbs reporting the same for Orthodoxy.[74] A stronger emphasis on ethnonationalism in the Serbian anti-gender movement is thus coherent with a stronger convergence of religious belief and national belonging in Serbia compared to Croatia. I have focused on the affirmative values of the movement since the illiberal politics of fear employed by anti-gender movement actors have been well-researched and are more openly expressed in 'back-stage' discourse. For example, movement

---

71 Shaban Darakchi, "'The Western Feminists Want to Make Us Gay': Nationalism, Heteronormativity, and Violence Against Women in Bulgaria in Times of 'Anti-Gender Campaigns'", *Sexuality & Culture* 23, no. 4 (2019): 1208–29, https://doi.org/10.1007/s12119-019-09611-9; Emilia Slavova, "Globalising Genderphobia and the Case of Bulgaria", *European Journal of English Studies* 26, no. 2 (2022): 176–96, https://doi.org/10.1080/13825577.2022.2091281.

72 Michael Minkenberg, *Transforming the Transformation? The East European Radical Right in the Political Process* (Routledge, 2015); Andrea L. P. Pirro, *The Populist Radical Right in Central and Eastern Europe: Ideology, Impact, and Electoral Performance* (London: Routledge Taylor & Francis Group, 2016).

73 Pew Research Centre, "Religious Belief and National Belonging in Central and Eastern Europe", 10 May 2017, https://www.pewresearch.org/religion/2017/05/10/religious-belief-and-national-belonging-in-central-and-eastern-europe/.

74 Pew Research Centre, "Religious Belief and National Belonging in Central and Eastern Europe".

actors have argued against the alleged subjugation of children to "homosexual torture" via sexual education,[75] advocated "curing" homosexuality,[76] and used transphobia to stoke anger around "gender".[77] While analysing hateful speech is important and harder to capture by researchers due to the insincerity of far-right self-representation,[78] we should not ignore the complexities of their affirmative values, motivation, and worldview.

Furthermore, although types of opposition to GSE change depending on the denominational differences I have highlighted, other factors surely also play a role. It could be argued that higher levels of social homophobia and lacking implementation of anti-discrimination legislation provides Serbian anti-gender actors with more discursive opportunities to openly rage against 'sodomy' compared to their Croatian counterparts. In addition, far-right actors in Serbia are predominantly concerned with issues such as statehood and territorial sovereignty due to the unresolved question of Kosovo. Issues related to gender and sexuality thus take a back seat or are framed more easily in an ethnonationalist way. Finally, while one could argue that the familialist turn is merely strategic whitewashing of homo/transphobia in a context of increasing social liberalisation, this argument prevents us from capturing long-term ideological change and internal movement diversification of anti-gender actors. Such an approach also ignores the importance of political theology and religious doctrine when researching ideological nuances and framing of religious-right movements. Future research should tackle whether more moderate anti-gender framing for broader audiences changes the movement's ideology, policy positions, and social composition over time.

---

75 TeenSTAR, "Šaljite dalje—svim roditeljima, odgojiteljima i ostalim građanima", OFS Kaptol, 8 January 2006, accessed 12 January 2022, http://kaptol.ofs.hr/saljite-dalje-svim-roditeljima-odgojiteljima-i-ostalim-gradanima/.

76 "Grozd preporučio učenicima: Na nastavu sa slikama golih žena", *Jutarnji List*, 15 February 2008, accessed on 12 January 2022, https://www.jutarnji.hr/naslovnica/grozd-preporucio-ucenicima-na-nastavu-sa-slikama-golih-zena-3867438.

77 Dunja Obajdin and Slobodan Golušin, "Narratives of Gender, War Memory, and EU-Scepticism in the Movement Against the Ratification of the Istanbul Convention in Croatia", in *Europeanisation and Memory Politics in the Western Balkans*, ed. Ana Milošević and Tamara Trošt (Cham: Palgrave Macmillan, 2021), 205–30, https://doi.org/10.1007/978-3-030-54700-4_9.

78 Kathleen Blee, "Where Do We Go from Here? Positioning Gender in Studies of the Far Right", *Politics, Religion & Ideology* 21, no. 4 (2020): 416–31, https://doi.org/10.1080/21567689.2020.1851870.

Appendix: List of Organizations Included in Interviews

Name	Type	Country
Croatia for Life	Anti-abortion organization	Croatia
Students for Life	Anti-abortion organization	Croatia
Betlehem	Anti-abortion organization	Croatia
Dalmatia for Life	Anti-abortion organization	Croatia
40 Days for life	Anti-abortion organization	Croatia
March for Life	Anti-abortion organization	Croatia
Center for Babies	Anti-abortion organization	Serbia
Choose Life	Anti-abortion organization	Serbia
Alliance for Life	Anti-abortion organization	Serbia
40 Days for Life – Novi Sad	Anti-abortion organization	Serbia
In the Name of Family	Anti-gender organization	Croatia
Association "Alojzije Stepinac"	Anti-gender organization	Croatia
Vigilare	Anti-gender organization	Croatia
Voice of Parents for Children	Anti-gender organization	Croatia
Parents Institute for Education	Anti-gender organization	Croatia
The Truth about the Istanbul Convention	Anti-gender organization	Croatia
Alliance of Orthodox Women	Anti-gender organization	Serbia
Coalition for the Natural Family	Anti-gender organization	Serbia
HRAST	Anti-gender party	Croatia
INF – Project Homeland	Anti-gender party	Croatia
Family Party	Anti-gender party	Croatia
Dveri	Anti-gender party	Serbia

Bibliography

Bellamy, A.J. (2002) The Catholic Church and Croatia's Two Transitions". *Religion, State and Society* 30, no. 1: 45–61.

Bieber, F. (2018). "Patterns of Competitive Authoritarianism in the Western Balkans". *East European Politics* 34, no. 3 (2018): 337–54.

Blee, K. (2020). "Where Do We Go from Here? Positioning Gender in Studies of the Far Right". *Politics, Religion & Ideology* 21, no. 4: 416–31.

Bustikova, L., and P. Guasti. (2017). "The Illiberal Turn or Swerve in Central Europe?" *Politics and Governance* 5, no. 4: 166–76.

Caiani, M., D. Della Porta, and C. Wagemann. (2012). *Mobilizing on the Extreme Right: Germany, Italy, and the United States*. Oxford: Oxford University Press.

Carlson, A.C. (2016). "The Universal Declaration on the Family and Marriage". The International Organization for the Family. Retrieved on February 12. https://www.upfdeutschland.de/files/The_Cape_Town_Declaration_on_the_Family_and_Marriage-2016.pdf.

Casanova, J. (1994). *Public Religions in the Modern World*. University of Chicago Press.

Collier, D., and J.E. Mahon. (1993). "Conceptual "Stretching" Revisited: Adapting Categories in Comparative Analysis". *American Political Science Review* 87, no. 4: 845–55.

Corredor, E.S. (2019). "Unpacking 'Gender Ideology' and the Global Right's Antigender Countermovement". *Signs: Journal of Women in Culture and Society* 44, no. 3: 613–38.

Croatian Episcopal Conference. (2012). *Za život svijeta. Pastoralne smjernice za apostolat vjernika laika u Crkvi i društvu u hrvatskoj*. Glas Koncila.

Darakchi, S. (2019). "'The Western Feminists Want to Make Us Gay': Nationalism, Heteronormativity, and Violence Against Women in Bulgaria in Times of 'Anti-Gender Campaigns'". *Sexuality & Culture* 23, no. 4: 1208–29.

Dowland, S. (2009). "'Family Values' and the Formation of a Christian Right Agenda". *Church History* 78, no. 3: 606–31.

Gergorić, M. (2020). Antirodni Pokreti u 21. Stoljeću". *Anali Hrvatskog Politološkog Društva* 17, no. 1: 149–67.

Grzymala-Busse, A. (2012). "Why Comparative Politics Should Take Religion (More) Seriously". *Annual Review of Political Science* 15, no. 1: 421–42. https://doi.org/10.1146/annurev-polisci-033110-130442.

Hennig, A. (2018). "Poltiical Genderphobia in Europe: Accounting for Right-Wing Political-Religious Alliances against Gender-Sensitive Education Reforms since 2012". *Zeitschrift Für Religion, Gesellschaft Und Politik* 2, no. 2: 193–219. https://doi.org/10.1007/s41682-018-0026-x.

Hodžić, A., J. Budesa, A. Štulhofer, and J. Irvine. (2012). "The Politics of Youth Sexuality: Civil Society and School-Based Sex Education in Croatia". *Sexualities* 15, no. 3–4: 494–514. https://doi.org/10.1177/1363460712439656.

Holzleithner, E. (2022). "Reactionary Gender Constructions in Illiberal Political Thinking". *Politics and Governance* 10, no. 4: 6–15. https://doi.org/10.17645/pag.v10i4.5537.

Jovanović, S.M. (2018). "The Dveri Movement through a Discursive Lens. Serbia's Contemporary RightWing Nationalism". *Sudosteuropa* 66, no. 4: 481–502. https://doi.org/10.1515/soeu-2018-0038.

Juroš, T.V. (2020). "The Rise of the Anti-Gender Movement in Croatia and the 2013 Marriage Referendum". *Europe-Asia Studies* 72, no. 9: 1523–53. https://doi.org/10.1080/09668136.2020.1820956.

Kahlina, K. (2020). "On Behalf of the Family and the People: The Right-Wing Populist Repertoire in Croatia". In: M. Kranert (ed) *Discursive Approaches to Populism Across Disciplines*. Cham: Palgrave Macmillan. Pp. 227–50. https://doi.org/10.1007/978-3-030-55038-7_9.

Kehrberg, J.E. (2015). "The Demand Side of Support for Radical Right Parties". *Comparative European Politics* 13, no. 5: 553–76. https://doi.org/10.1057/cep.2014.6.

Korolczuk, E., and A. Graff. (2018). "Gender as 'Ebola from Brussels': The Anticolonial Frame and the Rise of Illiberal Populism". *Signs: Journal of Women in Culture and Society* 43, no. 4: 797–821. https://doi.org/10.1086/696691.

Kuhar, R., and D. Paternotte. (2017). *Anti-Gender Campaigns in Europe: Mobilizing Against Equality*. London: Rowman & Littlefield International.

Kulenović, E. (2004). Ratzinger Protiv Rawlsa: Propast Preklapajućeg Konsenzusa". *Politička Misao* 40, no. 1: 55–61.

Mancini, S., and N. Palazzo. (2021). "The Body of the Nation: Illiberalism and Gender". In: S. Holmes, A.Sajo, and R. Uitz (eds.). *Routledge Handbook of Illiberalism*. Routledge. Pp. 403–422. https://papers.ssrn.com/abstract=3835305.

Minkenberg, M. (2015). *Transforming the Transformation? The East European Radical Right in the Political Process*. Routledge.

Minkenberg, M. (2017). *The Radical Right in Eastern Europe: Democracy under Siege?* New York: Palgrave Macmillan.

Möser, C., J. Ramme, and J. Takács, eds. (2022). *Paradoxical Right-Wing Sexual Politics in Europe*. Cham: Springer International Publishing. https://doi.org/10.1007/978-3-030-81341-3.

Mudde, C. (2000). *The Ideology of the Extreme Right*. Manchester: Manchester University Press.

Mudde, C. (2007). *Populist Radical Right Parties in Europe*. Cambridge: Cambridge University Press.

Naess, A. (1980). "Ideology and rationality". In: Maurice William Cranston, and Peter Mair (eds.). *Ideology and Politics*. Alphen aan den Rijn: Sijthoff.

Nikodem, K., and S. Zrinščak. (2019). "Etno-religioznost: Religioznost, nacionalni identitet i političke orijentacije u hrvatskom društvu". In: J. Šimunović, and S. Migles (eds.). *Uzvjerovah, zato besjedim*. Zagreb: Denona.

Norocel, O.C., and A. Giorgi. (2022). "Disentangling Radical Right Populism, Gender, and Religion: An Introduction". *Identities* 29, no. 4: 417–28. https://doi.org/10.1080/1070289X.2022.2079307.

Obajdin, D., and S. Golušin. (2021). "Narratives of Gender, War Memory, and EU-Scepticism in the Movement Against the Ratification of the Istanbul Convention in Croatia". In: A. Milošević and T. Trošt (eds.). *Europeanisation and Memory Politics in the Western Balkans*. Cham: Palgrave Macmillan. Pp. 20530. https://doi.org/10.1007/978-3-030-54700-4_9.

Oliver, P., and H. Johnston. (2000). "What a Good Idea! Ideologies and Frames in Social Movement Research". *Mobilization: An International Quarterly* 5, no. 1: 37–54. https://doi.org/10.17813/maiq.5.1.g54k222086346251.

Paternotte, D., and R. Kuhar. (2018). "Disentangling and Locating the 'Global Right': Anti-Gender Campaigns in Europe". *Politics and Governance* 6, no. 3: 6–19. https://doi.org/10.17645/pag.v6i3.1557.

Perica, V. (2002). *Balkan Idols: Religion and Nationalism in Yugoslav States*. Oxford University Press.

Pew Research Centre. (2017). "Religious Belief and National Belonging in Central and Eastern Europe". 10 May 2017. Accessed 20 September 2023. https://www.pewresearch.org/religion/2017/05/10/religious-belief-and-national-belonging-in-centraland-eastern-europe/.

Philpott, D. (2007). "Explaining the Political Ambivalence of Religion". *The American Political Science Review* 101, no. 3: 505–25.

Pirro, A.L.P. (2016). *The Populist Radical Right in Central and Eastern Europe: Ideology, Impact, and Electoral Performance*. London: Routledge Taylor & Francis Group.

Potz, M. (2020). *Political Science of Religion: Theorising the Political Role of Religion*. Cham: Palgrave Macmillan. https://doi.org/10.1007/978-3-030-20169-2.

Ramet, S.P., ed. (1999). *Gender Politics in the Western Balkans: Women and Society in Yugoslavia and the Yugoslav Successor States*. University Park, Pa: Pennsylvania State University Press.

Schmidt-Gleim, M., R. Smilova, and C. Wiesner, eds. (2022). *Democratic Crisis Revisited: The Dialectics of Politicisation and Depoliticisation*. 1st ed. Baden-Baden: Nomos.

Sekulić, B. (2022). *Ethnoreligiosity in the Contemporary Societies of the Former Yugoslavia: The Veils of Christian Delusion*. Lanham, MD: Lexington Books/Fortress Academic.

Shiffman, J., M. Skrabalo, and J. Subotic. (2002). "Reproductive Rights and the State in Serbia and Croatia". *Social Science and Medicine* 54, no. 4: 625–42. https://doi.org/10.1016/S0277-9536(01)00134-4.

Slavova, E. (2022). "Globalising Genderphobia and the Case of Bulgaria". *European Journal of English Studies* 26, no. 2: 176–96. https://doi.org/10.1080/13825577.2022.2091281.

Šljivić, D., and M. Mlinarić. (2019). "Sexual Othering and Democracy in Post-Yugoslav Societies: A Comparison of Dveri and U Ime Obitelji". In: S. Goll, M. Mlinariæ, and J. Gold (eds.). *Minorities under Attack: Othering and Right-Wing Extremism in Southeast European Societies*. Harrassowitz Verlag. Pp. 103–28. https://doi.org/10.2307/j.ctvc770t5.9.

Sremac, S., and R.R. Ganzevoort, eds. (2015). *Religious and Sexual Nationalisms in Central and Eastern Europe: Gods, Gays, and Governments*. Leiden: Brill.

Stojiljković, Z., and Dušan Spasojević. (2018). "Populistički Zeitgeist u 'Proevropskoj' Srbiji". *Politička Misao* 55, no. 3: 104–28. https://doi.org/10.20901/pm.55.3.04.

Tranfić, I. (2022). "Framing 'Gender Ideology': Religious Populism in the Croatian Catholic Church". *Identities* 29, no. 4: 1–17. https://doi.org/10.1080/1070289X.2022.2037899.

Tranfić, I., and T. Koch. (2022). "From Discourses to Actors: How Analyzing the Christian Right Can Further Our Understanding of Anti-Gender Mobilization". *Engenderings* (blog). London School of Economics, 12 December 2022. https://blogs.lse.ac.uk/gender/2022/12/12/from-discourses-to-actorshow-analyzing-the-christian-right-can-further-our-understanding-of-anti-gender-mobilization/. Last accessed 22 September 2022.

Vaggione, J.M. (2005). "Reactive Politicization and Religious Dissidence: The Political Mutations of the Religious". *Social Theory and Practice* 31, no. 2: 233–55. https://doi.org/10.5840/soctheorpract200531210.

Van der Tol, M.D.C., and P.S. Gorski. (2022). "Secularisation as the fragmentation of the sacred and of sacred space". *Religion, State and Society* 50, no. 5: 495–512. https://doi.org/10.1080/09637494.2022.2144662.

Veković, M. (2022). *Democratization in Christian Orthodox Europe: Comparing Greece, Serbia and Russia*. 1st Ed. Routledge.

Vigilare. (2015). "Statut udruge". Registar udruga Republike Hrvatske. Ministrastvo pravosuđa i uprave. Accessed 12 January 2023. https://registri.uprava.hr/.

Vukov, T. (2013). "Pokret Dveri". In: Z. Stojiljković, G. Pilipović, and D. Spasojević (eds.). *Nedemokratsko Redizajniranje Političkih Partija u Srbiji*. Beograd: Konrad Adenauer Foundation. Pp. 409–418.

Zaharijević, A. (2018). "Habemus Gender: The Serbian Case". *Feministiqa*. accessed 22 September 2022. https://feministiqa.net/wp-content/uploads/2018/05/2018_fem01_zaharijevic.pdf.

CHAPTER 10

The Orthodox Church and the Greek Solution Party: A Stunted Political Relation between Adjacent Ideological Platforms

Konstantinos Papastathis and Anastasia Litina

1   Introduction

The electoral success of the Greek Solution (GS) party did not come out of the blue. Under the leadership of the ultra-nationalist journalist Kyriakos Velopoulos, the party entertains an openly xenophobic outlook, advocating a nativist, law-and-order-oriented, and socially conservative agenda. The family ethics value frame is blended with a conspiracy theory mindset and a pro-Russian political affinity, even advocating that Greece should veto both within the EU and NATO of all support for Ukraine.[1] It seems that the central factors for the party's growth were: a) the imprisonment of the dominant radical-right (RR) party of the Golden Dawn (GD), which created a representation deficit that allowed the party to fill the produced political gap; b) the centrality in the party's electoral campaign of opposing the so-called Prespes Agreement, which ended the historic controversy between Greece and Northern Macedonia concerning the latter's official name. This agreement allowed Velopoulos to capitalize on his nationalist profile, especially within the region of Greek Macedonia, as well as the subsequent electoral shrinkage of the Independent Greeks (ANEL) radical-right party, which participated in the coalition government with SYRIZA.

A topic of special interest regarding this development is the possible role of the Orthodox Church of Greece (OCG, or the Church). This is because it historically forms an established religious institution and a highly influential interest group in party politics and policy making. Overall, this status is founded on the high level of religiosity within the society, the effectiveness of the religiosity cleavage, the strong symbolic capital of the OCG, due to its equation with

---

1 "Greek Solution on Ukraine: Make it Clear that no one Can Murder Greeks and Go Unpunished", *Naftemporiki*, 14 February 2022, accessed 9 October 2023, https://www.naftemporiki.gr/politics/1297574/elliniki-lysi-gia-oukrania-na-ginei-safes-oti-oudeis-borei-na-dolofonei-ellines-kai-na-menei-atimoritos/.

national identity, and the very close relationship between church and state. This chapter aims to empirically elaborate on the standpoint of the Greek-Orthodox Church, vis-à-vis the GS in relation to the political attitude of anti-immigration, as well as to explore the electoral behaviour of the religious body towards the party, guided by the following research questions:

RQ 1: What is the interplay at a micro-level between religiosity and two central ideological features of GS, i.e., nativism, and islamophobia? In other words, does religiosity makes one more or less likely to think that Muslim immigrants are a threat? Our research hypothesis is that religiosity has a positive effect in relation to Islamophobia and nativism. Analytically, this means that as people become more religious, they are likely to show more negative feelings towards Islam and a stronger preference for their own country and culture over others. RQ 2: what is the correlation between religiosity and GS voting? Did the religious electorate vote for the party or not? To get the broad picture of the RR voting, we examine the possible alignment of the religious electorate to the other members of the party family. Our research hypothesis is that the religious electorate supports the party family due to its ideological overlap with the Church.

To investigate this research question, the paper utilizes data collected from all rounds of the World Values Survey (WVS), a large-scale international survey conducted at different time intervals. We focus on examining the relationship between the measure of church attendance and two other variables: nativism and Islamophobia. Overall, Islamophobia encompasses a range of anti-Islamic (religion, culture) and anti-Muslim (faithful) sentiments, spanning everyday behaviours, attitudes, and feelings, as well as discourses and practices that propagate derogatory views towards Muslims.[2] Nativism is generally understood as the ideology that "seeks to exclude rather than include",[3] since the states should be inhabited exclusively by born members of the national group, while special emphasis is put on the protection of the "native" population's cultural identity vis-à-vis the alleged threats posed from the foreign outgroups as well as the priority of the nationa's economic and security interests over those of immigrants.[4] For RQ 2, i.e. the religious voting, we use the last round of the

---

2 Didem Doganyilmaz Duman, "Religious Idenities in Times of Crisis: an Analysis of Europe", in *Routledge International Handbook of Religion in Global Society*, eds. Jayeel Cornelio, François Gauthier, Tuomas Martikainen, and Linda Woodhead (London: Routledge, 2021), 435–436.
3 Benjamin Moffitt, "Liberal Illiberalism? The Reshaping of the Contemporary Populist Radical Right in Northern Europe", *Politics and Governance* 5, no. 4 (2017): 112–122., https://doi.org/10.17645/pag.v5i4.996.118.
4 Cas Mudde, *Populist Radical Right Parties in Europe* (Cambridge: Cambridge University Press, 2007), 19.

European Elections Studies, which allows us to get a broader perspective on RR voting and explore the voting "from the heart", which is better expressed in the European Elections than the national ones, in which other factors are involved as well (e.g. government formation).[5] We conduct regression analysis, i.e., a statistical technique used to model and understand the relationship between a dependent variable (in this case, the measure of church attendance) and one or more independent variables (nativism and Islamophobia). By employing regression analysis, we attempt to determine whether there is a relationship between church attendance and the other variables and, if so, the nature and strength of that relationship.

This article is divided in four parts following this introduction. In the next section, we explore the relation between the Church and the GS party in terms of discourse. The third section explores RQ 1, i.e. the attitude of the religious body vis-à-vis anti-immigration. Then we elaborate empirically on RQ 2, i.e. the religious voting for the GS. Finally, we summarise our conclusions and refer to possible extension of our research.

2   The GS Discourse on Religion

Overall, the GS party employs religion to further identitarian politics, following the "devout and conservative immersion format",[6] in which nationalism has a central place. For the GS party, religion is represented as the basis of cultural unity, and as such inextricably linked to national belonging; in effect, it forms a criterion for cultural self-determination, a marker of identity to define the hostile other for collective homogeneity. As such, it is perceived as an integral part of the nativist narrative against the Islamic East.[7] In other words, Islam is viewed as the external 'intruder' that would jeopardize the local culture and threaten state security.[8] In particular, the GS party has made an effort to

---

5   Mark Franklin, "The Fading Power of National Politics to Structure Voting Behaviour in Elections to the European Parliament", (Paper prepared for the Budapest Conference on the European Election Study, May 2005).

6   Ulf Hedetoft, "Nationalism and the Political Theology of Populism: Affect and Rationality in Contemporary Identity Politics", in *Religion and Neo-Nationalism in Europe*, eds. Florian Höhne and Torsten Meireis (Baden-Baden: Nomos, 2020), 104.

7   Rogers Brubaker, "Between Nationalism and Civilizationism: The European Populist Moment in Comparative Perspective", *Ethnic and Racial Studies* 40, no. 8 (2017): 1208, https://doi.org/10.1080/01419870.2017.1294700.

8   Jeffrey Haynes, "Right-Wing Populism and Religion in Europe and the USA", *Religions* 11, no.10 (2020): 13, https://doi.org/10.3390/rel11100490.

construct a political profile of the supposed custodian of the imagined unity between Greek national and religious identity, its vote-seeking strategy targeting the institutionally faithful electoral audience as the alleged authority of church affairs. The invocation of Christianity, thus, is not more about "belonging" than "belief", as in the case of its Western European counterparts,[9] but the party's agenda is equally founded on "belonging" as well as in "faith".[10]

To this end, GS put emphasis on church affairs and religious everyday life, stressing issues such as the closing of church schools or the burglary of parish churches,[11] and supports pro-clerical policies, such as the close relation between church and state, state funding for the OCG, and the payment of wages to the clergy. For the GS, the instruction of religious courses should be structured in confessional and catechetical lines and be obligatory in primary and secondary education. Morning prayer should be mandatory as well.[12] As stated in its program, the party aims at "revitalizing the Greek education for the development of Hellenism and Orthodoxy",[13] and "protecting the cultural and religious heritage".[14] Last but not least, in line with conservative religious circles, GS stands against the full implementation of the human rights value framework, articulating an anti-LGBT rhetoric.[15]

---

9   Nadia Marzouki, Duncan McDonnell, and Oliver Roy, eds., *Saving the People: How Populists Hijack Religion* (London: Hurst, 2016).

10 Konstantinos Papastathis and Anastasia Litina, "Orthodoxy as Exclusivist Identity in the Greek Radical Right: Discourse Analysis and Electoral Behavior", in *Illiberal Politics and Religion in Europe and Beyond: Concepts, Actors, and Identity Narratives*, eds. Anja Hennig and Mirjam Weiberg-Salzmann (Frankfurt: Campus, 2021), 295.

11 Greek Solution, "Closure of the Ecclesiastical School of Chania", 15 June 2022, accessed 31 October 2022, https://elliniki-lisi.gr/thema-titloi-telous-gia-tin-ekklisiastiki-scholi-sta-chania; Greek Solution, "Burglars attacked the church of Agia Paraskevi in Artemida of Attica", 2 May 2022, accessed 31 October 2022, https://elliniki-lisi.gr/thema-stochos-diarrikton-i-ekklisia-tis-agias-paraskevis-stin-artemida-attikis.

12 Kyriakos Velopoulos, "Parliamentary Speech on 21 January 2020", Greek Solution, accessed 31 October 2022, https://elliniki-lisi.gr/kyriakos-velopoulos-topothetisi-stin-olomelia-gia-themata-pedias.

13 Greek Solution, "The 12 points of Greek Solution programme", 11 May 2019, accessed 31 October 2022, https://elliniki-lisi.gr/ta-12-simeia-tou-programmatos-tis-ellinikis-lisis.

14 Greek Solution, "Founding Declaration", accessed 31 October 2022, https://elliniki-lisi.gr/idritiki-diakiriksi.

15 Greek Solution, "Press Release: the Greek Solution MP in European Parliament was the only representative of a Greek Party Downvoting LGBT Marriage and Adoption", 19 September 2021, accessed 31 October 2022, https://elliniki-lisi.gr/anakoinosi-typou-o-efrovoulevtis-tis-ellinikis-lysis-o-monos-ekprosopos-ellinikou-kommatos-pou-katapsifise-ton-gamo-kai-tin-apoktisi-paidion-apo-loatki.

The Covid-19 pandemic was seen as an opportunity for GS to create strong bonds with the religious target audience via a signature anti-vax campaign issue and representation of itself as the political protector of ecclesiological correctness. At the same time, GS structured its argumentation on the typical RR ideological features of islamophobia, phyletism and anti-globalization, constructing in parallel the coinage of *christianophobia*, i.e. "the racial standpoint against a group of people due to its Christian faith",[16] as their ideological opposite, which allegedly forms in turn the core feature of the party's antagonists. Within this framework, GS reacted against measures supposedly against Eastern Orthodoxy, such as entering the church with a mask, while "allowing hundreds of illegal mosques to operate illegally".[17] The other parties were projected as a fifth column of cosmopolitanism, "demonizing the church, the holy communion and the Orthodox faith which annoys globalization".[18] Moreover, Greece was perceived as a state under invasion, where the political establishment allows the "islamization" of the country by illegal immigrant intruders, who pose an existential threat to the national language, culture, and religion.[19] To conclude, the GS uses religion to construct the ingroup/outgroup distinction as part of an exclusionary political agenda. In this way, however, religion is actually instrumentalized to serve the party's nativist frame, while the alleged custodian of theological accuracy eventually ends up secularizing its own content.

However, the GS pro-religious agenda has not produced effective cooperation with the Church leadership; on the contrary, they are on bad terms. The polemic of the GS neither targets the Church as an institution, nor the upper hierarchy at large, but exclusively archbishop Hieronymus and his team. Since the party's establishment, the archbishop was reluctant to endorse it and was unwilling even to meet with Velopoulos. This might be explained by the

---

16   Greek Solution, "Press Release: Proposal for Amending Law 927/1979 concerning Christianophobia and Blasphemy", 3 September 2020, accessed 31 October 2022, https://elliniki-lisi.gr/anakoinosi-typou-i-elliniki-lysi-katethese-protasi-nomou-gia-tin-syblirosi-tou-nomou-927-1979-opos-tropopoiithike-apo-ton-nomo-4285-2014-anaforika-me-tin-christianofovia-kai-tin-prosvoli-kai-exyvri.

17   Greek Solution, "Press Release: Orthodoxy is targeted by the Government and the Opposition", 5 November 2021, accessed 31 October 31, https://elliniki-lisi.gr/anakoinosi-typou-protofanis-i-stochopoiisi-tis-orthodoxias-apo-kyvernisi-kai-antipolitefsi.

18   Greek Solution, "Press Release: Nea Democratia and Syriza Target the Church one more time", 2 November 2020, accessed 31 October 2022, https://elliniki-lisi.gr/anakoinosi-typou-i-ekklisia-akoma-mia-fora-sto-stochastro-neas-dimokratias-kai-syriza.

19   Greek Solution, "An Overview of the Greek Solution Founding Principles", 5 March 2019, principle 8, accessed 31 October 2022, https://elliniki-lisi.gr/sinopsi-ton-programmatikon-theseon-tis-ellinikis-lisis.

publication of his book *Jesus and Zeus* (2003), in which Velopoulos propagated the problematic assertion that paganism is related to Christianity, as well as the distorted profile of a Hellenized Jesus as a means to "purify" him from his Jewish ancestry. This antisemitic concept was not new, but dominant within extreme-right circles since the Nazi era, while it had a self-deceptive purpose as well, working to foster the symbolic capital of the Greek nationalist ideology. The book was condemned by various Church officials as blasphemous, which eventually forced Velopoulos to revise it. Particularly, he added more than a hundred pages in the introduction to idealize his thesis and even changed the subtitle from "Orthodoxy or Dodecatheon" (the twelve Olympian Gods of ancient Greece) to "Orthodoxy and Dodecatheon", to demonstrate that they do not form separate and uncongenial religious systems but are closely linked.[20]

Moreover, the relationship between GS and the Church deteriorated when certain officials from both the Ecumenical Patriarchate of Constantinople and the Church of Greece publicly denounced Velopoulos, who is a professional telemarketer, for deceiving the viewers by selling forged manuscript letters of Christ.[21] On the other hand, it should be noted that despite Velopoulos trading these letters for months, the accusation was only made a few days before the general elections (July 2019), most probably in an effort to dissuade the religious electorate from voting GS and align it to the mainstream conservative party of New Democracy, with which the Church apparatus maintains strong political ties. Finally, it should be clear that this tension has not led the Church to participate in the *cordon sanitaire* against the party. This stance might be explained by three basic factors: first, the Church's past close relations with the extreme-right establishment and the dominance (until recently) of hierarchs aligned to the dictatorship (1967–1974);[22] second, the shared ideological core (nationalism, populism, exclusionism) between the two actors, especially under late Archbishop Christodoulos;[23] and third, the fact that at least a few

---

20   Dimitris Psarras, *A Little Bit of Nazism by Kyriakos Velopoulos* (Athens: Ekdoseis EFSYN, 2019); "The Blasphemous Book of Velopoulos", *EFSYN*, 28 May 2019, accessed 31 October 2022, https://www.efsyn.gr/politiki/201547_blasfimo-biblio-toy-belopoyloy.
21   "The Church Hammers Velopoulos", *Ta Nea*, 1 July 2019, https://www.tanea.gr/2019/07/01/politics/sfyrokopima-apo-tin-ekklisia-kata-velopoulou/.
22   Stavros Zoumboulakis, *Golden Dawn and the Church* (Athens: Polis, 2013).
23   Yannis Stavrakakis, "Politics and Religion: on the 'Politicization' of Greek Church Discourse", *Journal of Modern Greek Studies* 21, no. 2 (2003) 153–181, https://muse.jhu.edu/article/47675/pdf; Konstantinos Papastathis, "Religious Discourse and Radical Right Politics in Contemporary Greece, 2010–2014", *Politics, Religion and Ideology* 16, no. 2–3 (2015): 218–247, https://doi.org/10.1080/21567689.2015.1077705.

hierarchs still keep friendly relations with Velopoulos, eventually blocking a total political war by the Church against him from within.

The party, in return, criticized the church leadership for not properly protecting the church from "christianophobia",[24] and condemned the synodal decision to require attendees to take a rapid test before entering the church.[25] Moreover, Hieronymus is viewed as inadequate, as someone who cannot properly represent either the Greeks or the Christians and the clergy.[26] Last but not least, following the overall Russophile tendency of the party family, GS opposed the decision of the Ecumenical Patriarchate to officially acknowledge the establishment of the autocephalous Orthodox Church of Ukraine, which was condemned by the Moscow Patriarchate as an uncanonical act.[27] On the other hand, GS could not afford closing the door to the Church and the religious constituency. From an ideological perspective, the 'mono-cultural' rationale of the Church allows the definition of the 'us vs. them' distinction along religious lines; thus, it establishes a framework according to which Islam is demonised and should be treated as a corrupting element.

Especially under archbishop Christodoulos, the Church participated directly in the generation of orientalist stereotypes socially directed to the exclusion of Islam, perceived as the "hostile" alien. This development had an indirect legitimizing effect on the overall radical-right framework in the public sphere: by establishing the nationalist discourse as part of the mainstream, it allowed the gradual de-stigmatization of the party family. Moreover, to avoid the accusation of anti-clericalism, GS became close to the fundamentalist circles within the Church, as well as the electorally important community of the Old Calendar. It also cultivated relations with some influential Mount Athos elders, which, in contrast to the institutional Church, constitute the authentic agents

---

24 Greek Solution, "Press Release on the Holy Synod Declaration", 16 November 2020, accessed 31 October 2022, https://elliniki-lisi.gr/anakoinosi-typou-gia-tin-anakoinosi-tis-ieras-synodou-epi-ton-syntonismenon-sykofantion-kata-tis-ekklisias.

25 Velopoulos, "Parliamentary Speech".

26 Kostas Chittas, "The Head of our Church is Inadequate—He does not Represent the Greeks", *Maronnews*, 11 July 2020, Audio, 5:39, accessed 31 October 2022, https://maronnews.gr/%ce%ba%cf%8e%cf%83%cf%84%ce%b1%cf%82-%cf%87%ce%ae%cf%84%ce%b1%cf%82-%ce%b1%ce%bd%ce%b5%cf%80%ce%b1%cf%81%ce%ba%ce%ae%cf%82-%ce%bf-%cf%80%cf%81%ce%bf%ce%ba%ce%b1%ce%b8%ce%ae%ce%bc%ce%b5%ce%bd%ce%bf/.

27 Kyriakos Velopoulos, "The Ukrainian Autocephaly was a Mistake of the Patriarch", *Vima Orthodoxias*, 20 January 2021, https://www.vimaorthodoxias.gr/nea/velopoylos-quot-lathos-toy-patriarchi-i-aytokefalia-stin-oykrania-mpikame-sto-mati-tis-rosias-quot-vinteo/.

of Orthodox faith in the popular religious perception. The question that arises then is whether this type of relationship between GS and the Church produces actual electoral effects, i.e. the alignment or not of the religious voters to the party. To this end, the next sections explore the correlation between religiosity and political attitudes as well as GS voting.

3   Religiosity and RR Attitudes on an Individual Level

This section explores the interaction of religiosity with nativism and Islamophobia, which form central elements of the RR platform. The WVS analysis uses the measure for the frequency of religious attendance, i.e. the question "Independently of marriages and funerals, how often do you attend religious services?" where the respondents respond on a scale from "more than once a week" to "practically never". To focus on anti-immigration attitudes, we used the following questions:

a. On this list are various groups of people. Could you please mention any that you would not like to have as neighbours? (Answer: Immigrants/foreign workers)
b. When jobs are scarce, employers should give priority to people of this country over immigrants. Do you agree, disagree or neither agree nor disagree with the following statements?
c. Immigration policy preference: How about people from other countries coming here to work. Which one of the following do you think the government should do? (Answer: Let anyone come/ As long as jobs available/ Strict limits/ Prohibit people from coming)

For measuring Islamophobia, we use the question:

d. On this list are various groups of people. Could you please mention any that you would not like to have as neighbours? (Answer: Muslims)

To factor in various socioeconomic differences, we also control for additional individual variables such as the age and the gender of the respondent, his/her educational level and employment status. Last, we introduce wave of the survey fixed effects, to capture the role of potential time specific shocks. Overall, the empirical findings demonstrate that there is systematic effect of church attendance on nativist attitudes in Greece. As Figure 10.1 shows, in Greece, more religiosity is positively and significantly associated with anti-immigration and Islamophobia. Analytically and in relation to each question illustrated in the graph, the more religious people become a) the more likely they are to mention that they do not want foreign neighbours; b) the more likely they are to agree

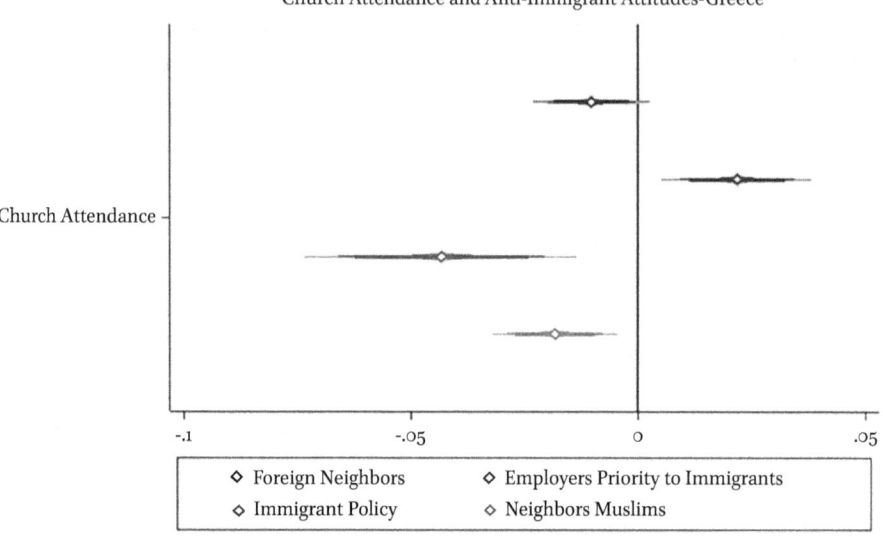

FIGURE 10.1 Church Attendance and Anti-Immigrant Attitudes in Greece
The figure illustrates graphically how church attendance affects anti-immigrant attitudes in Greece. Each line (indicated by different shades of grey) illustrates a different result. To facilitate the interpretation the lines in the figure appear in the same order as in the legend. The first line indicates attitudes towards foreign neighbours, the second line indicates attitudes towards whether employers should give priority to natives or immigrants, the third indicates attitudes towards immigrant policy, and the last indicates attitudes towards having Muslims as neighbours.

with the statement that priority of employers should be given to natives; c) the stricter immigrant policy they want; and d) the more likely they are to mention that they do not want Muslim neighbours.[28]

---

28 To "read" the plot, note that it is a "coefplot". In a coefplot, the estimated effects of an independent variable on various dependent variables are illustrated. Here, church attendance is considered the independent variable to understand its impact on different attitudes about immigrants, which are the dependent variables. The diamonds on the plot show the estimated impact of church attendance on each attitude. If a diamond is to the right of the central zero line, it suggests that higher church attendance might be associated with more of that particular attitude; a diamond to the left would suggest an association with less of that attitude. However, the reliability of these associations is determined by the horizontal lines, or confidence intervals, that stretch from each diamond. If these lines cross the zero point, it means the association isn't statistically significant and we can't be sure that church attendance is really affecting those attitudes. In this plot, most of the lines do not cross the zero line, which indicates statistical significance. The one that crosses the zero point does so marginally, indicating significance at the 5% level.

4 Religious Voting for the GS

4.1 The Data

The analysis employs data from the European Election Studies dataset which corresponds to the last European parliamentary elections of 2019. The analysis uses a measure of religious attendance, i.e., the frequency of attendance at religious services. As far as RR voting is concerned, our dependent variable is based on the question: "Which party did you vote for in the recent European Parliament elections?". All the main political parties are mentioned in the answer. To focus on RR voting, we used the responses to construct a binary variable. The variable takes the value 1 if the individual has voted for one of the RR parties with parliamentary representation in 2019, i.e., the Golden Dawn (GD), Independent Greeks (IG) and the GS and 0 otherwise. We call this constructed variable "Radical Right Voting". Finally, the EES also provides information about several demographics such as the age of the respondent, the gender, the occupation, and the level of education achieved. We also have information about the region in which the respondent lives, this we control for regional fixed effect capturing unobservables at the regional level.

4.2 Empirical Strategy

In this section we implement a regression analysis to estimate the effect of religiosity on RR voting for the European Parliament.

Regression analysis is a statistical method used to examine the relationship between a dependent variable and one or more independent variables. In our case, the dependent variable of interest is voting behavior for the European Parliament, specifically the vote share for a particular political party or group. The independent variable of interest is religiosity.

To estimate the effect of religiosity on voting behavior we construct a regression model that predicts the vote share for the European Parliament based on the level of religiosity among individuals. The regression model allows us to estimate the relationship between religiosity and voting behavior while controlling for other relevant factors, such as demographics.

The estimated model for regressing the 2019 voting and the religiosity variables is given by

$$RW_{ig} = \alpha_0 + \alpha_1 R_{ig} + \alpha_2 I_i + \alpha_3 RG_g + \varepsilon_{ig}$$

Where RW_i is a measure of RR voting for the European Parliament (EP) election of individual i, residing in region g of Greece, who participated in the 2019

EES round. R_{ig} is a measure of religiosity as captured by attendance of religious services for individual I, residing in region g. The analysis controls for a vector of individual controls, I_i such as age, age square, gender, occupation, and educational level. RG_g is a regional fixed effect capturing unobserved heterogeneity at the regional level. ε_{ig} is an individual specific error term. The analysis employs robust standard errors.

4.3 Religiosity and the Vote for the Radical Right in Greece: Empirical Findings

Table 10.1 illustrates the results for the 2019 election for the EP. In particular, Column (1) regresses the measure of RR voting in the year 2019 on the degree of religiosity while controlling only for the full set of individual characteristics. The findings suggest that the coefficient for religiosity is statistically significant. Column (2) augments the analysis by introducing a set of regional fixed effects that capture unobserved regional characteristics of regions in Greece. We refer to Column (2) as the benchmark specification that contains the full set of controls. In Columns (1) and (2) we run Ordinary Least Squares regressions. The findings of Column (2) suggest that there is a significant effect of religiosity on RR voting. Column (3) replicates the analysis using a Probit model and confirms the findings of the benchmark specification. However, despite the

TABLE 10.1 Religious attendance and radical right voting-2019 (1)

Dep. var: Radical right voting	(1)	(2)	(3)
Religious attendance	0.044***	−0.036***	−0.034***
	(0.008)	(0.009)	(0.010)
Obs	884	761	761
R-Squared	0.028	0.114	

Summary: This table establishes that stronger religiosity has significant effect on the probability of the individual to vote for a radical-right party in the 2019 EP elections. However, the magnitude of the effect is rather small. The analysis controls for individual characteristics such as age, educational level, occupation and regional fixed effects that capture region specific unobservable shocks.

Note: (i) Robust standard error estimates are reported in parentheses; (ii) *** denotes statistical significance at the 1 percent level, ** at the 5 percent level, and * at the 10 percent level, all for two-sided hypothesis tests.

statistical significance, it is crucial to find out about the actual significance of the results. To interpret the magnitude of the coefficient we use the results of Column (3) that are easier to interpret as probabilities. When we estimate the marginal effect, we find that it is rather low (0.01), i.e., a unitary change in the religiosity index (which takes values from 1–7) is associated with 0.01 higher probability to vote for the Radical Right. *Therefore, this effect is rather small or even trivial.* We thus need to be cautious about the actual interpretation of our findings.

We further break down our findings in Table 10.2, by testing whether religiosity affects the probability of voting for each of the radical-right parties separately for the 2019 EP elections. Column (1) employs as the dependent variable the probability to vote for the GS, Column (2) for GD and Column (3) for ANEL. All three columns employ the full set of controls as in the benchmark specification and use a Probit model. Interesting it is only Column (1) that appears to yield a statistically significant effect of religiosity on the probability to vote for the GS. However, if we estimate the marginal effect (-0.004) we notice that this effect is also rather small, i. e. a change of one unit in the religiosity variable is associated with a 0.004 change in the probability to vote for the GS.

TABLE 10.2   Religious attendance and radical right voting-2019 (2)

	(1)	(2)	(3)
Dep. var: Voting for	GS	GD	ANEL
religious attendance	−0.010**	−0.007	0.001
	(0.004)	(0.005)	(0.001)
Obs	761	761	761
Region FE	Yes	Yes	Yes

Summary: This table establishes that stronger religiosity has a positive significant effect on the probability of the individual to vote for GS in the 2019 EP elections, but not for GD or ANEL (higher values of the religious attendance variable indicate lower attendance). However, the magnitude of the effect is rather small. The analysis controls for individual characteristics such as age, age square, gender, educational level, occupation and regional fixed effects that capture region specific unobservable shocks.

Note: (i) Robust standard error estimates are reported in parentheses; (ii) *** denotes statistical significance at the 1 percent level, ** at the 5 percent level, and * at the 10 percent level, all for two-sided hypothesis tests.

5   Conclusions

The relation between populism and religion has ideological, political, electoral, social and economic aspects. It is of course not only a current Greek phenomenon, nor is it linked solely to the Eastern Orthodox countries, but forms a constitutive feature of US politics, has strong links to the development of political Islam, and is closely related to movements attached to various religious traditions. Moreover, it is not only political populist actors that employ religion, but religious agents that have articulated a populist discourse as well. The present chapter, therefore, does not cover this broad thematic, but focuses on the current dominant populist radical-right party in Greece, i.e. Greek Solution, empirically studying the possible acceptance by the religious body of its central ideological features, namely nativism and Islamophobia. Moreover, the article elaborates on the theme of religious voting and particularly whether the religious electorate aligned to the Greek Solution party or not. Overall, the findings of the research confirm from a quantitative perspective the view that the religious discourse has an overall positive effect for the legitimization of the RR ideological frame. In particular, the empirical evidence suggests that our hypothesis that religiosity is positively correlated to Islamophobia and xenophobia is correct. However, this effect has not signified a political alignment of the religious electorate to the RR party family in 2019 election.

The Covid-19 pandemic and the war in Ukraine have posed challenging questions for the Greek Radical Right and GS in particular, since it formed the political representative of the anti-vax movement and has kept an openly pro-Russian stance both in relation to the war in Ukraine as well as to the autocephaly question of the Ukrainian Church, for which the institutional Church has followed the complete opposite path. Moreover, the last national elections (2023) were marked by the rise of the radical-right party Niki (Victory), which set religion, family values, and traditional values among its signature issues, thereby gaining substantial support from the religious constituency. This development renders Niki a political rival to the GS, with which it must compete for acquiring the issue ownership over the religious nationalist agenda. Whether, therefore, the GS political positioning might drive the religious voting in its favor remains to be seen. In any case, the volatility of Greek party politics during the last decade suggests that any political realignment, even that of the traditionally cemented religious constituency, might not be highly probable, but it should at least not come as a surprise.

Bibliography

(2019). "The Church Hammers Velopoulos". *Ta Nea*, 1 July 2019 https://www.tanea.gr/2019/07/01/politics/sfyrokopima-apo-tin-ekklisia-kata-velopoulou/.

(2022). "Greek Solution on Ukraine: Make it Clear that no one Can Murder Greeks and Go Unpunished". *Naftemporiki*, 14 February 2022. Accessed 9 October 2023. https://www.naftemporiki.gr/politics/1297574/elliniki-lysi-gia-oukrania-na-ginei-safes-oti-oudeis-borei-na-dolofonei-ellines-kai-na-menei-atimoritos/.

(2024). "The Blasphemous Book of Velopoulos". *EFSYN*, 28 May 2019. Accessed 31 October 2022. https://www.efsyn.gr/politiki/201547_blasfimo-biblio-toy-belopoyloy.

Brubaker, R. (2017). "Between Nationalism and Civilizationism: The European Populist Moment in Comparative Perspective". *Ethnic and Racial Studies* 40, no. 8: 1191–1226. https://doi.org/10.1080/01419870.2017.1294700.

Chittas, K. (2020). "The Head of our Church is Inadequate—He does not Represent the Greeks". *Maronnews*, 11 July. Audio, 5:39. Accessed 31 October 2022. https://maronnews.gr/%ce%ba%cf%8e%cf%83%cf%84%ce%b1%cf%82-%cf%87%ce%ae%cf%84%ce%b1%cf%82-%ce%b1%ce%bd%ce%b5%cf%80%ce%b1%cf%81%ce%ba%ce%ae%cf%82-%ce%bf-%cf%80%cf%81%ce%bf%ce%ba%ce%b1%ce%b8%ce%ae%ce%bc%ce%b5%ce%bd%ce%bf/.

Doganyilmaz Duman, D. (2021). "Religious Identities in Times of Crisis: an Analysis of Europe". In: J. Cornelio, F. Gauthier, T. Martikainen, and L. Woodhead (eds.). *Routledge International Handbook of Religion in Global Society*. London: Routledge. Pp. 432–443.

Franklin, M. (2005). "The Fading Power of National Politics to Structure Voting Behaviour in Elections to the European Parliament". Paper prepared for the Budapest Conference on the European Election Study, May 2005.

Greek Solution. (2019a). "An Overview of the Greek Solution Founding Principles". 5 March 2019. Accessed 31 October 2022. https://elliniki-lisi.gr/sinopsi-ton-programmatikon-theseon-tis-ellinikis-lisis.

Greek Solution. (2019b). "The 12 points of Greek Solution programme". 11 May 2019. Accessed 31 October 2022. https://elliniki-lisi.gr/ta-12-simeia-tou-programmatos-tis-ellinikis-lisis.

Greek Solution. (2020a). "Press Release: Proposal for Amending Law 927/1979 concerning Christianophobia and Blasphemy". 3 September 2020. Accessed 31 October 2022. https://elliniki-lisi.gr/anakoinosi-typou-i-elliniki-lysi-katethese-protasi-nomou-gia-tin-syblirosi-tou-nomou-927-1979-opos-tropopoiithike-apo-ton-nomo-4285-2014-anaforika-me-tin-christianofovia-kai-tin-prosvoli-kai-exyvri.

Greek Solution. (2020b). "Press Release: Nea Democratia and Syriza Target the Church one more time". 2 November 2020. Accessed 31 October 2022. https://elliniki-lisi.gr/anakoinosi-typou-i-ekklisia-akoma-mia-fora-sto-stochastro-neas-dimokratias-kai-syriza.

Greek Solution. (2020c). "Press Release on the Holy Synod Declaration". 16 November 2020. Accessed 31 October 2022. https://elliniki-lisi.gr/anakoinosi-typou-gia-tin-anakoinosi-tis-ieras-synodou-epi-ton-syntonismenon-sykofantion-kata-tis-ekklisias.

Greek Solution. (2021a). "Press Release: the Greek Solution MP in European Parliament was the only representative of a Greek Party Downvoting LGBT Marriage and Adoption". 19 September 2021. Accessed 31 October 2022. https://elliniki-lisi.gr/anakoinosi-typou-o-efrovoulevtis-tis-ellinikis-lysis-o-monos-ekprosopos-ellinikou-kommatos-pou-katapsifise-ton-gamo-kai-tin-apoktisi-paidion-apo-loatki.

Greek Solution. (2021b). "Press Release: Orthodoxy is targeted by the Government and the Opposition". 5 November 2021. Accessed 31 October 31. https://elliniki-lisi.gr/anakoinosi-typou-protofanis-i-stochopoiisi-tis-orthodoxias-apo-kyvernisi-kai-antipolitefsi.

Greek Solution. (2022a). "Burglars attacked the church of Agia Paraskevi in Artemida of Attica". 2 May 2022. Accessed 31 October 2022. https://elliniki-lisi.gr/thema-stochos-diarrikton-i-ekklisia-tis-agias-paraskevis-stin-artemida-attikis.

Greek Solution. (2022b). "Closure of the Ecclesiastical School of Chania". 15 June 2022. Accessed 31 October 2022. https://elliniki-lisi.gr/thema-titloi-telous-gia-tin-ekklisiastiki-scholi-sta-chania.

Greek Solution. (N.d.). "Founding Declaration". Accessed 31 October 2022. https://elliniki-lisi.gr/idritiki-diakiriksi.

Haynes, J. (2020). "Right-Wing Populism and Religion in Europe and the USA". *Religions* 11, no. 10: 490. https://doi.org/10.3390/rel11100490.

Hedetoft, U. (2020). "Nationalism and the Political Theology of Populism: Affect and Rationality in Contemporary Identity Politics". In: F. Höhne and T. Meireis (eds.). *Religion and Neo-Nationalism in Europe*. Baden-Baden: Nomos. Pp. 99–114.

Marzouki, N., D. McDonnell, and O. Roy, eds. (2016). *Saving the People: How Populists Hijack Religion*. London: Hurst.

Moffitt, B. (2017). "Liberal Illiberalism? The Reshaping of the Contemporary Populist Radical Right in Northern Europe". *Politics and Governance* 5, no. 4: 112–122. https://doi.org/10.17645/pag.v5i4.996.

Mudde, C. (2007). *Populist Radical Right Parties in Europe*. Cambridge: Cambridge University Press.

Papastathis, K. (2015). "Religious Discourse and Radical Right Politics in Contemporary Greece, 2010–2014". *Politics, Religion and Ideology* 16, no. 2–3: 218–247. https://doi.org/10.1080/21567689.2015.1077705.

Papastathis, K., and A. Litina. (2021). "Orthodoxy as Exclusivist Identity in the Greek Radical Right: Discourse Analysis and Electoral Behavior". In: A. Hennig and M. Weiberg-Salzmann (eds.). *Illiberal Politics and Religion in Europe and Beyond: Concepts, Actors, and Identity Narratives*. Frankfurt: Campus. Pp. 291–316.

Psarras, D. (2019). *A Little Bit of Nazism by Kyriakos Velopoulos*. Athens: Ekdoseis EFSYN.

Stavrakakis, Y. (2003). "Politics and Religion: on the 'Politicization' of Greek Church Discourse". *Journal of Modern Greek Studies* 21, no. 2: 153–181. https://muse.jhu.edu/article/47675/pdf.

Velopoulos, K. (2020). "Parliamentary Speech on 21 January 2020". Greek Solution. Accessed 31 October 2022. https://elliniki-lisi.gr/kyriakos-velopoulos-topothetisi-stin-olomelia-gia-themata-pedias.

Velopoulos, K. (2021). "The Ukrainian Autocephaly was a Mistake of the Patriarch", *Vima Orthodoxias*, 20 January 2021. https://www.vimaorthodoxias.gr/nea/velopoylos-quot-lathos-toy-patriarchi-i-aytokefalia-stin-oykrania-mpikame-sto-mati-tis-rosias-quot-vinteo/.

Zoumboulakis, Stavros. (2013). *Golden Dawn and the Church*. Athens: Polis.

CHAPTER 11

Belonging without Attending? National Identity and Contemporary Religious Patterns in Serbia

Marko Veković

1   Introduction

In the days when Serbia was part of the communist Yugoslavia, people often joked about religion and religiosity. They would say something like "the only time when a Serb goes to Church is when he or she is sick", or "when it is raining outside". Yet Serbia has been free of the communist regime for over three decades now, and during that period a lot of things have changed. Perhaps one of the most important changes that Serbian society has experienced is the "resurgence of religion",[1] a widely recognised phenomenon in the post-communist countries across Eastern Europe and the globe,[2] and a process also referred to as the "de-secularization".[3]

Today, Serbia is a multi-religious country with the total population of 6.6 million (without Kosovo and Metohija). The latest 2022 census data show that 81% of the total population identify with Orthodox Christianity, 3.9% with Catholicism, 0.8% with Protestantism, and 4.1% with Islam. A small minority of

---

1   See Monica Toft, Daniel Philptt, and Timothy Shah, *God's Century, Resurgent Religion and Global Politics* (New York: W.W. Norton & Company, 2011); Pippa Norris and Ronald Inglehart, *Sacred and Secular: Religion and Politics Worldwide* (Cambridge: Cambridge University Press, 2004); Miroljub Jevtić, "Political Science and Religion", *Politics and Religion Journal* 1, no. 1 (2007): 59–69.

2   See Ani Sarkissian, "Religious Reestablishment in Post-Communist Polities", *Journal of Church and State* 51, no. 3 (2009): 472–501; Jonathan Fox, *Introduction to Religion and Politics, Theory and Practice* (London: Routledge, 2018); Marko Veković, *Democratization in Christian Orthodox Europe: Comparing Greece, Serbia and Russia* (London: Routledge, 2021); Jonathan Fox, *A World Survey of Religion and the State* (New York: Cambridge University Press, 2008); Mirko Blagojević, "Desecularization of Contemporary Serbian Society", *Occasional Papers on Religion in Eastern Europe* 28, no. 1 (2008): 37–50; Mirko Blagojević, "Revitalization of Religion and Religiousness in Serbia: Reality of a Myth?", *Filozofija i društvo* 20, no. 2 (2009): 97–117.

3   Peter Berger, *The Desecularization of the World: Resurgent of Religion and World Politics* (Grand Rapids, MI: William B. Eerdmans Publishing Company, 1999); Jose Casanova, *Public Religions in the Modern World* (Chicago: University of Chicago Press, 1994).

the population are Jewish, 1% are atheists, and 2.5% did not declare their religiosity, while 5.3% declared their religiosity as "unknown".[4] This is in accordance with most relevant international surveys, including the most recent European Values Study (EVS) of 2017.[5] Thus, even though several religions are present in Serbia, the Serbian Orthodox Church (SOC, or the Church) is a "dominant religious actor in the country".[6] Nevertheless, if you take a stroll down the streets of Belgrade, or any other city or village in Serbia on a Sunday morning, you will find (mostly) empty Orthodox Christian churches. This chapter explores the question: why do Serbs not attend church regularly?

It is logical to presume that the answer lies in trust. If people do not trust the Church, it is more likely that they will not attend religious services; and vice versa, if people do trust the Church, they are more likely to attend. And yet it is quite the opposite in Serbia: studies show that since the fall of communism, the SOC is one of the most trusted institutions in the country.[7] This chapter argues that religiosity in Serbia is dominantly understood as a part of a national identity, culture, and tradition. Serbs belong to the SOC as a matter of 'belonging', but for historical and political reasons, this is not reflected in church attendance. Moreover, the significance of the church lies primarily in culture, tradition, and identity, and as such could be understood as 'belonging without attending'. The notion of belonging without attending, together with close church-state relations, explains why the SOC can assert its political significance and even instrumentalise its connections with the political elite to pursue its own interests. Such patterns are present in various post-communist states where Orthodoxy is the dominant religion, including Russia, Bulgaria, Ukraine, Romania and Moldova.

Various chapters within this volume help us understand these issues in a more detailed fashion, particularly the Russian case. For example, Veronica Cibotaru claims that there is a shared ideological discourse by the Russian government and the Russian Orthodox Church, while Dmitry Bintsarovskyi analyses the political instrumentalization of Russian Orthodox philosophy. Also, a

---

4 Statistical Office of the Republic of Serbia, "2022 Census of Population, Households and Dwellings on the population of the Republic of Serbia by ethno-cultural characteristics", accessed 22 June 2023, https://popis2022.stat.gov.rs/en-US/5-vestisaopstenja/news-events/20230616-st.
5 European Values Study, accessed 15 January 2023 https://europeanvaluesstudy.eu/.
6 Veković, *Democratization in Christian Orthodox Europe*, 71.
7 See, for example, Miloš Jovanović and Danijela Gavrilović, "Trust and Legitimation", in *Social and Cultural Capital in Western Balkan Societies*, eds. Predrag Cvetičanin and Ana Birešev (Niš: Center for Empirical Cultural Studies of South-East Europe and The Institute for Philosophy and Social Theory, 2012), 138–40.

more general insights into these issues can be found in the chapter by Petr Kratochvíl, who analyses the relationship between religion and populism and argues that the anti-liberal stances of the new populists are a consequence of the populist politics of faith. Finally, Jenny Leith explores how the forms of national belonging and community can be fostered by the relationship of national churches to national space and identity, suggesting that Churches can identify national spaces as their ecclesial identity—which is particularly important for the Serbian case.

The goals of this chapter are threefold. Expected findings include a relatively high level of belonging as well as believing in Serbia—but significantly low scores on church attendance. This fact is of particular importance to the argument that low church attendance is of utmost importance for understanding patterns of believing without attending in Serbia, especially in light of the liturgically important Sunday service, which in the Orthodox tradition is understood to be "mandatory act which is the only rightful way of making a connection with God".[8] Secondly, this chapter explains why Serbs do not attend church regularly, based on an ethnographic survey of Sunday liturgy in 33 Churches across Serbia in April and May of 2022. Finally, this chapter explores why the Serbian Orthodox Church can operate as a dominant religious actor in Serbia, considering the low attendance rates. If the strength of the relationship between religion, politics, and society depends on how thoroughly religious *values* are embedded in public opinion, political institutions, and public policy,[9] then organised religion would be the most obvious *institutional* purveyor of such values. This chapter argues that the social and political significance of the SOC is perhaps overrated, and that the influence it enjoys is solely a consequence of close church-state relations in Serbia.

The Serbian case holds relevance to the overall theme of this volume for several reasons. As indicated by the 2017 Pew study, religion plays a pivotal role in shaping the national identity in Serbia. This study shows that 78% of respondents considers that being an Orthodox Christian is very important or somewhat important for national identity, with 76% expressing a special connection with other Orthodox Christians in the world. Additionally, an overwhelming 95% express immense pride in their identity based on Orthodox

---

8 Mirko Blagojević, "Revitalization of Religion and Religiousness in Serbia: Reality of a Myth?", *Filozofija i društvo* 20, no. 2 (2009): 111–12.
9 Rada Drezgić, "Religion, politics, and gender in the context of nation-state formation: The case of Serbia", *Third World Quarterly* 31, no. 6 (2010): 955–70; Barbara-Ann J. Rieffer, "Religion and Nationalism: Understanding the Consequences of a complex relationship", *Ethnicities* 3, no. 2 (2003): 215–42; Paul A. Djupe and Brian R. Calfano, "Religious value priming, threat, and political tolerance", *Political Research Quarterly* 66, no. 4 (2012): 768–80.

Christianity.¹⁰ However, despite the strong attachment to religious identity, Serbs do not attend church regularly and show relatively low scores of religious observance. This disparity is compensated by the state in the post-communist era, with state acting as sort of a bridge between the SOC as an institution, and the people. Consequently, religion has become a tool often used by political elites for legitimization of their own agendas, by leveraging the significance of the SOC in the political, historical and historical spheres. However, it is also to be noted that the influence of the SOC extends well beyond Serbia's borders, encompassing Serbs in Montenegro and Republika Srpska (entity in the Bosnia and Herzegovina). This is a vivid illustration of the shared spatial imagination of the "Serbian World", recently embraced by several political parties in Serbia and the SOC, which does make a solid argument about the Orthodox Christian geopolitics in the region. The concept of the "Serbian World" is very similar to the concept of the "Russian World", which has been discussed in several contributions to this volume.

2   Theoretical Rationale

The downfall of communist Yugoslavia was a point when religion and religious actors became a part of the public space in all former Yugoslav republics. Whether it was the SOC in Serbia, the Catholic Church in Croatia, or Muslims in Bosnia, religion became a part of once rigidly secular spaces. From a theoretical point of view, it seems that the idea that these spaces nowadays are neither secular nor sacred is valid, and that spaces might contain "various ascriptions of meaning, even inherently incompatible ones".¹¹ In other words, public space in Serbia became "trans-liminal", containing a vivid example of the nexus between religion and nationalism. In her study on Islam in Türkiye, Gülay Türkmen illuminated the interconnection of ethnicity and religion, suggesting the possible priority of ethnicity over religion.¹² Her concept of ethno-religious nationalism is salient in that it "signifies and affirms the importance of both ethnicity and religion to the issue of belonging, while acknowledging that ethnic belonging

---

10   "Religious Beliefs and National Belonging in Central and Eastern Europe", PEW Research Center, 2017: 1–176.
11   M.D.C. van der Tol and P.S. Gorski, "Secularization as the fragmentation of the sacred and of sacred space", *Religion, State & Society* 50, no. 5 (2022): 508.
12   See: Gülay Türkmen, *Under the Banner of Islam: Turks, Kurds, and the Limits of Religious Unity* (Oxford University Press, 2021).

might take precedence over religious belonging".[13] In post-Yugoslav countries, and particularly in Serbia, it seems that ethnic belonging often equates to religious belonging, and, even though religious belonging to the SOC is often a key for ethnic and national identity, the churches across Serbia are mostly empty.

Even though measuring religiosity comes with several liabilities,[14] quantitative studies of religion are at the core of modern sociology of religion;[15] as Peter Farago argues, it still remains the "gold standard" of sociology of religion.[16] Such an approach facilitates a deeper understanding of important socio-cultural changes in a given society over time, and also to explore these changes longitudinally, to compare and analyse them alongside different socio-political contexts. The usual methodology for measuring religiosity is often expressed as the "three B's of religion", namely "believing, behaving, and belonging".[17] In short, *believing* refers to a set of questions aimed at finding out whether someone is a religious person, and whether they believe in God, life after death, heaven, and hell. It is important to note that this set of questions is mostly employed for research in the Western world and areas dominated by the three monotheistic religions. However, its employability in other parts of the world, such as Asia or Africa, is often criticised (see for example the critics of the 2021 Pew research on religion in India).[18] Meanwhile, *behaving* typically refers to a

---

13 Cited in Viktória Kóczián, "'This nest is for all kinds of birds'? National identity questions in the refugee reception of the Reformed Church in Hungary", *Religion, State & Society* 50, no. 5 (2022): 563.

14 Adam B. Cohen, Gina L. Mazza, and Jonathan E. Cook, "Theorizing and Measuring Religiosity Across Cultures", *Personality and Social Psychology Bulletin* 43, no. 12 (2017): 1724–36; Dobroslawa Wiktor-Mach, "Measuring Muslims: The Problems of Religiosity and Intra-Religious Diversity", *Annual Review of the Sociology of Religion* 3 (2012): 207–27.

15 See: Joseph H. Fichter, "Social Measurement of Religiosity", *Review of Religious Research* 10, no. 3 (1969): 169–177; Stefan Huber and Odilo W. Huber, "The Centrality of Religiosity Scale (CRS)", *Religions* 3, no. 3 (2012): 710–24; Steve Bruce, "Defining Religion: A Practical Response", *International Review of Sociology* 21, no. 1 (2011): 107–20; Ronald Jonhstone, *Religion in Society A Sociology of Religion* (New York: Routledge, 2015).

16 Peter Farago, "Foreword", in *Values and Identities in Europe Evidence from the European Social Survey,* ed. Michael Breen (London & New York: Routledge, 2017), XXI.

17 As suggested by Lyman A. Kellstedt, John C. Green, Jamel L. Guth and Corwin E. Smidt, "Is there a culture war? Religion and the 1996 election" (Paper presented at the Annual Meeting of the American Political Science Association, Washington DC, 28–31 August 1997). However, it should be noted that recent studies include the fourth B of religion, namely *bonding*. See more in Vassilis Saroglou, "Believing, Bonding, Behaving, and Belonging: The Big Four Religious Dimensions and Cultural Variation", *Journal of Cross-Cultural Psychology* 42, no. 8: 1320–40.

18 Neha Sahgal et al, "Religion in India: Tolerance and Segregation", Pew Research Centre, 29 June 2021, https://www.pewresearch.org/religion/2021/06/29/religion-in-india-tolerance-and-segregation/. This report initiated a debate and critiques of the methods

set of questions aimed at finding out the frequency of church attendance, fasting, praying, religious symbols, and participation in other religious practices. Once again, it works best in the areas dominated by the monotheistic religions. It is to be noted that church attendance is one of the most important indicators for religious behaving, which is often employed in the scientific study of religion as a key variable for predicting, for example, different political attitudes, or as a control variable.[19] Finally, *belonging* refers to the question of whether someone belongs to a religious organisation. Despite the common critiques of this approach, it is still true that by analysing these three sets of data we can learn a lot about religion and religiosity in a given society.

This approach has helped scholars of religion to make a significant impact in the field by analysing and comparing these three sets of data on religiosity, to come to a deeper understanding of the contemporary world. When Grace Davie argued that the future of religion in Great Britain can be described as "believing without belonging",[20] she actually claimed that we are witnessing the *de-institutionalisation of Christianity* on the one hand, and the *spiritualisation of religion,* on the other.[21] Her work made a significant impact in the field of sociology of religion, and not only that, further studies tested her claims: scholars went a step further and developed new ideas. For example, Tromp, Pless and Houtman tested the "believing without belonging" thesis across twenty European countries, and concluded that the foregrounded version of Davie's theory, the *"de-institutionalization of Christianity* needs to be rejected, while the typically unnoticed version of a *spiritualization of religion*

---

used: "The problem with surveys such as the latest one by Pew is the Abrahamic-modern idea of religion imposed upon a civilisation and country that has no equivalent word for it" (Makarand R. Paranjape, "Dharma is not the same as religion", *The Indian Express*, 24 July 2021, accessed 4 December 2022, https://www.newindianexpress.com/opinions/columns/2021/jul/24/dharma-is-not-the-same-as-religion-2334479.html).

19 See: Alan S. Gerber, Jonathan Gruber, and Daniel M. Hungerman, "Does Church Attendance Cause People to Vote? Using Blue Laws' Repeal to Estimate the Effect of Religiosity on Voter Turnout", *British Journal of Political Science* 46, no. 3 (2016): 481–500; Cristiano Vezzoni and Ferruccio Biolcati-Rinaldi, "Church Attendance and Religious Change in Italy, 1968–2010: A Multilevel Analysis of Pooled Datasets", *Journal for the Scientific Study of Religion* 54, no. 1 (2015): 100–118; Miloš Bešić and Marko Veković, "Image of God and Democratic Orientation: What kind of God Matters?" *Nordic Journal of Religion and Society* 36, no. 1 (2023): 4–18.

20 Grace Davie, "Believing without Belonging: Is this the Future of Religion in Britain?" *Social Compass* 37, no. 4 (1990): 455–69.

21 See: Paul Tromp, Anna Pless and Dick Houtman, "'Believing without Belonging' in Twenty European Countries (1981–2008) De-institutionalization of Christianity and Spiritualization of Religion", *Review of Religious Reseach* 62 (2020): 509–31.

is supported".[22] Needless to say, the "believing without belonging" thesis has been further tested in various outlets, and in different settings—resulting in different conclusions.[23]

For example, several studies suggest that it is better to use the phrase "belonging without believing" in analysing contemporary religiosity. That is why McIntosh flips Davie's idea in her analysis of the church as a community in a digital age. She claims that that there is a "significant move towards belonging without believing".[24] Furthermore, Oakes asks whether a person "can participate in religion without being a believer?" and concludes that "belonging without believing" is the best summary of this kind of believer.[25] A similar conclusion comes from Marchisio and Pisati as they analysed contemporary Italy, concluding that "while the Catholic Church has maintained its pre-eminent position in Italy's internal religious market, it has lost ground in recent decades and at present must contend with a considerable lack of both vitality and orthodoxy".[26] In his ethnographic study, Bullock focused on the secular congregation Sunday Assembly London, and concludes that those people "are still seeking to belong, but do not want to believe in a religious doctrine".[27] This specific pattern of religiosity Wollschleger and Beach call "subjective religious hypocrisy", in other words, belonging to a religious group but not believing in its tenets.[28] Finally, Mountford argues in *Christian Atheist: Belonging without Believing* that there are people who "value the cultural heritage of

---

22 Tromp, Pless and Houtman, "'Believing without Belonging' in Twenty European Countries".
23 See: Grace Davie, "Believing without Belonging: A Liverpool Case Study", *Archives de Sciences Sociales des Religions* 38, no. 81 (1993): 79–89; David Voas and Alasdair Crockett, "Religion in Britain: Neither Believing nor Belonging", *Sociology* 39, no. 1 (2005): 11–28; Jyoti Sahi, "Believing without Belonging? Some Reflections", *International Review of Mission* 92, no. 365 (2003): 227–40; John Vinod, *Believing without Belonging? Religious Beliefs and Social Belonging of Hindu Devotees of Christ* (Eugene: Pickwick Publications, 2020); Kerry Gallagher, "Dichotomy of Believing and Belonging—An Irish Context", *Journal of Sociological Research* 1, no. 1 (2009): 1–23.
24 Esther McIntosh, "Belonging without Believing: Church as Community in an Age of Digital Media", *International Journal of Public Theology* 9, no. 2 (2015): 131–55.
25 Kaya Oakes, "Belonging without Believing", *CrossCurrents* 65, no. 2 (2015): 229–38.
26 Roberto Marchisio and Maurizio Pisati, "Belonging without Believing: Catholics in Contemporary Italy", *Journal of Modern Italian Studies* 4, no. 2 (1999): 236–55.
27 Josh Bullock, "The Sociology of the Sunday assembly: 'belonging without believing' in a post-Christian context" (PhD thesis, Kingston University, 2018).
28 Jason Wollschleger and Lindsey R. Beach, "Religious Chameleons: Exploring the Social Context for Belonging without Believing", *Rationality and Society* 25, no. 2 (2013): 178–97.

Christianity—the language, art, music, moral compass, sense of transcendence—without actually believing in God".[29]

The phrase "belonging without attending" refers to a specific pattern of religiosity where people tend to claim to be part of or belong to a religious organisation primarily as a focal point of their national identity, show relatively high scores of believing in major doctrinal tenets, followed by (very) low scores on church attendance. What is particularly important here is the fact that such a religious pattern is mostly present in the post-communist countries of South-Eastern Europe (with one important outlier, namely Greece).[30] The PEW study on "Religious Belief and National Belonging in Central and Eastern Europe" illuminates this pattern:

> Many Central and Eastern Europeans might be described as 'believing and belonging, without behaving' … Survey shows that majority of adults across the region believe in God and identify with Orthodox Christianity, conventional measures of Christian religious behavior—such as levels of daily prayer and weekly worship attendance—are relatively low.[31]

And yet, scholars from the region tend to claim that the major religious pattern in Serbia is "belonging without believing". For example, Radmila Radić claims that "increased religiosity in Serbia [after the fall of communism] registered in censuses and surveys does not imply that it represents anything more than ethno-national identification, and is a consequence of ideological and political circumstances and not of any deeper personal beliefs and values".[32] Milan Vukomanović adds to this argument that "in case of Serbia, due to the significance of religious affiliation for the collective identity, we could speak of belonging without (deeper) believing, particularly when we analyse data

---

29 Brian Mountford, *Christian Atheist: Belonging without Believing* (Alresford: O-Books, 2011), 1.
30 The Greek case has been elaborated by Papasthatis and Litina in this volume. They wonder whether religiosity is correlated with two central ideological features of the right-wing "Greece Solution Party"—namely, nativism and islamophobia. They conclude that there is a positive correlation between religiosity and islamophobia in Greece, and that there is a shift within their voters towards pro-Russian stances on the war in Ukraine, and on the autocephality of the Ukrainian Orthodox Church.
31 Pew Research Centre, "Religious Belief and National Belonging in entral and Eastern Europe", 10 May 2017, pg. 7, https://www.pewresearch.org/religion/2017/05/10/religious-belief-and-national-belonging-in-central-and-eastern-europe/.
32 Radmila Radić, "Pripadanje bez verovanja i poznavanja", *Europe* 28, no. 1 (2008): 129.

from religious affiliation and genuine religiosity".[33] However, if we compare the level of *believing* in Serbia with other European countries covered in the EVS, we will not find any significant differences. The only significant difference is in *attending*.

3 Results and Discussion

In order to analyse the religiosity and consequently the religious pattern in contemporary Serbia, this section employs data from the 2017 EVS survey, focussing primarily on the set of questions regarding religiosity, and particularly *believing*. Descriptive statistics on these questions is showed in Tables 11.1 to 11.5. The first question addresses the self-understanding of people in Serbia, do they identity as a religious person, or as something else? Table 11.1 shows the results for the question: "Independently of whether you go to church, would you say you are …" 1) a religious person; 2) not a religious person; 3) a convinced atheist; 4) don't know; 5) no answer. The results show that 79.8% of people say they are a religious person, 13.9% say that they are not a religious person, and 6.3% are declared atheists. This data is in accordance with the 2011 census, and the 2015 PEW Study.

TABLE 11.1 Religious person: Data showing how people in Serbia identify in terms of religiosity, including categories such as religious, non-religious, or convinced atheist

		Frequency	Percent	Valid percent	Cumulative percent
Valid	A religious person	1112	74.2	79.8	79.8
	Not a religious person	193	12.9	13.9	93.7
	A convinced atheist	88	5.9	6.3	100.0
	Total	1393	92.9	100.0	
Missing	No answer	29	1.9		
	Don't know	77	5.1		
	Total	106	7.1		
Total		1499	100.0		

---

33 Milan Vukomanović, "Srpska pravoslavna crkva, desekularizacija i demokratija", *Poznanskie Studia Slawistyczne* 10 (2016): 269–79.

The second question, "Which, if any, of the following do you believe in?" comes with the possible answers God, life after death; hell; and heaven (Tables 11.2 to 11.5). According to sociological surveys, these items represent the core of the monotheistic belief system(s). When it comes to God, 85.4% believe, compared to 14.6% who do not. From a comparative Eastern European perspective, and from the perspective of the 2015 PEW survey, the data on whether people believe in God are not unusual or peculiar to Serbia.

In terms of *believing,* in life after death, hell, and heaven, the numbers from Serbia are significantly lower. For example, the majority of people, 59%, do not believe in life after death—something which is often emphasised as a core Christian belief—compared to 41% who do.

TABLE 11.2 Belief in God: Data showing the percentage of people in Serbia who believe in God

		Frequency	Percent	Valid percent	Cumulative percent
Valid	No	206	13.7	14.6	14.6
	Yes	1202	80.2	85.4	100.0
	Total	1408	93.9	100.0	
Missing	No answer	19	1.3		
	Don't know	72	4.8		
	Total	91	6.1		
Total		1499	100.0		

TABLE 11.3 Belief in life after death: Data showing the percentage of people in Serbia who believe in life after death

		Frequency	Percent	Valid percent	Cumulative percent
Valid	No	745	49.7	59.0	59.0
	Yes	518	34.6	41.0	100.0
	Total	1263	84.3	100.0	
Missing	No answer	26	1.7		
	Don't know	210	14.0		
	Total	236	15.7		
Total		1499	100.0		

TABLE 11.4 Belief in hell: Data showing the percentage of people in Serbia who believe in hell

		Frequency	Percent	Valid percent	Cumulative percent
Valid	No	801	53.4	63.1	63.1
	Yes	469	31.3	36.9	100.0
	Total	1270	84.7	100.0	
Missing	No answer	32	2.1		
	Don't know	197	13.1		
	Total	229	15.3		
Total		1499	100.0		

TABLE 11.5 Belief in heaven: Data indicating the percentage of people in Serbia who believe in heaven

		Frequency	Percent	Valid percent	Cumulative percent
Valid	No	743	49.6	58.2	58.2
	Yes	534	35.6	41.8	100.0
	Total	1277	85.2	100.0	
Missing	No answer	31	2.1		
	Don't know	191	12.7		
	Total	222	14.8		
Total		1499	100.0		

The difference is even more present when it comes to belief in hell. The majority of people in Serbia, 63.1%, do not believe in hell, compared to 39.9% who do believe in hell.

Finally, the percentage of people who believe in heaven, 41.8%, is also smaller compared to those who do not believe in heaven, 58.2%.

Of course, descriptive statistics come with certain disadvantages. However, these numbers give insight into general religious processes in Serbia since the fall of communism. From a comparative perspective, the lower numbers for *believing* in Serbia are nothing new when compared to other post-communist societies in Eastern Europe. Thus, the Serbian case does not affirm Tromp, Pless and Houtman's observation about the de-institutionalisation of Christianity. And yet, they also argue in favour of the spiritualisation of religion argument, which is supported in Western Europe. From the 2017 EVS data on Serbia, it appears that this thesis too should be rejected. The low level of believing in Serbia is such that the spiritualisation of religion is not supported by data. At the same time, from a comparative perspective it seems that the level of *believing* in Serbia is in accordance with the European context, and specifically with other post-communist countries.

Based on these data, it follows that the vast majority of the population in Serbia considers themselves religious, and that majority of population believes in God. On the other hand, EVS, PEW and the 2022 census data show that the majority of the Serbian population *belongs* to a religious organisation (mostly to the dominant religious organisation, the Serbian Orthodox Church), and that the level of *believing* is not significantly different from that of other European countries. Thus, one should expect the level of church attendance, as the main indicator of *behaving*, to be in accordance with these two categories. However, the data show that Serbs do not attend church frequently. The EVS questionnaire has a specific question on church attendance (q.15): "Apart from weddings, funerals, and christenings, about how often do you attend religious services these days?" Results from the Serbian case are given in the Table 11.6.

TABLE 11.6 How often do you attend religious services: Data reflecting the frequency of church attendance in Serbia, showing how often individuals participate in religious services

		Frequency	Percent	Valid percent	Cumulative percent
Valid	More than once a week	23	1.5	1.6	1.6
	Once a week	98	6.5	6.6	8.2
	Once a month	216	14.4	14.7	22.9
	Only on special holy days/Christmas/Easter days	494	33.0	33.5	56.4
	Once a year	120	8.0	8.1	64.5
	Less often	235	15.7	15.9	80.5
	Never, practically never	288	19.2	19.5	100.0
	Total	1474	98.3	100.0	
Missing	No answer	16	1.1		
	Don't know	9	.6		
	Total	25	1.7		
Total		1499	100.0		

Of the total population, 19.5% never, or practically never, goes to church, followed by 15.9% of those who say that they attend religious services less often than once a year. The most frequent attendance of religious services in Serbia is on special holy days (namely Christmas and Easter), which accounts for about 33.5% of the total sample. However, the most striking results are that only 1.6% attend religious services more than once a week, and only 6.6% attend religious services once a week. Although church attendance is low among Serbs, most of the Serbian Orthodox Christian families celebrate their family's patron saint (*slava*), and most of them attend church on the day of *slava*.[34] Thus, the data suggest that religious patterns in contemporary Serbia can be best described as 'belonging without attending', and yet, it still remains unclear why this is the case.

This question is addressed on the basis of fieldwork carried out in 2022 surrounding the Sunday liturgy in 33 churches across Serbia. The guiding questions were: "How many people attended the Sunday liturgy?", "How many people participated in holy communion or the Eucharist?", and "Why do people not attend church more often?" The first two questions were addressed through participant observation, while semi-structured interviews with priests illuminated the third, as summarised below.

The general impression was that the churches in Serbia are *mostly empty* on Sunday morning. The number of people who attended the Sunday liturgy varied from 4 to 110, depending on the demographics of the area where a given church is located. The number of people who participated in holy communion or the Eucharist was even lower. Also, the *urban versus rural* variable did not work. It was expected that attendance in rural areas would be higher compared to urban areas, however, this was not the case. This can be explained by the fact that the Serbian villages are getting emptier as people tend to move to the urban areas. One of the interviews indicated that the Church struggles to appoint priests to work in rural areas and that the Church pays them extra to work there. The *age variable* did not work either: Though it was expected that the older generations would attend church more frequently, the data show quite the contrary. The majority of people who attended the Sunday

---

34 *Slava* (celebration, or christened celebration) is a family custom of annual celebration of a patron saint. Celebration of slava distinguishes Serbs from all other Christian communities. According to Sabina Hadžibulić, "Besides Christmas and Easter the slava is one of the most important celebrations in the life of every family. Its unique status was recognised internationally, in November 2014, when the slava celebration was included in the UNESCO's Lists of Intangible Cultural Heritage, thus becoming the first Serbian intangible cultural asset to be registered" (Sabina Hadžibulić, "The *Slava* celebration: A Private and a Public Matter", *Temenos* 53, no. 1 (2017): 31).

liturgy in Serbia are younger. Furthermore, the data show that women attend church more frequently than men, which was expected.

Some of the interviews took place after the liturgy. As was expected, not all of them wanted to participate and discuss the matter of church attendance. Their reasoning was usually the lack of blessing from their Bishop, as it is quite common in the SOC that a priest should always ask for a blessing first if he wanted to participate in something that is not a part of his duties as a clergyman. This is why it is so hard to do interviews with many of the SOC's clergy. Every single priest who wanted to take part in the survey and reply to the questions wanted to remain anonymous. Of the 33 churches surveyed, about twenty priests agreed to the interview. Every single priest agreed that church attendance is quite low, but the rationale they offered varied significantly. Some of the answers were amusing, for example that people do not attend the church because it is early in the morning, or that people usually have something else planned for Sunday. One priest told me that "going to a liturgy is not fancy". However, it seems to be that SOC's clergy is widely concerned by the fact that people, in general, do not understand the very meaning of the liturgy.

Thus, part of the survey results is in line with the priests' concerns, as they argued that "people don't understand what liturgy is, what it represents, and why it is so central for the Church". Some clergy are "worried about how the Church communicates with the people"; on my remark that might be because the Church is so focused on the state and the politics, I received a confirmatory nodding of the head. However, it seems that the most common answer to the question of why Serbs do not regularly attend church lies in the communist heritage. Most of the interviewed priests agreed that the main reason for the low church attendance in Serbia is actually the communist heritage, and the lack of traditional and continuous family attendance which could be passed on from generation to generation. Therefore, most of them were very pleased to see that younger people, born in the mid-1990s and later, are the among the most frequent church goers in Serbia.

4 Why Does it Matter?

The data provide a strong case for understanding the contemporary religious pattern in Serbia as a "belonging without attending" and suggest that the major driving force for the low religious attendance in Serbia is the communist heritage. However, why does it matter? Besides trying to understand the general religiosity in Serbia, the set of data provided in this chapter can illuminate the political role of the SOC in Serbia. It is logical to presume that the political power of a religious actor is primarily based in the religiosity of the people and in the extent to which thoroughly religious values are embedded in public opinion, political institutions, and public policy. For this reason, religious attendance is an important predictor of political behaviour in the United States, for example.[35] Also, religious attendance is an important factor in explaining political socialisation in the United States.[36] In other words, churches need people to attend their services to assert themselves as a political actor. However, what happens if the churches are empty?

Elizabeth Prodromou claims that the Orthodox Christian churches serve as a focal point of identity across South-Eastern Europe for doctrinal as well as historical reasons:[37] *doctrinal,* in that the church is autocephalous or autonomous, in that its borders are often aligned with state borders, and in that the church is regarded as a national church; *historical,* in that Eastern European countries have often been under occupation of foreign states and empires, and that these circumstances created a strong alliance between ethnicity, church and state. That is why the SOC has a specific position in the Serbian society and serves as a focal point of the national identity.[38]

It is quite possible that the political significance of the SOC is overrated, as it is not based in the religiosity of the people, but in the need of political actors to have the support of the Church. This is backed up by the fact that political behaviour in Serbia is mostly dependent on variables such as education, income, rural versus urban, and not by religiosity per se. This is relevant to various political issues, including but not limited to membership of the European Union, the status of LGBTQIA+ community, the status of Kosovo and Metohija, and, at the present time, to Russian aggression in Ukraine. However, the political role of the SOC cannot be overestimated in the field of political legitimization in contemporary Serbia. As Jonathan Fox puts it: "Religion is one of the few things that can legitimate nearly anything".[39] This is particularly important

---

35   See: John Green, *The Faith Factor: How Religion Influences American Elections* (Westport: Praeger Publishers, 2007); Robert Putnam and David Campbell, *American Grace: How Religion Divides and Unites Us* (New York: Simon & Shuster, 2012); Corwin E. Smidt, "The Role of Religion in 2016 American presidential elections", *Z Religion Ges Polit* 133, no. 1 (2017): 133–62.
36   Kenneth Wald and A. Calhoun-Brown, *Religion and Politics in the United States* (Lanham, MD: Rowman and Littlefield, 2011).
37   Elizabeth Prodromou, "Christianity and Democracy: The Ambivalent Orthodox", *Journal of Democracy* 15, no. 2 (2004): 62–75.
38   See a more detailed analysis in: Veković, *Democratization in Christian Orthodox Europe,* 63–71.
39   Fox, *Introduction to Religion and Politics, Theory and Practice,* 60.

for the Serbian context, where religion is seen as a key part of the national identity, and the SOC is close to the state, particularly since 2012.

The close relationship between church and state in Serbia has been strongly relayed in the state media and affirmed by visits of President Aleksandar Vučić to the SOC and its Patriarch Porfirije. From the perspective of the State, such an alliance is needed for the wider legitimisation of its authoritarian policies and is based on the shared idea of defending the core values and identity of the Serbian people. This fact can be best seen from the notable silence of the SOC during the mass protests against the regime in Serbia since 2018. At the same time, the SOC did not raise its voice against the decline of democracy in Serbia in recent years, and the rising authoritarian tendencies. Finally, the SOC is one of the few Orthodox churches that did not condemn the Russian invasion of Ukraine, similarly to the position of the Serbian State. It could be also noted that the SOC did not raise concerns about the recently developed idea of the "Serbian World", which, as noted before, has some striking similarities with the "Russian World".

5 Conclusions

This chapter explored the religious pattern in contemporary Serbia by using data from the 2017 EVS, and from my own fieldwork done in 2022. This study shows two distinctive conclusions, and one possible fresh look into the political significance of the Serbian Orthodox Church. First, the data show that religiosity is primarily understood as part of Serbian national identity, where people tend to belong to the dominant religion of Orthodox Christianity, have relatively high level of believing, and yet they show significantly low level of church attendance. Thus, this chapter argues that the dominant religious pattern in Serbia is best described as 'belonging without attending'. Fieldwork data helped me understand why Serbs do not regularly attend church, and data from the semi-structured interviews suggest that the dominant reason for this is the communist heritage. However, this study shows that younger generations are more inclined towards attending church, which can be a significant predictor for the future of religiosity in Serbia. Furthermore, low church attendance suggests that the political significance of the Serbian Orthodox Church is mostly based on the close church-state relationship in Serbia, and that the church does not have a base for sharing its values and ideas within the society from the 'bottom up', from society itself. Rather, its political role comes from 'above'.

That is why it is of utmost importance to consider the role of the state as a bridge between the SOC and the people. Such arrangement made it possible for the state to silence the SOC particularly in the recent decade which has been marked by the decline of democracy, rising authoritarian and populist tendencies, and antidemocratic values in the society. At the same time, the primarly political concern of the SOC is the status of Kosovo and Metohija. Consequently, the dominant narrative in Serbia is that the Kosovo and Metohija is the "heart and the soul" of the Serbian people, as late Patriarch Irinej emphasized in 2015 by saying "What is Serbia without Kosovo and Metohija? It is a corpse without a soul and heart. Holy Serbia can exist only together with Kosovo and Metohija".[40] Such a narrative affects the anti-Western values in Serbia, as there is a shared belief held by the state and the SOC that the loss of Kosovo is directly caused by the West. Compared to the Russian case, there is a striking similarity with the Putin's narrative about the war in Ukraine. Putin concluded his two-hours long interview with the American journalist Tucker Carslon in February 2024 by saying that Ukrainian authorities are dismantling the Ukrainian Orthodox Church because "it brings together not only the territory, it brings together our souls. No one will be able to separate the soul".[41] From this point of view, there is a striking similarity between the concepts of the "Russian" and "Serbian" worlds, in addition to the shared anti-Western and anti-liberal discourse.

Finally, 'belonging without attending' as a theoretical concept has a broader use. It is not reserved for the Serbian case, and it should be further tested in other settings, primarily in the dominant Orthodox Christian countries of Eastern Europe. Future comparative studies in this field could help us to better understand the ethno-religious nexus across the region, and the cultural, traditional and above all political significance of Orthodox Christian Churches.

Bibliography

(2024). "Exclusive: Tucker Carlson Interviews Vladimir Putin". 6 February 2024. https://www.youtube.com/watch?v=fOCWBhuDdDo.

Berger, P., ed. (1999). *The Desecularization of the World: Resurgent of Religion and World Politics*. Grand Rapids, MI: William B. Eerdmans Publishing Company.

Bešić, M., and M. Veković. (2023). "Image of God and Democratic Orientation: What kind of God Matters?" *Nordic Journal of Religion and Society* 36, no. 1: 4–18.

---

40 Hieromonk Ignaty Shestakov, "Serbia Without Kosovo is Like a Corpse Without a Soul and Heart, Patriarh Irinej says", *Orthodox Christianity*, 29 June 2015, https://orthochristian.com/80356.html.

41 This part of the interview starts at 2:06:30. See "Exclusive: Tucker Carlson Interviews Vladimir Putin", February 6, 2024, https://www.youtube.com/watch?v=fOCWBhuDdDo.

Blagojević, M. (2008). "Desecularization of Contemporary Serbian Society". *Occasional Papers on Religion in Eastern Europe* 28, no. 1: 37–50.

Blagojević, M. (2009). "Revitalization of Religion and Religiousness in Serbia: Reality of a Myth?" *Filozofija i društvo* 20, no. 2: 97–117.

Bruce, S. (2011). "Defining Religion: A Practical Response". *International Review of Sociology* 21, no. 1: 107–20.

Bullock, J. (2018). "The Sociology of the Sunday assembly: 'belonging without believing' in a post-Christian context". PhD Thesis, Kingston University.

Casanova, J. (1994). *Public Religions in the Modern World*. Chicago: University of Chicago Press.

Cohen, A.B., G.L. Mazza, and J.E. Cook. (2017). "Theorizing and Measuring Religiosity Across Cultures". *Personality and Social Psychology Bulletin* 43, no. 12: 1724–36.

Davie, Grace. (1990). "Believing without Belonging: Is this the Future of Religion in Britain?" *Social Compass* 37, no. 4: 455–69.

Davie, Grace. (1993). "Believing without Belonging: A Liverpool Case Study". *Archives de Sciences Sociales des Religions* 38, no. 81: 79–89.

Djupe, Paul A., and Brian R. Calfano. (2012). "Religious value priming, threat, and political tolerance". *Political Research Quarterly* 66, no. 4: 768–80. https://doi.org/10.1177/1065912912471203.

Farago, P. (2017). "Foreword". In: Michael Breen (ed.). *Values and Identities in Europe Evidence from the European Social Survey*. London: Routledge. Pp. 21–2.

Fichter, J.H. (1969). "Social Measurement of Religiosity". *Review of Religious Research* 10, no. 3: 169–77.

Fox, J. (2008). *A World Survey of Religion and the State*. New York: Cambridge University Press".

Fox, J. (2018). *Introduction to Religion and Politics, Theory and Practice*. 2nd ed. London: Routledge.

Gallagher, K. (2009). "Dichotomy of Believing and Belonging—An Irish Context". *Journal of Sociological Research* 1, no. 1: 1–23.

Gerber, A.S., J. Gruber, and D.M. Hungerman. (2016). "Does Church Attendance Cause People to Vote? Using Blue Laws' Repeal to Estimate the Effect of Religiosity on Voter Turnout". *British Journal of Political Science* 46, no. 3: 481–500.

Green, J. (2007). *The Faith Factor: How Religion Influences American Elections*. Westport: Praeger Publishers.

Hadžibulić, S. (2017). "The *Slava* celebration: A Private and a Public Matter". *Temenos* 53, no. 1: 31–53.

Hieromonk Ignaty Shestakov. (2015). "Serbia Without Kosovo is Like a Corpse Without a Soul and Heart, Patriarh Irinej says". *Orthodox Christianity*, 29 June 2015. https://orthochristian.com/80356.html.

Huber, S., and O.W. Huber. (2012). "The Centrality of Religiosity Scale (CRS)". *Religions* 3, no. 3: 710–72.

Jevtić, M. (2007). "Political Science and Religion". *Politics and Religion Journal* 1, no. 1: 59–69.

Jonhstone, R. (2015). *Religion in Society A Sociology of Religion*. New York: Routledge.

Jovanović, M., and D. Gavrilović. (2012). "Trust and Legitimation". In: P. Cvetičanin, and A. Birešev (eds.). *Social and Cultural Capital in Western Balkan Societies*. Niš: Center for Empirical Cultural Studies of South-East Europe and The Institute for Philosophy and Social Theory. Pp. 133–44.

Kellstedt, L.A., J.C. Gree, J.L. Guth, and C.E. Smidt. (1997). "Is there a culture war? Religion and the 1996 election". Paper presented at the Annual Meeting of the American Political Science Association, Washington DC, 28–31 August 1997.

Kóczián, V. (2022). "'This nest is for all kinds of birds'? National identity questions in the refugee reception of the Reformed Church in Hungary". *Religion, State and Society* 50, no. 5: 553–68.

Marchisio, R., and M. Pisati. (1999). "Belonging without Believing: Catholics in Contemporary Italy". *Journal of Modern Italian Studies* 4, no. 2: 236–55.

McIntosh, E. (2015). "Belonging without Believing Church as Community in an Age of Digital Media". *International Journal of Public Theology* 9, no. 2: 131–55.

Mountdord, B. (2011). *Christian Atheist: Belonging without Believing*. Alresford: O-Books.

Norris, P., and R. Inglehart. (2004). *Sacred and secular: Religion and politics worldwide*. Cambridge: Cambridge University Press.

Oakes, K. (2015). "Belonging without Believing". *CrossCurrents* 65, no. 2: 229–38. https://doi.org/10.1111/cros.12124.

Paranjape, M.R. (2021). "Dharma is not the same as religion". *The Indian Express*. 24 July 2021. https://www.newindianexpress.com/opinions/columns/2021/jul/24/dharma-is-not-the-same-as-religion-2334479.html.

Pew Research Centre. (2017). "Religious Belief and National Belonging in Central and Eastern Europe". 10 May 2017. https://www.pewresearch.org/religion/2017/05/10/religious-belief-and-national-belonging-in-central-and-eastern-europe/.

Prodromou, E. (2004). "Christianity and Democracy: The Ambivalent Orthodox". *Journal of Democracy* 15, no. 2: 62–75.

Putnam, R., and D. Campbell. (2012). *American Grace: How Religion Divides and Unites Us*. New York: Simon & Shuster.

Radić, R. (2008). "Pripadanje bez verovanja i poznavanja". *Europe* 28, no. 1: 107–26.

Rieffer, B.-A.J. (2003). "Religion and Nationalism: Understanding the Consequences of a complex relationship". *Ethnicities* 3, no. 2: 215–42.

Sahgal, N., J. Evans, A.M. Salazar, K.J. Starr, and M. Corichi. (2021). "Religion in India: Tolerance and Segregation". Pew Research Centre. 29 June 2021. https://www.pewresearch.org/religion/2021/06/29/religion-in-india-tolerance-and-segregation/.

Sahi, J. (2003). "Believing without Belonging? Some Reflections". *International Review of Mission* 92, no. 365: 227–40.

Sarkissian, A. (2009). "Religious Reestablishment in Post-Communist Polities". *Journal of Church and State* 51, no. 3: 472–501.

Saroglou, V. (2011) "Believing, Bonding, Behaving and Belonging: The Big Four Religious Dimensions and Cultural Variation". *Journal of Cross-Cultural Psychology* 42, no. 8: 1320–40.

Smidt, C.E. (2017). "The Role of Religion in 2016 American presidential elections". *Z Religion Ges Polit* 133, no. 1: 133–62.

Statistical Office of the Republic of Serbia. (2022). "2022 Census of Population, Households and Dwellings on the population of the Republic of Serbia by ethno-cultural characteristics". https://popis2022.stat.gov.rs/en-US/5-vestisaopstenja/news-events/20230616-st.

Toft, M., D. Philpott, and T. Shah. (2011). *God's Century, Resurgent Religion and Global Politics.* New York: W.W. Norton & Company.

Tromp, P., A. Pless, and D. Houtman. (2020). "'Believing without Belonging' in Twenty European Countries (1981–2008) De-institutionalization of Christianity and Spiritualization of Religion". *Review of Religious Research* 62: 509–31.

Türkmen, G. (2021). *Under the Banner of Islam: Turks, Kurds, and the Limits of Religious Unity.* Oxford: Oxford University Press.

Van der Tol, M.D.C., and P.S. Gorski. (2022). "Secularisation as the fragmentation of the sacred and of sacred space". *Religion, State and Society* 50, no. 5: 495–512.

Veković, M. (2021). *Democratization in Christian Orthodox Europe: Comparing Greece, Serbia and Russia.* London: Routledge.

Vezzoni, C., and F. Biolcati-Rinaldi. (2015). "Church Attendance and Religious Change in Italy, 1968–2010: A Multilevel Analysis of Pooled Datasets", *Journal for the Scientific Study of Religion* 54, no. 1: 100–18.

Vinod, J. (2020). *Believing without Belonging? Religious Beliefs and Social Belonging of Hindu Devotees of Christ.* Eugene, OR: Pickwick Publications.

Voas, D., and A. Crockett. (2005). "Religion in Britain: Neither Believing nor Belonging". *Sociology* 39, no. 1: 11–28.

Vukomanović, M. (2016). "Srpska pravoslavna crkva, desekularizacija i demokratija". *Poznanskie Studia Slawistyczne* 10: 269–79.

Wald, K., and A. Calhoun-Brown. (2011). *Religion and Politics in the United States.* Lanham, MD: Rowman and Littlefield.

Wiktor-Mach, D. (2012). "Measuring Muslims: The Problems of Religiosity and Intra-Religious Diversity". *Annual Review of the Sociology of Religion* 3: 207–27.

Wollschleger, J., and L.R. Beach. (2013). "Religious Chameleons: Exploring the Social Context for Belonging without Believing", *Rationality and Society* 25, no. 2: 178–97.

CHAPTER 12

The Danish People's Party and the Heritage of Tidehverv: A National Example of a European Tendency

Erik Sporon Fiedler

1 Introduction

This chapter investigates the impact of the Lutheran movement *Tidehverv* ('the turn of the times') on the rise of Christian nationalism in Denmark. Tidehverv has been instrumental in key transformations and developments in Danish politics from the end of the 1990s to the present day and has been called the most important development in twentieth-century Danish theology.[1] However, there is little research on the movement, even as its entwinement with nationalist politics has in many ways been a laboratory of European populists' use of religion.[2] Historically, the movement centered around an eponymous journal, which focused on theological and later also political struggles, and articulated itself over against a range of others: Cultural Christianity, liberalism, Marxism, multiculturalism, and immigration. This chapter shows how religion was historically constitutive of Christian nationalism in Denmark, even as in its contemporary manifestation, its Christian roots have become more symbolic, expressive of 'belonging' more than of 'belief'. It shows that the role of

---

1 Martin Schwarz Lausten, *A Church History of Denmark* (Taylor and Francis, 2017), 292.
2 Torben Bramming, *Tidehvervs Historie* (Frederiksberg: Anis, 1993); Mette Kathrine Grosbøll, *Teologisme—om Tidehvervs vej til Christiansborg* (Frederiksberg: Anis, 2007); Torben Bramming, "Tidehverv og velfærdsstaten-tre generationers kritik", in *I himlen således også på jorden? Danske kirkefolk om velfærdsstaten og det moderne samfund*, eds. Jørn Henrik Petersen and Klaus Petersen (Odense: Syddansk Universitetsforlag, 2010), 101–27; Klaus Petersen and Jørn Henrik Petersen, "The Good, the Bad, or the Godless Society?: Danish'Church People' and the Modern Welfare State", *Church History* 82 no.4 (2013): 904–40; Morten Axel Pedersen, "The politics of paradox: Kierkegaardian theology and national conservatism in Denmark", in *Distortion: Social Processes Beyond the Structured and Systemic*, ed. Nigel Rapport (London: Routledge, 2017), 84–106; Morten Axel Pedersen, "Becoming what you are: faith and freedom in a Danish Lutheran movement", *Social Anthropology/Anthropologie Sociale* 26, no. 2 (2018): 182–96; Henrik Back, *Konfrontationskurs: Tidehverv og den guddommelige komedie* (Copenhagen: Gyldendal, 2018).

religion is both contextual and dynamic, and that the role of religion in nationalism today needs to be understood as part of longer historical processes.

Tidehverv was originally founded in 1926 and still constitutes a major theological branche within the state-supported Evangelical-Lutheran Danish People's Church (*Folkekirken*). The impact beyond the church, however, is palpable, especially through the affiliation of several Tidehverv leaders with the right-wing populist party the Danish People's Party (*Dansk Folkeparti*). The liaison was epitomized by the priest and theologian Søren Krarup (1937–2023) who was editor of the *Tidehverv*-journal from 1984 to 2012, and Member of Parliament for the Danish People's Party from 2001 to 2011. Krarup, together with his cousin Jesper Langballe (1939–2014), fellow party member and co-editor of *Tidehverv*, shaped the ideological position of the Danish People's Party significantly. Their legacy has been taken up by the current leader of the Danish People's Party, Morten Messerschmidt, who seeks to advance Christian nationalism by re-actualising the heritage of Tidehverv in the party. His fusing of religion and politics, the sacred and the secular, is at once particular to the Danish context, as well as reflective of right-wing populism in Europe, particularly in Poland, Hungary, and Sweden.[3]

This chapter returns to the origins of the Tidehverv movement and the three theological doctrines that are central to its gradual politicisation. The chapter then analyses the Danish People's Party's stance on Christianity and its relationship to the Tidehverv movement. To understand the politicisation of Tidehverv and the Christianisation of the Danish People's Party, this chapter will focus on Søren Krarup, the key broker of this relationship. Subsequently, the chapter explores Messerschmidt's claims to Christianity as his assertion of Christianity as constitutive of the party's core values and policy. The chapter discusses the interplay of both continuity and change when it comes to Messerschmidt's appropriation of the Tidehverv legacy. It then reflects on the sacralisation of nationhood and politicisation of religion, the relationship between the secular and the sacred, and its ramifications for the study of Christian nationalism in Denmark and elsewhere in Europe.

---

3 Nadia Marzouki and Duncan McDonnell, "Populism and Religion", in *Saving the People: How Populists Hijack Religion*, eds. Nadia Marzouki, Duncan McDonnell and Olivier Roy (London: Hurst and Company, 2016), 1–11; Ulrich Schmiedel and Joshua Ralston, eds. *The Spirit of Populism: Political Theologies in Polarized Times*. (Leiden: Brill, 2022); Jakob Schwörer and Belén Fernández-García, "Religion on the Rise Again? A Longitudinal Analysis of Religious Dimensions in Election Manifestos of Western European Parties" *Party politics* 27, no.6 (2021): 1160–71; Efe Peker, "Finding Religion: Immigration and the Populist (Re)Discovery of Christian Heritage in Western and Northern Europe", *Religions* 13, no.2 (2022): 158–77.

2 Tidehverv: A Danish Lutheran Movement of the Twentieth Century

Tidehverv arose out of an intra-ecclesiastical struggle within Denmark's Christian Student Union (*Danmarks Kristelige Studenterforbund*) where the founders of *Tidehverv* opposed the idealistic Christianity of YMCA (*KFUM*) and the personalised evangelicalism of Inner Mission (*Indre Mission*). Tidehverv came into being in 1926 when a group of young theologians founded the journal *Tidehverv* and began organising annual summer meetings. The Tidehverv movement was and still is a form of theological working collective centred around the journal and related events. This means that Tidehverv does not have a formal leadership nor members in a traditional sense but is instead constituted by the people who write in the journal and participate in the summer meetings. Despite the loose structure, there have always been people who particularly shaped the movement. Among the first generation are the journal's editor Niels Ivar Heje (1891–1971) and the co-founders Gustav Brøndsted (1885–1959), Kristoffer Olesen Larsen (1899–1964), Tage Schack (1892–1945), and later Vilhelm Krarup (1904–1999).

They were inspired by the theology of crisis that developed around the journal *Zwischen den Zeiten* in the German-speaking world in the wake of the First World War. Aligned with the Dialectical Theology of primarily Karl Barth (1886–1968), Eduard Turneysen (1888–1974) and Rudolf Bultmann (1884–1976), Tidehverv was severely critical of liberal theology, idealism and cultural optimism. Although the influence of Dialectical Theology is important, theologically Tidehverv is profoundly Lutheran with a Danish influence from the existentialist thought of Søren Kierkegaard (1813–1855) and the work of the priest, politician and poet Nikolai F.S. Grundtvig (1783–1872). At the centre of Tidehverv's anti-idealistic theology is an emphasis on the concrete realities of human existence and of God as something completely and qualitatively different from humanity.[4] Humans are sinners who can only believe in God's salvation: good works and outward piety mean nothing, as humans are always facing God on their own, and only God—terrifying, strict, and forgiving—brings salvation. Trust in humanity's rational capabilities and innate potential for progress and prosperity were thus discarded in favour of a profound Lutheranism focusing on the teachings of the gospel.

Tidehverv has always had an ethos of conflict and contestation. Being born out of theological struggles in the 1920s and 1930, it also engaged in political resistance, in the 1940s against the Nazi occupation of Denmark and the

---

4   Karl Barth, *Der Römerbrief, zweite Fassung, 1922* (Zürich: Theologische Verlag, 2010).

cooperative Danish politics of the time. After the war, its attention shifted to liberal cultural Christianity, humanistic values and the rising welfare state in the 1950s, then to the youth movement and to Marxism in the 1960s and 1970s. From the 1980s the movement asserted itself against the European Union, multiculturalism and immigration. This ethos of conflict and contestation has been defining and expresses itself in its negative critiques of church, culture, and society, rather than in a constructive vision of what these institutions could be. In the 1980s, under the leadership of Krarup and Langballe, the movement became increasingly politically oriented, culminating in the political involvement of Krarup and Langballe in the Danish People's Party since 2000. Krarup argued that the cultural battle against liberalism and multiculturalism necessitated him to enter politics, and even compared his situation to that of the resistance during World War II.[5] This brought the legacy of Tidehverv into a completely new context, a political one to be precise, and in doing so, it also departed from the non-political ethos that defined earlier generations of the Tidehverv movement.[6]

Besides the radical alterity between God and humans, Tidehverv's interpretation of the Lutheran doctrines of vocation and the three estates is of prime importance. Humans are bound to the concrete context of their lives understood as the God-given framework determining human existence. This means that one is born into a specific nation and a specific people with a specific history constituted by and constituting the nation and the people. The nation is the given reality that one is committed to as a Christian. This concreteness comes to the fore in Tidehverv's reading of Grundtvig, through which their Lutheran Christianity is given a Danish national inclination with a strong emphasis on the Danish people. This entails a narrow interpretation of the commandment of brotherly love, which is discussed in the chapter by Zoran Grozdanov elsewhere in this volume. To Tidehverv the commandment is confined to concern those with whom one shares the concrete experiences of one's life, thus limiting it to the concrete neighbour in the national reality and rejecting it as a universal concept. Lastly, the inspiration from Kierkegaardian thought and key notions such as 'the individual', 'the decision', 'the moment', and 'the leap'[7] underlines the existential sincerity of Tidehverv and the importance of staying true to oneself. This means to stand one's ground and

---

5 Søren Krarup, "Søren Krarups tale ved Dansk Folkepartis årsmøde 2011: Danmark i 73 år", *Danske Taler*, 17 September 2011, https://dansketaler.dk/tale/danmark-i-73-aar/; Søren Krarup, *I min levetid: 60 års Danmarkshistorie* (Copenhagen: Spektrum, 1999).
6 Mette Kathrine Grosbøll, *Teologisme*, 36.
7 Petersen, "Becoming what you are", 182–196.

speak one's mind, no matter the consequences.[8] These three elements of Tidehverv's theology have all, in time, contributed as a foundation to the Christian nationalism that came to fruition once attached to the Danish People's Party.

3   The Danish People's Party

The Danish People's Party came into existence in 1995 when the Progress Party (*Fremskridtspartiet*) imploded. The Progress Party, which was founded in 1972, presented as a libertarian anti-tax party and entered the Danish parliament the following year with 15.9% of the vote, making it among the first European populist parties to make a significant electoral impact. In the 1980s, their profile grew as an anti-immigration and anti-multicultural party. After significant internal controversy, several leading figures left and founded the Danish People's Party. Combining a strong anti-immigration and anti-multicultural right-wing value policy with a classic social democratic welfare policy, the Danish People's Party positioned itself as the defender of both the Danish nation and the Danish welfare state, drawing a parallel between the two. The success of the Danish People's Party was imminent and immediately shaped the political agenda. The relationship between Danish culture and multiculturalism and the problematisation of immigration went from somewhat marginal issues to becoming a central feature in Danish politics for years to come. At the election in 2001, the Danish People's Party, with 12% of the vote, came to hold the decisive mandates supporting a government coalition between the Liberal Party (*Venstre*) and the Conservative People's Party (*Konservative folkeparti*) overturning almost a decade of Social Democrat-led coalition governments.

Søren Krarup referred to this electoral impact as "the Change of System" (*Systemskiftet*),[9] interpreting it as a decisive change of direction in the ongoing cultural battle between the nationalist Danish people and the left-wing cultural-liberal elite.[10] The success of the Danish People's Party continued until the election in 2015, when they became the second-largest party with 21.1 % of the vote. Thereafter the curve broke and the party experienced a severe crisis, receiving only 8.7 % of the vote in 2019, and only 2.6 % in 2022, barely making the threshold. Through most of the party's upswing the Tidehverv wing of the party, most prominently represented by Krarup and Langballe, was central

---

8   Petersen, "Becoming what you are", 184–186.
9   Søren Krarup, *Systemskiftet: i kulturkampens tegn* (Copenhagen: Gyldendal, 2006).
10   Søren Krarup, "Søren Krarups tale ved Dansk Folkepartis årsmøde 2011: Danmark i 73 år".

and provided the Danish People's Party an ideological and intellectual grounding based on their theological position. In 2000, Krarup officially joined the party, running for Parliament the following year and partaking in the party's success by being elected. But already in 1997, Krarup had appeared as a guest speaker at the party's annual meeting with a speech that was subsequently printed in *Tidehverv*.[11] The early impact of Krarup is also visible in the Danish People's Party's program of political principles that was drafted in 1997. Here it is declared "[W]e love our fatherland and we feel a historical obligation to protect the Danish heritage".[12] The Danish heritage that the Danish People's Party endorses is intimately linked to Evangelical-Lutheran Christianity:

> Christianity has centuries of primacy in Denmark and is inseparable from the life of the people. The meaning Christianity has had and is having is immense. It has left its mark on the Danish way of life and the legislation. Throughout the ages, it has been a guide and a signpost for the people.[13]

From early on, Christianity thus played an important role as the foundation of the core values and policies of the party; something that makes the Danish People's Party differ from other anti-immigration populist parties founded across Europe in the late 1990s that initially tended to be much more secular.[14] However, despite the close connection to Tidehverv, the Danish People's Party has not traditionally been understood as a Christian party. Polls made by Gallup throughout the years have shown that the party's voters are among the least participatory when it comes to church attendance. In a poll from 2007, only 2,6 % of churchgoers said they were voting for the party.[15] In another poll from 2016, only 2,5 of the party's voters said they attended church 1–3 times a month while 80,8 % answered that they never or rarely attended church.[16]

---

11 Søren Krarup, "Hetz", *Tidehverv* 71 (1997): 201; Søren Krarup, "I undergangens angst", *Tidehverv* 71 (1997): 202–5.
12 All quotes are translated from Danish by the author unless otherwise stated; Dansk Folkeparti, *Partiprogram* (Copenhagen: DFs folketingsgruppe, 1997), 4.
13 Dansk Folkeparti, *Partiprogram*, 14.
14 Olivier Roy, *Is Europe Christian?* (Oxford: Oxford University Press, 2019), 107.
15 "Venstre fylder mest på kirkebænkene" https://www.kristendom.dk/danmark/venstre-fylder-mest-på-kirkebænkene.
16 Morten Rasmussen, "DF-vælgere går sjældnere i kirke end de fleste", *Kristendom.dk*, 26 October 2007, https://www.kristeligt-dagblad.dk/danmark/df-vaelgere-gaar-sjaeldnere-i-kirke-end-de-fleste.

4 The Politicization of Tidehverv and the Christianization of the Danish People's Party

In 1984, Søren Krarup, son of the theologian, priest and editor of *Tidehverv* Vilhelm Krarup, succeeded his father as editor of the journal. Although Tidehverv had been engaged in a theologically grounded critique of culture and society since its foundation, that critique became, with Krarup's centrality in the movement, more tied to a fixed nationalist and conservative position on the political right. Earlier, people connected to Tidehverv had been politically active across the political specter and without drawing parallels between their political engagement and religious convictions.[17] With Krarup this changed, and in 1981 he wrote: "Our Lord *must* be used in politics, as it is only the preaching of Christianity that keeps politics in its place as politics".[18] Here Krarup referred to what he saw as the dominant form of modern liberal politics. A political ideology that has made politics into a religion that worships the human and claims universality and therefore must be fought.[19]

The opponents in this struggle can be summarised as the liberal elites and immigrants, bringing Krarup's position into line with populist narratives generally.[20] Through Krarup's battling of these antagonists, which he saw as representing the anthropocentric liberal religion of politics and threatening the Danish culture and people, Tidehverv became overtly political. This political dimension of Krarup's Tidehverv can be understood as a nationalist form of conservatism anchored in Christianity reminiscent of Edmund Burke's counter-enlightenment conservatism.[21] Krarup has described it accordingly:

> [F]rom the beginning I have had a deep loathing for all abstract systems, for all global idealism. ... And because, on the contrary, I have known myself to be bound by the concrete, the historically given, the heritage and obligation that applies to me as this particular human being in this particular context.[22]

---

17 Henrik Bach, *Konfrontationskurs: Tidehverv og den guddommelige komedie* (Copenhagen: Gyldendal, 2018), 271–275.
18 Søren Krarup, quoted in Bach, *Tidehverv*, 269.
19 Søren Krarup, "Tidehverv", *Tidehverv* 58 (1984): 1.
20 Jan Werner Müller, *What is Populism?* (Philadelphia: University of Pennsylvania Press, 2016), 7–8; Rogers Brubaker, "Why Populism?" *Theory and society* 46, no. 5 (2017): 362.
21 Edmund Burke, *Reflections on the Revolution in France* (Oxford: Oxford University Press, 2009).
22 Søren Krarup, "Den konservative eksistens", in *Forandre for at bevare? Tanker om konservatisme*, ed. Anders Ehlers Dam (Copenhagen: Gyldendal, 2003).

Echoes of Tidehverv's interpretation of Luther's doctrine of vocation and estate as a national grounding of human existence are clear in this description, and so is the opposition to the universal principles that sprang from the French Revolution and shaped the liberal tradition. Krarup's conservative Christian nationalism was evident in the main topics he promoted within the Danish People's Party which could be summarised as three main stances: anti-refugees and migrants, anti-European Union, and anti-humanistic values.[23] These stances were closely related to the three elements of Tidehverv's theology that were presented earlier: the narrow interpretation of the commandment of brotherly love, the focus on existence as bound by the concrete reality of the nation and the obligation to speak up against what is perceived as a liberal elite whose politics threaten the people.

To explain their joining of the Danish People's Party, Krarup and Langballe argued that they were simply carrying out their Christian vocation by serving the people in 'the Kingdom of Man', distinguishing between law and gospel in accordance with the Lutheran doctrine of the two kingdoms. Interestingly, Krarup's and Langballe's vocation took the form of politics, but they stressed that they were not acting as politicians but doing the people's work, which is a Christian duty. Accordingly, Krarup has talked about his political commitment as a member of parliament as a "conscription".[24] Representing the Danish people as politicians are thus according to Krarup and Langballe in accordance with staying faithful to the given national reality of their existence and speaking truth to power. Therefore, they interpreted their political involvement as a nationalistic act *and* a theological duty, not a political one. Krarup's joining of the party was followed by an editorial nota bene in the Tidehverv-journal arguing of the validity of the liaison: "That a Lutheran minister takes a life in vocation and estate seriously and engages himself in the people's work ought to be quite obvious and is seen before, e.g. during the German occupation".[25] By invoking the German occupation, the urgency of the cultural battle against the liberal elites to counter multiculturalism becomes a battle where the survival of Denmark and the Danish people is at stake. As Krarup stated at the Danish People's Party's annual meeting in 1997, he feared "that our descendants will not live in Denmark and like Danes".[26] On another occasion asking: "Is Copenhagen a Danish city in 50 years? Can the Danes continue to be a people,

---

23 Torben Bramming, "Tidehverv og velfærdsstaten", 111.
24 Søren Krarup, *National værnepligt: politisk ekskurs* (Copenhagen: Gyldendal, 2009).
25 Redaktionen "NB!" *Tidehverv* 74, (2000), 232.
26 Søren Krarup, "I undergangens angst", 202.

when language, history and religion are no longer commonly shared?"²⁷ Interestingly, these statements by Krarup anticipated and contributed to the demographic conspiracy theory that was popularized over a decade later under the moniker of the great replacement theory by the French author Renaud Camus and is now central in the Identitarian movement and among radical right-wing supporters across Europe.²⁸

The close connection between Tidehverv and the Danish People's Party was underlined by the fact that Krarup's and Langballe's speeches in Parliament were subsequently published in the *Tidehverv* journal, thus making it hard to distinguish the two. With Krarup's politicization of Tidehverv, the 'will to confront' primarily came to expression in contemporary cultural battles, while simultaneously defending and promoting an imagined condition of concord between Danishness and Christianity. Thus, a theological-ecclesiastical battlefield was exchanged for a cultural-political one. There is no doubt that Krarup was the central link that enabled first the politicization of Tidehverv in a national conservative direction and then the Christianization of a political party on the political right, namely the Danish People's Party. Interestingly, according to the chronology of the development of this example, it is not initially religion that is being instrumentalized, but rather convictions rooted in theology that became politicized. Elsewhere in this volume Kratochvíl discusses the structural proximity between religion and populism arguing that there is a deeper linkage than mere instrumentalization. However, since Krarup and Langballe retired, Tidehverv has somewhat distanced itself from the close political ties to the Danish People's Party. Simultaneously the visibility of Christianity in the party diminished. With the expanding crisis of the party and the increasingly central role of Morten Messerschmidt, this again changed.

5 Morten Messerschmidt's Danish Christianity

The Danish People's Party's leader Morten Messerschmidt entered politics as a declared atheist. However, in a 2010 interview, he confessed a newfound Christian faith, and ten years later he became the party's vice-chair and part of an attempt to reinvigorate the party by relaunching its political profile with

---

27 Søren Krarup, *I min levetid*, 247.
28 Renaud Camus, *Le Grand Remplacement* (Plieux: Chez l'auteur, 2011).

a renewed focus on Christianity.²⁹ Messerschmidt's political mobilisation of Christianity began in the summer of 2020 when he in a range of interviews and debate pieces explicitly connected himself and the line of the party to Evangelical-Lutheran Christianity and a specific national cultural heritage formed by Lutheran Christianity. In other words, a Danish Christian nationalism. This was followed by the book *The Christian Heritage* (*Den kristne arv*),³⁰ where he developed his understanding of Danish Christianity. The first intervention by Messerschmidt was a grandly staged interview with the Danish newspaper *Politiken* wherein he stated that the electoral losses by the Danish People's Party since 2015 were because the party had failed the Christian heritage of the Tidehverv theologians Krarup and Langballe and that this must be remedied.³¹

This political analysis mirrors a larger narrative, where the roots of the West's civilizational crisis are found in the loss of Christian values and accordingly the remedy is found in re-establishing those values.³² In 2021 the Christian nationalism that Messerschmidt had paved the way for in his interviews and writings came partially to political expression in a pamphlet of cultural-political initiatives titled "Defend Danish Culture: A Reply to Identity Politics" (*Forsvar dansk kultur—et modsvar til identitetspolitikken*).³³ Therein the Danish People's Party wanted the teaching of Christianity in primary schools strengthened and made obligatory in upper secondary education. Further, the singing of songs from the Danish Hymnbook should be made compulsory in primary schools. The underlying argument being that "Christianity has shaped our values and way-of-life",³⁴ and that "the given conditions and communities we Danes are born into have been under strong pressure over the past 150 years".³⁵ The initiatives reproduce the idea of an ongoing cultural struggle propagated by Krarup and attempts at consolidating a Danishness that is portrayed as threatened while equating it with Christianity.

---

29   Morten Messerschmidt, "Sådan er livet: Med kristendommen under huden", interview with Else Marie Nygaard, *Kristeligt Dagblad*, 12 November 2010, https://www.kristeligt-dagblad.dk/kirke-tro/med-kristendommen-under-huden.
30   Morten Messerschmidt, *Den kristne arv* (Frederiksberg: Eksistensen, 2021).
31   Morten Messerschmidt, "Morten Messerschmidt om DF's krise: Jeg kan måske være en del af redningen", *Politiken*, 30 July 2020.
32   Jayne Svenungsson, "Christianity and Crisis: Uses and Abuses of Religion in Modern Europe". *Eco-ethica* 8 (2019), 13.
33   Dansk Folkeparti, *Forsvar dansk kultur—et modsvar til identitetspolitikken* (København: Dansk Folkeparti, 2021).
34   Dansk Folkeparti, *Forsvar dansk kultur*, 16.
35   Dansk Folkeparti, *Forsvar dansk kultur*, 3.

However, it is not just in the political dimension that Messerschmidt follows Krarup. In Messerschmidt's own words, Krarup and Langballe were his mentors in Christianity.[36] Although he has only been vaguely involved in Tidehverv, having published only one article in the journal,[37] he connects himself to its theological heritage through Krarup and Langballe. In his utterances, Messerschmidt is less theological than Krarup, but there is a strong emphasis on the most profound elements of Krarup's understanding of Tidehverv. Messerschmidt continuously speaks of Danish Christianity coupling Evangelical-Lutheran Christianity with Danish nationalism: "Naturally, Danishness is closely linked to Christianity. Not Hungarian, Polish or other Catholicism, but Danish Christianity".[38] Developing this Messerschmidt writes:

> While becoming Christian a thousand years ago brought us into the European tradition, the Reformation 500 years ago brought us on track of a Danish Christianity. With Luther the Christian faith became national. The power of the pope disappeared, and the Danish king took over. The language changed from Latin to Danish. The Bible was translated, and we got songs and psalms. Everywhere the new faith flourished, grounded in what is Danish. Out of this soil grew the thoughts that still lay the foundations for Denmark.[39]

The influence of Tidehverv on Messerschmidt's Danish Christianity is clear. It is Lutheran Christianity focusing on its specific theological developments in a Danish national context and influenced by the thoughts of Kierkegaard and Grundtvig as they are interpreted by Tidehverv.[40] Therefore, we also see that Messerschmidt has embraced the three theological elements that Krarup politicized. With Messerschmidt's focus on Danish Christianity the nation conditions everything and it constitutes the concrete given reality of existence:

> To be Danish is neither an idea nor an ideology. It is to devote oneself to what is given. We talk about a mother-tongue because it is given to us. We have a fatherland because we are born into it ... It is given to us before we can do anything else but receive. Before we even understand

---

36   Messerschmidt, *Den kristne arv*, 33.
37   Morten Messerschmidt, "EU-domstolens undergraven af demokratiet", *Tidehverv* 87 (2013).
38   Messerschmidt, *Den kristne arv*, 19.
39   Messerschmidt, *Den kristne arv*, 99.
40   Messerschmidt, *Den kristne arv*, 62–63.

what we have been given ... In the Christian reality, we are bound to the given. To our baptism. To our parents, our language and the nation.[41]

In Messerschmidt's Danish Christian nationalism, he has maintained the specific interpretation of Danishness and of Danish history that the national conservative political theology formed by Krarup and Langballe propagated. In continuation of this, the commandment of brotherly love is interpreted narrowly from a national perspective: "The neighbour and the fatherland go together. Because, of course, the one with whom we share the gift of fatherland is our neighbour".[42] Further, Messerschmidt's focus on Danish Christianity makes the obligation to stay true to oneself a question about courage. Dare one to stand one's ground when facing those who oppose the national and Christianity. Like Krarup, Messerschmidt sees an ongoing struggle where the latest instances of "Christian Denmark's real antagonist"[43] are post-modernism and identity politics. Therefore, he asks: "Dare we be true to our heritage? Do we dare to be Christians?"[44]

Theologically, Messerschmidt is clearly inspired by Krarup and Langballe, however, the specific history of Tidehverv which was of key importance to Krarup and Langballe is left out. Krarup and Langballe viewed their political involvement in the Danish People's Party as a theological duty and as the natural continuation of Tidehverv's history of conflict and contestation. However, Messerschmidt's Danish Christianity is more focused on identity than theology. It is as much about belonging as it is about believing. As he writes: "Danish Christianity is fundamentally about belonging".[45] Identity markers are therefore of prime importance to Messerschmidt: "Only by knowing your heritage can you maneuver confidently in this world. That's why I'm calling for more Christianity—in the school curriculum and in the public sphere".[46] Messerschmidt's Danish Christianity is thus more akin to a national identity marker than it is to religion: "Whether you are a member of the Church or not is not for anyone to judge. Whether you believe or not is not the issue at all. My concern is that we should know who we are—not just as individuals, but as part of the 1000-year-old history".[47] As such Danish Christianity is a Christian nationalism tied to a project of national conservative culture formation.

---

41 Messerschmidt, *Den kristne arv*, 77.
42 Messerschmidt, *Den kristne arv*, 78–79.
43 Messerschmidt, *Den kristne arv*, 38.
44 Messerschmidt, *Den kristne arv*, 112.
45 Messerschmidt, *Den kristne arv*, 25.
46 Messerschmidt, *Den kristne arv*, 25.
47 Messerschmidt, *Den kristne arv*, 26–27.

As such, Messerschmidt's Danish Christianity is what Mattias Martinson has called a monumentalized form of religion, as it is reduced and reified as a national identity marker shaping a we against the others.[48] Therefore, Messerschmidt's endeavour at mobilising Christianity as a national identity marker is more akin to other European populists' use of Christianity than it is to the history of Tidehverv. However, Krarup is the connecting link through whom the theology of Tidehverv intersected with the Danish People's Party, creating the possibility of the Christian nationalism that comes to expression in Messerschmidt's administration of the heritage of Tidehverv in his Danish Christianity.

6   Blurring the Distinction between Politics and Religion

The fusing of Christian imaginaries and symbols with a Danish national framework and narrative is clear in the case of Messerschmidt's Danish Christianity. As Van der Tol and Gorski argue, "Nationalism has a specific territorial aspect, in which the national space functions as a secular-sacred space".[49] The public space in a national framework is not just a secular formation but a field of tension, where religion plays a part in an ongoing negotiation and construction.[50] This is seen in Messerschmidt's call for more Christianity in the public sphere. The Danish case thus challenges a conceptual framework of politics and religion that sees the categories of the secular and the sacred as constructing an oppositional binary. By ascribing a religious meaning to the nation, the national institutions and the public space, Krarup's and Messerschmidt's Christian nationalism challenges the idea of a purely secular modern state. There is an intriguing ambivalence to the ways both Krarup and Messerschmidt insist on keeping religion and politics separate, condemning the sacralisation of politics, while simultaneously politicising religion and sacralising nationhood.

The ambiguity of Messerschmidt's position is visible in some seemingly contradictory utterances made in August 2020. On the one hand, Messerschmidt states that "Christianity must play a greater role in Danish society in general,

---

48   Mattias Martinson, "Towards a 'Theology' of Christian Monumentality: Post-Secular Reflections on Grace and Nature", in *Monument and Memory*, ed. Jonna Bornemark, Mattias Martinson, Jayne Svenungsson (Berlin: LIT, 2015), 21–42; Mattias Martinson, *Sekularism, populism, xenofobi: En essä om religionsdebatten* (Malmö: Eskaton, 2017), 55.

49   M.D.C. Van der Tol and P.S. Gorski, "Secularisation as the fragmentation of the sacred and of sacred space", *Religion, State and Society* 50, no. 5 (2022): 499.

50   Van der Tol and Gorski, "Secularisation as the fragmentation of the sacred and of sacred space", 507.

and that begins with articulating it politically",[51] while on the other hand, he distances himself from political opponents who talk about the commandment of brotherly love in relation to an inclusive refugee and migrant policy, claiming that they "conflate faith and politics".[52] By doing so, he acts in line with Matthias Martinson's analysis of populism's monumentalized Christianity: Other ways of utilizing Christianity are being dismissed as destroying the monument and desecrating the Christian identity.[53] Messerschmidt is fully aware that he redraws the boundary between the sacred and the secular, religion and politics, and how he in this redrawing privileges Christianity as something that belongs within the secular: "In the last 20–30 years, there has been a reluctance to talk about the Christian faith, Christian identity and Christian values in the political debate; there has been a misunderstanding of the concept of secularisation, that you cannot talk about religion in politics, but of course you can".[54] And similarly: "Although we live in what can largely be considered secular and non-religious societies, the echoes of Christianity as a carrier of culture and society can be heard in almost every part of our society".[55] Further, Messerschmidt denounces Islam as "a conflation of the political and the religious in the sense that the democratic is set aside and religion itself gains political strength",[56] thus constructing a counter-image to his Danish Christianity. This strategy of claiming Islam to be at odds with Christian-European values, amongst them keeping politics and religion separate, while at the same time presenting Christian nationalism as corresponding with these values, is common among European right-wing populists.[57] In this way, the public space for other religious traditions than the inherently Christian culture is being restricted.[58]

---

51   Morten Messerschmidt, "Debatinterview. Morten Messerschmidt indleder kristen værdikamp: Enhver, der konverterer til kristendommen, konverterer til friheden", interview with Johan Storgaard Jespersen, *Kristeligt Dagblad*, 4 August 2020, https://www.kristeligt-dagblad.dk/debat/morten-messerschmidt-indleder-kristen-vaerdikamp-enhver-der-konverterer-ind-i-kristendommen.
52   Morten Messerschmidt, "Nej, jeg sammenblander ikke religion og politik" *Kristeligt Dagblad*, 15 August 2020, https://www.kristeligt-dagblad.dk/debatindlaeg/morten-messerschmidt-nej-jeg-sammenblander-ikke-religion-og-politik.
53   Mattias Martinson, "Towards a 'Theology' of Christian Monumentality: Post-Secular Reflections on Grace and Nature", 21–42.
54   Messerschmidt, "Debatinterview. Morten Messerschmidt indleder kristen værdikamp".
55   Messerschmidt, *Den kristne arv*, 114.
56   Messerschmidt, "Debatinterview. Morten Messerschmidt indleder kristen værdikamp".
57   Olivier Roy, *Is Europe Christian?* 103–124; Jayne Svenungsson, "Christianity and Crisis: Uses and Abuses of Religion in Modern Europe", *Eco-ethica* 8 (2019), 13–30.
58   Jayne Svenungsson, "Christianity and Crisis: Uses and Abuses of Religion in Modern Europe", 14.

Comparative cases to the Danish example are the preambles to the Hungarian Constitution of 2011 drafted by Fidesz, which reads "We are proud that our king Saint Stephen built the Hungarian State on solid ground and made our country a part of Christian Europe one thousand years ago", and the Polish Constitution amended in 2009 where "the Christian heritage of the Nation" is underlined. Although the state and church are separated according to Article 7 of the Hungarian Constitution and Article 25 of the Polish Constitution, the preambles serve as political imaginaries.[59] Christianity is privileged and implicitly claimed to be the foundation of the separation of church and state in the Christian nation that are also part of a Christian civilizational identity. We find similarities to these constitutional narratives, in Messerschmidt's and Krarup's claim of a 1000–year-old history of Christianity in Denmark and in the dual emphasis on a Christian national heritage and a Christian civilizational complex in Messerschmidt's talk of "The European tradition" on the one hand, and "Danish Christianity" on the other.[60] Within the domain of Lutheran Christianity, Jayne Svenungsson has shown how in Sweden, the Sweden Democrats make use of the same strategies.[61] Further, Mattias Martinson has, also in a Swedish context, argued how specific elements of Lutheran cultural heritage are prone to being developed into a xenophobic discourse when it is tied to questions of secularism.[62]

The Danish example of Tidehverv and the Danish People's Party shows the importance in right-wing populist politics of the emphasis on Christian roots and values to Christian secular culture. This occurs across European populism, in particular Hungary, Poland, and Sweden, as is discussed in numerous chapters across this volume. To better understand what is happening now politically, it is thus important to challenge and reconsider theoretical dichotomies such as that between politics and religion that reproduces a sharp distinction between what is secular and what is sacred. An important part of the populist strategy of instrumentalizing religion is exactly to conflate Christianity with secularism[63] as Messerschmidt and others do when they claim Christianity to be the foundation of secular ideals. When applying this strategy, strong lines of

---

59 Nomi Claire Lazar, "Time Framing in the Rhetoric of Constitutional Preambles", *Law and literature* 33, no. 1 (2021): 1–21.
60 Messerschmidt, *Den kristne arv*, 99.
61 Jayne Svenungsson, "Christianity and Crisis: Uses and Abuses of Religion in Modern Europe", 24–25.
62 Mattias Martinson, "Lutheran Secularism as a Challenge for Constructive Theology: A Swedish Perspective, a Foucauldian Proposal" in *Dialog: a journal of theology* 56 (2017), 233–237.
63 Jayne Svenungsson, "Christianity and Crisis: Uses and Abuses of Religion in Modern Europe", 25–26.

demarcation are drawn in the public sphere against the religious other that do not adapt to this version of Christian secularism.[64]

7 Conclusion

This article analysed the influence of the Danish Lutheran movement Tidehverv on the Danish populist right-wing party the Danish People's Party, especially through the work of Søren Krarup, who initially made the connection between Tidehverv and the Danish People's Party, and on the current party leader Morten Messerschmidt. This closer look at the Danish example of populist intertwinement of religion and politics shows that Denmark has in many ways been a laboratory of European populist parties' use of religion. The Danish People's Party's clear references to Christianity in their foundational policy documents from the late 90s precede many European right-wing populist parties where references to Christianity in their politics first began a decade later.[65] As does Krarup's invocation, as early as 1997, of ideas similar to the great replacement theory, where Islam and multiculturalism are regarded as an existential threat to Danish and Christian culture. To understand the specificity of the Danish case, however, it is crucial to focus on the historical background and the importance that the Lutheran movement of Tidehverv has had on the political developments. The connection with Tidehverv gave the Danish People's Party an intellectual grounding in a theological tradition that shaped their politics. Krarup and Langballe succeeded in interweaving church and Christianity in the cultural battle of values that took place in Denmark in the 2000s. The culmination perhaps being the program of the government formed by the liberal Lars Løkke Rasmussen in 2015, *Together for the Future* (*Sammen for fremtiden*), where it was stated that "Denmark is a Christian country".[66] This formulation, which is reminiscent of the value-based constitutionalism of Poland and Hungary, was claimed to be the doing of the Danish People's Party and underlines the immense transformative impact that Tidehverv has had on Danish politics.[67]

---

64 See Talal Asad, *Formations of the Secular: Christianity, Islam, Modernity*. (Stanford: Stanford University Press, 2003).
65 Rosario Forlenza, "Abendland in Christian Hands: Religion and Populism in Contemporary European Politics", in *Populism and the Crisis of Democracy*, ed. Gregor Fitzi, Juergen Mackert and Bryan Turner (Routledge, 2019), 135.
66 Regeringen, *Sammen for fremtiden—regeringsgrundlag 2015* (Copenhagen: Regeringen, 2015), 29.
67 Christian Birk, "Langballe: Vi står bag formuleringen om et kristent Danmark", *Kristeligt Dagblad*, 15 July 2015, https://www.kristeligt-dagblad.dk/danmark/christian-langballe-df-vi-staar-bagformuleringen-om-et-kristent-danmark.

The coupling of Tidehverv and the Danish People's Party formed a politics grounded in Christianity that was so closely related to nationalism that it now lives on, decoupled from its theological grounding. With Messerschmidt's Danish Christianity and its focus on Christianity as a national identity marker where belonging is more important than believing, we now find similarities in other contemporary European right-wing populist parties and their use of Christianity as a civilizational identity marker,[68] rather than in the history and tradition of Tidehverv. For Tidehverv, including Krarup and Langballe, Christianity is never just a cultural identity marker, but more of a dogmatic truth.[69] Krarup himself resigned from the party shortly before his death. Looking at the popular impact of Messerschmidt's Danish Christianity, a poll made by the polling institute YouGov showed that 49% of respondents agreed with Messerschmidt's proposal of obligatory singing of psalms in primary schools.[70] However, even though he succeeded in setting the agenda when it came to religion and politics, it did not result in electoral success. The parliament election of 2022 gave the Danish People's Party the worst result in the party's history. Therefore, Denmark might for now be compared to Britain which Timothy Peace has described as an "infertile breeding ground for populists wishing to use religion to advance their cause".[71] The voter potential for a Christian-religious right-wing populism simply does not seem to be there in Denmark at the moment, although some of the national conservative value-policies attached to it do seem to resonate with voters.

Bibliography

Asad, T. (2003). *Formations of the Secular: Christianity, Islam, Modernity*. Stanford: Stanford University Press.

Bach, H. (2018). *Konfrontationskurs: Tidehverv og den guddommelige komedie*. Copenhagen: Gyldendal.

---

[68] Rogers Brubaker, "Between Nationalism and civilizationism: The European Populist Moment in Comparative Perspective", *Ethnic and racial studies* 40, no. 8 (2017): 1199.

[69] Mark Sedgwick, "Something Varied in the State of Denmark: Neo-nationalism, Anti-Islamic Activism, and Street-level Thuggery" in *Politics, Religion & Ideology* 14, no.2 (2013): 220.

[70] Jens From Lyng, "Hver anden dansker vil have salmesang i folkeskolen", *Kristeligt Dagblad*, 3 September 2020, https://www.kristeligt-dagblad.dk/kirke-tro/flertal-af-befolkning-vil-have-salmesang-i-folkeskolen.

[71] Timothy Peace, "Religion and Populism in Britain: an infertile breeding ground?" in Marzouki, McDonnell, and Roy, *Saving the People*, 107.

Barth, K. (2010). *Der Römerbrief, (zweite Fassung), 1922*. Zürich: Theologische Verlag.
Birk, C. (2015). "Langballe: Vi står bag formuleringen om et kristent Danmark". *Kristeligt Dagblad*, 15 July 2015. Accessed 13 March 2024. https://www.kristeligt-dagblad.dk/danmark/christian-langballe-df-vi-staar-bagformuleringen-om-et-kristent-danmark.
Bramming, T. (1993). *Tidehvervs Historie*. Frederiksberg: Anis.
Bramming, T. (2010). "Tidehverv og velfærdsstaten – tre generationers kritik". In: J. Henrik Petersen, and K. Petersen (eds.). *I himlen således også på jorden? Danske kirkefolk om velfærdsstaten og det moderne samfund*. Odense: Syddansk Universitetsforlag. Pp. 101–27.
Brubaker, R. (2017a). "Why Populism?" *Theory and society* 46, no. 5: 357–85.
Brubaker, R. (2017b). "Between Nationalism and Civilizationism: The European Populist Moment in Comparative Perspective". *Ethnic and racial studies* 40, no. 8: 1191–226.
Burke, E. (2009). *Reflections on the Revolution in France*. Oxford: Oxford University Press.
Camus, R. (2011). *Le Grand Remplacement*. Plieux: Chez l'auteur.
Dansk Folkeparti. (1997). *Partiprogram*. Copenhagen: DFs folketingsgruppe.
Dansk Folkeparti. (2021). *Forsvar dansk kultur – et modsvar til identitetspolitikken*. Copenhagen: Dansk Folkeparti.
Forlenza, R. (2019). "Abendland in Christian Hands: Religion and Populism in Contemporary European Politics". In: G. Fitzi, J. Mackert, and B. Turner (eds.). *Populism and the Crisis of Democracy*. Routledge. Pp. 133–49.
Grosbøll, M.K. (2007). *Teologisme—om Tidehvervs vej til Christiansborg*. Frederiksberg, Anis.
Holm, T.A. (2017). "DF-vælgere går sjældnere i kirke end de fleste". *Kristeligt Dagblad*, 21 February, 2017. Accessed 13 March 2024. https://www.kristeligt-dagblad.dk/danmark/df-vaelgere-gaar-sjaeldnere-i-kirke-end-de-fleste.
Krarup, S. (1984). "Tidehverv". *Tidehverv* 58: 1.
Krarup, S. (1997a). "Hetz". *Tidehverv* 71: 201.
Krarup, S. (1997b). "I undergangens angst". *Tidehverv* 71: 202–5.
Krarup, S. (1999). *I min levetid: 60 års Danmarkshistorie*. Copenhagen: Spektrum.
Krarup, S. (2003). "Den konservative eksistens". In: Anders E. Dam (ed.). *Forandre for at bevare? tanker om konservatisme*. Copenhagen: Gyldendal.
Krarup, S. (2006). *Systemskiftet: i kulturkampens tegn*. Copenhagen: Gyldendal.
Krarup, S. (2009). *National værnepligt: politisk ekskurs*. Copenhagen: Gyldendal.
Krarup, S. (2023). "Søren Krarups tale ved Dansk Folkepartis årsmøde 2011: Danmark i 73 år". *Danske Taler*, 17 September 2011. Accessed 13 March 2024. https://dansketaler.dk/tale/danmark-i-73-aar/.
Lausten, M.S. (2017). *A Church History of Denmark*. Taylor and Francis.

Lazar, N.C. (2021). "Time Framing in the Rhetoric of Constitutional Preambles". *Law and literature* 33, no. 1: 1–21.

Lyng, J.F. (2020). "Hver anden dansker vil have salmesang i folkeskolen". *Kristeligt Dagblad*, 3 September 2020. Accessed 13 March 2024. https://www.kristeligt-dagblad.dk/kirke-tro/flertal-af-befolkning-vil-have-salmesang-i-folkeskolen.

Martinson, M. (2015) "Towards a 'Theology' of Christian Monumentality" in J. Bornemark, M. Martinson, and J. Svenungsson (eds.). *Monument and Memory*. Berlin: LIT. Pp. 21–42.

Martinson, M. (2017a). *Sekularism, populism, xenofobi: En essä om religionsdebatten*. Malmö: Eskaton.

Martinson, M. (2017b). "Lutheran Secularism as a Challenge for Constructive Theology: A Swedish Perspective, a Foucauldian Proposal: Lutheran Secularism as a Challenge for Constructive Theology". *Dialog: a journal of theology* 56: 233–243.

Marzouki, N., and D. McDonnell. (2016). "Populism and Religion". In: N. Marzouki, D. McDonnell, and O. Roy (eds.). *Saving the People: How Populists Hijack Religion*. London: Hurst and Company. Pp. 1–11.

Marzouki, N., D. McDonnell, and O. Roy, eds. (2016). *Saving the People: How Populists Hijack Religion*. London: Hurst and Company.

Messerschmidt, M. (2010). "Sådan er livet: Med kristendommen under huden". Interview with E.M. Nygaard. *Kristeligt Dagblad*, 12 November 2012. Accessed 13 March 2024. https://www.kristeligt-dagblad.dk/kirke-tro/med-kristendommen-under-huden.

Messerschmidt, M. (2013). "EU-domstolens undergraven af demokratiet". *Tidehverv* 87.

Messerschmidt, M. (2020a). "Morten Messerschmidt om DF's krise: Jeg kan måske være en del af redningen". *Politiken*, 30 July 2020.

Messerschmidt, M. (2020b). "Debatinterview. Morten Messerschmidt indleder kristen værdikamp: Enhver, der konverterer til kristendommen, konverterer til friheden". *Kristeligt Dagblad*, 4 August 2020. Accessed 13 March 2024. https://www.kristeligt-dagblad.dk/debat/morten-messerschmidt-indleder-kristen-vaerdikamp-enhver-der-konverterer-ind-i-kristendommen.

Messerschmidt, M. (2020c). "Nej, jeg sammenblander ikke religion og politik". *Kristeligt Dagblad*. 15 August 2020. Accessed 13 March 2024. https://www.kristeligt-dagblad.dk/debatindlaeg/morten-messerschmidt-nej-jeg-sammenblander-ikke-religion-og-politik.

Messerschmidt, M. (2021). *Den kristne arv*. Frederiksberg: Eksistensen.

Müller, J.-W. (2016). *What is Populism?* Philadelphia: University of Pennsylvania Press.

Peace, T. (2016). "Religion and Populism in Britain: an infertile breeding ground?" In: N. Marzouki, D. McDonnell, and O. Roy (eds.). *Saving the People: How Populists Hijack Religion*. London: Hurst and Company. Pp. 95–108.

Pedersen, M.A. (2017). "The politics of paradox: Kierkegaardian theology and national conservatism in Denmark" In: N. Rapport (ed.). *Distortion: Social Processes Beyond the Structured and Systemic*. (London: Routledge). Pp. 84–106.

Pedersen, M.A. (2018). "Becoming what you are: faith and freedom in a Danish Lutheran movement". *Social Anthropology/Anthropologie Sociale* 26, no. 2: 182–96.

Peker, E. (2022). "Finding Religion: Immigration and the Populist (Re)Discovery of Christian Heritage in Western and Northern Europe". *Religions* 13, no. 2: 158–77.

Petersen, J.H., and K. Petersen. "The Good, the Bad, or the Godless Society?: Danish 'Church People' and the Modern Welfare State" *Church History* 82, no.4 (2013): 904–40.

Rasmussen, M. (2007) "Venstre fylder mest på kirkebænkene". *Kristendom.dk, 26 October 2017.* accessed 13 March 2024. https://www.kristendom.dk/danmark/venstre-fylder-mest-på-kirkebænkene.

Redaktionen. (2000). "NB!" *Tidehverv* 74: 232.

Regeringen. (2015). *Sammen for fremtiden—regeringsgrundlag 2015*. Copenhagen: Regeringen.

Roy, O. (2019). *Is Europe Christian?* Oxford: Oxford University Press.

Schmiedel, U., and J. Ralston, eds. (2022). *The Spirit of Populism: Political Theologies in Polarized Times*. Leiden: Brill.

Schwörer, J., and B. Fernández-García. (2021). "Religion on the Rise Again? A Longitudinal Analysis of Religious Dimensions in Election Manifestos of Western European Parties". *Party Politics* 27, no. 6: 1160–71.

Sedgwick, M. (2013). "Something Varied in the State of Denmark: Neo-nationalism, Anti-Islamic Activism, and Street-level Thuggery". *Politics, Religion & Ideology* 14, no.2: 208–33.

Svenungsson, J. (2019). "Christianity and Crisis: Uses and Abuses of Religion in Modern Europe". *Eco-ethica* 8: 13–30.

Van der Tol, M.D.C., and P.S. Gorski. (2022). "Secularisation as the fragmentation of the sacred and of sacred space". *Religion, State and Society* 50, no. 5: 495–512. https://doi.org/10.1080/09637494.2022.2144662.

CHAPTER 13

Christianity, Religion and Christian Democracy

Katharina Kunter and Leon van den Broeke

1   Introduction

The existence of Christian political parties in Europe raises questions about their nature from a political, social, as well as religious perspective. While questions about the relationship between religion, politics, and society are not new,[1] the rise of right-wing populist parties challenge the position of Christian political parties in a post-secular age. This chapter explores the self-understanding of Christian Democrats. With the erosion of the political 'Centre', Christian Democrats have sustained significant electoral losses in several countries, including in Germany, Italy, France, and the Netherlands. Such electoral losses relate to both country-specific factors and broader political and social developments in Europe, such as increasing secularisation, the fragmentation of the political landscape, the disintegration of classical party structures, social and religious pluralisation, and the decline of institutionalised religion. Under these diverse conditions, the question arises to what extent Christian Democratic parties remain indispensable to the consolidation of democracy, and to which extent Christianity will continue to shape them in the 21st century.

This chapter provides an comparative overview that analyses, juxtaposes and compares previous research on the religious foundations of two Christian

---

1   Cf. among others: Augustine, *The City of God against the Pagans*, 7 vols., ed. George Englert MacCracken (London: Heinemann, 1957–1972); George Harinck, Roel Kuiper and Peter Bak, eds., *De Antirevolutionaire partij 1829–1980* (Hilversum: Verloren, 2001); Rienk Janssens, *De opbouw van de Antirevolutionaire Partij 1850–1888* (Amsterdam, Hilversum: Verloren, 2001); Andries Hoogerwerf, *Christelijke denkers over politiek: Een oogst van 20 eeuwen* (Baarn: Ten Have, 1999); G.G. de Kruijff, *Waakzaam en nuchter: Over christelijke ethiek in een democratie* (Baarn: Ten Have, 1994); Arnold A. van Ruler, *Religie en politiek* (Nijkerk: G.F. Callenbach, 1945); A.J. Rasker, *Christelijke politiek: Gesprek over de theocratie* (Nijkerk: G.F. Callenbach, 194?); Reinhold Zippelius, *Staat und Kirche: Von der Antike bis zur Gegenwart* (Mohr Siebeck: Tübingen, 2009); Paul Miktat, ed., *Kirche und Staat in der neueren Entwicklung* (Darmstadt: Wissenschaftliche Buchgesellschaft, 1980); Charles Odahl, *Constantine and the Christian Empire* (London: Routledge, 2010); Zsolt Enyedi and John T.S. Madeley, eds., *Church and State in Contemporary Europe* (London: Frank Cass Publications, 2003).

Democratic parties:[2] 1) the German Christian Democratic Union (*Christlich Demokratische Union*, CDU) which has led various majority-coalitions; and 2) the historically significant but now declining Dutch Christian Democratic Appeal (*Christen-Democratisch Appèl*; CDA).[3] Both parties are rooted in cross-denominational political alliances and articulate their Christian profile in two countries that have historically been shaped by the Protestant Reformation and by Protestantism more generally. The starting points of this discussion are both historical and theological, as the chapter addresses the question: to what extent Christianity or a religious narrative still plays a role in the self-description of two Christian democratic parties in the Netherlands and Germany in the twenty-first century?

In this context, the heterogeneity of the two countries and the developments of their relevant Christian Democratic parties, as well as their similar political convictions and positions in the party spectrum of their respective countries must be kept in mind. Building on the interdisciplinary project "A Factor of the Past? Christian Democracy in Europa 1989–2022" this chapter first identifies and analyses some significant observations, features, and national specificities relating to religion and Christian democracy in Germany and the Netherlands. Second, this chapter evaluates and discusses these dimensions in two separate sections on Germany and the Netherlands.[4] Third, this chapter returns to the research question and formulates a working hypothesis on the 'death' of Christian Democracy in Europe, before articulating concluding reflections in the final section.

Although this contribution focusses on Christian Democratic parties in Germany and the Netherlands, it needs to be considered in the context of the changing or changed political landscape in not only these two countries, but in the European Union, and in the geopolitical context. The erosion of the political centre as a result of polarisation and the left-right distinction challenge the future of democracy in general and of Christian democracy specifically.

---

2 Already published but with no explicit reference to religion: Jurijn Timon de Voss, *Christendemocratie en identiteit. Nederland en Duitsland vergeleken (2000–2017)* (Münster: Verlag readbox publishing GmbH, 2019).
3 CDU, "CDU", accessed 20 September 2023, https://www.cdu.de/; CDA, "CDA", accessed 20 September 2023, https://www.cda.nl/.
4 The European People's Party Group (EPP Group) in the European Parliament falls outside the scope of this chapter.

2 Christianity and Christian Democracy

The interdisciplinary research project "A Factor of the Past? Christian Democracy in Europa 1989–2022" examines the meaning and role of Christianity and religion for Christian democrats in Europe over the last thirty years. It probes the question whether, and if so, to what extent, the Christian undertone of current Christian democracy may have contributed to this loss of significance or, in a completely different sense, whether it was precisely this Christian or religious grounding that 'saved' the Christian democratic parties from an even worse decline. This would presuppose that their constituencies still largely see themselves as Christian or religious, or inclined towards a Christian social policy, and that Christian democracy still offers a political home for these people and voters. In this line of thought, secularisation might offer an important explanation for the loss of votes.[5] This frame, however, would come with limitations concerning knowledge of these voters' core ideas, their hidden agendas and imprints.[6] Instead, growing religious pluralism and party-political alternatives needs to be included in the analysis.

While the history of Christian democracy after 1945 may be considered well-researched in various countries,[7] this has not been the case for the most recent years. Historical comparisons show that Christian democracy in continental Europe developed into a dominant political movement between social democracy on the one hand and liberalism on the other hand. This chapter's interest

---

5 Among others Detlef Pollack, Christel Gärtner and Karl Gabriel, eds., *Umstrittene Säkularisierung: Soziologische und historische Analysen zur Differenzierung von Religion und Politik* (Berlin: Berlin University Press, 2012); Detlef Pollack, "Religious Change in Europe: Theoretical Considerations and Empirical Findings", *Social Compass* 55 (2008): 168–86; Steve Bruce, *God is Dead: Secularization in the West* (Oxford: Wiley-Blackwell, 2002).

6 See e.g. Jeffrey Haynes, *The Routledge Handbook to Religion and Political Parties* (London: Routledge, 2021); Martin H.M. Steven, *Christianity and Party Politics* (London: Routledge, 2011).

7 For Germany see e.g. Norbert Lammert, ed., *Handbuch zur Geschichte der CDU* (Darmstadt: Wissenschaftliche Buchgesellschaft, 2021); Maria Mitchell, *The Origins of Christian Democracy: Politics and Confession in Modern Germany* (Michigan: University of Michigan Press, 2012); Frank Bösch, *Die Adenauer-CDU: Aufstieg und Krise einer Erfolgspartei (1945–1969)* (München: Deutsche Verlagsanstalt, 2001); Thomas Kselman and Thomas Buttigieg, eds., *European Christian Democracy: Historical Legacies and Comparative Perspectives* (Notre Dame: University of Notre Dame Press, 2003). For the Netherlands for example: Dik Verkuil, *Een positieve grondhouding: De geschiedenis van het CDA* ('s-Gravenhage: Sdu Uitgeverij, Koninginnegracht, 1992); Hans-Martien Th.D. ten Napel, *'Een eigen weg': De totstandkoming van het CDA (1952–1980)*, (Kampen: Vbk Media, 1992); Hans van Spanning, *De Christelijk-Historische Unie 1908–1980: Enige hoofdlijnen uit haar geschiedenis*, 2 vols. (Amsterdam: Scheltema & Holkema, 1988).

is in the period from 1989 to 2022, when the Cold War ended and Europe entered a new phase of democratisation, globalisation, and liberalisation, followed by a period of nationalist and isolationist tendencies. Between these phases, the significance of religion and classical institutions, such as churches and political parties has fundamentally changed. The same is true for Christian Democratic parties and their Christian profiles. What it meant to be a 'Christian' Democratic party is important to the question whether one can speak of the 'death' of Christian Democracy in Germany and in the Netherlands in the twenty-first century.

3 Christianity and the Christian Democratic Party in Germany

3.1 *The CDU's Founding*

The foundation of the German Christian Democratic Party, the *Christlich Demokratische Union Deutschlands* (CDU), on 21 June 1945 was a result rooted in German religious history and the German context since the sixteenth century. In particular, the nineteenth century and the antagonisms between Catholicism and Protestantism were formative to the development of Christian Democracy, which historian Olaf Blaschke and others have characterised as Germany's "second confessional age".[8] The CDU, and its regional affiliate in Bavaria, the CSU (*Christlich Soziale Union*), were grounded as a supra-confessional party, specifically to overcome confessional competition between Protestants and Catholics.[9] At the same time, it was important to emphasise human dignity along with its Christian character, so as to mark a break with the anti-Christian and anti-individual ideology of National Socialism. It was one of the reasons why the Allied forces regarded the churches as important to the reconstruction and democratisation of Germany. Because both Christian

---

8   Olaf Blaschke, *Konfessionen im Konflikt: Deutschland zwischen 1800 und 1970. Ein zweites konfessionelles Zeitalter* (Göttingen: Vandenhoeck & Ruprecht, 2002); Olaf Blaschke and Frank Michael Kuhlmann, eds., *Religion im Kaiserreich: Milieus—Mentalitäten—Krisen*, 2nd ed. (Gütersloh Gütersloher Verlagshaus 2002); Helmut Walser Smith, ed., *Protestants, Catholics and Jews in Germany 1800–1914* (Oxford: Berg Publishers, 2002).

9   Cf. among others Maria D. Mitchell, *The Origins of Christian Democracy: Politics and Confession in Modern Germany*, (Ann Arbor: University of Michigan Press, 2012); Ulrich Lappenküper, "Zwischen 'Sammlungsbewegung' und 'Volkspartei': Die CDU 1945–1969", in *Christdemokratie in Europa im 20. Jahrhundert*, eds. Michael Gehler, Wolfram Kaiser, and Helmut Wohnout (Wien: Böhlau, 2001), 385–98.

churches benefitted from this Allied moral and social trust,[10] the experiment of a Christian party, unique in German history up to that time, seemed forward-looking.

The CDU was founded at a time when the vast majority of the German population belonged to one of the two denominations, so "Christian" had the appeal of a broader people's party (*Volkspartei*). Nevertheless, in the initial phase under the Catholic Federal Chancellor Konrad Adenauer, Catholics saw it primarily as their party-political home, while Protestants remained more distanced from the Federal Republic. Protestants tended to focus on the future of the Eastern Zone, the later German Democratic Republic (GDR). For this reason, the Protestant Working Group of the CDU (*Evangelischer Arbeitskreis der CDU, EAK*) was founded in 1952, driven by the Protestant CDU politician Herman Ehlers.[11] The EAK would give the Protestant members of the CDU an ideal home for reflection, while it provided a meaningful space where the party, Protestant churches, and other Protestant organisations could interact. Even if in the beginning only 19% of the CDU were Protestants,[12] prominent Protestants shaped the profile of the CDU in the second half of the twentieth century with, for example, former presidents Richard von Weizsäcker and Roman Herzog, the longstanding Federal interior minister Wolfgang Schäuble, and the Federal Chancellor from 2005 to 2021 Angela Merkel, a pastor's daughter who hailed from Eastern Germany.[13]

3.2 CDU *Party Members and Their Christian Ties*

From its foundation, the CDU attempted to balance conservative Christian and liberal orientations. The focus of the Christian Democratic programme

---

10 See among others Siegfried Hermle and Harry Oelke, eds., *Protestantismus in der Nachkriegszeit (1945–1961)* (Leipzig: EVA, 2021); Martin Greschat, *Die evangelische Christenheit und die deutsche Geschichte nach 1945: Weichenstellungen in der Nachkriegszeit* (Stuttgart: Kohlhammer, 2002); Thomas Sauer, ed., *Katholiken und Protestanten in den Aufbaujahren der Bundesrepublik* (Stuttgart: Kohlhammer, 2000); Jochen-Christoph Kaiser and Anselm Döring-Manteuffel, eds., *Christentum und politische Verantwortung: Kirchen im Nachkriegsdeutschland* (Stuttgart: Kohlhammer, 1990).

11 Among others Martin Albrecht, Gottfried Mehnert and Christian Meißner, *Der Evangelische Arbeitskreis der CDU/CSU 1952–2002: Werden, Wirken und Wollen* (Rheinbach: UBG-Betriebs GmbH, 2012); Konrad Adenauer Stiftung, "Der Evangelische Arbeitskreis (EAK)", accessed 20 September 2023, https://www.kas.de/de/web/geschichte-der-cdu/evangelischer-arbeitskreis-eak-.

12 Gerhard Besier, "Christliche Parteipolitik und Konfession. Zur Entstehung des Evangelischen Arbeitskreises der CDU/CSU", *Kirchliche Zeitgeschichte* 3 (1990): 166–87.

13 Cf. now among others Kati Marton, *The Chancellor: The Remarkable Odyssey of Angela Merkel* (New York: Simon and Schuster, 2021).

primarily concerned the democratic orientation of the Federal Republic towards Western Europe, rather than some profound vision of (re)Christianisation. However, what was initially a successful model changed over the course of decades.[14] Increasing secularisation and declining church membership of the Federal Republic of Germany, as well as the de-Christianised areas of East Germany following reunification, developed into a major challenge for the CDU; because CDU members were often denominationally bound, active members of their church. New research shows that the proportion of churchgoers both among the population and among CDU supporters is declining, and even that most of them rarely or never go to church.[15] This also has an impact on voting behaviour, because the higher the frequency of churchgoing, the higher the tendency to vote for the CDU.

Declining church membership in society means that the CDU needs to engage differently with traditional 'Christian' issues. On the one hand, polarising identitarian discussions developed around the apparent de-Christianisation of Germany and the CDU. This included, for example, the crucifix controversy in 2010, which was triggered by the then new Minister for Social Affairs and Integration in Lower Saxony, Aygül Özkan (CDU). She was the first female head of department of Turkish origin in Germany and had spoken out against crosses and headscarves in public schools—which led to heated debates in the CDU and Özkan eventually had to withdraw her vote.[16] On the other hand, however, an increasingly pluralistic Christian profile became more and more apparent in the CDU, such that religiosity would in itself no longer imply a certain stance on a range of ethical decisions. This was particularly evident in 2015 during the refugee crisis, when the then German Chancellor Angela Merkel explicitly justified her refugee policy of open borders on the basis of a Christian ideal of human dignity.

Her empathic statement "We can do it" ("Wir schaffen das!") found support within the CDU, but also drew criticism, such as from the Catholic Horst Seehofer, then CSU-Minister of the Interior from Bavaria. Seehofer called to limit the intake of refugees and promoted the idea of a Christian *Leitkultur* in the face of a supposed Islamic dominance (*Überfremdung*). That a homogenous

---

14   Further Benjamin Ziemann, "Säkularisierung und Neuformierung des Religiösen. Religion und Gesellschaft in der zweiten Hälfte des 20. Jahrhundert", *Archiv für Sozialgeschichte* 51 (2011): 3–36.
15   Viola Neu, "Religiosität und Wahlverhalten", Konrad Adenauer Stiftung, 18 September 2020, accessed 20 September 2023, https://www.kas.de/de/analysen-und-argumente /detail/-/content/religiositaet-und-wahlverhalten.
16   Aygül Özkan, "Özkan rückt vom Kruzifix-Verbot ab", Die *Zeit*, 26 April 2010, accessed 20 September 2023, https://www.zeit.de/politik/deutschland/2010-04/oezkan-kruzifixe-cdu.

conservative, Christian social-ethical position in the CDU was no longer possible was also visible in 2017, when the 'marriage for all' was introduced. A total of 75 CDU parliamentarians voted in favour, and 225—three quarters—voted against.[17] Both groups included confessing Christians. Some cited the compatibility of the new law with Article 6 of the German Basic Law as a reason for their vote, which states that marriage is under special state protection and is defined as the union of one man and one woman. Christian references, such as the idea of a 'created order' or direct references from the Bible were not invoked either by those in favour or those voting against.

Another area where one can trace the changing religious orientations of CDU members is in their declared denominational affiliations. Catholics are still overrepresented in the CDU compared to the population as a whole, with about half of the CDU members being Catholic, a third Protestant, and about 17% non-denominational or of another religion.[18] In the population, there is a different distribution: nationwide, about one-third professes one of the two major denominations each.[19] There are nevertheless significant regional differences: in the former GDR federal states, originally the 'country of the Reformation', only about 6% belongs to the Catholic Church and 38% to the Protestant Church.[20] At the same time, some of the guest workers who arrived since the 1960s have become active members in the CDU.

As empirical surveys among CDU voters confirm, these demographical changes have impacted on the self-understanding of a party that respects religious values: the title 'Christian' does not seem to have a discriminatory effect but is rather interpreted as having an affinity with religion (probably in contrast to the Social Democrats, who are perceived as a more secular party). This seems to make the CDU a trustworthy party even for non-Christians. An empirical survey of CDU members according to their religious affiliation in 2019 shows that the proportion of Muslims in the CDU is about the same as the Muslim population in Germany (around 5%).[21] At the same time, it is evident that Catholics, Protestants and, to an above-average extent, Muslims in the

---

17 See Deutscher Bundestag, "Eheschließung für Personen gleichen Geschlechts", accessed 22 December 2022, https://www.bundestag.de/parlament/plenum/abstimmung/abstimmung/?id=486.
18 Viola Neu, "Die Mitglieder der CDU", Konrad Adenauer Stiftung, 26 October 2010, accessed 20 September 2023, https://www.kas.de/de/zukunftsforum-politik/detail/-/content/die-mitglieder-der-cdu.
19 Neu, "Die Mitglieder der CDU", 11–14.
20 Neu, "Die Mitglieder der CDU", 11–14.
21 Konrad Adenauer Stiftung, "Datensammlung April 2021, Monitor Wahl- und Sozialforschung, Tabellen und Grafiken Religion und Wahlverhalten", April 2021, p.5, accessed

CDU describe themselves as somewhat or very religious, with twice as many Muslims as Protestants describing themselves as very religious.[22]

From this, it can be derived that the CDU is perceived as a party in which political and civic engagement and religious practice are not seen as in contradiction with each other. It remains an open question, however, to what extent this finding corresponds with the self-perception of CDU voters, but also to that of political representatives in state and federal governments. According to their multi-religious membership, every tenth CDU official would have to be held by either a Muslim or a Christian Eastern Orthodox. A look at the CDU's current parliamentary group in the Bundestag shows that this is by no means the case—there are none.[23] The former German CDU-Interior Minister Wolfgang Schäuble invented the first German Islam Muslim Conference (*Deutsche Islam Konferenz*) in 2006.[24] It was intended to initiate long-term dialogue between the German state and Muslims living in Germany, with specific reference to the religious and socio-political integration of the Muslim population. As a result of this dialogue, which was shaped by Christian ethics, Schäuble claimed, Islam would find its place in Germany.[25] These efforts did not reach the CDU's broader base, especially since the rise of *Alternative für Deutschland* (the AfD) with its anti-Islamic rhetoric and policy caused the CDU deprioritise this dialogue.

Moreover, Germany has seen a dramatic rise in anti-Semitism and anti-Semitic crimes since the 2010s. In the first nine months of 2018, the number of incidents with an anti-Semitic background in south-western Germany increased by 38.1 per cent to 87 offences compared with the previous year,

---

20   September 2023, https://www.kas.de/de/analysen-und-argumente/detail/-/content/religiositaet-und-wahlverhalten.
22   Konrad Adenauer Stiftung, "Datensammlung April 2021, Monitor Wahl- und Sozialforschung, Tabellen und Grafiken Religion und Wahlverhalten", 8.
23   Deutscher Bundestag, "Parliament: CDU/CSU-Fraktion", 23 November 2022, accessed 20 September 2023, https://www.bundestag.de/parlament/fraktionen/cducsu. The twenty members are only Catholic and Protestant members.
24   Die Bundesregierung, "Regierungserklärung des Bundesministers des Innern, Dr. Wolfgang Schäuble, zur Deutschen Islamkonferenz vor dem Deutschen Bundestag am 28. September 2006 in Berlin", 28 September 2006, accessed 20 September 2023, https://www.bundesregierung.de/breg-de/service/bulletin/regierungserklaerung-des-bundesministers-des-innern-dr-wolfgang-schaeuble--797464.
25   Die Bundesregierung, "Regierungserklärung des Bundesministers des Innern, Dr. Wolfgang Schäuble, zur Deutschen Islamkonferenz vor dem Deutschen Bundestag am 28. September 2006 in Berlin".

including one violent offence.[26] In response, the Jewish Forum of the CDU Baden-Württemberg was established in 2018.[27] It is intended to promote social networking and intercultural dialogue. The Jewish Forum of the CDU followed Germany's official policy, expressed as a special historical responsibility of Germany for Israel's existence and security as a result of the Holocaust. In 2008, in a speech in the Knesset in Jerusalem, CDU Chancellor Angela Merkel described this as part of Germany's "*Staatsräson*" or reason of state.[28] In line with this official German policy, the preamble of the Jewish Forum declares its support for Israel's right to exist and opposes discrimination against Jews. Michael Hagel, the initiator of the Jewish Forum, justified the special responsibility of the CDU Baden-Württemberg towards the Jews and Jewish culture in Germany on the basis of Christian values, such as responsibility and tolerance. As a further step, the CSU condemned all forms of anti-Semitism at its party congress in Munich in 2019.[29]

Both examples demonstrate that religion is an important issue for the CDU. The party cannot afford to exist solely as a monolithic Christian conservative party, but caters to more diverse Christian, religious, and non-religious constituencies. However, low numbers of religiosity within the party are not further differentiated between conservative or progressive forms of religiosity. Arguably, a conservative Christian orientation is no longer a given. This is due to the loss of Christian socialisation among politicians and the pluralisation of Christianity in Germany in the post-war period. However, it is worth considering whether the CDU's 'Christianity' is being replaced by a more ambiguous or pluralistic orientation. In light of the recent federal elections in 2024, one might wonder

---

26 "Antisemitismus Beauftragter warnt vor Verschwoerungsmythen", *Süddeutsche Zeitung*, 1 July 2019, accessed 20 September 2023, https://www.sueddeutsche.de/politik/extremismus-stuttgart-antisemitismus-beauftragter-warnt-vor-verschwoerungsmythen-dpa.urn-newsml-dpa-com-20090101-190701-99-873388.

27 Stefanie Ball, "Neue Plattform Will Judentum Sichtbarer Machen", *Jüdische Allgemeine*, 22 July 2019, accessed 22 December 2022, https://www.juedische-allgemeine.de/unsere-woche/neue-plattform-will-judentum-sichtbarer-machen/.

28 Angela Merkel, speech before the Knesset, Jerusalem, 18 March 2008, https://www.bundesregierung.de/breg-de/service/newsletter-und-abos/bulletin/rede-von-bundeskanzlerin-dr-angela-merkel-796170.

29 CSU, "Müncher Erklärung gegen jede Form von Antisemitismus", accessed 20 September 2023, https://www.csu.de/common/csu/content/csu/hauptnavigation/dokumente/2019/Leitantrag-Muenchner-Erklaerung.pdf; Beauftragter der Bayerischen Staatsregierung für jüdisches Leben und gegen Antisemitismus, für Erinnerungsarbeit unde geschichtliches Erbe, "Tätigkeitsbericht des Beauftragten", CSU, 6 February 2020, accessed 20 September 2023, https://www.csu.de/common/csu/content/csu/hauptnavigation/partei/parteiarbeit/aks/Taetigkeitsbericht_Antisemitismusbeauftragter.pdf.

whether non-religious CDU voters will have a greater influence on the party in the future, and whether the CDU will continue to attract more religious voters.

4 Christianity and the Christian Democracy in the Netherlands

4.1 A Broad Field: Christian Parties in the Netherlands and the Emergence of the CDA

This section discusses the place of the *Christen Democratisch Appèl* (CDA) in Dutch politics and its relationship with Christianity and religion. It explores the self-understanding of the CDA, its importance in the political domain, developments with regard to its members, voters, and the number of seats of the party in the second chamber of the government. It also explores the role of the Child Care Benefit scandal and the departure of one of its most popular Parliamentarians, Pieter Omtzigt in 2021.

In contrast to Germany, there are several other political parties that see themselves as Christian, even though they do not belong to the family of Christian Democratic parties. These include a conservative Reformed political party, the SGP (*Staatkundige Gereformeerde Partij*),[30] which was established in 1918 and holds certain theocratic ideals. The more centrist Christian Union or CU (*ChristenUnie*)[31] was established in 2000 as a merger between two smaller Protestant parties, the former Reformed Political Alliance (*Gereformeerd Politiek Verbond*, GPV)[32] and the Reformed Political Federation (*Reformatorische Politieke Federatie*, RPF). The CU and the CDA have both been part of the most recent Rutte-administration (2022–2023). Apart from the Christian political parties presented above, religion is a broader feature in Dutch party politics. For example, religious people are also active in the eighteen non-Christian political parties which are represented in the Senate and the House of Representatives, as well as in regional and local politics.[33]

The CDA itself was founded in 1980 as a merger between three Christian parties: the Christian-Historical Union (*Christelijk-Historische Unie*, CHU) which was established in 1908, the Anti-Revolutionary Party (*Anti-Revolutionaire Partij*, ARP) which was founded in 1879, and the Catholic People's Party

---

30 SGP, "SGP", accessed 20 September 2023, https://sgp.nl.
31 CU, "CU", accessed 20 September 2023, https://www.christenunie.nl/.
32 George Harinck, "Het ontstaan van het Gereformeerd Politiek Verbond 1945–1949", in Harinck, Kuiper, and Bak, *De Antirevolutionaire partij 1829–1980*, 223–38.
33 Parlement, "Partijen in Eerste en Tweede Kamer", accessed 20 September 2023, https://www.parlement.com/id/vh8lnhrpfxut/partijen_in_tweede_en_eerste_kamer.

(*Katholieke Volkspartij*, KVP) which was instituted in 1945.[34] The CDA participated in several administrations until the 1990s and again since the 2000s, and has transformed itself tremendously.[35] Their decline in seats in the Dutch House of Representatives (*Tweede Kamer*) started in 2010 and since then it appears that the CDA plunged into a free fall. This decline is also visible in its membership. Apart from a few gains in membership, the CDA has lost more and more members. In 2020 the party had about 50,000 members, sustaining a loss of about 80,000 members over 35 years.

The downward trend has accelerated since 2010. The next section explores the reasons for this decline, including the Child Care Benefit scandal (*toeslagenaffaire*), declining trust in the government, cultural secularism in the Netherlands, anti-democratic tendencies[36] and counter-democracy,[37] which affect and even threaten the democratic rule of law and "the interface of public welfare policy and private morality".[38] Sara Kalm, Lisa Strömbom, and Anders Uhlin state that "Counter-democracy is manifested in the institutions, agents and functions that are committed to overseeing ruling institutions, expressing mistrust and channelling dissent. Importantly, counter-democracy is not contrary to democracy, but a vital and perennial aspect of it".[39]

4.2 CDA and Religion

Although the CDA is rooted in Christianity, both in Roman Catholicism and in Protestantism, religion plays a marginal, and even implicit role.[40] This does

---

34 D.Th. Kuiper, *Christen-democratie* (Leiden: Stichting Burgerschapskunde, 1988); Van Spanning, *De Christelijk-Historische Unie 1908–1980*; RUG/DNPP, "Anti-Revolutionaire Partij (ARP)", accessed 20 September 2023, https://www.rug.nl/research/dnpp/politieke-partijen/arp/; RUG/DNPP, "Katholieke Volkspartij (KVP)", accessed 20 September 2023, https://www.rug.nl/research/dnpp/politieke-partijen/kvp/.
35 D.Th. Kuiper, *Christen-democratie*.
36 Rijksoverheid, "Direct verbod op antidemocratische organisaties mogelijk", 22 June 2021, accessed 23 April 2024, https://www.rijksoverheid.nl/actueel/nieuws/2021/06/22/direct-verbod-op-antidemocratische-organisaties-mogelijk.
37 Sara Kalm, Lisa Strömbom, and Anders Uhlin, "Civil Society Democratising Global Governance? Potentials and Limitations of ‚Counter-Democracy'", *Global Society* 33:4 (2019), 499–519, https://doi.org/10.1080/13600826.2019.1640189; Pierre Rosavallon and Arthur Goldhammer, *Counter-Democracy: Politics in an Age of Distrust* (Cambridge: Cambridge University Press, 2010).
38 David Hanley, ed., *Christian Democracy in Europe: A Comparative Perspective* (London: Pinter Publishers, 1994), 213; Hans-Martien ten Napel Adams and Maarten Neuteboom, eds., "Democratie in ademnood?" Special Issue, *Christen Democratische Verkenningen* 32, no. 4 (Winter 2012).
39 Kalm, Strömbom and Uhlin 2019, 499.
40 Cf. Martin Terpstra, "De religieuze dimensie van democratie", *Christen Democratische Verkenningen* 32, no. 4 (2012): 70–77.

not necessarily mean that personal faith is absent in the membership, its politicians, or the party more in general. Similarly to the CDU in Germany, Muslims also participate in the CDA.[41] Some have become members of the municipal council, provincial councils or the House of Representatives. Since the 2000s, the CDA even has informal deliberations for theologians, the so-called Theologians' Council (*Theologenberaad*).[42] The notion of religion in the political party nevertheless is not so explicit, but more implicit at present. This is apparent from the position of the Theologians' Council, which is somewhat informal, and which draws limited interest among CDA Parliamentarians. It also appears, for example, from the overview of the standpoints of the CDA on a range of societal and political topics. These topics include health care, education, agriculture, fishery, and the national anthem. However, religion or faith is not included.[43] In this regard, secularisation across society is also visible within the CDA.

4.3 Case Study: The Child Care Benefit Scandal

At this point it is helpful to bring in the Child Care Benefit scandal, which was exposed by a very popular CDA Parliamentarian, Pieter Omtzigt, who left the party following a fallout in 2021. His work on the scandal brought to light that the taxation department of the government wrongfully accused about 26,000 citizens of fraudulent use of child care benefits in the period 2004 to 2019, affecting about 70,000 children. The Tax and Customs Administration violated the fundamental principles of the rule of law, causing significant hardship for the families involved, including because of ethnic profiling and discriminating of Dutch citizens with non-Dutch surnames. After a high-profile Parliamentary investigation of the matter, families were promised financial compensation, although problems continue to arise as many families still suffer.

The political party leadership feared that Omtzigt's popularity might lead him to establish a new political party that would compete with the traditional CDA constituency. When the third Rutte-administration resigned in January 2021, formally in response to the Child Care Benefit scandal, it became clear that the CDA – as part of the government – would share the blame for the scandal. While the CDA obtained 15 of the 150 seats in the House of Representatives in March 2021, Omzigt received many preferential votes. When the new

---

41 CDA, "Gedeelde waarden: Moslims in het CDA", accessed 20 September 2023, https://www.cda.nl/leden/publicaties/gedeelde-waarden-moslims-in-het-cda.
42 Gerrit-Jan KleinJan, "Theologenberaad buigt zich over de 'C' van het CDA", *Trouw*, 8 February 2011.
43 CDA, "Standpunten op alfabet", accessed 30 November 2021, https://www.cda.nl/standpunten/op-alfabet/.

coalition negotiations were underway, it was suggested that Omtzigt might be offered a position 'elsewhere'. He then decided to work as an independent Parliamentarian until the electoral year of 2023, when he founded a new political party, New Social Contract or NSC (*Nieuw Sociaal Contract*). NSC won 20 of the 150 seats (12,8% of the votes), whereas the CDA only won 5 seats (3,3% of the votes), signalling that Omzigt was able to attract support from among a significant number of CDA voters.[44]

4.4 *The Decline of Membership of the CDA*

In general, between 1977 and 2021 the percentage of CDA voters went from 31.89% of the electorate in 1977 to 9.5% in 2021. There have also been some increases, in 1986 it was 34.59% and in 1989 even 35.39% of the total electorate. In 2012 the percentage was even lower than in 2021, namely 8.51%. This is reflected in actual seats won. In 1977 they won 49 of the 150 seats in the House of Representatives, almost one third of the total seats of House of Representatives. In 1986 and 1989 the number of seats was the highest, with 54 seats. In 2021 this number was 15, one tenth of the total number of seats of the House.

Despite the ongoing contestation of the future orientation of the party – should it pursue a more left-wing or right-wing identity – the CDA had been and still is considered a political party of the centre or centre-right.[45] The party is, however, no longer in the centre of political power. Rather, it has become a party which no longer appears on the list of the largest or most influential parties, although in 2021 it still held the fourth position in the list of 17 political parties, after two liberal parties (VVD and D66) and a right-wing populist party (PVV).[46] The CDA would gain no more than five seats, at least according to the polls of political analyst Maurice de Hond from 18 December 2022.[47]

On 16 March 2022, elections for city councils were held in the Netherlands. Although both the VVD and the CDA were, from a national perspective, the two largest political parties in the city councils, the CDA lost 240 seats in total. The VVD lost 145 seats. In 2018, both the VVD and the CDA had more than 13% of the vote, and in 2022 11.5% and 11.2% respectively. Both the VVD and the CDA were

---

44 NOS, "Zetelverdeling Tweede Kamer", accessed 21 February 2023, https://app.nos.nl/nieuws/tk2023/.

45 CDA, "De uitgangspunten van het CDA", accessed 20 April 2024, https://www.cda.nl/standpunten/uitgangspunten; BNR, "CDA-achterban wil centrumrechtse, pro-EU-opvolger Buma", accessed 20 April 2024, https://www.bnr.nl/nieuws/politiek/10378665/cda-achterban-wil-centrumrechtse-pro-eu-opvolger-buma.

46 Parlement, "Samenstelling Tweede Kamer na de verkiezingen van 17 maart 2021—totaaloverzicht", March 2021, accessed 20 September 2023, https://www.parlement.com/id/vlfkldqdjwmw/samenstelling_tweede_kamer_na_de.

47 Peilingen Nederland, "Peilingen Ipsos", accessed 12 January 2023, https://www.peilingennederland.nl/alle-peilingen.html.

and are part of the government administrations under Rutte III (2017–2021) and Rutte IV (from 2022).

To close, according to an even more recent poll of 26 March 2024, the CDA would have only six seats in the House of Representatives.[48] With recent changes in the leadership and reflection on the notion of Christian democracy by new leader Henri Bontenbal (*1982), the party is regaining its appeal.[49] The most recent poll of 14 April 2025 shows that the CDA would have eighteen seats, and NSC two. This was four days before Omtzigt announced his departure from national politics.[50]

5   The Death of Christian Democracy?

With the increasing political separation of church and state and the growing acceptance of secular political and social state structures, different confessional Christian parties emerged throughout Europe from the so-called long nineteenth century onwards.[51] After the humanitarian catastrophe of the Second World War, Christian Democratic parties re-established themselves in several European countries. Although they often came from the Roman Catholic tradition, they now consciously saw themselves as Christian, that is, non-denominational, parties. They assumed governmental and democratic responsibility in many countries and formed an important pillar of the emerging European communities. The commitment to the social market economy and a Christian-inspired European welfare model were important contributions of the Christian parties in post-war Europe.

At the same time, there was fundamental theological criticism of this Christian party commitment, often from within Protestant circles. One of the harshest critics was the Swiss Reformed theologian Karl Barth (1886–1968) who criticised the notion of Christian politics, because of what he considered as a major distinction between God and human beings. He feared the politicisation of the divine; though this did not mean he thought that the church and Christians can be politically indifferent.[52] The European successes of Christian

---

48   Peilingen Nederland, "Peilingen Ipsos", accessed 20 April 2024, https://www.peilingennederland.nl/alle-peilingen.html.
49   CDA, "Henri Bontenbal: Politiek leider CDA", accessed 21 February 2021, https://www.cda.nl/henri.
50   Peilingen Nederland, "Peilingen Ipsos", accessed 23 April 2025, https://www.peilingennederland.nl/alle-peilingen.html.
51   Enyedi and Madeley, *Church and State in Contemporary Europe*; Karl Barth, *Der Römerbrief* (Zürich: Theologischer Verlag Zürich, 1985); Karl Barth, *Christengemeinde und Bürgergemeinde* (*Kirche und Staat*) (Zollikon-Zürich: Evangelischer Verlag, 1946).
52   Barth, *Christengemeinde und Bürgergemeinde*.

Democracy in the post-war period as well as the voices concerned for the sanctity of the Christian church, such as Barth's, seem out of date nowadays, but they reflect an important contestation of the Christian identity of Christian Democracy.

In our brief overview, this chapter showed that the two Christian Democratic parties in Germany and the Netherlands have very different histories, but also, that their understanding of 'Christian' developed differently. The meaning of the 'C', the notion of Christianity specifically or of religion in general in the CDA and CDU, has changed over the years. It has become less prominent and explicit, more ambivalent, and in some ways, more inclusive. Christian believers can be found in other Christian political parties, but also in neutral political parties, although the CDA has an informal Theologians' Council. The CDU is considered trustworthy by a range of religious and non-religious voters, although the party emerged from a conservative Christian orientation. One cannot say that the CDA has ceased to be Christian, but it has become Christian in a very different way, more of a generally religious party. However, it is hard to understand what the nature of religion is in Christian Democracy. In general, it might express a particular register of Luckmann's "invisible religion".[53] There are also elements of what Hjelm calls "the new visibility of religion".[54]

Against this background, the question of the causes of the decline or even death of the Christian democrats cannot be answered in a general European way either but must address the specific developments and particularities of both countries. Nevertheless, it is appealing to consider further the argument of Jan-Werner Müller. He stated in 2014 that today's Europe is "a creation of Christian Democrats", since they "were the architects of European integration and of postwar Atlanticism".[55] This reveals something about the history and the nature of the European Union. We also have to face the current

---

53 T. Luckmann, *The Invisible Religion: The Problem of Religion in Modern Society* (New York: Macmillan, 1967).

54 Titus Hjelm, "Understanding the New Visibility of Religion", *Journal of Religion in Europe* 7, no. 3-4 (2014): 203–22, https://doi.org/10.1163/18748929-00704002. Cf. among others T. Cremer, *Defenders of the Faith? Religion, National Populism and the Rise of Right-Wing Identity Politics* (London: Routledge, 2022); Katharina Kunter and Leon van den Broeke, "Religion, Populism and Politics: The Notion of Religion in Election Manifestos of Populist and Nationalist Parties in Germany and The Netherlands", *Religions* 12, no. 3 (2021): 1–15, https://doi.org/10.3390/rel12030178.

55 Jan-Werner Müller, "The End of Christian Democracy: What the Movement's Decline Means for Europe", *Foreign Affairs*, 15 July 2014, accessed 20 September 2023, https://www.foreignaffairs.com/articles/western-europe/2014-07-15/end-christian-democracy.

and future challenges of the European Union in the context of geopolitics. The increasing questioning of democracy in general and the decline of Christian democracy in Europe affects the future of Europe and post-war Atlanticism, events in Ukraine in the context of the geopolitical stage, since it demonstrates the ongoing potency of non-democratic powers. Focussing on the changing or changed political landscape in Germany and the Netherlands needs to be understood in the context of the East-West division propagated by illiberal politics in Russia, Europe and the United States of America. Moreover, the erosion of the political centre under the influence of polarisation and the left-right distinction is posing a challenge to the future of democracy – not just in Germany and the Netherlands, but also in Europe.

Müller hints at the search for a synthesis of Christianity and modern democracy.[56] His concept of Christianity is fundamentally a Roman Catholic one. From a historical perspective he pointed out three strategies in order to reach such a synthesis: 1) to apply the French Revolution and to form a Christian nation; 2) to make democratic institutions Christian in nature; and, 3) to form Christian political parties respectful of modern democratic rule of law. However, it is not (only) the influence of secularisation which has a negative effect on Christian political parties, such as the Christian Democratic parties, but also the rise of new nationalist and populist political parties that challenge the values of Christian Democracy.[57] This illiberal turn translates into meaningful threats to democracy and the rule of law across Europe.[58]

The decline of Christian Democracy and the threats to democracy in Europe can be considered as a wake-up call for Christian Democratic political parties in Europe. Michael Meyer-Resende, executive director of Democracy Reporting International, a non-partisan NGO which supports political participation, concluded his article on the slow death of Christian Democracy and the rise of national and populist political parties with these words: "As the extreme right is discrediting itself in many countries, Christian Democrats should be more confident in their own political offer".[59]

The decline of Christian Democracy is not an isolated phenomenon. Many classical or traditional political parties are going through a hard time. In the

---

56 Jan-Werner Müller, "Towards a new history of Christian Democracy", *Journal of Political Ideologies* 18, no. 2 (2013): 243–55, https://doi.org/10.1080/13569317.2013.784025.

57 Cf. Michael Meyer-Resende, "The slow death of EU Christian Democracy", *EU Observer*, 3 June 2020, accessed 20 September 2023, https://euobserver.com/opinion/148527.

58 Cf. Carlo Invernizzi Accetti, *What Is Christian Democracy? Politics, Religion and Ideology* (Cambridge: Cambridge University Press, 2019).

59 Meyer-Resende, "The slow death of EU Christian Democracy".

Netherlands the same goes for the Labour Party (*Partij van de Arbeid*, PvdA).[60] In his new book, Joop van den Berg, emeritus professor parliamentary history, states that, since the 1990s, the Netherlands faces three plagues: 1) floating voters who are no longer familiar with fixed political parties or loyalty to such parties; 2) the coarsening of the behaviour of politicians in the political arena and in the media or on social media; and, 3) the fragmentation of political parties.[61] Furthermore, it is not only Christian democracy which faces exhaustion, but even democracy in general.[62]

6   Conclusions

With the start of the Russian war against Ukraine, a period of democratic and liberal openness that began with the collapse of the Communist regimes and the Soviet Union in 1991 came to its end. What were the characteristics of this period for the Christian Democratic parties? To what extent was a period of openness possibly rather obstructive for their Christian profile? These are important questions for future research. This chapter discussed the development of Christian Democracy and its connection with Christianity and religion in Germany and the Netherlands in the post-Cold War context until 2021.

After the Second War the CDU became a strong Christian political party in West Germany. More than half a century later, many members and voters are less Christian, but have an affinity with religion. For example, about 5% of the CDU today are Muslim. Moreover, members and voters do not consider themselves as Christian but appreciate the intertwinement of Christian democratic values or religious practice and civic engagement. Compared to the Dutch CDA, the two groups—Roman Catholic and Protestant—are more prominent. This appears, for example, in the process of choosing the successor of the Protestant Angela Merkel. For the CDU the question is whether it will be a home in the future for more strongly Christian, religious, or non-religious members and voters.

Much of this resembles the situation of the Dutch CDA, which has become a shadow of its former self. In 1977 the CDA had one third of the seats in the second chamber of Dutch Parliament; in 2021 it had less than ten percent. The CDA is competing with traditional liberal and socialist parties, but also faces

---

60   PvdA, "PvdA", accessed 20 September 2023, https://www.pvda.nl/.
61   Joop van den Berg, *Humeurig volk, verkrampte politiek en hoe het anders kan* (Amsterdam: Prometheus-Bert Bakker, 2022).
62   Maurice Adams et al., *Democratie in ademnood* (Amsterdam: Boom, 2012).

significant challenges from nationalist and populist parties, and by internal challenges, as the Omtzigt case demonstrated. These developments beg further reflection from within the party. Even if core values such as stewardship, solidarity, public justice, and distributed responsibility continue to shape the party, the question is in what way the CDA distinguishes itself from other parties; and moreover, how to walk the talk as political leader(s), politicians, members, and voters in the CDA for the benefit of Dutch society, and how to demonstrate moral, inspired and inspiring leadership, and cast away the nature of a political party which is focused on political power.

If indeed Europe is a creation of Christian Democracy, the geopolitical and national developments provide much homework for Christian Democratic political parties in Germany and the Netherlands.[63]

Bibliography

(2019). "Antisemitismus Beauftragter warnt vor Verschwoerungsmythen". *Süddeutsche Zeitung*, 1 July 2019. Accessed 20 September 2023. https://www.sueddeutsche.de/politik/extremismus-stuttgart-antisemitismus-beauftragter-warnt-vor-verschwoerungsmythen-dpa.urn-newsml-dpa-com-20090101-190701-99-873388.

Accetti, C.I. (2019). *What Is Christian Democracy? Politics, Religion and Ideology.* Cambridge: Cambridge University Press.

Accetti, C.I. (2020). "The European Union as a Christian democracy: a heuristic approach". *Journal of European Public Policy* 27, no. 9: 1329–48.

Adams, H.-M. ten N., and M. Neuteboom, eds. (2012). "Democratie in ademnood?" Special Issue, *Christen Democratische Verkenningen* 32, no. 4.

Adams, M, et al. (2012). *Democratie in ademnood.* Amsterdam: Boom.

Albrecht, M., G. Mehnert, and C. Meißner. (2012). *Der Evangelische Arbeitskreis der CDU/CSU 1952–2002: Werden, Wirken und Wollen.* Rheinbach: UBG-Betriebs GmbH.

Augustine. (1957–1972). *The City of God against the Pagans.* 7 Vols. Ed. George Englert MacCracken. London: Heinemann.

Ball, S. (2019). "Neue Plattform Will Judentum Sichtbarer Machen". *Jüdische Allgemeine*, 22 July 2019. Accessed 22 December 2022. https://www.juedische-allgemeine.de/unsere-woche/neue-plattform-will-judentum-sichtbarer-machen/.

Barth, K. (1946). *Christengemeinde und Bürgergemeinde (Kirche und Staat).* Zollikon-Zürich: Evangelischer Verlag.

---

63 Accetti, "The European Union as a Christian democracy"; François Foret, *Religion and Politics in the European Union: The Secular Canopy* (New York: Cambridge University Press, 2015); Müller, "The End of Christian Democracy".

Barth, K. (1985). *Der Römerbrief.* Zürich: Theologischer Verlag Zürich.

Beauftragter der Bayerischen Staatsregierung für jüdisches Leben und gegen Antisemitismus, für Erinnerungsarbeit unde geschichtliches Erbe. (2020). "Tätigkeitsbericht des Beauftragten". CSU, 6 February 2020. accessed 20 September 2023. https://www.csu.de/common/csu/content/csu/hauptnavigation/partei/parteiarbeit/aks/Taetigkeitsbericht_Antisemitismusbeauftragter.pdf.

Besier, G. (1990). "Christliche Parteipolitik und Konfession. Zur Entstehung des Evangelischen Arbeitskreises der CDU/CSU". *Kirchliche Zeitgeschichte* 3: 166–87.

Blaschke, O. (2002). *Konfessionen im Konflikt: Deutschland zwischen 1800 und 1970. Ein zweites konfessionelles Zeitalter.* Göttingen: Vandenhoeck & Ruprecht.

Blaschke, O., and F.M. Kuhlmann, eds. (2002). *Religion im Kaiserreich: Milieus—Mentalitäten—Krisen.* 2nd Ed. Gütersloh: Gütersloher Verlagshaus.

Bösch, F. (2001). *Die Adenauer-CDU: Aufsteig und Krise einer Erfolgspartei (1945–1969).* München: Deutsche Verlagsanstalt.

Bruce, S. (2002). *God is Dead: Secularization in the West.* Oxford: Wiley-Blackwell.

CDA. (n.d.). "Gedeelde waarden: Moslims in het CDA". Accessed 20 September 2023. https://www.cda.nl/leden/publicaties/gedeelde-waarden-moslims-in-het-cda.

CDA. (n.d.). "Standpunten op alfabet". Accessed 30 November 2021. https://www.cda.nl/standpunten/op-alfabet/. No longer accessible.

Cremer, T. (2022). *Defenders of the Faith? Religion, National Populism and the Rise of Right-Wing Identity Politics.* London: Routledge.

CSU. (2019). "Müncher Erklärung gegen jede Form von Antisemitismus". accessed 20 September 2023. https://www.csu.de/common/csu/content/csu/hauptnavigation/dokumente/2019/Leitantrag-Muenchner-Erklaerung.pdf.

De Kruijff, G.G. (1994). *Waakzaam en nuchter: Over christelijke ethiek in een democratie.* Baarn: Ten Have.

De Voss, J.T. (2019). *Christendemocratie en identiteit: Nederland en Duitsland vergeleken (2000–2017).* Münster: Verlag readbox publishing GmbH.

Deutscher Bundestag. (2022). "Parliament: CDU/CSU-Fraktion". 23 November 2022. Accessed 20 September 2023. https://www.bundestag.de/parlament/fraktionen/cducsu.

Deutscher Bundestag. (N.d.). "Eheschließung für Personen gleichen Geschlechts". Accessed 22 December 2022. https://www.bundestag.de/parlament/plenum/abstimmung/abstimmung/?id=486.

Die Bundesregierung. (2006). "Regierungserklärung des Bundesministers des Innern, Dr. Wolfgang Schäuble, zur Deutschen Islamkonferenz vor dem Deutschen Bundestag am 28. September 2006 in Berlin". 28 September 2006. Accessed 20 September 2023. https://www.bundesregierung.de/breg-de/service/bulletin/regierungserklaerung-des-bundesministers-des-innern-dr-wolfgang-schaeuble--797464.

Distrust. Cambridge: Cambridge University Press.

Enyedi, Z., and J.T.S. Madeley, eds. (2003). *Church and State in Contemporary Europe*. Frank Cass Publications.

Foret, F. (2015). *Religion and Politics in the European Union: The Secular Canopy*. New York: Cambridge University Press.

Greschat, M. (2002). *Die evangelische Christenheit und die deutsche Geschichte nach 1945: Weichenstellungen in der Nachkriegszeit*. Stuttgart: Kohlhammer.

Hanley, D. (ed.). (1994). *Christian Democracy in Europe: A Comparative Perspective*. London: Pinter Publishers.

Harinck, G. (2001). "Het ontstaan van het Gereformeerd Politiek Verbond 1945–1949". In: G. Harinck, R. Kuiper, and P. Bak (eds.). *De Antirevolutionaire partij 1829–1980*. Hilversum: Verloren. Pp. 223–38.

Harinck, G., Roel K., and P. Bak, eds. (2001). *De Antirevolutionaire partij 1829–1980*. Hilversum: Verloren.

Haynes, J. (2021). *The Routledge Handbook to Religion and Political Parties*. London: Routledge.

Hermle, S., and H. Oelke, eds. (2021). *Protestantismus in der Nachkriegszeit (1945–1961)*. Leipzig: EVA.

Hjelm, T. (2014). "Understanding the New Visibility of Religion". *Journal of Religion in Europe* 7, no. 3–4: 203–22. doi:10.1163/18748929-00704002.

Hoogerwerf, A. (1999). *Christelijke denkers over politiek: Een oogst van 20 eeuwen*. Baarn: Ten Have.

Janssens, R. (2001). *De opbouw van de Antirevolutionaire Partij 1850–1888*. Amsterdam: Verloren.

Kaiser, J.-C., and A. Döring-Manteuffel, eds. (1990). *Christentum und politische Verantwortung: Kirchen im Nachkriegsdeutschland*. Stuttgart: Kohlhammer.

Kalm, S., L. Strömbom, and A. Uhlin. "Civil Society Democratising Global Governance?

KleinJan, G.-J. (2011). "Theologenberaad buigt zich over de 'C' van het CDA". *Trouw*, 8 February 2011.

Konrad Adenauer Stiftung. (2021). "Datensammlung April 2021, Monitor Wahl- und Sozialforschung, Tabellen und Grafiken Religion und Wahlverhalten". April 2021. Accessed 20 September 2023. https://www.kas.de/documents/291186/291235/Religion+und+Wahlverhalten.pdf/fc0e178c-cbd6-e2ef-9255-3f35d64a3eb8?version=1.0&t=1618913055535.

Konrad Adenauer Stiftung. (n.d.). "Der Evangelische Arbeitskreis (EAK)". Accessed 20 September 2023. https://www.kas.de/de/web/geschichte-der-cdu/evangelischer-arbeitskreis-eak-.

Kselman, T., and T. Buttigieg, eds. (2003). *European Christian Democracy: Historical Legacies and Comparative Perspectives*. University of Notre Dame Press.

Kuiper, D.Th. (1988). *Christen-democratie.* Leiden: Stichting Burgerschapskunde.

Kunter, K., and L. van den Broeke. (2021). "Religion, Populism and Politics: The Notion of Religion in Election Manifestos of Populist and Nationalist Parties in Germany and The Netherlands". *Religions* 12, no. 3: 1–15. https://doi.org/10.3390/rel12030178.

Lammert, Norbert, ed. (2021). *Handbuch zur Geschichte der CDU.* Darmstadt: Wissenschaftliche Buchgesellschaft.

Lappenküper, Ulrich. (2001). "Zwischen 'Sammlungsbewegung' und 'Volkspartei': Die CDU 1945–1969". In Michael Gehler, Wolfram Kaiser, and Helmut Wohnout (eds.). *Christdemokratie in Europa im 20. Jahrhundert,* Vienna: Böhlau. Pp. 385–98.

Luckmann, T. (1967). *The Invisible Religion: The Problem of Religion in Modern Society.* New York: Macmillan.

Marton, K. (2021). *The Chancellor: The Remarkable Odyssey of Angela Merkel.* New York: Simon and Schuster.

Meyer-Resende, M. (2020). "The slow death of EU Christian Democracy". *EU Observer,* 3 June 2020. Accessed 20 September 2023. https://euobserver.com/opinion/148527.

Miktat, P., ed. (1980). *Kirche und Staat in der neueren Entwicklung.* Darmstadt: Wissenschaftliche Buchgesellschaft.

Mitchell, M. (2012). *The Origins of Christian Democracy: Politics and Confession in Modern Germany.* University of Michigan Press.

Müller, J.-W. (2013). "Towards a new history of Christian Democracy". *Journal of Political Ideologies* 18, no. 2: 243–55. https://doi.org/10.1080/13569317.2013.784025.

Müller, J.-W. (2014). "The End of Christian Democracy: What the Movement's Decline Means for Europe". *Foreign Affairs,* 15 July 2014. Accessed 20 September 2023. https://www.foreignaffairs.com/articles/western-europe/2014-07-15/end-christian-democracy.

Neu, V. (2010). "Die Mitglieder der CDU". Konrad Adenauer Stiftung, 26 October 2010. accessed 20 September 2023. https://www.kas.de/de/zukunftsforum-politik/detail/-/content/die-mitglieder-der-cdu.

Neu, V. (2020). "Religiosität und Wahlverhalten". Konrad Adenauer Stiftung, 18 September 2020. Accessed 20 September 2023. https://www.kas.de/de/analysen-und-argumente/detail/-/content/religiositaet-und-wahlverhalten.

Odahl, C. (2010). *Constantine and the Christian Empire.* London: Routledge.

Özkan, A. "Özkan rückt vom Kruzifix-Verbot ab". *Die Zeit,* 26 April 2010. accessed 20 September 2023. https://www.zeit.de/politik/deutschland/2010-04/oezkan-kruzifixe-cdu.

Parlement. (2021). "Samenstelling Tweede Kamer na de verkiezingen van 17 maart 2021—totaaloverzicht". March 2021. Accessed 20 September 2023. https://www.parlement.com/id/vlfkldqdjwmw/samenstelling_tweede_kamer_na_de.

Parlement. (N.d.). "Partijen in Eerste en Tweede Kamer". accessed 20 September 2023. https://www.parlement.com/id/vh8lnhrpfxut/partijen_in_tweede_en_eerste_kamer.

Peilingen Nederland. (n.d.). "Peilingen Ipsos". Accessed 20 September 2023. https://www.peilingennederland.nl/alle-peilingen.html.

Pollack, D. (2008). "Religious Change in Europe: Theoretical Considerations and Empirical Findings". *Social Compass* 55: 168–86.

Pollack, D., C. Gärtner, and K. Gabriel, eds. (2012). *Umstrittene Säkularisierung: Soziologische und historische Analysen zur Differenzierung von Religion und Politik*. Berlin: Berlin University Press.

Potentials and Limitations of ‚Counter-Democracy'". *Global Society* 33:4 (2019), 499–519. https://doi.org/10.1080/13600826.2019.1640189.

Rasker, A.J. (194?). *Christelijke politiek: Gesprek over de theocratie*. Nijkerk: G.F. Callenbach.

Rijksoverheid. (2021). "Direct verbod op antidemocratische organisaties mogelijk". 22 June 2021. Accessed 23 April 2024. https://www.rijksoverheid.nl/actueel/nieuws/2021/06/22/direct-verbod-op-antidemocratische-organisaties-mogelijk.

Rosavallon, P., and A. Goldhammer. (2010). *Counter-Democracy: Politics in an Age of.*

RUG / DNPP. (n.d.). "Katholieke Volkspartij (KVP)". Accessed 20 September 2023. https://www.rug.nl/research/dnpp/politieke-partijen/kvp/.

RUG/DNPP. (n.d.). "Anti-Revolutionaire Partij (ARP)". Accessed 20 September 2023. https://www.rug.nl/research/dnpp/politieke-partijen/arp/.

Sauer, T., ed. (2000). *Katholiken und Protestanten in den Aufbaujahren der Bundesrepublik*. Stuttgart: Kohlhammer.

Smith, H.W., ed. (2002). *Protestants, Catholics and Jews in Germany 1800–1914*. Oxford: Berg Publishers, 2002.

Steven, M.H.M. (2011). *Christianity and Party Politics*. London: Routledge, 2011.

Ten Napel, H.-M.Th.D. (1992). *'Een eigen weg': De totstandkoming van het CDA (1952–1980)*. Kampen: Vbk Media.

Terpstra, M. (2012). "De religieuze dimensie van democratie". *Christen Democratische Verkenningen* 32, no. 4: 70–77.

Van den Berg, J. (2022). *Humeurig volk, verkrampte politiek en hoe het anders kan*. Amsterdam: Prometheus-Bert Bakker.

Van der Tol, M.D.C., and P. Gorski (2022). "Secularisation as the fragmentation of the sacred and of sacred space", *Religion, State and Society* 50, no. 5: 495–512. https://doi.org/10.1080/09637494.2022.2144662.

Van Ruler, A.A. (1945). *Religie en politiek*. Nijkerk: G.F. Callenbach.

Van Spanning, H. (1988). *De Christelijk-Historische Unie 1908–1980: Enige hoofdlijnen uit haar geschiedenis*. 2 Vols. Amsterdam: Scheltema & Holkema.

Verkuil, D. (1992). *Een positieve grondhouding: De geschiedenis van het CDA*.'s-Gravenhage: Sdu Uitgeverij, Koninginnegracht.

Wikipedia. (n.d.). "Christen-Democratisch Appèl". Accessed 20 September 2023. https://nl.wikipedia.org/wiki/Christen-Democratisch_App%C3%A8l.

Ziemann, B. (2011). "Säkularisierung und Neuformierung des Religiösen. Religion und Gesellschaft in der zweiten Hälfte des 20. Jahrhundert". *Archiv für Sozialgeschichte* 51: 3–36.

Zippelius, R. (2009). *Staat und Kirche: Von der Antike bis zur Gegenwart*. Mohr Siebeck: Tübingen.

CHAPTER 14

The European Union as a Space of (In)Securities: Analysing Political Reasoning by Lithuanian Catholics

Rosita Garškaitė-Antonowicz

1 Introduction

"Let's not delude ourselves, we have not entered paradise, nor the Gardens of Eden, but only the fair of opportunities. ... This fair of opportunities is also a great moral challenge. The question will arise even more sharply, more painfully, more frequently: for what purpose do we use freedom and prosperity?" These are the words of the former archbishop of Vilnius, Audrys Juozas Bačkis, transmitted via television and radio on the occasion of Lithuania's accession to the European Union in 2004. He also expressed his joy and pride for the fact that Lithuanian people finally came back to the 'European home', which was in line with general support for integrationist ideas from Catholic bishops. The year before, in the EU membership referendum, the Catholic Church used its, at the time, authoritative voice and nationwide network to encourage citizens' participation and voting 'Yes'. However, the warning in the above quote demonstrates the defensive disposition towards the EU characteristic of official Catholic discourse. Right from the beginning, the hierarchy was cautious about the effects of integration into Europe on Lithuanian society. Another thing worth noting in the above quote is a vivid spatial imagination. The European Union is more than a political entity; it is a space simultaneously perceived as home and a challenging fair of opportunities.

Scholars have repeatedly shown that Catholics are among the 'warmest' towards the European Union compared to believers affiliated with other or no religious traditions, especially in countries where Catholicism is dominant.[1]

---

[1] Brent F. Nelsen and James L. Guth, *Religion and the Struggle for European Union: Confessional Culture and the Limits of Integration* (Washington, D.C.: Georgetown University Press, 2015); Brent F. Nelsen, James L. Guth, and Brian Highsmith, "Does Religion Still Matter? Religion and Public Attitudes toward Integration in Europe", *Politics and Religion* 4, no. 1 (April 2011): 1–26; Brent F. Nelsen, James L. Guth, and Cleveland R. Fraser, "Does Religion Matter?: Christianity and Public Support for the European Union", *European Union Politics* 2, no. 2 (June 29, 2001): 191–217; Margarete Scherer, "The Religious Context in Explaining Public Support for

Although Catholicism as a confessional culture has ceased to provide support for the EU among millennials, the positive influence of religious commitment on support persists.[2] This is not surprising, considering the Vatican's pro-EU position and the historical role that Christian Democrats played in the construction of the EU.[3]

Yet contradictions arise between their religious worldview and the values of the 'secular and secularising'[4] polity regarding sexual morality and reproductive matters, the regulation of religious affairs in the public sphere, and issues of institutional memory such as the refusal to mention the 'Christian roots' of Europe in the failed European Constitution, and later in the Treaty of Lisbon. Moreover, the EU is presented as a threat to religious and national values in some Catholic discourse, most notably in Poland,[5] and right-wing populists employ references to Christianity as an identity marker to shape antagonism between their nation and the EU elites not only in the Eastern part of Europe.[6]

---

the European Union", *Journal of Common Market Studies* 53, no. 4 (2015): 893–909; Willfried Spohn, Matthias Koenig, and Wolfgang Knöbl, *Religion and National Identities in an Enlarged Europe. Religion and National Identities in an Enlarged Europe* (London: Palgrave Macmillan, 2015); Siobhan McAndrew, "Belonging, Believing, Behaving, and Brexit: Channels of Religiosity and Religious Identity in Support for Leaving the European Union", *British Journal of Sociology* 71, no. 5 (2020).

2   Brent F. Nelsen, and James L. Guth, "Losing Faith: Religion and Attitudes toward the European Union in Uncertain Times", *JCMS: Journal of Common Market Studies* 58, no. 4 (July 1, 2020): 909–24.

3   Petr Kratochvíl, and Tomáš Doležal, *The European Union and the Catholic Church* (Palgrave Macmillan UK, 2015); Carlo Invernizzi Accetti, *What Is Christian Democracy?: Politics, Religion and Ideology* (Cambridge University Press, 2019); Wolfram Kaiser, *Christian Democracy and the Origins of European Union* (Cambridge University Press, 2007).

4   François Foret, *Religion and Politics in the European Union: The Secular Canopy* (Cambridge University Press, 2015), 280.

5   Agnieszka Szumigalska, "The Polish Catholic Church's Perception of the Processes of EU Integration and Europeanisation in the Context of Traditional Norms and Values", *Religion, State and Society* 43, no. 4 (October 2, 2016): 342–56; Guerra, Simona, "Religion and the EU: A Commitment under Stress", in *Euroscepticism as a Transnational and Pan-European Phenomenon*, eds. John FitzGibbon, Benjamin Leruth, and Nick Startin (Abingdon: Routledge, 2017); Joanna Konieczna-Sałamatin, and Maja Sawicka, "The East of the West, or the West of the East? Attitudes toward the European Union and European Integration in Poland after 2008", *East European Politics and Societies: And Cultures* 35, no. 2 (June 4, 2020): 363–83.

6   Christian Lamour, "Orbán Urbi et Orbi: Christianity as a Nodal Point of Radical-Right Populism", *Politics and Religion*, 2021, 1–27; Andrea Molle, "Religion and Right-Wing Populism in Italy: Using 'Judeo-Christian Roots' to Kill the European Union", *Religion, State and Society* 47, no. 1 (January 1, 2019): 151–68; Marta Kotwas and Jan Kubik, "Symbolic Thickening of Public Culture and the Rise of Right-Wing Populism in Poland", *East European Politics and Societies and Cultures* 33, no. 2 (April 16, 2019): 435–71.

In Lithuania, far-right political actors also attempt to portray themselves as defenders of 'Christian values' inherent to the Lithuanian nation from allegedly foreign and threatening ideologies originating from the EU: globalism, multiculturalism, and 'genderism'.[7] However, they do not target the EU *per se* or Lithuania's membership thereof, because neither mainstream political parties nor the society in general are polarised on the EU issue. Since the restoration of independence in 1990, Lithuanians have been among the most supportive of EU membership.[8] Up to this day, the European project does not suffer from a lack of legitimacy, and even the 2008 financial crisis did not shake Lithuanians' confidence in the EU.[9] It is no surprise that political manifestations of Euroscepticism are marginal in a small post-communist country neighbouring the Russian Federation.[10] Because of size, historical experience, and geographic location, security concerns motivate pro-European stances among political elites and broader society.[11]

Against this background, I ask how Catholics in Lithuania perceive and navigate possible tensions around European integration. Regarding religion, most Lithuanians affiliate with the Roman Catholic Church (74%, according to the 2021 Census), but as in most European countries, the individualisation and privatisation of religion are present.[12] The description of "belonging without attending" introduced by Marko Veković in his chapter on Serbia suits to characterise religiosity among Lithuanian Catholics as well. The majority are so-called cultural or nominal Catholics, whereas active or devout believers who practise

---

7   Rosita Garškaitė, and Jogilė Ulinskaitė, "In the Name of the Family", in *CBEES State of the Region Report 2021: The Many Faces of the Far Right in the Post-Communist Space. A Comparative Study of Far-Right Movements and Identity in the Region*, ed. Ninna Mörner (Centre for Baltic and East European Studies, CBEES, Södertörn University, 2022), 140–142.
8   Cladas Gaidys, "25-Eri Požiūrio į Lietuvos Narystę Europos Sąjungoje Tyrimų Metai: 1991–2016", *Filosofija. Sociologija*, no. 4 (2016): 305–307.
9   Mažvydas Jastramskis, "Lietuvos Visuomenės Ir Politinių Partijų Nuostatos ES Atžvilgiu 2009–2013 M", in *Lietuva Europos Sąjungoje: Metraštis 2009–2013 Metais*, (2014), 18–22.
10 Ingrida Unikaitė-Jakuntavičienė, "Eurosceptics in Lithuania : On the Margins of Politics?" *European Quarterly of Political Attitudes and Mentalities* 3, no. 4 (2014): 19, https://nbn-resolving.org/urn:nbn:de:0168-ssoar-403079.
11 Gediminas Vitkus, "Small Is Small: Euroscepticism in Lithuanian Politics", in *Euroscepticism in the Baltic States: Uncovering Issues, People and Stereotypes*, eds. Karlis Bukovskis and Aldis Austers (Riga: Latvian Institute of International Affairs, Friedrich Ebert Stiftung, 2017); Ramūnas Vilpišauskas, "Lithuania and the EU: Pragmatic Support Driven by Security Concerns", in *The Future of Europe: Views from the Capitals*, eds. P. Kaeding, M., Pollak, and J. Schmidt (Cham: Palgrave Macmillan,2019).
12 Rūta Žiliukaitė,"Religinės Vertybės", in *Lietuvos Visuomenės Vertybių Kaita per Dvidešimt Nepriklausomybės Metų*, eds. Rūta Žiliukaitė, Arūnas Poviliūnas, and Aida Savicka (Vilnius: Vilniaus universiteto leidykla, 2016), 164–165.

their faith regularly constitute less than 13%.[13] In this chapter, I focus on the latter group because the more deeply one is embedded in a religious community, the more 'being a religious person' will take priority in one's social identity, and consequently in interpreting politics.

2 Theoretical-Methodological Approach and Data

To achieve an in-depth understanding of lay political reasoning about the EU and its interplay with Catholic identity, I start from two essential premises. First, religion provides individuals with cultural resources to articulate their relations to themselves, to others, and to mundane phenomena such as politics. As Ann Swidler puts it: "culture has enduring effects on those who hold it, not by shaping the ends they pursue, but by providing the characteristic repertoire from which they build lines of action".[14] Second, everyday[15] political thinking is not the internal, passive, and solitary affair illustrated by the famous Rodin sculpture 'Le Penseur'. According to Michael Billig, it is socially constructed because we employ cultural resources that are available to us and it is discursive, occurring in conversation with oneself or others.[16] Hence, drawing on the rhetorical-discursive approach in which "the words of the discourse are the thoughts, and the pattern of the argument is a record of the activity of thinking".[17]

The empirical data consists of in-depth interviews with 40 devout Lithuanian Catholics: people who attend Mass at least every Sunday, take active part in their parish life or other faith-based community and prioritise their religious identity. In *Schützian* terms, they can be positioned in the continuum between 'men (and women) on the street' and 'well-informed citizens'.[18] Although none of them were experts, some were highly interested in politics and aspired to

---

13   Eglė Laumenskaitė, *Krikščioniškumas Kaip Socialinių Laikysenų Veiksnys Totalitarinėje Ir Posovietinėje Visuomenėje* (Vilnius: Lietuvių katalikų mokslo akademija, 2015), 70–98.
14   Ann Swidler, "Culture in Action: Symbols and Strategies", *American Sociological Review* 51, no. 2 (April 1986): 284.
15   I use 'everyday' to describe thinking and talking produced by non-experts in non-formal interactions that do not have to occur daily.
16   Michael Billig, *Arguing and Thinking: A Rhetorical Approach to Social Psychology*, 2nd ed (Cambridge: Cambridge University Press, 1996), 142–145; 228–229.
17   Michael Billig, *Ideology and Opinions: Studies in Rhetorical Psychology* (Sage Publications, 1991), 191.
18   Alfred Schütz, "The Well-Informed Citizen: An Essay on the Social Distribution of Knowledge", *Social Research* 13, no. 4 (1946): 465–467, https://www.jstor.org/stable/40958880.

have a well-informed opinion, but the level of their interest varied. I recruited informants through parishes in two small towns and through religious communities in the capital city Vilnius. They aged from 19 to 68, the median age of the participants at the time of the interview was 45. Distributed rather representatively in terms of locality and gender (23 women and 17 men), most of the informants had completed higher education, only 4 participated with secondary and 2 with vocational training. In addition, informants differed in professional profile (including students and retired people) and partisanship. All were born and educated in Lithuania; some lived abroad for educational or professional reasons and came back for good.

Interviews were conducted in 2020–2022; they were tape-recorded and lasted from half an hour to an hour and a half. I aspired to collect interviews that resembled spontaneous conversational discourse. The topic guide contained questions and prompts on the meanings of European integration, Lithuanian membership, Brexit, European identity, connection of faith to politics, etc. My role was that of a good listener, offering a topic to discuss from time to time or guiding participants back to the main subject, but mainly asking them to expand on their points, explain what they meant, give examples of generalisations they made or – vice versa – spell out the implications of examples. After the first round of interviews, I also started to bring up the positions articulated by previous informants (some people said to me that …) in order to encourage a more argumentative style of reasoning.

Inductive interpretive analysis grew out of a search for patterns across interviews. I started by closely reading the transcripts and conducting a thematic analysis to identify the main themes through which positive or negative orientation towards the EU is constructed. Following the thematic overview, I carried out a more detailed rhetorical analysis of the discourse based on the Catholic repertoire, examining the argumentative lines, tropes, and commonplaces that anchored it.

3   Interpretive Findings

3.1   *Security Dilemma*

One of the most salient themes structuring everyday reasoning about the EU was "benefit". The importance of the utilitarian dimension in popular EU support has been well-researched,[19] and the primacy of pragmatic motives in the

---

19   For overviews see Anders Ejrnæs, and Mads Dagnis Jensen, "Divided but United: Explaining Nested Public Support for European Integration", *West European Politics* 42, no. 7

Central-Eastern European context has been demonstrated repeatedly.[20] Individuals who perceive economic gain from EU membership on a personal or state level tend to be the most supportive. My informants illustrated this well-established finding by talking at length about "opportunities" provided by the EU for them or their milieu to travel, study and work abroad as well as the financial support their country received through membership. Closely related was a national security theme encompassing both economic and political aspects.

For instance, when discussing Brexit, informants implicitly compared the United Kingdom to Lithuania by emphasising that the former "is not going to disappear", "will survive", and "can manage on its own". The latter, on the contrary, is not big, strong, rich, and powerful, therefore "it would be afraid to withdraw". They described their own country primarily as "small", but also "weak", "insignificant", and even "poor". In addition, discussion of Lithuanian EU membership was organised around such key phrases as "sense of security" and "there is no other way for us". My interlocutors argued that we are better off "under the EU wing" because: a) small states, in general, have to "pal up" with bigger ones to persist in the hostile international arena, b) EU membership protects Lithuania from the military threat of Russia, and c) it helps to overcome the negative "heritage" of the Soviet past in many areas of private and public life. Quite often the comparison with Belarus occurred, a neighbouring post-communist country and a stark contrast economically and politically with the European path taken by Lithuania in 2004.

Even before Russia launched its full-scale invasion of Ukraine on 24 February 2022, some informants mentioned that, if not for EU membership, Lithuania would be in Ukraine's stead. Since 2014 when Russia annexed Crimea and started an undeclared war in the Donbas region, a condition of "sovereign uncertainty" became characteristic of political rhetoric, public space and everyday life in Lithuania.[21] Although no actual armed conflict is taking place here, there is heightened insecurity. This condition was vividly articulated in

---

(November 10, 2019): 1390–1419; Sara B. Hobolt, and Catherine E De Vries, "Public Support for European Integration", *Annual Review of Political Science* (2016).

20 Piret Ehin, "Determinants of Public Support for EU Membership: Data from the Baltic Countries", *European Journal of Political Research* 40, no. 1 (August 1, 2001): 31–56; Matthew Loveless, "Agreeing in Principle: Utilitarianism and Economic Values as Support for the European Union in Central and Eastern Europe", *Journal of Common Market Studies* 48, no. 4 (September 1, 2010): 1083–1106.

21 Neringa Klumbytė, "Sovereign Uncertainty and the Dangers to Liberalism at the Baltic Frontier", *Slavic Review* 78, no. 2 (June 1, 2019): 337.

the accounts of those research participants who had lived under Soviet occupation and evaluated that period negatively. One interlocutor in her early seventies told me that she was very worried about the UK leaving the EU and then about the conflict in Ukraine, because she felt "this threat of disappearance, this fear".

Another salient theme concerned the change of values in Lithuanian society due to EU integration. Informants spoke about the positive (openness, respect for self and others, various freedoms etc.) and negative aspects of this process, the latter chiefly related to sexual morality, secularity, and to a lesser extent – national culture.[22] The verbs employed were revealing, for instance, in cases of perceived positive change, the EU "recommends", "teaches", "shows example" and we "learn", "take example", "assimilate"; in the negative context, the EU "propagates", "pushes", "intervenes", "makes demands", "instructs" etc. The minority of informants celebrated all changes associated with the EU as an inevitable part of becoming more like the West and as healthy for their country; whereas the majority expressed a strong to slight feeling of unease. They emphasised that the change of values "depresses", "worries", "frightens" them, or makes them feel "animosity", "hurt" or "a sense of insecurity".

Generally, my interlocuters deplored secularity as privatisation of religion. In their view, Christianity is "diminished, pushed away" or "not respected, valued enough" in the EU. The examples given involve EU institutions not being willing to prioritise Christianity, debates around Christian symbols in public places, and a general trend in public opinion to celebrate dechristianisation. Spatial imagination was behind this discourse, as Eastern Europe is treated as less secular, with Poland being the finest example. Expressing their fears of living in secularised space, they drew on sacred-secular dichotomy, although these layers do not have to be mutually exclusive and can co-exist, as a form of transliminal space.[23]

Chronological imagination was also present when informants spoke about the importance of religious freedom by linking the possible future of Lithuania in the EU with the past in the USSR. They were afraid of being forced to privatise their beliefs or even renounce them as they or their parents and grandparents were obliged to under Soviet occupation. Some informants shared their

---

22 Some conveyed concerns over the status of the Lithuanian language or globalisation in general, saying that people in Europe are becoming more alike and national differences are melting away, but they were not as prevalent. Interestingly, a few informants reflected on how their worries about national culture they have had before accession were not confirmed.

23 Marietta van der Tol and Philip Gorski, "Secularisation as the Fragmentation of the Sacred and of Sacred Space", *Religion, State & Society* 50, no. 5 (2022): 495–512.

personal experiences of feeling intimidated to talk from their Christian perspectives in Lithuania already. It can be inferred that this possibility of becoming a religious minority is terrifying for the better part of them.

In recent years, as heated debates about the Istanbul Convention and the gender-neutral civil partnership bill[24] have received much attention in the media, the theme of sexual morality has anchored discontent with the EU. Here is how one informant in his mid-fifties built an opposition between the EU and Christianity while talking about the notion of family: "The EU views it in a liberal way and the Christian world – contrary to that". Many of the interlocutors were concerned that legal recognition of same-sex relationships would threaten their right to speak their minds freely about sexual morality or raise their children in line with the Catholic understanding of a family as a union of man and woman. They markedly drew on Catholic repertoire[25] in talking about homosexual acts as sinful and in stressing the importance of gender complementarity. In the interviews, the EU was often depicted as only "caring for sexual minority rights" instead of "defending the family", and LGBT+ people were defined as the collective 'other' as if their aspirations and those of Catholics are mutually exclusive. It can be said that this constructed antagonism elucidates the centrality of sexual morality norms in defining the symbolic boundaries of Lithuanian Catholic identity.

In addition, many informants were prone to present these norms as distinctive part of national culture, implying that any changes regarding sexual morality would destroy a valuable part of Lithuanian culture. One informant, a young man in his mid-thirties, put it like this: "In some countries, people do not have problems with these sensitive issues [life, abortion, family], in Belgium, Luxembourg, Netherlands. That's fine – let them live happily. But in Lithuania, Latvia, Poland, and Hungary, we see that people think differently; therefore, [the EU] should not try to reconstruct their country, culture and attitudes". In his view, Lithuania can integrate into Europe in various spheres, but the 'national culture' is a red line which cannot be crossed. As observed by Petr Kratochvíl in the second chapter of this volume, the nation is seen as a "commonsensical bulwark" against liberal tendencies. It's a well-known populist strategy to "naturalise" certain conventions or communities and promise to

---

24 In Lithuania there is no legal recognition of same-sex relationships to this day, and the Istanbul Convention, although signed, is not yet ratified.

25 This does not mean that the resources mentioned are the only ones provided by Catholicism. As do all real cultures, it "contain diverse, often conflicting symbols, rituals, stories, and guides to action" (Swidler. "Culture in Action", 277). For example, few of my informants while talking about same-sex unions drew on the principles of human dignity and charity backed by stories from the life of Jesus.

defend them because they are allegedly under attack. This stress on the natural resonated well among many Catholics I interviewed.

Hence, despite the manifested EU support, latent scepticism lurks in connection to perceived threats to their Catholic identity. Against the backdrop of the concept of ontological security, increasingly used by International Relations scholars to analyse the European polity,[26] I argue that the EU is simultaneously understood by my informants as providing existential safeguards and posing ontological threats. Borrowing from Giddens,[27] who defines ontological security as a subjective sense of order and continuity in regard to an individual's biography, IR research extrapolates a state's need for it from the individual level and introduces additional dimensions to security (in this academic field traditionally understood as physical). A sharp distinction is drawn between "security as survival" and "security not of the body but of the self".[28]

Existential security may be seen by my informants as having been achieved through EU membership. Still, the normative threats associated with it are viewed as undermining the capacity to maintain a sense of continuity and certainty. A fragment from an interview with a young, educated woman in her late twenties vividly illustrates this security dilemma:

> Sometimes we talk with friends that the Soviet Union,[29] the Russian side, is to be feared, but the same is true of the European side. We are cautious about it [EU] because it brings its beliefs, and you have to obey. That is the feeling. ... The fact that we are physically free is fantastic, thank God. But whether we are spiritually free, I don't know. And which of the captivities is worse – that is a good question.

---

26 Christian Kaunert, Joana de Deus Pereira, and Mike Edwards, "Thick Europe, Ontological Security and Parochial Europe: The Re-Emergence of Far-Right Extremism and Terrorism after the Refugee Crisis of 2015", *European Politics and Society* 23, no. 1 (2022): 42–61; Catarina Kinnvall, Ian Manners, and Jennifer Mitzen, "Introduction to 2018 Special Issue of European Security: 'Ontological (in)Security in the European Union'", *European Security* 27, no. 3 (2018): 249–6; Vincent Della Sala, "Homeland Security: Territorial Myths and Ontological Security in the European Union", *Journal of European Integration* 39, no. 5 (2017): 545–58.

27 Anthony Giddens, *Modernity and Self Identity: Self and Society in the Modern Age* (Stanford, California: Stanford University Press, 1991), 311.

28 Jennifer Mitzen, "Ontological Security in World Politics: State Identity and the Security Dilemma", *European Journal of International Relations* 12, no. 3 (July 24, 2006): 344.

29 The informant was well aware that the Soviet Union no longer exits; mentioning it should be interpreted as negative labelling of contemporary Russia.

3.2 *Navigating Security Dilemma*

Despite this prevalent security dilemma, only 2 out of 40 research participants were hard Eurosceptics, insisting that economic and security benefits are inadequate compensation for the perceived harm to Christian and national values and no longer seeing any point in EU membership. The more significant part of my interlocutors who considered pros and cons during the interviews could be described as more or less critical supporters. One commonplace which structured their observations (and also their support) was the founding narrative of Europe. Some informants referred to the abstract "Christian roots" or "Christian foundation" of the EU, while others expressed knowledge either about the founding fathers – Christian Democrats (Robert Schuman, Konrad Adenauer) or about the Christian symbolism of the EU flag. Moreover, the EU was represented as acting in accordance with Christian principles (such as taking care of the weaker, going beyond self-interest, living peacefully and in communion).

I argue that this narrative about the EU as a Christian project circulating among active Catholics strengthens their identification with a polity and allows them to 'own it'. Even if confusion or outright disappointment was expressed about the EU renouncing its Christian roots, the foundation was still appreciated, and the concern about the future was deeply ingrained. The economic and security benefits, together with this narrative from the Catholic repertoire, function as the primary sources of support for the EU. For instance, an informant, 63, convinced that Europe is collapsing as a consequence of low morality and religiosity, also expressed a strong attachment to this polity. He sees himself as a peacemaker who has a responsibility to calm down his own peers in criticising the EU. In his mind, one has to fight for "Christian values" but in a peaceful manner to avoid destruction. The Polish example is inspiring for him:

> I will support [the EU] no matter what because I will always find people who think alike. Now I see Poles. Most of them want to remain in the EU. ... I am truly for us living in the united Europe, but our distinctiveness should not be touched. I don't know how to say it ... I certainly feel European, and I support being a part of the EU. Because ... What can you do alone? You would not be able to show yourself. No withdrawal. By no means. We need to communicate ...

To navigate between existential and ontological needs, informants also drew on the Catholic repertoire. The belief in a world supposed to be hostile to the followers of Christ was very useful because, if Christians 'do not belong to the world', challenges to their faith or even persecutions are inevitable. In the interview material, ontological threats linked to the EU are interpreted as consolidating and purifying their own faith and preventing a comfortable Catholic life, even referred to as a "gift". In Western Europe, the faith is challenged – a parish priest told me – therefore, it can be more 'authentic'. The following excerpt from a conversation with a young woman working in a Catholic institution demonstrates how spiritual benefit shines through the negative political trends:

> Christ has already won, His victory is already here. That brings peace [to my mind]. It's very difficult with a Christian – you can kill him, but he will still enter eternal life and even gain a crown of martyrdom. The challenge is not what keeps you away from believing. On the contrary, a challenge is something that strengthens your faith. You have more work to do. And sometimes, it is even easier this way. I think the very bad times were when the Church had lots of power. Hypocrisy was present. The challenge, I think, purifies us, and you see more clearly where you have to go to be an apostle, where you have to go to speak to people because they don't know Christ, they don't know the way.

According to the above-quoted interlocutor, this type of mindset is the first of two things allowing her to accept the undesirable change of values in Lithuanian society. The second is also substantiated by referring to faith. Only God can rule justly and faultlessly, but Jesus did not try to rule over an earthly kingdom. Consequently, it is impossible for human governments to be perfect. As another informant, a father of four, put it:

> I support the EU, but I keep my identity, I have my own opinion, I want to be part of the process, I want to vote, I want to be able to have a different opinion, I want to raise my children according to my moral values. But still, there is my support … Because this is not a paradise where everything is perfect.

The remaining strategies for mitigating ontological threats were of a different kind. Some participants counterbalanced their concerns by affirming that the EU itself should not be blamed for changing values, as responsibility is borne by part of the elite or by particular political powers. Furthermore, some blame was put on the modern world itself, referring to "the spirit of the times" or the "West". One more strategy was to emphasise the agency of the Lithuanian elite. Here are examples from three separate conversations:

> (*Sighs*). But aren't the same things happening *elsewhere in the world*, not necessarily in the EU? I think there is some kind of global problem in the world where people want to be very free.
>
> It is not the European Union itself, but *certain trends* [that are hostile]. After all, the European Union was founded on Christianity. Its founding fathers were also Catholic. And that flag, as far as I understand it, is also a sign of the Virgin Mary.
>
> Today I am pro-EU [...] As for these threats and fears, I think *I am more afraid of my government* here than I am of the government there. The Poles, for example, they can still ... If the local government has the backbone, they can stand up for their own things.

Finally, the security dilemma was navigated by weighing the economic and security benefits and other opportunities that the participants personally or the country received against disappointments and concerns. The following examples demonstrate two different modes. The first informant chose existential security over ontological because in her (and some others) thinking such a small and poor state is always a part of a bigger state's sphere of influence. If one does not want to "return to Russians" or "become dependent on China", one has to prioritise EU membership. The second interlocutor also spoke a lot in these geopolitical terms as well as economic benefits. In her opinion, the "value change" is a price Lithuania has to pay for all the goods received. By employing a logic of exchange, she stayed ambiguous towards the EU. Yet at the end of the interview, when asked whether she would vote in a hypothetical membership referendum 'Yes', as she did two decades ago, her answer was affirmative.

> I think it is very easy to say 'no' [to the EU], but to whom to say 'yes'? Since I don't have anyone to say yes to, I don't resist. And I teach my children that. They tell me: 'I don't want that, I don't want that.' And I say: 'So what do you want?' That's bad, that's bad, and who knows what's good. You have to have a proposal. Give me an alternative. *I don't know what the alternative is* ... You still *have to be united with somebody*.
>
> I think the value change is invisible, but it is happening intensively. This is the downside of the European Union. *It's like an exchange*: you want the benefit, the support, but you are forced to follow the rules of the game that ... are not good. You wouldn't say that you sell your soul, but fundamentally it is like that. You sell your values.

4 Conclusions

The bottom-up perspective invoked in this chapter enables one to go beyond the discourse of far-right populists who claim to speak on behalf of 'ordinary people' and target the EU by referencing to Christianity. It also challenges simplistic explanations for citizens' political opinions and inclinations which assign them to clear-cut categories of 'euro-optimists' or 'eurosceptics'. In fact, people who participated in this study weaved quite varied combinations of views – critical as well as appreciative – into intelligible perspectives.

The interpretive analysis of in-depth interviews with active Lithuanian Catholics suggests that their faith can both generate normative concerns related to the EU and contribute to the mitigation of perceived threats. On the one hand, integration into Europe is blamed for the shrinking status of Christianity and sexual freedom at odds with religious morality. On the other, a narrative about the Christian roots of Europe creates a strong attachment to the EU despite the disappointment with the EU 'turning its back' on it. The understanding of Christians as not of this world also contributed to a more moderate view towards some of the political concerns. These are just a few examples from the Catholic repertoire employed in everyday political reasoning.

Specific to many Lithuanian Catholics is a security dilemma in which the EU is simultaneously perceived as a space of existential security and ontological insecurity. Although the financial aspect of EU support is not very sustainable (the Lithuanian economy is growing, and from 2028, the country is supposed to transition from net beneficiary to net payer to the EU budget), the security aspect will remain relevant. EU as existential safeguard is expected to anchor Lithuanian political thinking because neither the size of the country nor its geographical position is going to change. Moreover, in the face of global challenges such as pandemics, rapid technological advancement, climate crisis, growing inequalities, etc., a politically unified Europe may be trusted more to solve constantly emerging new issues.

As long as Catholics do not choose the "Benedict Option" (a defensive withdrawal from contemporary society proposed by influential American Christian and far-right thinker Rod Dreher), we can expect them to prioritise existential needs of their fellow citizens over their own unease with the EU values. While currently their views on sexual freedoms coincide with the majority of society, the young generation in Lithuania is much more liberal-minded[30] and much

---

30 Ainė Ramonaitė, "Laisvės Partijos Fenomenas: Naujumo Efektas Ar Naujos Vertybinės Takoskyros Pradžia?" *Politologija* 102, no. 2 (October 18, 2021): 23–24.

less religious.[31] Even if the dominant mode of Catholicism does not change, believers will definitely find themselves in a very different political landscape in two decades or so.

Finally, this particular Lithuanian case illustrates a broader temptation for defensive attitudes vis-à-vis the EU that many Christians in Europe face. Although it does not necessarily convert to explicit Euroscepticism, a political imaginary of 'Christian Europe' is strongly lamented together with normative superiority. My analysis shows that a good deal of Catholics are not ready to adopt a new minority status in transliminal European space, which is neither sacred nor secular but layered with "various ascriptions of meaning, even inherently incompatible ones".[32] In this chapter, the analysis focused on what I believe is a rather dominant security dilemma regarding the EU among Catholics in Lithuania. Nonetheless, alternative voices, more open to the idea of different layers of meaning co-existing in the European space, are by no means to be explored in further research. It is worth deliberatively examining the diversity within the Catholic tradition.

Bibliography

Accetti, C.I. (2019). *What Is Christian Democracy?: Politics, Religion and Ideology*. Cambridge University Press.

Billig, M. (1991). *Ideology and Opinions: Studies in Rhetorical Psychology*. Sage Publications.

Billig, M. (1996). *Arguing and Thinking: A Rhetorical Approach to Social Psychology*. 2nd ed. Cambridge: Cambridge University Press.

Ehin, P. (2001). "Determinants of Public Support for EU Membership: Data from the Baltic Countries". *European Journal of Political Research* 40, no. 1 (August 1): 31–56.

Ejrnæs, A., and M.D. Jensen. (2019). "Divided but United: Explaining Nested Public Support for European Integration". *West European Politics* 42, no. 7 (November 10): 1390–1419.

---

31 According to Pew Research Center, adults younger than 40 in Lithuania still highly affiliate with religion, but the percentage of them praying daily is 4 times smaller and the share attending the Church weekly is 6 times smaller compared to older generations. As in many other nations, the age gap in religious commitment is rather large. See Pew Research Center, "The Age Gap in Religion Around the World", 13 June 2018, https://www.pewresearch.org/religion/2018/06/13/the-age-gap-in-religion-around-the-world/.

32 Van Der Tol and Gorski, "Secularisation as the Fragmentation of the Sacred and of Sacred Space", 508.

Foret, F. (2015). *Religion and Politics in the European Union: The Secular Canopy. Religion and Politics in the European Union: The Secular Canopy*. Cambridge University Press.

Gaidys, V. (2016). "25-Eri Požiūrio į Lietuvos Narystę Europos Sąjungoje Tyrimų Metai: 1991–2016". *Filosofija. Sociologija*, no. 4: 304–12.

Garškaitė, R., and J. Ulinskaitė. (2022). "In the Name of the Family". In: N. Mörner (ed.). cbees *State of the Region Report 2021: The Many Faces of the Far Right in the Post-Communist Space. A Comparative Study of Far-Right Movements and Identity in the Region*. Centre for Baltic and East European Studies, cbees, Södertörn University. Pp. 106–14.

Giddens, A. (1991). *Modernity and Self Identity: Self and Society in the Modern Age*. Stanford, California: Stanford University Press.

Guerra, S. (2017). "Religion and the EU: A Commitment under Stress". In: J. FitzGibbon, B. Leruth, and N. Startin (eds.). *Euroscepticism as a Transnational and Pan-European Phenomenon*. Abingdon: Routledge.

Hobolt, S.B., and C.E. De Vries. (2016). "Public Support for European Integration". *Annual Review of Political Science*.

Jastramskis, M. (2014). "Lietuvos Visuomenės Ir Politinių Partijų Nuostatos ES Atžvilgiu 2009–2013 M". In: *Lietuva Europos Sąjungoje: Metraštis 2009–2013 Metais*. Pp. 9–32.

Kaiser, W. (2007). *Christian Democracy and the Origins of European Union. Christian Democracy and the Origins of European Union*. Cambridge University Press.

Kaunert, C., J. de Deus Pereira, and M. Edwards. (2022). "Thick Europe, Ontological Security and Parochial Europe: The Re-Emergence of Far-Right Extremism and Terrorism after the Refugee Crisis of 2015". *European Politics and Society* 23, no. 1: 42–61.

Kinnvall, C., I. Manners, and J. Mitzen. (2018). "Introduction to 2018 Special Issue of European Security: 'Ontological (in)Security in the European Union.'" *European Security* 27, no. 3: 249–65.

Klumbytė, N. (2019). "Sovereign Uncertainty and the Dangers to Liberalism at the Baltic Frontier". *Slavic Review* 78, no. 2 (June 1): 336–47.

Konieczna-Sałamatin, J., and M. Sawicka. (2020). "The East of the West, or the West of the East? Attitudes toward the European Union and European Integration in Poland after 2008". *East European Politics and Societies: And Cultures* 35, no. 2 (June 4): 363–83.

Kotwas, M., and J. Kubik. (2019). "Symbolic Thickening of Public Culture and the Rise of Right-Wing Populism in Poland". *East European Politics and Societies and Cultures* 33, no. 2 (April 16): 435–71.

Kratochvíl, P., and T. Doležal. (2015). *The European Union and the Catholic Church. The European Union and the Catholic Church*. Palgrave Macmillan UK.

Lamour, C. (2021). "Orbán Urbi et Orbi: Christianity as a Nodal Point of Radical-Right Populism". *Politics and Religion*: 1–27.

Laumenskaitė, E. (2015). *Krikščioniškumas Kaip Socialinių Laikysenų Veiksnys Totalitarinėje Ir Posovietinėje Visuomenėje*. Vilnius: Lietuvių katalikų mokslo akademija.

Loveless, M. (2010). "Agreeing in Principle: Utilitarianism and Economic Values as Support for the European Union in Central and Eastern Europe". *Journal of Common Market Studies* 48, no. 4 (September 1): 1083–1106.

Mälksoo, M. (2017). "Kononov v. Latvia as the Ontological Security Struggle over Remembering the Second World War". In: U. Belavusau and A. Gliszczyńska-Grabias (eds.). *Law and Memory: Towards Legal Governance of History*. Cambridge University Press. Pp. 91–108.

McAndrew, S. (2020). "Belonging, Believing, Behaving, and Brexit: Channels of Religiosity and Religious Identity in Support for Leaving the European Union". *British Journal of Sociology* 71, no. 5.

Mitzen, J. (2006). "Ontological Security in World Politics: State Identity and the Security Dilemma". *European Journal of International Relations* 12, no. 3 (July 24): 341–70.

Molle, A. (2019). "Religion and Right-Wing Populism in Italy: Using 'Judeo-Christian Roots' to Kill the European Union". *Religion, State and Society* 47, no. 1 (January 1): 151–68.

Nelsen, B.F., and J.L. Guth. (2015). *Religion and the Struggle for European Union: Confessional Culture and the Limits of Integration*. Washington, D.C.: Georgetown University Press.

Nelsen, B.F., and J.L. Guth. (2020). "Losing Faith: Religion and Attitudes toward the European Union in Uncertain Times". *JCMS: Journal of Common Market Studies* 58, no. 4 (July 1): 909–24.

Nelsen, B.F., J.L. Guth, and B. Highsmith. (2011). "Does Religion Still Matter? Religion and Public Attitudes toward Integration in Europe". *Politics and Religion* 4, no. 1 (April): 1–26.

Nelsen, B.F., J.L. Guth, and C.R. Fraser. (2001). "Does Religion Matter?: Christianity and Public Support for the European Union". *European Union Politics* 2, no. 2 (June 29): 191–217.

Ramonaitė, A. (2021). "Laisvės Partijos Fenomenas: Naujumo Efektas Ar Naujos Vertybinės Takoskyros Pradžia?" *Politologija* 102, no. 2 (October 18): 8–37.

Sala, V.D. (2017). "Homeland Security: Territorial Myths and Ontological Security in the European Union". *Journal of European Integration* 39, no. 5: 545–58.

Scherer, M. (2015). "The Religious Context in Explaining Public Support for the European Union". *Journal of Common Market Studies* 53, no. 4: 893–909.

Schütz, A. (1946). "The Well-Informed Citizen: An Essay on the Social Distribution of Knowledge". *Social Research* 13, no. 4: 463–78.

Spohn, W., M. Koenig, and W. Knöbl. (2015). *Religion and National Identities in an Enlarged Europe. Religion and National Identities in an Enlarged Europe*. London: Palgrave Macmillan.

Swidler, A. (1986). "Culture in Action: Symbols and Strategies". *American Sociological Review* 51, no. 2 (April): 273–86.

Szumigalska, A. (2016). "The Polish Catholic Church's Perception of the Processes of EU Integration and Europeanisation in the Context of Traditional Norms and Values". *Religion, State and Society* 43, no. 4 (October 2): 342–56.

Unikaitė-Jakuntavičienė, I. (2014). "Eurosceptics in Lithuania : On the Margins of Politics?" *European Quarterly of Political Attitudes and Mentalities* 3, no. 4: 1–21.

Van der Tol, M., and P. Gorski. (2022). "Secularisation as the Fragmentation of the Sacred and of Sacred Space". *Religion, State & Society* 50, no. 5: 495–512.

Vilpišauskas, R. (2019). "Lithuania and the EU: Pragmatic Support Driven by Security Concerns". In: P. Kaeding, M., Pollak, and J. Schmidt (eds.). *The Future of Europe: Views from the Capitals*. Cham: Palgrave Macmillan. Pp. 69–71.

Vitkus, G. (2017). "Small Is Small: Euroscepticism in Lithuanian Politics". In K. Bukovskis and A. Austers (eds.). *Euroscepticism in the Baltic States: Uncovering Issues, People and Stereotypes*. Riga: Latvian Institute of International Affairs, Friedrich Ebert Stiftung. Pp. 38–50.

Žiliukaitė, R. (2016). "Religinės Vertybės". In: R. Žiliukaitė, A. Poviliūnas, and A. Savicka (eds.). *Lietuvos Visuomenės Vertybių Kaita per Dvidešimt Nepriklausomybės Metų*. Vilnius: Vilniaus universiteto leidykla. Pp. 135–65.

CHAPTER 15

Theopolitical Visions of National Belonging: Resisting the Totalising Tendencies of Inclusion

Jenny Leith

1 Introduction

This chapter is animated by an interest in understanding belonging to a nation—or, put otherwise, being a citizen—in terms of membership of a political community.[1] This exploration takes place in the context of widespread concern over the fragmentation of nationhood amidst deepening demographic diversity.[2] As a result, a search is underway for stable forms of national identity capable of sustaining bonds of loyalty between fellow citizens, as well as between citizens and state institutions. Yet the visions of communal identity and inclusion offered in response all too often seem to perpetuate and even generate new forms of civic exclusion and marginalisation.

This chapter seeks to get under the surface of this tendency, exploring it in dialogue with Susannah Ticciati's theological account of modes of inclusion within a body.[3] The argument is made that there are two failed attempts to form a national political community—with two concomitant modes of inclusion of members—that can be identified in contemporary theopolitical thought and policy. It is argued that the first version of national political membership, the 'expanding container' mode, can be seen when national life is pictured in terms of generously admitting new members to the political community. A second flawed mode of inclusion, termed the 'despatialised mode', meanwhile, can be recognised in the construal of national belonging in terms of the sharing of certain values. Both attempts end up falling into an unintended exclusionary logic and leave us looking for a way of imagining national political membership capable of resisting these totalising temptations. Having diagnosed why two dominant attempts at inclusion fail to foster rich relations

---

1 For more on this way of conceiving of citizenship, see Molly Farneth, *Hegel's Social Ethics: Religion, Conflict, and Rituals of Reconciliation* (Princeton: Princeton University Press, 2017), 116.
2 Whilst this chapter focuses on the UK context, this is, of course, a global phenomenon.
3 Susannah Ticciati, "Reconceiving the Boundaries of Home: The 'Oikology' of Ephesians", *International Journal of Systematic Theology* 21, no. 4 (2019): 408–30.

of national belonging, we set out some parameters for a national political community predicated on the ongoing participation of all members. It is argued that only such a mode of political belonging is capable of resisting the totalising tendencies of nationhood.

Running through this argument is an interest in theologically inflected conceptions of national space, and particularly when religion is intertwined with the state. This is explored through the particular example of the English nation, and with a specific interest in the role played by the national church of this particular body politic (the Church of England) in shaping the way belonging to the space of the nation is understood. Whilst less dramatically troubling than many of the theopolitical visions shaping European political life explored in this volume, the English religion-state regime is nonetheless intertwined with wider political usages of Christianity today (for example, with accounts of Christianity as ensuring religious and cultural uniformity in the nation). Looking at a more stable expression of religiously inflected national space can, therefore, help to shed some light on wider theopolitical trends and movements.

For there is a spatial imaginary at play here, with the political community of English church and nation imagined in relation to the territory it occupies. Moreover, this chapter comes to argue, the political community is defined by the way in which the space is to be inhabited. The implicit accounts operating here of the correct way in which to relate to the national space have the effect of rendering national belonging conditional upon a particular performance of national membership. In this way, these theopolitical imaginaries create not only external others (against whom the national body politic and its territory must be protected), but also internal others (those who fail against the conditions of membership).

Religion-state regimes in general, and this one in particular, might seem, then, to sharpen the totalising dangers of nationhood. It is tempting to look at contemporary intertwinings of religion and nationalisms and conclude that theology is best kept far away from any construals of national identity. Yet to do so would, this chapter argues, be to deprive the current conversation of vital constructive resources for disrupting and reshaping national projects of inclusion.

2   Two Ways Belonging Goes Wrong

We turn first, then, to Susannah Ticciati's theological account of modes of inclusion within a home, drawn from her reading of St Paul's Letter to the

Ephesians. This may not seem, at first glance, an obvious place to begin in setting out on a theological exploration of belonging within a national political community. Theological accounts of home and its goodness have, after all, been deeply contested down the centuries.[4] Yet Ticciati shares a concern with the same questions of spatial imagination and the shaping of membership and belonging that animate this volume. By stepping back from the presenting issues of our day to attend to the patterns of thought and belief implicit within these, we emerge better able to both recognise and respond to the contemporary context.

In charting the spatial imaginaries at play in the letter to the Ephesians, Ticciati sets up "being in" and "being" as twin poles which should guide a theological account of inclusion within a body. However, these poles must always be held in relation to each other: overemphasising one over the other leads to distorted understandings of inclusion and membership. There are, by this account, two main ways in which thinking about what it means to be included in the body of the church can go wrong—and these are modes which also carry a salutary warning for the ways we imagine theologically what it is for members of a nation to be included in the body politic.

2.1 'Being in'

The first way in which a theological account of inclusion of members in a body can go wrong, according to Ticciati, is through an overemphasis on 'being in' the body. By this way of thinking, the body is chiefly pictured as a container which members were once outside and are now inside. In Ephesians, the expansion of the container is to include gentiles within the body of Christ.

The problem with this mode of inclusion is that the form of the container is not shaped by the members it contains; rather, the form of the container is fixed and the fact of its boundary goes uncontested. It simply expands to include new members. As Ticciati argues, "the container mentality goes together with othering and domination": even when the container is enlarged so as in principle to include everything, the "logic of inclusion at play continues to be one of domination". In the expanded container there remains "a hidden imperialist vision …, and those who do not conform remain other even while on the inside".[5]

---

4 Augustine has been particularly central to the development of a theological wariness of accounting for an earthly home as good and desirable. For more on the way that Augustine has often been read and for a reparative reading, see Natalia Marandiuc, *The Goodness of Home: Human and Divine Love and the Making of the Self* (Oxford: Oxford University Press, 2018), 7–10.
5 Ticciati, "Reconceiving the Boundaries of Home", 313–4.

2.2 'Being'

Overemphasising 'being', meanwhile, has the effect of removing belonging to place as a meaningful part of membership of a body—of being at home. As Ticciati puts it:

> When being is emphasized at the expense of being-in, home is thus reduced to a moral community, abstracted from its habitat. This—ironically—is an inverse expression of the container mentality, now entirely despatialized, and construed in terms of membership in a moral community.[6]

Removing the container in this way has the effect of abstracting members from the places in which they inhabit their belonging, and instead putting the full weight of inclusion within the body on shared moral values. This has the effect of creating new 'in' and 'out' groups based on assent or not to these values:

> Once spatial rootedness is lost to view, the container mentality reasserts itself in metaphorical borders between peoples. This is, in fact, the other side of the same coin as the spatially expressed container mentality. When land is arbitrarily carved up, people are detached from it and habitat becomes neutral, non-relational space. Communal identity must be reimposed by way of (artificial) group boundaries.[7]

Here, the arbitrary nature of belonging to a specific structure or institution is rejected. Yet this rejection of the body only serves to splinter the population into equally arbitrary identities, and these different identities become essentialised. In short, both overemphases make it impossible for members to contest and meaningfully shape the collective identity.

3   Belonging in the National Body Politic

We turn now to consider belonging within the nation. Using this typology of inclusion within the church to illuminate what is going on in a national political community requires some unpacking of the extent to which the body of the church and the body of the nation can and should be understood analogously. This also requires thinking through what is implied in describing these polities as 'bodies'.

---

6   Ticciati, "Reconceiving the Boundaries of Home", 414.
7   Ticciati, "Reconceiving the Boundaries of Home", 414.

There are, of course, important differences between talking about inclusion and unity within the body of Christ and the body of the church (as discussed in Ephesians), and inclusion and unity within a national body politic (as is my concern here). Much has been written in recent political theology and political philosophy regarding these differences, often stressing the importance of keeping a proper distance between the ways these two bodies are imagined.[8] A great deal of the apprehension about naming the state as a body that is in some way analogous to the body of the church flows out of an awareness of the way in which, in medieval and early modern political theology, the mysticism of Christ's body 'migrated' first to the body of the church and to the Christian commonwealth, and then to the body of the monarch and thence to the state. As William Cavanaugh puts it, "the state borrowed theological body language to take on the trappings of a divinity".[9] The abuses that followed have been well-documented: as Chad Pecknold argues, drawing on the work of Sheldon Wolin, "borrowed mysticism in politics gives rise to nationalism as a tool for collecting human allegiances into a new unified body called the nation state".[10] Mysticism becomes a halo, a reason to not question the nature of the political community. In such a totalising national body—framed as a new redemptive community—individuals are sacrificed for "the distinctive identity of the political whole".[11]

Overall, worries about analogy-making between the body of the church and the body of the nation or state stem from an awareness of the way such analogies have paved the way to, firstly, make the church subordinate to the state (or vice versa), and, secondly, to collect the consent of citizens to the legitimacy of a nation, to which they are then subordinated and sacrificed. So, whilst there

---

8   Henri de Lubac's work has been a galvanising force here, in his tracing of the history of the *corpus mysticum*, as has Ernst Kantororwicz's *The King's Two Bodies: A Study in Medieval Political Theology* (Princeton, NJ: Princeton University Press, 2016). Contemporary studies of the relationship between medieval sacramental theology on contemporary political theory and practice include: Chad Pecknold's *Christianity and Politics: A Brief Guide to the History* (Oregon: Cascade, 2010); William Cavanaugh's *Field Hospital: The Church's Engagement with a Wounded World* (Michigan: Eerdmans, 2016); and Graham Ward's *Cities of God* (Abingdon: Routledge, 2000).

9   Cavanaugh, *Field Hospital*, 22.

10 Chad Pecknold, *Christianity and Politics*, xix–xx and 139, citing Sheldon Wolin, *Democracy Incorporated: Managed Democracy and the Spectre of Inverted Totalitarianism* (Princeton: Princeton University Press, 2008).

11 Pecknold, *Christianity and Politics*, 131. See also William Cavanaugh on the domestication of the body of Christ to produce unity—with the state made possible through individuals bound by contract: *Theopolitical Imagination: Christian Practices of Space and Time* (London: T&T Clark, 2001): 9, 39, 73–4.

is undoubtedly a freighted history when it comes to speaking of the nation as a body—and one that is in some ways analogous to the body of the church—drawing on such language does not in itself necessitate these dangers. In fact, we will come to argue that 'body' language can open up distinctively generative ways of understanding what the national political community both should and should not be.[12]

Spending time considering the analogous logics of inclusion within these bodies can help us, then, to better understand how political theologies of membership operate in both. Ticciati's framework can enable us to identify underlying patterns and commonalities in ostensibly diverse postures towards to national polity—both in political theologies of the Church of England and in features of contemporary political discourse and policy.

So, we return to Ticciati's account of the dangers of an overemphasis on 'being in' in conceptualising inclusion within the body of the church. Thinking of liberal democratic regimes in Europe in which a national religion has been understood as providing a holding structure for the nation, we can see this logic of expansion in the container of the state being expanded over the centuries to include plural expressions of faith and belief (amongst other forms of diversity). This vision overlaps and resonates with understandings of national identity which rest upon incorporation within a communal heritage.[13]

With this tendency to imagine a political community as neatly nestled within a container in mind, we can shed some light on what is going wrong today when a national religion is still understood as providing a holding structure for the nation.[14] To take the example of the Church of England,

---

12 Wolin is chief amongst the critics of the alienating and dehumanising effects of applying "borrowed mysticism" to the nation state; and yet it is in his work that we will find resources for retrieving the language of the body in such a way that renders the national body politic fundamentally dependent on the thorough-going participation of all its members.

13 Tobias Müller identifies this as an approach to nationhood highlighted and critiqued by what he calls "critical secularism studies". He notes that this school of secularism studies also offers a relevant analytical lens when it comes to 'shared values' discourse and policies. In both modes, the coherence of national identity, as constructed through what Müller calls a "religion-culture-citizenship" nexus, requires a racial other. See Tobias Müller, "Conscripts of secularism: nationalism, Islam and violence", *Religion, State and Society* 50, no. 5 (2022): 513–31, https://doi.org/10.1080/09637494.2022.2123691. For an in-depth typology of the intersection of ethnicity, religiosity, and secularism with nationalism, see Gülay Türkmen, *Under the Banner of Islam: Turks, Kurds, and the Limits of Religious Unity* (Oxford: Oxford University Press, 2021).

14 It is worth saying here that I am not trying to neatly categorise any one religion-state regime wholly within either of these camps—either historically or in the present. Rather,

this container mindset can be seen in the expectation that national civic life depends on members finding their place within this preestablished ecclesial territory—which is both a physical space and a spiritual and cultural imaginary. This container has been enlarged over the centuries through the shift from the systemic exclusion of non-Anglicans from public life to post-liberal theological accounts of church-state relationship which cast the Church of England as 'host' of the nation.[15] More people are now 'welcomed' by this host to participate in national life, but the container has only become larger: the Church of England is still the framing mechanism, and is so still regulating who can belong and what this demands.

As Lauren Morry's chapter also highlights, these 'guest-host' dynamics often shape relationships with other intermediate associations in a locality, with Anglicans tending to cast their Church in the role of 'host' and so presenting the parish as the Church's 'home' into which 'guests' are invited. It is increasingly widely noted in theological and sociological scholarship that UK Christians in general, and the Church of England in particular, are most comfortable with forms of civic action which puts the Church in a position of giving charitably to neighbours—most notably over the past decade, through food banks.[16] When local Churches do enter into seemingly equal partnership with other organisations, the same tendencies are often evident. We see this in the assumption that the vicar of the parish ought by default to chair a local interfaith body, for example, or that their approval must be required for government-funding for interfaith initiatives.[17] This 'hosting' can also take the form of offering education to local children through Church schools, but with

---

I am trying to unearth what is going on theologically and politically in national churches and their respective nations.

15 See, for example, John Milbank and Adrian Pabst, "The Anglican Polity and the Politics of the Common Good", *Crucible: The Christian Journal of Social Ethics*, no. 1 (2014): 7–15. For more on the established church exercising this kind of hospitality, see Jonathan Chaplin, *Beyond Establishment: Resetting Church-State Relations in England* (London: SCM, 2022), 28–31.

16 See, for example, Chris Allen, "Food Poverty and Christianity in Britain: A Theological reassessment", *Political Theology* 17, no. 4 (2016): 361–77.

17 As is the case, for example, the Near Neighbours programme, which is administered by Church Urban Fund, the Church of England's social action charity. For a fuller critique of this Anglican mentality, see Al Barrett, *Interrupting the Church's Flow: A radically receptive political theology in the urban margins* (London: SCM, 2020). More on the Near Neighbours programme can be found here: https://www.near-neighbours.org.uk/about. See also Jonathan Chaplin, *Beyond Establishment*, 23.

this school attendance conditional on parents displaying certain forms of outward conformity to Anglican faith.[18]

There are implications here too for the way the participation of each member in democratic life is imagined. In John Milbank's iteration of the Church of England hosting national polity, for example, the flourishing of democratic life ultimately depends on the guiding of a virtuous elite—who are to be supplied by the church.[19] In Church of England political theology as a whole, there is a tendency to err on the side of a predetermined form of political life (in both the life of the church and in public life), rather than one that is contingent upon wide, diverse participation and common deliberation. The polity and its members are formed through their form, with roles flowing *from* what is common to the community *to* the individual members. This often takes on a top-down and static vision of political life. So, while Oliver O'Donovan, for example, affirms that a people is "a community constituted by participation in the common good", this community is nonetheless called forth in response to a conception of the common good that is received from the political authorities above (rather than through common deliberation).[20]

These are, then, some of the dangers of imagining political belonging primarily in terms of 'being in' the national body politic. Secondly and more

---

18 For more on this, see Mairi Levitt and Linda Woodhead, "Choosing a faith school in Leicester: admissions criteria, diversity and choice", *British Journal of Religious Education* 42, no. 2 (2020): 224–41. There are resonances here with historic understandings of the national boundary as a token of divine reward. This is also relevant when thinking of the despatialising use of boundaries in colonialism—see, for example, Rowan Strong on Anglican understandings of providence in the British empire in *Anglicanism and the British Empire, c.1700–1850* (Oxford: Oxford University Press, 2007).

19 John Milbank, *The Future of Love* (London: SCM Press, 2009), 245. For Milbank, while hierarchies within liberalism are competitive and utilitarian and therefore destroy the common good, the 'spiritual hierarchy' has its *telos* rooted in excellence rather than utility and is not a hierarchy of the privileged but is rather made up of a portion of society that has dedicated life to education and the pursuit of excellence. See *The Future of Love*, XII and XIV. See also "Liberality versus Liberalism" in *The Future of Love*, 242–63; and *Being Reconciled: Ontology and Pardon* (London: Routledge, 2003), 132–3. True democracy requires, Milbank argues, "sacramental ordination" and "a guiding virtuous elite" formed in intermediate communities (particularly the church). See *The Future of Love*, XII–XIII, 245.

20 Related to this is O'Donovan's account of ethical and civic formation taking place at the 'pre-political' level of social life, within associations such as the church and the family. Citizens chiefly influence their community, O'Donovan argues, "by exercising the pre-political social virtue on which any good community is founded". There is a separation of the architecture of political processes and political ethics, whereby when citizens do participate politically it is primarily with an acceptance of existing power structures. Oliver O'Donovan, *The Ways of Judgement* (*The Bampton Lectures, 2003*) (Grand Rapids, MI: Wm B. Eerdmans, 2005), 138.

briefly, Ticciati's account of the danger of overemphasising a community's life as 'being', can also help us to see something of what is going on in conceptions of national polity in which there is a turn away from the old religious and cultural container and an attempt to create a despatialised political community bound by shared moral values.

We can see this kind of logic at work in the discourse around 'British values' in contemporary UK political life, for instance, and the various policies that have flowed from the resultant reimposition of artificial group boundaries. This project of forming a moral community can perhaps be seen most strikingly in the UK Government's creation of the category of "non-violent extremism", by which whole strata of the citizenry become suspected of not truly belonging to the nation unless they can demonstrate their assent to "British values".[21]

The quest for shared national values is also recognisable in what Jonathan Chaplin terms "state-church public service partnership"—particularly that which features the aims of curbing 'extremism' and strengthening 'cohesion' and 'social capital'.[22] Near Neighbours can again be understood as part of this project of forming a moral community, as can the types of social action encouraged by the Big Society-agenda of the early 2010s (holiday clubs in school holidays; food banks and community kitchens; and so on).

This brief exploration of distorted inclusions has allowed us, then, to identify certain commonalities in the ways belonging to the national 'home' is construed in both the Church of England's theological imagination and in the thinking and policies of the state. As Ticciati argues:

> If being-in without being results in the arbitrary carving up of space as a neutral container, then being without being-in results in the carving up of people into in-groups and out-groups. These are two sides of the same coin: the detachment of people from their habitats results in the artificial division of both—into (despatialized) peoples and (neutrally spatialized) containers.[23]

---

21 See, for example, this 2018 House of Commons Library brief on counter-extremism policy in English schools, for a discussion of the place of British values in education policy: https://commonslibrary.parliament.uk/research-briefings/cbp-7345/.

22 Jonathan Chaplin, *Beyond Establishment*. Theological support for the development of this type of shared moral community include Sean Oliver-Dee, "Integration, Assimilation and Fundamental British Values: Invested Citizenship and 21st Century 'Belonging'", *Cambridge Papers* 26, no. 3 (2017); and Julian Rivers, "Fundamental British Values and the Virtues of Civic Loyalty", *Ethics in Brief* 21, no. 5 (2016) (initially drafted for the Church of England's Higher Education Development Group).

23 Ticciati, "Reconceiving the Boundaries of Home", 420.

In other words, both these modes of inclusion end up displaying a totalising logic, whereby the individual citizen or member is fitted within a prefigured whole and cut off from deep solidarity with fellow members. Whilst at first glance there seem to be divergences over the space allowed for plural beliefs, in both the theological and secular account sketched there is in fact a shared sense that the national container or set of values to be shared are set in advance: the character of the national political community is not open to contestation or disruption by the bonds between its members.

4 Belonging as Disruptive Joining

If both of these ways of construing inclusion within a body are insufficient, and even politically dangerous, is there a way of imagining membership of a national political community that avoids these dangers? A way that is capable of holding together the need for members to both 'be' a body politic and to 'be in' that body?

Ticciati's answer to this question comes through exploring the language of *oikos* in the letter to the Ephesians. She highlights the way in which this language of belonging to a 'home' combines both economic and cultural connotations *and* natural connotations. This leads to a conception of home "not as a neutral container to be filled, but as relations to be configured and reconfigured: in terms of joining".[24] This can set some helpful parameters for thinking about a national 'home'.

The place of home in a spatial imaginary is, as we have already noted, a fraught topic. Some see home as the ultimate experience of place, and as that which connotes proper inhabitation and belonging.[25] Yet there are all sorts of ways in which talk of 'home' can cause problems, theologically and politically. Critiques often build from a concern that positive usages of 'home' are only possible through ignoring the lived reality for many of that which is designated as home, with feminist scholars such as the geographer Gillian Rose cautioning that many would not recognise home as caring or nurturing.[26] Others have argued that to make home an end to be pursued is an invitation to close one's eyes to the extent to which the very ideal of home rests on and props up

---

24 Ticciati, "Reconceiving the Boundaries of Home", 417.
25 See, for example, Gaston Bachelard, *The Poetics of Space*, trans. Maria Jolas (Boston: Beacon Press, 1969), 5.
26 Gillian Rose, *Feminism and Geography: The Limits of Geographical Knowledge* (Cambridge: Polity Press, 2007), 53–6.

capitalist, patriarchal, and heteronormative systems of oppression.[27] There are also, of course, particular concerns about ethnonationalist accounts of what it means to belong to a home country.[28]

As with the language of the body, the argument here is that whilst these dangers are real, they are not inherent to talking of a nation as, in some sense, a home. Indeed, the turn here to Ticciati's usage of home is precisely because of the resources offered for an account of a national home actively alert and resistant to these dangers. As with the language of the body, 'homely' language is generative for thinking about political relationships in the nation. Concretely, this concept can have a constructive theopolitical valence if rendered relationally rather than spatially. As we noted just now, not all relationships and attachments are oriented towards forming modes of belonging in which flourishing is possible for all, which is why it important to attend to Ticciati's call for relations of "joining" in which relations are "configured and reconfigured".[29] The 'homely' patterns of members relating to a national body politic should properly allow for ongoing configuration and reconfiguration; that is to say, belonging to a nation must involve ongoing negotiation and contestation if it is to resist the totalising logics of inclusion explored above.[30]

---

[27] For a fuller discussion of this see Siobhán Garrigan, "The Hermeneutics of Intersubjectivity: A Study of Theologies of Homelessness", in *Grace, Governance and Globalization*, eds. Stephan van Erp, Martin G. Poulsom, and Lieven Boeve (London: Bloomsbury Academic, 2017), 62–76.

[28] On the dangers of the language of a national home from a sociological perspective see Jan Willem Duyvendak, *The Politics of Home: Belonging and Nostalgia in Europe and the United States* (Hampshire: Palgrave Macmillan, 2011).

[29] For more in this vein, see Natalia Marandiuc's chapter "The Goodness of Home: Attachment as Anthropological and Pneumatogical Middle Space" for an account of the role of the Holy Spirit as 'third middle term', inhabiting and holding the attachment space between human beings and so making possible the sustenance of a relational home resistant to oppression (in *The Goodness of Home*, 181–198). See also Willie James Jennings on what such joining might look like in the context of theological education in *After Whiteness: An Education in Belonging* (Grand Rapids, MI: Eerdmans, 2020).

[30] The language of *oikos* is, of course, intrinsically tied to that of *polis* when used to describe the political character of the nascent church, in such a way that both terms are reconceptualised and the private-public division invoked by these terms in the classical world recast. In contemporary political philosophy, meanwhile, it is worth noting the dangers of using the language of *oikos* to disrupt established ways of imagining political communities. Giorgio Agamben and Roberto Esposito are amongst those who situate economics as a rival to political power—an opposition that merely abides by a different (but no less totalising) logic. In exploring the possibilities offered by the term *oikos,* therefore, I am not intending to imply that the language of *polis* is not necessary in conceptualising the polities of church and nation.

To experience being at home in a nation, then, is always at the same time to experience a search for home. As Robert Mugerauer puts it, it "turns out that our dwelling is nothing static at all. Dwelling is no lapse into dormancy but a becoming at home as a constant homecoming, achieved by our constant travel".[31] There is, in other words, a dynamism and incompleteness or excess to belonging to a home, where this belonging—or dwelling—is something that we are always arriving at anew. The dynamism of the ongoing joining and disruption involved in this kind of home-making resonates with the radical democratic thought of Sheldon Wolin and Romand Coles—who can help us to fill out the forms of political relationship involved in belonging to such a home.

4.1 *Belonging as Disruption*

As we have already noted, Wolin is (rightly) preoccupied with the dangers of the state collecting the consent of its citizens so as to then distance these members from deep participation in political decision-making. Wolin's democracy is famously "fugitive", always fleeing forces which seek to "manage" it, to render it less participatory and therefore more unpredictable than it should properly be. By this account, any political form that collects consent but rejects wide participation fails to allow for the full flourishing of humanity, and the life of a polity ought not, therefore, be tamed into a settled, over-arching system.[32]

Members of a democratic body politic must, therefore, resist what Wolin calls "disciplines of detachment", fostered by the neoliberal state and market, if they are to avoid the collective life of the body politic becoming tamed and made static—its structures fixed to a particular shape that is not contingent upon the political participation of each member.[33] Seen from this perspective, the life of a national body politic is not defined by a fixed state form, but is rather a polity in which ordinary people are active political actors. So, more positively, this restlessness means that the political is located in a quality of relationality, not in any fixed institutional structure. Political acts, understood in this way, "are always dynamically responsive to a world that always exceeds our terms and settled institutional forms".[34]

---

31 Robert Mugerauer, *Heidegger and Homecoming; The Leitmotif in the Later Writings* (Toronto: University of Toronto Press, 2008), 397.
32 Wolin, *Democracy Incorporated.*
33 Pecknold, *Christianity and Politics*, citing Wolin, *Democracy Incorporated.*
34 Romand Coles and Stanley Hauerwas, 'Introduction' in *Christianity, Democracy, and the Radical Ordinary: Conversations Between a Radical Democrat and a Christian* (Eugene, OR: Wipf and Stock, 2008), 3, note 4.

4.2 *Belonging as Joining*

From this follows a commitment to a more diffuse and local form of politics. This form of politics is the "first best hope" because of the way ordinary people, not systems or institutions, are understood as the primary political actors.[35] So, local and contingent settings are where the heart of political life is expected to be unfolding. Accordingly, this democratic project invites us to attend to our own local ways of "knowing and naming the political", to the politics of the everyday.[36] Indeed, Wolin's project can be characterised as a "'politics of tending' in which citizens attend to a political culture that cares for the habits, dispositions, practices, and forms of life worth sharing and sustaining".[37] Coles too describes radical democracy as referring to "political acts of tending to common goods and differences".[38] Joining at this scale emerges, then, as being at heart of what is required to overcome divisions arising from shared values discourse.

4.3 *Snapshots of National Belonging*

Both disruption and joining are required, we can see, for meaningful membership of the national body politic. Yet this does not mean that that both disruption and joining must both be always simultaneously expressed to the same extent in any given political action. Both must be present for false modes of inclusion to be resisted, yet there are times when contestation will properly be more to the fore than relationships of joining—and vice versa.

So, what might it look like to resist such detachment and to enact belonging through ongoing contestation of a national home?[39] And is it possible for a religion-state regime to foster this kind of national belonging?[40]

---

35 Sheldon Wolin, *The Presence of the Past: Essays on the State and the Constitution* (Baltimore, MD: Johns Hopkins University Press, 1989), 78.

36 Chad Pecknold, "Migrations of the Host: Fugitive Democracy and the Corpus Mysticum", *Political Theology* 11, no. 1 (2010): 97; Coles and Hauerwas, "Introduction", 4.

37 Molly Farneth, "A Politics of Tending and Transformation", *Studies in Christian Ethics* 32, no. 1 (2019): 114. See Sheldon Wolin, "Tending and Intending a Constitution", in *The Presence of the Past*, 82–99; and also Coles, *Beyond Gated Politics*.

38 Coles and Hauerwas, "Introduction", 3, note 4.

39 Wolin is mainly interested in what democracy needs to flee from. And I am sympathetic to this negative emphasis: resisting the temptation to fill out the content of democratic life in advance. But even an account of political community that stresses the need for ongoing negotiation of that community by its members in ways that render all structures of belonging provisional needs to be able to identify some images of what this kind of national political community might look like.

40 We can catch another glimpse of the difference this makes by turning our attention away from the UK and looking at the presence of Ukrainian Orthodox and Greek-Catholic

Coles writes strikingly of political community resting upon, and also making possible, the binding hope of a sense of common fate: a belonging together in the future that emerges "through self-discovery of common concerns and modes of action for realising them" in the present.[41] The discovery of common concerns will often emerge through, and entail, modes of action which seek to disrupt prevailing systems through which citizens' representation is limited. An established religion's ties to centres of economic and political power can mitigate against such disruption of established systems. Yet this positioning also heightens the power of established religion when it does engage in disruptive action.

This ambivalence is captured in the Church of England's response to the Occupy London movement of October 2011–January 2012, during which a camp was set up in the churchyard of St Paul's Cathedral. Whilst the Chapter (governing body) of St Paul's supported the eviction of protestors from church land, the Canon Chancellor of the Cathedral, Giles Fraser resigned from his position over the threat of what he saw as violence against a valid political action. This was followed by the then Archbishop of Canterbury, Rowan Williams, expressing sympathy for the aims of the protestors—and particularly for the establishment of a Financial Transactions Taxes (known as the Robin Hood Tax).[42] This intra-church debate fuelled and complexified national discussion about the role of financial corporations in public life.

For all that this awareness of sharing a common fate—a fate that endures across time and is shared between generations—might be most obviously evident in participation in the disruptive actions of groups like Occupy or

---

priests, monks, and believers at the Maidan protests in Kyiv in 2014. Whilst not wishing to over-simplify all that was at play in these protests, I think we can see something of what it looks like to seek a home for all through contestation in the way believers (primarily of the Kievan Patriarchate and Autocephalous Church and the Greek-Catholic Church) participated in the protests against state corruption and for a more deeply participative form of democracy for their nation. This included leading singing of the Lord's Prayer, celebrating the eucharist, and offering the monastery of St. Michael as a dormitory and field hospital. The sociologist Marat Shterin is amongst those who have drawn attention to the role of sacred imagery and ritual in the protests—both by those opposing the Yanukovich regime and those gathered in the regime's defence. For a discussion of the complexities of the political stances of Ukrainian national churches post-Maidan see Heleen Zorgdrager, "Ukrainian churches in defence of 'traditional values': two case studies and some methodological considerations", *Religion, State and Society* 48, nos. 2–3, 90–106.

41 Coles, *Democracy and the Radical Ordinary*, 114, 118.
42 For a timeline of key moments in the protests, see "Occupy London: timeline of the St Paul's Cathedral protest camp", *The Guardian*, 18 January 2012, accessed 12 June 2023, https://www.theguardian.com/uk/2012/jan/18/occupy-london-timeline-protest-camp.

Extinction Rebellion, it is not exhausted in disruption.[43] The kind of attention to, and nurturing of, local and quotidian political culture will also be predictable and stable in certain ways: for Anglicans, it will involve voting (and making one's church hall available as a polling station); serving on Church School governing bodies; taking part in community organising and/or development through one's church; and so forth. Joining with others in these quotidian ways will mean learning to pay close attention to what is truly going on in the community around us: attending to the messiness and irregularity of community life, rather than just slotting these encounters into our prior narrative of what life together should look like.

In these actions, then, we can see something of what national belonging can look like in a religion-state regime in which membership of the nation is understood to be expressed not in conformity within a prefigured theological container nor within a fixed set of values but rather in ongoing disruptive joining.

5 Conclusion

This is an all too brief sketch of national political belonging, but one which hopefully indicates what can be hoped and worked for in forms of religion-state regime in which democratic action is understood to shape the overarching form of the nation and in which bonds between citizens rest on the sense of sharing a common fate. In drawing upon Ticciati's account of the ways inclusion within a body can go wrong—and so end up generating new forms of exclusion—we have unearthed how these dynamics are at play in dominant conceptions of national belonging. Setting up the typology of the 'expanding container' and the 'despatialised values' has helped to highlight the dangers implicit in the forms of civic membership fostered through these approaches to inclusion.

Tracing an analogical relationship between the body of Christ and of the nation has also allowed the proposal of a constructive vision, highlighting the need for any national political community to be radically contingent upon the participation of all members. This kind of polity will be one characterised by relations between members which forge new forms of solidarity and so disrupt established processes of governance. Working with a theological framework

---

43   Extinction Rebellion is a UK-headquartered ecological movement. It describes itself as using "non-violent civil disobedience in an attempt to halt mass extinction and minimize the risk of social collapse". For more, see "About", Extinction Rebellion, accessed 12 June 2023, https://extinctionrebellion.uk/the-truth/about-us/.

of inclusion has also brought into view a mode of membership within the national body politic which the Church of England can help to foster, and which will, in turn, teach the Church more deeply about the nature of belonging to a body. In this way, paying attention to the need to reconceptualise the borders of the church has helped us to rethink the borders of the nation, in the hope that this will, in turn, continue to unsettle the imagined boundaries of the body of Christ.

Bibliography

Allen, C. (2016). "Food Poverty and Christianity in Britain: A Theological reassessment". *Political Theology* 17, no. 4: 361–77.

Bachelard, G. (1969). *The Poetics of Space*, trans. Maria Jolas. Boston: Beacon Press.

Barrett, A. (2000). *Interrupting the Church's Flow: A Radically Receptive Political Theology in the Urban Margins*. London: SCM.

Cavanaugh, W. (2001). *Theopolitical Imagination: Christian Practices of Space and Time*. London: T&T Clark.

Cavanaugh, W. (2016). *Field Hospital: The Church's Engagement with a Wounded World*. Michigan: Eerdmans.

Chaplin, J. (2022). *Beyond Establishment: Resetting Church-State Relations in England*. London: SCM.

Coles, R. (2005). *Beyond Gated Politics: Reflections for the Possibility of Democracy*. Minneapolis: University of Minnesota Press.

Coles, R., and S. Hauerwas. (2008). *Christianity, Democracy, and the Radical Ordinary: Conversations Between a Radical Democrat and a Christian*. Eugene, OR: Wipf and Stock.

Duyvendak, J.W. (2011). *The Politics of Home: Belonging and Nostalgia in Europe and the United States*. Hampshire: Palgrave Macmillan.

Farneth, M. (2017). *Hegel's Social Ethics: Religion, Conflict, and Rituals of Reconciliation*. Princeton: Princeton University Press.

Farneth, M. (2019). "A Politics of Tending and Transformation". *Studies in Christian Ethics* 2, no. 1: 113–18.

Garrigan, S. (2017). "The Hermeneutics of Intersubjectivity: A Study of Theologies of Homelessness". In: S. van Erp, M.G. Poulsom, and L. Boeve (eds). *Grace, Governance and Globalization*. London: Bloomsbury. Pp. 62–76.

Jennings, W.J. (2020). *After Whiteness: An Education in Belonging*. Grand Rapids, MI: Eerdmans.

Kantorowicz, E. (2016). *The King's Two Bodies: A Study in Medieval Political Theology*. Princeton, NJ: Princeton University Press.

Levitt, M., and L. Woodhead. (2020). "Choosing a faith school in Leicester: admissions criteria, diversity and choice". *British Journal of Religious Education* 42, no. 2: 224–41.

Marandiuc, N. (2018). *The Goodness of Home: Human and Divine Love and the Making of the Self.* Oxford: Oxford University Press.

Milbank, J. (1990). *Theology and Social Theory: Beyond Secular Reason.* Oxford: Blackwell.

Milbank, J. (2003). *Being Reconciled: Ontology and Pardon.* London: Routledge.

Milbank, J. (2009). *The Future of Love: Essays in Political Theology.* Eugene, OR: Cascade Books.

Milbank, J., and A. Pabst. (2014). "The Anglican Polity and the Politics of the Common Good". *Crucible: The Christian Journal of Social Ethics*, no. 1: 7–15.

Mugerauer, R. (2008). *Heidegger and Homecoming: The Leitmotif in the Later Writings.* Toronto: University of Toronto Press.

Müller, T. (2022). "Conscripts of secularism: nationalism, Islam and violence". *Religion, State and Society* 50, no. 5: 513–531. https://doi.org/10.1080/09637494.2022.2123691.

O'Donovan, O. (1996). *The Desire of the Nations: Rediscovering the Roots of Political Theology.* Cambridge: Cambridge University Press.

O'Donovan, O. (2005). *The Ways of Judgement: The Bampton Lectures, 2003.* Grand Rapids, MI: Eerdmans.

Oliver-Dee, S. (2017). "Integration, Assimilation and Fundamental British Values: Invested Citizenship and 21st Century 'Belonging'". *Cambridge Papers* 26, no. 3.

Pecknold, C. (2010). "Migrations of the Host: Fugitive Democracy and the Corpus Mysticum". *Political Theology* 11, no. 1: 77–101.

Pecknold, C. (2010). *Christianity and Politics: A Brief Guide to the History.* Eugene, OR: Cascade.

Rivers, J. (2016). "Fundamental British Values and the Virtues of Civic Loyalty". *Ethics in Brief* 21, no. 5.

Rose, G. (2017). *Feminism and Geography: The Limits of Geographical Knowledge.* Cambridge: Polity Press.

Siapera, E., ed. (2007). *Radical Democracy and the Internet.* London: Palgrave Macmillan.

Strong, R. (2007). *Anglicanism and the British Empire, c.1700—1850.* Oxford: Oxford University Press.

Temple, W. (1942). *Christianity and Social Order.* Harmondsworth: Penguin.

Ticciati, S. (2019). "Reconceiving the Boundaries of Home: The 'Oikology' of Ephesians". *International Journal of Systematic Theology* 21, no. 4: 408–430.

Türkmen, G. (2021). *Under the Banner of Islam: Turks, Kurds, and the Limits of Religious Unity* Oxford: Oxford University Press.

Ward, G. (2000). *Cities of God.* London: Routledge.

Ward, G. (2009). *The Politics of Discipleship: Becoming Postmaterial Citizens.* London: SCM Press.

Wolfson, E. (2018). *The Duplicity of Philosophy's Shadow–Heidegger, Nazism, and the Jewish Other.* New York: Columbia University Press.

Wolin, S. (1989). *The Presence of the Past: Essays on the State and the Constitution.* Baltimore, MD: Johns Hopkins University Press, 1989.

Wolin, S. (2008). *Democracy Incorporated: Managed Democracy and the Specter of Inverted Totalitarianism.* Princeton, NJ: Princeton University Press.

Zorgdrager, H. (2020). "Ukrainian churches in defence of 'traditional values': Two case studies and some methodological considerations". *Religion, State and Society* 48, no. 2–3: 90–106.

CHAPTER 16

The Contested Meanings of the Anglican Parish in Multireligious England

Lauren Morry

1   Introduction

In this chapter I examine the Church of England's spatial imaginary of the 'parish' and its implications for the politics of religious diversity in England. This chapter makes two arguments: one focuses on the parish itself; the other on the implications of studying it. The primary argument is as follows: the Church of England has intentionally doubled down on the importance of the parish as it has come to terms with the increasing religious diversity in England, choosing to subsume religious minorities into the Anglican view of space and thus into the patrimony/authority of the Church of England through the insistence that they are 'parishioners'. The Introduction of this volume speaks of spatial imaginaries as 'defences' against undesirable threats: in this case, for the national Church, the parish is a bulwark against the loss of the Church's influence. By counting all people as parishioners, the Church is bolstering its significance in multireligious England as the number of self-professed Anglicans declines. However, this directive on the parish, coming as it does from the Church's nationally produced reports, is diversified and challenged by local parish priests based on their everyday and localised encounters with religious minorities. This leads to my second conceit, which is an endorsement of the value of studying the local in addition to the national, and alongside this the importance of studying what is local to the scholar's own context.

Among the insights of this volume is the pressing fact that space is the nexus for the contestation of (theo)political ambitions for Europe's future. For many the parish is such a normative, seemingly innocuous part of English life that it is difficult to imagine how it might feature in this discussion, conjuring images of beautifully crumbling Norman churches amid England's mountains green. Yet it is for that precise reason—its normativity and even its 'quaintness'—that it ought to be examined. Bruce Lincoln reminds us that "Understanding the system of ideology that operates in one's own society is made difficult by two factors: (i) one's consciousness is itself a product of that system, and (ii) the system's very success renders its operations invisible, since one is so consistently immersed in and bombarded by its products that one comes to mistake them (and the apparatus through which they are produced and disseminated) for nothing other than 'nature'".[1] The reality is that the parish as a spatial imaginary is not a product of nature, but a continually evolving entity that has significant implications for multireligious England.

The Church of England[2] is the established church of the English nation, with entrenched ties to the state and to English national identity. The church-state settlement in England affords its Church the political advantages of twenty-six bishops in the House of Lords and the monarch as supreme governor of the Church. It also provides the Church with an enduring cultural influence, not least of which is the association of Anglicanism and the English identity, as its very name suggests. Such an association has consistently been encouraged by the Church; in his enthronement sermon as Archbishop of Canterbury in 1945, Geoffrey Fisher declared: "Church and nation have grown up together, and we see God's providence at work in both".[3] This is an attitude which endures today: "Anglicanism has continued to be associated with Englishness and the legacy of Empire, at least in the popular imagination".[4] That this cultural influence—the elision of Church and nation, or Anglicanism and Englishness—is incommensurate with the Church's membership is evidence of its ability to maintain power even without popular participation or assent.

Indeed, though it retains its status as the national church, the Church of England does not have a monopoly on the religious life of the nation. Islam is the fastest growing religion in England while Christian affiliation declines, and the 2021 census data shows that for the first time, the proportion of English people identifying as Christian has fallen below 50%—of which the Anglicans are only a fraction. This raises the question of how the Church of England has chosen to conceive of its role in twenty-first century multireligious England. In its national deliberations, those occurring in the upper echelons of the institution by task forces assembled in the name of the archbishops, the Church has chosen to entrench its identity as the national

---

1 Bruce Lincoln, "Theses on Method", *Method & Theory in the Study of Religion* 8, no. 3 (1996): 226.
2 Hereafter "the Church".
3 Matthew Grimley, "The Religion of Englishness: Puritanism, Providentialism, and 'National Character', 1918–1945" *Journal of British Studies* 46, no.4 (2007): 904.
4 Mark D. Chapman, Sathianathan Clarke, and Martyn Percy, "Introduction", in *The Oxford Handbook of Anglican Studies*, eds. Mark D. Chapman, Sathianathan Clarke, and Martyn Percy (Oxford: Oxford University Press, 2015), 6.

church, promulgating an understanding of itself as the leader among *all* of England's religions.[5] It has done this through the use of its parochial system, which is mapped onto all of England such that everyone lives within a parish. In the Church's spatio-theological understanding, all people in the country—Christians, Muslims, atheists, or otherwise—are 'parishioners' and thus in some capacity belong to the Church. Such is the approach of the Church *qua* institution, as represented by its official reports, to be discussed below. Locally however, the situation is more complex. My ethnographic interviews with Anglican clergy in the Church of England's Diocese of Birmingham, a highly religiously diverse diocese, found that some priests appreciate the notion of all English people as 'parishioners' while others find it unhelpful, paternalistic, or even patently false.[6]

Following the insights of the spatial turn, I consider the parish as a social product consisting of an interplay of the built environment, imagination, and the experiences which take place within its constantly negotiated boundaries.[7] While Chidester and Linenthal correctly write of space as containing "hierarchical power relations of domination and subordination, inclusion and exclusion, appropriation and dispossession",[8] I am most interested in how "symbolic orderings of space and time provide a framework ... through which we learn who or what we are as a society".[9] More than a simple division of space, for the Church of England the parish is the site on which the identity of the Church in multireligious England is wrought, negotiated, and lived. This is significant not merely for Anglicans, but for all people who have an interest in the religious landscape of England. As of 2021, the Church of England's endowment sat at £10.1 billion with an average annual return of 10.7% over the last ten

---

5   This has the effect of retaining and justifying its social role: so long as *any* religion matters in England, so will its established church. The same logic was seen *mutatis mutandis* in the Church's response to national discussions around pluralism in 1960s and 1970s, with Daniel Loss arguing that the Church "shored up its institutional position through the framework of communal pluralism" (Daniel S. Loss, "Missionaries, the Monarchy, and the Emergence of Anglican Pluralism in the 1960s and 1970s", *Journal of British Studies* 57 (2018): 563).

6   My interviews with clergy were on the subject of how Anglican-Muslim interreligious relations are pursued at the local level, collected for my doctoral thesis. The interviews were carried out from 2020–2021. All names have been pseudonymised.

7   Henri Lefebvre, *The Production of Space*, trans. D. Nicholson-Smith (Oxford: Blackwell, 1991).

8   David Chidester and Edward T. Linenthal, *American Sacred Space* (Bloomington: Indiana University Press, 1995), 17.

9   Pierre Bourdieu, *Outline of a Theory of Practice* (Cambridge: Cambridge University Press, 1977), 163.

years.¹⁰ The manner in which the Church of England decides to allocate its thousands of buildings, and billions of pounds in assets and its political influence affects all other religious bodies, directly or indirectly. An understanding of the Church's approach to England's religious diversity gives insight into this powerful actor and functions to illuminate the portrait of religion in England today.

2   The Parish

The Church of England is a territorial church; its boundaries are largely coterminous with the English borders.¹¹ Likewise, it is spatially organised through parishes, deaneries, archdeaconries, and dioceses. The spatial organisation of the church into these units, which are both administrative and redolent with theological understanding, reached fruition in the Middle Ages and survived many upheavals in England's religious life, including the Protestant Reformation.¹² Today, the parish in particular remains an axiomatic aspect of Anglican identity: "the most characteristic unit of Anglican church life".¹³

In the Church of England, the term 'parish' has a broader meaning than simply the church building. It refers not simply to a place of worship, but to the area surrounding it—and, crucially, to the people living in that area, whom the Church of England refers to as parishioners. The Church of England's parochial system is mapped onto all the country, such that there is not meant to be a house, meadow, or tube station that is not situated in a Church of England parish, however oblivious most of the population may be to this fact. Parishes are associated with the notion of the 'cure of souls', which in the Church's understanding refers to the parish priest's responsibility to pray for all who fall within the boundaries of his or her parish regardless of whether they choose to be affiliated with the parish church. This is a reality that is connected to

---

10   The Church Commissioners for England, *Supporting the Work and Mission of the Church of England: The Church Commissioners for England Annual Report 2021*, 2022, pg. 32, https://www.churchofengland.org/sites/default/files/2022-07/5950_cofe_church-commissioners_final-120522-1.pdf.
11   The exceptions to this are 'The Church of England abroad' (e.g., the Diocese of Europe), as well as a number of parishes in Wales that opted to remain in the Diocese of Hereford after the disestablishment of the Church of Wales.
12   Norman J.G. Pounds, *A History of the English Parish: The Culture of Religion from Augustine to Victoria* (Cambridge: Cambridge University Press, 2000).
13   Colin Buchanan. *Historical Dictionary of Anglicanism* (London: Rowman & Littlefield, 2015), 463.

England's church-state settlement: all people in England are entitled to baptism, marriage, and a funeral in their parish church.[14]

While its endurance is a testament to its dynamic nature, in England today the status of the parish is increasingly under scrutiny along with the Church to which it belongs. One aspect of this conversation is the question of who belongs to the parish, a question which has particularly salient ramifications in multireligious England. Since the boundaries of the spatial units of the Church of England are primarily geographical and only secondly theological or membership-based, there are no clear boundaries of belonging or exclusion. Instead, the membership of the parish is up for negotiation. As will be discussed below, for the Church of England's national task group on interreligious relations, non-Anglicans and non-Christians are "parishioners".

3 The Church's Reports

In 2005, the Church of England released a report entitled "Presence and Engagement: The churches' task in a multi Faith society".[15] This report, detailing the launch of its 'Presence and Engagement' programme, marked the emergence of a new era in the Church's approach to relations with people of other religions in England. Presence and Engagement represents the Church of England's attempt "… to think about the reality of religious diversity and how it might shape mission and ministry".[16] The Presence and Engagement task group has been publishing reports since 2005, designed to be read by both national church actors such as those sitting on General Synod, and local parish priests and laity.[17] These reports have yet to be analysed in depth by scholars and are of much importance. They are documentary evidence of the Church's ongoing attempts to understand—and actively construct—its place in light of the increasing presence of other religions in England. They cover a wide range

---

[14] It is worth noting that at the time of writing, the Church of England will not marry same-sex couples. Parishioners are also entitled to burial in the parish churchyard, if existent.
[15] "Churches" in the title refers to individual congregations, hence the spelling. The titles of the reports are not consistent in their style and capitalisation. I have presented them as the written by the Church of England.
[16] "About Presence and Engagement", The Church of England, accessed June 2023, https://www.churchofengland.org/about/building-relationships/interfaith-relations/presence-engagement.
[17] General Synod is the national legislative assembly of the Church of England. There are four successors to the first Presence and Engagement report, from 2009, 2010, 2011, and 2019.

of topics, such as the meaning of establishment, soteriology, evangelism, and the role of parishes and church buildings.

Running throughout the reports, especially the inaugural 2005 report, is the role of the parish in maintaining the Church of England's social status as a religious leader among all religions in England, or the "Church for the nation", in the words of the Bishop of Aston, a member of the group which prepared the Presence and Engagement report.[18] The parish is presented as intertwined with the state. For example, in a section of the 2005 report concerning "Reflections on Presence and Engagement", the authors write:

> [T]he Church of England has continued to understand itself to be called to be present corporately in all the localities of the country. At the heart of this self understanding [sic] is the parish church, a Christian community called to be present and to engage actively with all who live in the neighbourhood irrespective of their Faith or none. This comprehensive presence and duty of engagement with all via the shared charge of the 'cure of souls', has continued to be a foundational distinction of the Church of England *and an underpinning of its relationship with the State*.[19]

In this statement and in others to be discussed below, the Church of England demonstrates an attitude that it is the 'host' religion of the nation, whose role it is to welcome other religions on its own terms. Indeed, hospitality is a common theme across the Presence and Engagement reports and a frequent motif in interreligious relations writ large. The biblical imperative to love one's neighbour is often interpreted by Christians as welcoming guests, and in interreligious interactions, is often cited by Christians as an impetus to engage with people of other religions. Crucially however, hospitality tacitly relies on a system where it is clear who is the host and who is the guest. It also relies on a shared understanding of the parameters and ownership of the space in which the host/guest interaction is taking place.

The notion expressed in the quote above that the incumbent of a parish has the "cure of all souls" in that parish carries an implicit notion of hosting within the boundaries of the parish. This very notion is reinforced, and the boundaries of the hosting relationship extended nation-wide when the

---

18　The Archbishops' Council, "General Synod July 2005 Group of Sessions", *Report of Proceedings* 36, no. 2 (2005): 202.

19　The Church of England, "Presence and Engagement: The churches' task in a multi Faith society" (2005), pg. 11, https://www.churchofengland.org/sites/default/files/2019-05/Presence_and_Engagement_Report%202005.pdf. Emphasis mine.

Church's close relationship with the state is invoked. The phrasing used by the Church indicates an ongoing understanding of Anglicanism as a component of English identity. It is notable that this understanding has not broken down since the rise of religious diversity in the nation. For instance, in another section of the 2005 report, the authors state that: "the wider world of other Faiths has arrived on *our* doorstep and *Muslims, Sikhs and Hindu people are now parishioners* with the happy consequence that the universal is now more than ever encompassed within the local parish".[20]

An obvious sense of ownership is proffered through the use of "our". The "doorstep" is most readily understood as England itself, the birthplace and inheritance of the established church. Just as salient regarding Church-as-host is the insistence that Muslims, Sikhs, and Hindus are participants in the parochial system, a space invented by Christians and sustained by the Church of England.[21] Moreover, the assertion that these individuals are "encompassed" within the local parish presents the image of an absorption of their identities by the Church of England. The fact that "power relations always underlie the social construction of space"[22] is important here: through the invocation of this spatial system, the Church attempts to make other religions subjects in its own hierarchical divisions of space.

An anecdote from a parish priest quoted in the report supports the notion that the parish enables actors in the Church to have an attitude of ownership: "Yesterday at my local Sufi mosque we prayed together as usual. I am *their* priest. It is good".[23] The fact that the mosque fell within the parish boundaries enabled the priest to use possessive language: "my mosque". It also reinforced the priest's sense of identity in relation to the mosque: "I am "*their*" priest". The anecdote is enthusiastically listed under a section of the report called "Stories of creative engagement". That the Presence and Engagement felt that this was worth including is indicative of a host mentality in relation to the parochial system. The perspective of the mosque was not included in the report.

The Church's confidence in its status as host, or in continuing in previous ways of hosting, is not always as firm as the above quotes indicate. The authors of the 2005 report write:

---

20 Church of England, "Presence and Engagement", 21. Emphasis mine.
21 The parochial system originated with the Roman Catholic Church pre-Reformation and was carried forward in the modern instantiation of the Church of England.
22 Setha Low, *Spatializing Culture: The Ethnography of Space and Place* (New York: Routledge, 2017), 69.
23 Church of England, "Presence and Engagement", 58. Emphasis in original report.

> Rapid change in the surrounding context has been the norm for most parishes which are now in or moving towards a minority Faith position in the neighbourhood. In such situations anxiety and a loss of confidence can sap the ability of a congregation to remain people of outgoing hope and *hospitality* and turn them inwards. True confidence lies not in numbers or in power but in the way of the incarnation, the Cross and resurrection. The loss of status and position can be crucifying, but can also be the means for local churches to lead people *back to a confidence in God rather than in inherited structures and ways of doing things*.[24]

The invocation to remain "people of outgoing hope and hospitality" indicates that hospitality is a central duty for the Church, both in the past and going forward. These words of exhortation and encouragement might be addressed to those who worry about declining membership alongside the growth of other religious communities. These traditional measures of judging the health of the church are perhaps not considered viable or the truest measures according to the Church, as the latter part of the paragraph testifies. The opposition between "confidence in God" and "inherited structures" is notable: the host religion is the host because of inherited structures and ways of doing things.

The tone of encouragement in the above quote might be an attempt to address some of the experiences relayed to the Presence and Engagement task force in their gathering of stories from parishes around the country. One such story from Birmingham read:

> The Gurdwara has replaced the Church as the Established Church. It is they who have the processions and organise the street parties and they are superb. Our church used to fulfil this role 50 years ago. We are utterly irrelevant to their life–they would be ten times our size–but each Faith is well disposed to the other.[25]

In his seminal work on *The Symbolic Construction of Community*, anthropologist Anthony Cohen notes that community "both implies similarity and difference", since a community is relational as both a positive grouping of people with something in common and opposition to other social entities. In this sense, "the boundary marks the beginning and end of a community ... the boundary encapsulates the identity of the community". Yet boundaries are not objective, even when marked by physical elements such as a sea or wall. Boundaries are

---

24   Church of England, "Presence and Engagement", 17. Emphasis mine.
25   Church of England, "Presence and Engagement", 22.

symbolic in the sense that they are representative, and also because symbols "allow those who employ them to supply part of their meaning".[26] It follows from this that community boundaries such as parishes may be perceived in different ways even by those within the community. For some, the presence of people from other religions in 'their' parish is a positive opportunity, for others, a negative and a sign of the decline of Christianity in Britain.

In their inaugural report, the task force behind Presence and Engagement chose to encourage an expansive view of parochial 'belonging' that maintains the status of host. As the initiators and custodians of the Anglican parochial system, they are able to supply the meaning of parochial space. The Church of England nationally takes on the tone of a "church for the nation". As the English nation includes growing numbers of Muslims, Sikhs, Hindus, the implication is that they are the church for those communities. This is a striking claim, but it does not represent the entire picture. As will be seen in a case study of the Diocese of Birmingham, at the local level Anglican parish priests have different views about the parish and about how to engage with people of other religions.

4   Birmingham

As seen in the Presence and Engagement reports, the parochial system assumes that everyone who lives in England is a participant in the Church. This notion is reaffirmed in the Presence and Engagement reports, which refer to non-Anglicans and non-Christians as "parishioners". My ethnographic interviews carried out among twenty-five parish priests and Anglican leaders in the Church of England's Diocese of Birmingham aimed to identify how Anglicans pursued interreligious relations at the local level.[27] The parish emerged as a prominent theme in almost every interview.

Though the fact of its importance was agreed upon by my interlocutors, there was not unanimity of perspective about how the parish should be understood in light of religious diversity. For some, the notion of all people being parishioners was a sign of inclusivity, while for others it represented an uncomfortable paternalism. The diversity of viewpoints of Anglican priests in Birmingham were not reflected in the Church of England's national reports. In addition to giving a broader perspective, this functions as a reminder of the important of studying local, emic perspectives in addition to what is presented

---

26   Anthony Cohen, *The Symbolic Construction of Community* (London: Routledge, 1985), 14.
27   The names of my interlocutors and their parishes have been pseudonymised.

4.1 *The Reverend Nathaniel: Boundaries of Belief and Belonging*

The Reverend Nathaniel identifies himself and his congregation as "Bible-believing" Christians. His choice of label was borne out of a concern that the terms 'conservative' and 'evangelical' are ambiguous and risk being misleading, but he readily acknowledged that those labels would not be an inaccurate way of perceiving his congregation. For Revd. Nathaniel, there was great significance in the fact that the Church of England is a "confessional Church". By this, Revd. Nathaniel meant that the Church of England holds to the Thirty-Nine Articles and that it has "specific doctrines that are common ground for its membership, which define the boundaries of belief and belonging … there is a doctrine that you would be expected to sign up to, to be Anglican". As such, Revd. Nathaniel was concerned that a broad understanding of 'belonging' in the Church of England, including in the parish, limits its unique claims. He contrasted his viewpoint with those who say that being Anglican is just about attending Church of England services and furthermore said that:

> Some people even hold to the view that the Church of England consists of everyone who is English, which I find a strange notion because obviously, that would include everyone in my parish. And some of them would be surprised to find that they're part of the Church of England. The imam at the mosque might not want that.

Revd. Nathaniel's perspective was informed by a classical conservative evangelical view that to be a Christian is to accept Jesus into one's life and hold to an exclusive set of doctrines which are then reinforced through church attendance and living a Christian life. For him, the notion that anyone who lives in England is an Anglican, or has a part in the Church of England, is problematic because it undermines the need for Anglicans to affirm confessional claims which form the boundaries of what is and is not Anglican. Revd. Nathaniel's statement "the imam at the mosque might not want that" can be understood in two main ways. The first is a matter of respect: to not impose a religion on someone who does not wish to belong to it. The second is one of maintaining internal Christian boundaries so that the meaning of being a Christian is not reduced to being simply one who lives in a country with a Christian national church. Revd. Nathaniel's perspective highlights the axiomatic element of the parish: boundary, and particularly "boundaries of belief and belonging", in his own phrasing. The concepts of 'parish,' 'parishioner' 'Church of England'

and 'Anglican' can be construed in a multitude of ways depending on one's theology, social ethic, and concept of the nation and what it means to be the national church.

4.2 Father Adrian: An (un)traditional Understanding of the Parish?

Revd. Nathaniel's concerns about people who take a broad view of belonging in the parish were not abstract: they are represented by many of his colleagues in the same diocese. The Anglican parochial framework is bound up with a responsibility of the cure of souls. This language comes readily to some clergy. When I asked Father Adrian, one of my interlocutors, how large his parish was, with the intention to determine the *geographical* size, he replied with, "20,000 souls". Fr. Adrian is most readily identifiable with the 'liberal Catholic' wing of the Church of England. As such, it is the ecclesiological elements of the Church of England that are important to his identity as an Anglican, especially the parish, but he does not by default hold to an exclusivist theology. The religious identities of the 20,000 souls within his parish were not relevant to him. He animatedly shared with me:

> The cure of souls, which is given to a parish priest [by the bishop] is something that is really quite important. So I can go into a gurdwara, or a mosque or any building ... Or a pub! "I have come to visit as your parish priest". And they'll go, "Oh, but I'm Sikh" or whatever. "No, you are still within my cure of souls, I still have to look after you". And that's what everything is predicated on.

In Fr. Adrian's conceptual framework, the parish is defined by the souls within it. Belonging does not necessitate a Christian identity. The cure of souls for Fr. Adrian has a dual emphasis. Firstly, it encompasses everyone. He was at pains to emphasise that he had the cure of souls of everyone in his parish: "whatever they believe or think". The second is that the cure of souls ought to be exemplified through practical action. For Fr. Adrian, the cure of souls is not simply a matter of church doctrine but a living, everyday tradition. This is essential because it guides his approach to interfaith relations. He explained his perspective on his duty as a parish priest to marry *all* parishioners who approach him. This injunction means that non-Christians must be made comfortable, even if it means altering the prescribed services of the Church of England. His parish church is a grand, grade II listed building, and it is not an uncommon occurrence for non-Christians to ask to be married in its scenic location. He was approached by a Hindu couple and worked with them to find language that they were comfortable using during the ceremony: "If somebody wants something, the answer is 'Yes'. And then we work out how it can be done".

There are elements of Fr. Adrian's approach that clearly echo the Church of England's national reports on interreligious relations, especially his insistence that all people are parishioners. At one point in our conversation, he boldly proclaimed that "all people are parishioners, whether they like it or not". Such language might be striking but it is not fundamentally different from the assertion in the 2005 Presence and Engagement report that "... the wider world of other Faiths [sic] has arrived on our doorstep and Muslims, Sikhs, and Hindu people are now parishioners".[28] The weighty historical tradition of the English parish buttresses Fr. Adrian's ability to walk into any social situation and declare himself the parish priest. He is further supported by the Presence and Engagement reports, which bring this historical tradition to the present day. In other words, by virtue of belonging to the national church he is afforded a high degree of social currency. This is not true in all parishes, as will be seen below, and it is important to note that Fr. Adrian's parish has many Christians in it, which further supports his claims. However, his actions also demonstrate a departure from the Church of England's nationally dictated strategy on interreligious relations.

It is uncertain whether many in the hierarchy of the Church of England, namely those represented in Presence and Engagement task group, would be comfortable with the strategic limiting of Christian language in a marriage ceremony performed in an Anglican church. Yet it is by virtue of the very idea that they promulgate—that all people are parishioners—that Fr. Adrian insisted on accommodating a Hindu wedding in a Christian church: the couple were under his "cure of souls". This is indicative of the ambiguity of the space of the parish as it pertains to non-Anglicans. The ambiguity is experienced not only by actors outside the church, but by those within it, a fact which will be examined in a final case which shows an entirely different experience of the parish.

4.3 The Reverend Justin

The Reverend Justin's approach to ministry is driven by the Biblical ethic of loving one's neighbour. He believes that the Church of England's presence across the country, including in non-Christian majority areas demonstrates a commendable commitment to all people: "it says we care about you". However, Revd. Justin also uses the words "mad", "crazy", and "crackers" to describe the

---

28   Church of England, "Presence and Engagement", 21.

parochial system. He ministers in Carlington, an urban area of the Diocese of Birmingham where the parochial boundaries can seem arbitrary. He pointed to the fact that the next parish over has 25,000 people in it while his has 7,000. It is comical to Revd. Justin is how the division between the parishes runs down right down the middle of a street, according to the map. "If you're on one side you're *ours*, and if you're on the other side you're [St Anne's]! It's crackers!" While the notions of presence and responsibility for others is central for Revd. Justin, the parochial system itself is not.

According to the latest census data, the religious demographics of Revd. Justin's parish indicate that over two-thirds of the population are Muslims, with very few Christians. Revd. Justin is consistently reminded that his parish has many people of other religions, especially Muslims, due to the siting of a mosque directly across the street from his church. As I interviewed him, Revd. Justin indicated the proximity of the two places of worship with his hands held up parallel to each other: "In the room that I'm sitting in now, if I look that way, I see the church, which is probably about 40 feet away. And if I look that way, I see the mosque, and that's probably 50 feet away. So it's literally like THAT [hands held upright next to each other], you know?"

Revd. Justin's church enjoys a good relationship overall with the mosque, and while he says that some other churches "drew up the drawbridge" when waves of immigration brought many Muslims to the neighbourhood in the 1970s and 1980s, his church decided to help the new Muslim families by setting up a childcare centre that still thrives in the church to this day. As with any relationship however, there are sources of tension. On Fridays, Revd. Justin's parish fills up with hundreds, sometimes even thousands of people going to the mosque. He told me,

> One of the difficulties of living in this area is that you can feel overwhelmed and you can feel sort of displaced. And certainly on a Friday, you know, Friday prayers for half an hour, three quarters of an hour, the roads around here are almost impossible, because people will just park everywhere in order to make it to the prayer. ... So it can feel like you're either being overlooked just because you're a very small group, or it can feel like you're being squeezed out.

Often people going to the mosque will park in the church car park, which poses a problem when it blocks Revd. Justin's car in. His frustration became apparent when he told me,

> it ends up being the final straw that breaks the back of this sense of being an outsider, sort of, you know, the minority, you finally think, 'Well, this is

what you think of me, isn't it? You think I'm so unimportant that you can block my drive, or you can fill the church car park up so that it's literally every space—not just parking spaces—*every* space within the car park is taken'.

Revd. Justin is quick to emphasise that there are members of the mosque who oppose the behaviour of those who park without consideration for others, and that during Ramadan, when good deeds are especially valued—and when prayer attendance rises—there is permission asked to use the church's car park. He also says, after sharing the above, perhaps more to himself than me, "I mustn't get too carried away. It is only a car park". Still, it remains a source of tension, as does a lingering sense that if the childcare program at the church were to talk about Jesus too much, the local Muslim leaders might get upset with the church and stop allowing their families to take part.

The Church of England's idea of being a host and the parish system provide a lens through which Revd. Justin can understand why the Church of England is present in an area where he estimates only 2–3% of people are professing Christians. Yet the parochial system is not of help when the church car park is full because of the mosque across the street and his car is blocked in when he needs to drive to an appointment. Nor is the language of the "cure of souls" helpful when he feels limited in his own Christian speech. In other words, many of the privileges that are associated with belonging to the national Church of England are of little benefit to Revd. Justin in Carlington. The Presence and Engagement strategy of seeing all people as parishioners is not necessary for him to care about others—he would anyway—nor is it helpful in navigating tense social situations locally. In one way his congregation conforms to the national Church of England's host mentality: the childcare centre welcomes and helps many people. Yet this has little to do with belonging to the national Church and much to do with his congregation's own Christian ethic of love.

5 Conclusions

It will not come as a surprise to anyone with knowledge of the Church of England that it is theologically divided on the topic of interreligious relations and the meaning of the parish. These are only an example of many disputed issues in the Church. However, there are several points worth noting about the particular matter of the parish. The first is that there is a visible differentiation between the approach presented by what might be termed the 'national' or 'institutional' level of the Church versus the 'local' level. The national approach on this issue is unified and cohesive, which is not true for many other matters in the Church. It is at the local level, that of the parish priest, where the theology becomes diversified. A common motif across my interviews was the insistence of my interlocutors that every parish is unique. The logical outworking of this is that a localised and practical theological response is needed, one that responds to the needs of each context. My research found that it is the priests and those who they encounter in daily life who carry out this theological work. This functions as a reminder that when considering theological imaginaries—whether the Anglican parish or the Russian World—we must not merely consider the institutional but also the local. If we fail to do this then we risk acting as agents for those institutional figures or bodies which would have us believe that their position is not only authoritative but normative.

Like any social practice, interreligious relations are embedded in by complex matrices of power. When the interreligious encounter takes place, it is unlikely to be between individuals or communities with equal access to resources including finances, space for meeting and worship, social influence, and even security: "Interreligious dialogue never takes place 'on a clean slate'—rather, it is always already entangled with the politics of representation, which govern access to speech and conditions of visibility".[29] Take, for instance, the Church's notion that "A parishioner may equally be agnostic, atheist, Muslim, or Christian, but remain nevertheless a parishioner".[30] While ostensibly a welcoming sentiment, the insistence that non-Anglicans partake in a spatial system owned by the national Church can equally be seen as a statement of control.

The impelled inclusivity of the national Church's approach does not leave much room for a Muslim, a non-conforming Christian, or an atheist to say that she would rather *not* be a parishioner. In the context of this volume's examination of the Russian World, it is instructive to reflect on England's own historical entangling of national identity, imperial ambition, and religious authority – particularly through the Church of England's role in legitimating territorial and cultural dominance. Today, the Church of England claims jurisdiction – spiritual and symbolic – over all those within its borders, regardless of how they identify religiously. This assertion is arguably the inheritance of the colonial mentality of what might have once been called the British World. Conversely, the fact remains that non-Christians in England, especially Muslims, have

---

29 Judith Gruber, "Can women in interreligious dialogue speak? Productions of in/visibility at the intersection of religion, gender, and race", *Journal of Feminist Studies in Religion* 36, no.1 (2020): 68.
30 Church of England, "Presence and Engagement", 55.

been vocal about the benefits of a state Church as a bulwark against an otherwise bleak secularism.[31] In this sense the Church of England is right: the parish as a constituent part of the national Church has the potential to hold value for non-Anglicans. This aligns also with Jenny Leith's persuasive assertion in this volume that national churches in general, and the Church of England in particular, can provide a sense of belonging for all people. In sum, we are reminded that "The insistence on a particular meaning [of space] can marginalise other layers of meaning, especially when backed by the law or the force of power, but it does not change the capacity for space to contain multiple layers of meaning in principle".[32] The parish can contain as many layers of meaning as there are 'parishioners'—but there is at present a narrative from the institutional Church which would present a dominant view of what the parish should be. These two facts must be held in tension with one another.

In this chapter I have aimed to understand the mindset of the dominant religion in England as pertains to a spatial imaginary which illuminates its approach to religious minorities in England. The parish has emerged as a central theme. The ensuing task is to continue to explore the diversity within the Church, particularly voices such as Revd. Nathaniel or Revd. Justin who dispute the narrative that "all people are parishioners whether they like it or not". It is equally essential to understand how the Church of England's claims are understood by non-Anglicans. Only then can we understand the experiences of those on the Church of England's "doorstep".

Bibliography

Bourdieu, P. (1977). *Outline of a Theory of Practice*. Cambridge: Cambridge University Press.

Buchanan, C. (2015). *Historical Dictionary of Anglicanism*. 2nd ed. Lanham: Rowman & Littlefield, 2015.

---

31 See Modood and Meer: "... there is no evidence that the Anglican establishment actually alienates British Muslims ... there is no record of any criticism by a Muslim group in relation to the religious establishment. However, many Muslims do complain that Britain is too unreligious and anti-religious, too hedonistic, consumerist and materialist". 'Religious Pluralism in the United States and Britain: Its Implications for Muslims and Nationhood', *Social Compass* 62, no.4 (2015): 536.

32 Marietta van der Tol and Philip Gorski, "Secularisation as the fragmentation of the sacred and of sacred space", *Religion, State and Society* 50, no. 5 (2022): 499.

Chapman, M.D., C. Sathianathan, and M. Percy. (2015). "Introduction". In: M.D. Chapman, S. Clarke, and M. Percy (eds.). *The Oxford Handbook of Anglican Studies*. Oxford: Oxford University Press. Pp. 1–18.

Chidester, D., and E.T. Linenthal. (1995). *American Sacred Space*. Bloomington: Indiana University Press.

Cohen, A. (1985). *The Symbolic Construction of Community*. London: Routledge.

Grimley, M. (2007). "The Religion of Englishness: Puritanism, Providentialism, and 'National Character', 1918–1945". *Journal of British Studies* 46, no. 4: 884–906.

Gruber, J. (2020). "Can Women in Interreligious Dialogue Speak? Productions of in/Visibility at the Intersection of Religion, Gender, and Race". *Journal of Feminist Studies in Religion* 36, no. 1: 51–69.

Lefebvre, H. (1991). *The Production of Space*. Trans D. Nicholson-Smith. Oxford: Blackwell.

Lincoln, B. (1996). "Theses on method". *Method & Theory in the Study of Religion*, 8, no. 3: 225–227.

Loss, D.S. (2018). "Missionaries, the Monarchy, and the Emergence of Anglican Pluralism in the 1960s and 1970s". *Journal of British Studies* 57: 543–63.

Low, S. (2017). *Spatializing Culture: The Ethnography of Space and Place*. New York: Routledge.

Meer, N., and T. Modood. (2015). "Religious Pluralism in the United States and Britain: Its Implications for Muslims and Nationhood". *Social Compass* 62, no. 4: 526–40.

Pounds, N. (2000). *A History of the English Parish: The Culture of Religion from Augustine to Victoria*. Cambridge: Cambridge University Press.

The Archbishops' Council. (2005). "General Synod July 2005 Group of Sessions". *Report of Proceedings* 36, no. 2.

The Church Commissioners for England. (2022). *Supporting the Work and Mission of the Church of England: The Church Commissioners for England Annual Report 2021*. https://www.churchofengland.org/sites/default/files/2022-07/5950_cofe_church-commissioners_final-120522-1.pdf.

The Church of England. (2005). "Presence and Engagement: The churches' task in a multi Faith society". https://www.churchofengland.org/sites/default/files/2019-05/Presence_and_Engagement_Report%202005.pdf.

Van der Tol, M.D.C., and P.S. Gorski. (2022). "Secularisation as the fragmentation of the sacred and of sacred space". *Religion, State and Society* 50, no. 5: 495–512.

CHAPTER 17

Concluding Reflection: The Call for Political Theologies after Christendom

Marietta van der Tol, Petr Kratochvíl, Sophia Johnson, and Zoran Grozdanov

Processes of secularisation, de-institutionalisation, and individualisation have shaped Europe's transformation over the last number of decades, and for some conservative Christians, this has contributed to a profound sense of loss, disquiet, and anxiety. While these processes do not follow a linear trajectory and remain profoundly complex, there are meaningful questions to be asked about the relationship between the Christian tradition(s) and perceptions of transformation, change, and loss. These are old themes in the history of Christianity, stretching from St. Augustine's restless *Confessions* to Charles Taylor's *A Secular Age,* and they manifest again in our time. These themes of transformation, change, and loss also animate discourses across the contexts of populism, the European Far Right and Russian civilisationist discourse. In this context, it is perhaps not a surprise that forms of traditionalism, conservatism, and Christianity coalesce around them.

What that loss exactly entails, however, and how it is reflected in politics may not always be clear. While it may refer to secularisation, globalisation and the rise of the liberal international order as meta-narratives, it may also refer to the category of the personal in its engagement with gender, sexuality and the future of the traditional family, or to the reality of economic disadvantage present throughout Europe's social, political, and economic peripheries. Even if the category of 'loss' is ambiguous, it is recognisable and familiar enough to function as an important political frame, invoking at once the present, the past, and the future. Illiberal politics frames this in the mythologisation of a past, the dystopia of the present, and apocalyptic intimations of the future.[1] In this context of threat, loss might take on an existential meaning, making religion perhaps a likely frame of reference for addressing it. Further, the visibility of religion across the Far Right and in Russian civilisationist discourse is not accidental: even as European societies have secularised under the influence of

---

1 Jayne Svenungsson, "From Apocalyptic Demonization to Theological Responsibility", *Streit-Kultur. Journal für Theologie* (2023).

both liberalism and communism,[2] religion has always provided background political and social imaginaries and continues to offer them in the present.

What is new, is perhaps the contemporary transformation of the political role of religion. What is sometimes understood as a 'return of religion' is a much more differentiated and diffuse phenomenon, allowing for traditional religious attachments to institutions as well as for uses of religion that have long escaped the confines of Scripture, reason, and tradition. In this book, this transformation is explored through the lens of Christianism in its diverse forms. In the words of Rogers Brubaker, Christianism primarily referred to a "secularist posture", in which cultural and sometimes confessional Christianity is conscripted in support of a "philosemitic stance" and a "liberal defence" of freedom of speech, gender equality and gay rights.[3] While this characterisation perhaps focused on a type of right-wing populism in Western Europe, the transnational nationalism of today invites a more differentiated meaning to Christianism, one that is inclusive of the emerging bridge frames of contemporary illiberalism: being anti-liberal, anti-Western, anti-LGBT, anti-elitist, and anti-democratic, and which is not obviously or exclusively definable as a secularist posture.

The many faces of Christianism relate to their overlapping and distinct functions across national, transnational, and local spaces of political contestation. To say the least, the distinction between a civilizationist focus and a national(ist) one is meaningful as far as it captures the different political strategies Christianist actors opt for when entering the political arena. The Russian World ideology with its rhetoric of shared cultural and religious values is clearly distinct from those versions of Christianism that build on more ethno-centric and Atlanticist interests.[4] For this reason, geopolitical realities strike differently in the Baltic area, as is shown in the chapter by Garškaitė-Antonowicz. Othering plays an important role in all forms of Christianism, even as the category of 'the other' is adaptable to particular political struggles. While the language is, at first glance, defensive (after all, the recurrent theme is the protection of 'our families', 'our values', or 'our culture'), the Christianist re-appropriation of religion can be strongly offensive, as expressed in

---

2   Katharina Kunter, "Communism and European Christianity." *Entangling Web: The Fractious Story of Christianity in Europe* 4 (2024): 196.
3   Rogers Brubaker, "Between Nationalism and Civilisationalism: The European populist movement in comparative perspective", *Ethnic and Racial Studies* 40, no. 8 (2017): 1191–1226.
4   Nicola Guerra, "The Russian-Ukrainian war has shattered the European far right. The opposing influences of Steve Bannon and Aleksandr Dugin", *European Politics and Society* 25, no. 2 (2024): 421–439.

Schmitt-esque variations on political theology which are reproduced from the Russian World to the MAGA-movement in the USA.[5]

This othering concurrently aims at external as well as internal others, especially where 'disruptive' elements that are allegedly contributing to the destruction of 'our' families, nations and civilization arise from within. This is where gender, sexuality and reproduction emerge as central frames, as issues that threaten the traditional family – the locus for biological, cultural, and religious reproduction.[6] Besides gender, sexuality and reproduction is the issue of migration, which would lead to the 'dilution' of existing nations or in the words of Viktor Orbán, the "mixing of races".[7] Taken together, these issues nod to concerns over demographic decline, declining birthrates, and to threats perceived as stemming from globalisation. European integration, too, may be seen as part of the same problem. With the European Union's support for the free movement of people and its celebration of diversity, the EU is, from the Christianist point of view, exacerbating the problems Christianists are allegedly trying to solve. The articulation of 'the other' depends on the assertion of collective identities of particularism, typically revolving around the concepts of family, nation, culture, or civilization. The role of these frames for the Christianist argument (i.e. family, nation, civilization) is hard to overstate.

Chapters across this book wrestle with the transformation of the role of religion in politics, and the rise of religion in public and political space. The rise of Christianism is perhaps the most politically pertinent manifestation of the complex and hybrid re-arrangement of the secular-sacred, of this process of redrawing of their mutual boundaries and, indeed, their blurring. As such, this hybridity perhaps reflects the intrinsic rootlessness Charles Taylor ascribed to modern secularity.[8] Individually and collectively, the chapters raise political, sociological, and theological questions about the transforming interrelation of politics and religion. In their interdisciplinary character, chapters sometimes build on each other, filling out the picture or drawing the reader's attention to different dimensions of Christianism. Sometimes, they point to contradictions

---

5   Ulrich Schmiedel, *Terror und Theologie: Der religionstheoretische Diskurs der 9/11-Dekade* (Mohr Siebeck, 2021).
6   Phillip Ayoub and Kristina Stoeckl, "The Global Resistance to LGBTIQ Rights", *Journal of Democracy* 35, no. 1 (2024): 59–73; Petr Kratochvíl and Míla O'Sullivan, "A war like no other: Russia's invasion of Ukraine as a war on gender order", *European Security* 32, no. 3 (2023): 347–366.
7   Alexander Faludy, "The troubling Christian roots of Orbán's rhetoric", *Church Times*, 19 August 2022, accessed 9 April 2024, https://www.churchtimes.co.uk/articles/2022/19-august/comment/opinion/the-troubling-christian-roots-of-orbans-rhetoric.
8   Charles Taylor, *A Secular Age* (Cambridge, MA: Belknap Press, 2007).

which cannot quite be resolved. This is pertinent in the encounter between political science and sociology on the one hand, and theology on the other, particularly where doctrinal distinctions that matter in theology seem to take a backseat in political or sociological writings. In many ways, these encounters are reflective of a puzzle: when we focus on a handful of pieces, it is not always imminently clear how they fit together unless we grant them the time and attention to see the fuller picture emerge.

The pieces of the puzzle, in this volume, pertain to theoretical and theological reflections on the role of religion in politics, the gradual and multipolar development of the 'Russian World', and ensuing chapters on Christianity and the Far Right. Taken together, the chapters invoke a sense that contemporary issues, such as the war in Ukraine, have exacerbated tensions that shaped up over a long period of time and cannot be contained in simple categories of good or evil. These chapters also invite further political theological reflection, about the role of the churches, incentives for their participation in illiberal politics, and the ways in the liberal political order has opened an avenue for the Far Right to align itself with conservative Christianity in its contestation of the liberal political order, and for conservative Christianity to align itself with the Far Right in its contestation of the secular.

Taken together, the chapters on the Russian World and the Far Right in Europe show that the transformation of the role of religion in politics is not merely one of assertion of decline. However, this dynamic is in many ways asymmetrical, first because only a subset of Christianity is represented in this endeavour, and second, because the Far Right has successfully shaken off the Christian sources of authority, namely scripture, tradition, reason, and ecclesial structure, as normative sources of correction, and reinterpreted the Christian message in an idiosyncratic way, suitable for its political purposes.[9] This leaves Christianity vulnerable to the whims of political appropriation, especially where churches remain silent or ambivalent over their claim to Christianity.[10] Of course, a similar claim concerning the transformed relationship between religious authority and religious tradition is true beyond the West and beyond Christianity as well, being visible in Indian Hindutva, the Netanyahu administration in Israel, and arguably in various forms of Islamism.

---

9   Tobias Cremer, "Defenders of the Faith? How shifting social cleavages and the rise of identity politics are reshaping right-wing populists' attitudes towards religion in the West", *Religion, State and Society* 50, no. 5 (2022): 532–552.

10 Hannah Strømmen and Ulrich Schmiedel, *The Claim to Christianity: Responding to the Far Right* (London: SCM Press, 2020).

Contestation of both the secular and the liberal political order are squarely in the interest of the Kremlin, as is the growth of the Far Right across Europe and the United States. The Kremlin's overt 'symphonic' reliance on Russian Orthodoxy, and the tremendous resources poured into the rise of a transnational Christian Right,[11] shore up its geopolitical interests. Hungary's position is perhaps more central to this effort than is often thought. Not only does Hungary export illiberalism to the USA, Israel, and to a range of European states, it has also become a hub for the illiberal intelligentsia to meet and greet. Examples include the connections between American Conservative Union's CPAC conferences in the USA and in Hungary and the Edmund Burke Foundation's Scruton-esque National Conservatism.[12] In recent years, the pro-Orbán Danube Institute has hosted postliberal opinion makers such as Rod Dreher (Orthodox convert),[13] who posted a conversation series on Youtube with the highly influential Orthodox Metropolitan Hilarion Alfeyev (before Hilarion was repositioned from Budapest to Karlovy Vary in the Czech Republic in 2025).[14] This is significant: Alexandar Mihailovic noted that "on several occasions" Hilarion Alfeyev "appealed to traditionalists in the West to form a 'common front' against atheism and secularism".[15] The choice for Budapest was perhaps not as accidental, as the context provides ample opportunity to build traditionalist coalitions.

Sometimes the alliances come with electoral or financial benefits to the churches: Putin has invested in the renovation of Russian Orthodox churches, and Orbán has directed money towards the construction of Reformed and

---

11 Kristina Stoeckl and Dmitry Uzlaner, *The Moralist International: Russia in the Global Culture Wars* (New York: Fordham University Press, 2022); Gionathan Lo Mascolo, *The Christian Right in Europe: Movements, Networks, and Denominations* (New York: Transcript, 2023).

12 Kristina Stoeckl, "Europe's New Religious Conflicts: Russian Orthodoxy, American Christian Conservatives and the Emergence of a European Populist Christian Right-Wing", in *The Power of Religion/Religion and Power* (Walter de Gruyter, 2023), 53–60; Guillem Colom, "An International Far-Right Alliance? A Comparative Analysis of the Linkages Between the Republican Party and European Far-Right Parties" (26 February 2024), http://dx.doi.org/10.2139/ssrn.4739346.

13 Jamie Whyte, "The postliberal confusion", *Economic Affairs* 43, no. 1 (2023): 109ff. For more on American interest in Orthodoxy, see Sarah Riccardi-Swartz, *Between heaven and Russia: religious conversion and political apostasy in Appalachia* (Fordham University Press, 2022).

14 Alar Kilp and Jerry G. Pankhurst, "Religious Leadership and Critical Junctures in the 2022 Russian Invasion of Ukraine: 104 War Days of Metropolitan Hilarion", *Occasional Papers on Religion in Eastern Europe* 42, no. 7 (2022): 3.

15 Alexandar Mihailovic, *Illiberal Vanguard: Populist Elitism in the United States and Russia* (University of Wisconsin Pres, 2023).

Catholic church buildings and seminaries as well, both inside Hungary and beyond its borders. Furthermore, this support does come at a meaningful price: lending political legitimacy to secular claims to Christianity, holding back public critique, and stifling internal political disagreement. These traditions are not intellectually and politically free, even if the lack of freedom is not immediately apparent because of their current political alignment with the Kremlin and the Orbán-administration. Moreover, such financial support is only available for 'chosen' churches in Hungary, while minority churches or churches these states do not fully recognise face significant political, financial, and social disadvantages, including the limitation of their religious freedom.[16] In the case of Russia and the Russian-occupied territories of Ukraine, it is well-documented that disfavoured religious groups face open persecution under the guise of counter-extremist and counter-terrorist legislation.[17]

The benefits of these 'unholy' alliances are not merely material, however. Other short-term interests include the gratification of a need for affirmation that conservative Christians are not alone in some of the anti-liberal values they hold. This perhaps signals a deeper-seated issue about the transformed role of previously significant churches as now smaller societal players, and even as social minorities. The search for social relevance is shared by many churches in secularised countries in Europe; however, there is a difference between finding one's voice as a new minority and raising one's voice because of a need to re-emerge as normatively superior. Even so, where confessional Christianity supports the Far Right, it entails little more than a radical subset of conservative Christianity, whereas the major public support stems from cultural Christianity, which may or may not be committed to regular church attendance, or "belonging without attending", as Veković calls it in this volume.

An understanding of the secular-sacred moorings of Christianism is indispensable to understanding the sacralisation of belonging in the imaginaries of both European nationalism as well as Russian civilisationalism. Secularisation as the fragmentation of the sacred has created the very space for new and primarily secular assertions of sacrality, including on the political communal

---

16   Marietta van der Tol, *Constitutional Intolerance: The Fashioning of the Other in Europe's constitutional Repertoires* (Cambridge: Cambridge University Press, 2025).

17   Tatiana Vagramenko and Francisco Arqueros, "Criminotheology: Persecution of Jehovah's Witnesses in Putin's Russia", *International Journal for Religious Freedom* 16, no. 2 (2023): 83–103; Aram Terzyan, "The state of religious freedom in Russia: towards Orthodox monopoly", *Journal of Liberty and International Affairs* 9, no. 2 (2023): 507–519; Oleksandra Kovalenko, "Religious freedom and war: Ukrainian realities", *International Journal for Religious Freedom* 16, no. 2 (2023): 1–12.

level.¹⁸ It is the very fluidity of ideas rooted in both the secular and the sacred that prohibits their definitive categorisation as secular or religious: European nationalism and Russian civilisationalism are not conclusively anchored in either: they are 'transliminal'. This transliminality makes it especially difficult to discern whether these political movements are compatible with Christian traditions. This complexity puts public and political theology to the task of meaningful engagement with other disciplines, and vice versa, especially sociology, anthropology, international relations, and comparative politics.

Western European theology after the World War II positioned itself as socially and politically critical. It engaged with the sense of transformation, change and loss of the traditional forms and impact of Christianity on the societies and political communities of its time. The response of that theology was the articulation of a "new political theology" by the Catholic theologian Johann Baptist Metz (1928–2019) and Protestant theologians Jürgen Moltmann (1926–2024) and Dorothee Sölle (1929–2003)¹⁹ and it was concentrated on the deprivatization of Christian faith and the assertion of its tradition as a socially and politically critical force. It was not political in the sense of theological legitimization of political orders, but focused its criticism on the political, social (and religious) forms of oppression. This deprivatization and kind of 'politicisation' of Christianity was, according to them, needed due to the self-imposed privatization of religious language and doctrines on the part of theology and the churches. However, few decades later, and after the supposed 'return of the religion', there seems a need for a 'new new political theology' which will reflect on the role of religion in the formation of political enmity and polarisation, considering and reconsidering the way politically oppressive regimes use its religious repertoires.

It is in this spirit that several conferences of the Protestant Political Thought-project have drawn attention to the rise of Christian nationalism, the Far Right, and what is now known as the 'Russian World'. The conferences sought to bring together critiques of democratic backsliding and constructive accounts of democracy across Protestantism, Catholicism and Orthodoxy.²⁰ After the

---

18   M.D.C. Van der Tol and P.S. Gorski, "Secularisation as the fragmentation of the sacred and of sacred space", *Religion, State and Society* 50, no. 5 (2022): 495–512.

19   See for instance Jürgen Moltmann, *Religion, Revolution, and the Future* (New York: Charles Scribner's Sons, 1969); Johann Baptist Metz, *Faith in History and Society: Toward a Practical Fundamental Theology* (New York: Herder, 1977; Dorothee Sölle, *Political Theology* (Minneapolis: Fortress, 1974).

20   Pantelis Kalaitzidis, *Orthodoxy and Political Theology* (Geneva: WCC Publications, 2015); Cyril Hovorun, *Political Orthodoxies: The unorthodoxies of the Church coerced* (Fortress Press, 2018); Luke Bretherton, *Christ and the common life: political theology and the case*

full-scale invasion of Ukraine by Russia, it seems that political theologies that are pro-democracy still need a deeper engagement with the contemporary legacies of Christendom and how they shape (geo)political enmity in a post-secular world. It asks for a reckoning with the experience of those who have suffered from political violence, atrocities, and exclusion, but also with Christianist claims on the past to do with forgone empires, lost territories or historical traditions of national or civilisational greatness. Even if complicity in political violence is a legacy that contemporary Christians cannot undo, 'new new political theologies' might engage in an exercise of what Miroslav Volf calls "remembering rightly", to develop political theologies situated as 'after Christendom'.[21]

Such 'political theologies after Christendom' can build on long traditions of thinking about the bonds between religion, politics, and violence. Historical traditions have reflected deeply on the issue of political violence and war and have offered conditions under which Christians can legitimately participate in war, if at all.[22] Hence, it is not true that every alliance with power necessarily leads to complicity in violence, but it takes discernment where a line has been crossed. In doing so, political theologies after Christendom might build on thinking about the 'Two Kingdoms' in unsettling monopolising claims on the sacred, taking seriously how positionality is reflected in political theologies that shore up or critique the bonds between religion, politics, and violence. In doing so, it will need to reckon with that theological antisemitism that is often implied in accounts of the kingdoms.[23] Critiques of 'symphonia' in Orthodoxy might in its current context seek to offer alternatives to 'Putinism', for example

for democracy (Wm. B. Eerdmans Publishing, 2019); José Casanova, *Public religions in the modern world* (University of Chicago Press, 2011); David P. Gushee, *Defending Democracy from Its Christian Enemies.* (Wm. B. Eerdmans Publishing, 2023); Miroslav Volf, and Ryan McAnnally-Linz, *Public faith in action: How to engage with commitment, conviction, and courage* (Brazos Press, 2017); John Heathershaw, *Security after Christendom: Global Politics and Political Theology for Apocalyptic Times* (Wipf and Stock Publishers, 2024); Cyril Hovorun and Jonathan Chaplin, *Beyond Establishment: Resetting Church-State Relations in England* (London: SCM, 2022).

21 Miroslav Volf, *The end of memory: Remembering rightly in a violent world* (Wm. B. Eerdmans Publishing, 2021).

22 M. Rowley and N. Hodgson, eds., *Miracles, Political Authority and Violence in Medieval and Early Modern History* (Abingdon: Routledge, 2022); M. Rowley, *God, Religious Extremism and Violence* (Cambridge University Press, 2024).

23 Sophia R. C. Johnson, ""We the People of Israel": Covenant, Constitution, and the Supposed Biblical Origins of Modern Democratic Political Thought", *Journal of the Bible and its Reception* 8, no. 2 (2021): 247–268, https://doi.org/10.1515/jbr-2021-0005; Eran Shalev, "The Old and the New Israel: The Cultural Origins of the Special Relationship", *Journal of the Bible and its Reception*, vol. 8, no. 2 (2021): 229–246, https://doi.org/10.1515/jbr-2021-0006.

in the work of Cyril Hovorun. In critiquing the Russian World or Christian nationalism both sides of the Atlantic and defending democracy, these discourses may feed of each other, as might the reconstructive work that political theologies after Christendom will necessitate.

Bibliography

Ayoub, P., and K. Stoeckl. (2024). "The Global Resistance to LGBTIQ Rights". *Journal of Democracy* 35, no. 1: 59–73.

Bretherton, L. (2019). *Christ and the common life: political theology and the case for democracy*. Wm. B. Eerdmans Publishing.

Brubaker, R. (2017). "Between Nationalism and Civilisationalism: The European populist movement in comparative perspective". *Ethnic and Racial Studies* 40, no. 8: 1191–1226.

Casanova, J. (2011). *Public religions in the modern world*. University of Chicago press.

Chaplin, J. (2022). *Beyond Establishment: Resetting Church-State Relations in England*. London: SCM.

Colom, G. (2024). "An International Far-Right Alliance? A Comparative Analysis of the Linkages Between the Republican Party and European Far-Right Parties". 26 February 2024. http://dx.doi.org/10.2139/ssrn.4739346.

Cremer, T. (2022). "Defenders of the Faith? How shifting social cleavages and the rise of identity politics are reshaping right-wing populists' attitudes towards religion in the West". *Religion, State and Society* 50, no. 5: 532–552.

Garamvolgyi, F., and P. Walker. (2023). "Viktor Orbán-influenced university plans outpost in London" *The Guardian*. 28 August 2023. Accessed 1 September 2023. https://www.theguardian.com/politics/2023/aug/28/viktor-orban-influenced-university-plans-outpost-in-london.

Guerra, N. (2024). "The Russian-Ukrainian war has shattered the European far right. The opposing influences of Steve Bannon and Aleksandr Dugin". *European Politics and Society* 25, no. 2: 421–439.

Gushee, D.P. (2023). *Defending Democracy from Its Christian Enemies*. Wm. B. Eerdmans Publishing.

Heathershaw, J. (2024). *Security after Christendom: Global Politics and Political Theology for Apocalyptic Times*. Wipf and Stock Publishers.

Hovorun, C. (2018). *Political Orthodoxies: The unorthodoxies of the Church coerced*. Fortress Press.

Johnson, S.R.C. (2021). ""We the People of Israel": Covenant, Constitution, and the Supposed Biblical Origins of Modern Democratic Political Thought". *Journal of the Bible and its Reception* 8, no. 2: 247–268. https://doi.org/10.1515/jbr-2021-0005.

Kalaitzidis, P. (2015). *Orthodoxy and Political Theology*. Geneva: WCC Publications.

Kilp, A., and J.G. Pankhurst. (2022). "Religious Leadership and Critical Junctures in the 2022 Russian Invasion of Ukraine: 104 War Days of Metropolitan Hilarion." *Occasional Papers on Religion in Eastern Europe* 42, no. 7: 3.

Kovalenko, O. (2023). "Religious freedom and war: Ukrainian realities." *International Journal for Religious Freedom* 16, no. 2: 1–12.

Kratochvíl, P., and M. O'Sullivan. (2023). "A war like no other: Russia's invasion of Ukraine as a war on gender order". *European Security* 32, no. 3: 347–366.

Kunter, K. (2024). "Communism and European Christianity." *Entangling Web: The Fractious Story of Christianity in Europe* 4: 196.

Lo Mascolo, G. (2023). *The Christian Right in Europe: Movements, Networks, and Denominations*. New York: Transcript.

Mihailovic, A. (2023). *Illiberal Vanguard: Populist Elitism in the United States and Russia*. University of Wisconsin Pres.

Riccardi-Swartz, S. (2022). *Between heaven and Russia: religious conversion and political apostasy in Appalachia*. Fordham University Press.

Rowley, M. (2024). *God, Religious Extremism and Violence*. Cambridge University Press.

Rowley, M., and N. Hodgson, eds. (2022). *Miracles, Political Authority and Violence in Medieval and Early Modern History*. Abingdon: Routledge.

Schmiedel, U. (2021). *Terror und Theologie: Der religionstheoretische Diskurs der 9/11-Dekade*. Mohr Siebeck.

Shalev, E. (2021). "The Old and the New Israel: The Cultural Origins of the Special Relationship". *Journal of the Bible and its Reception*, vol. 8, no. 2; 229–246. https://doi.org/10.1515/jbr-2021-0006.

Stoeckl, K. and D. Uzlaner. (2022). *The Moralist International: Russia in the Global Culture Wars*. New York: Fordham University Press.

Stoeckl, K. (2023). "Europe's New Religious Conflicts: Russian Orthodoxy, American Christian Conservatives and the Emergence of a European Populist Christian Right-Wing". In: *The Power of Religion/Religion and Power*. Walter de Gruyter. Pp. 53–60.

Strømmen, H., and U. Schmiedel. (2020). *The Claim to Christianity: Responding to the Far Right*. London: SCM Press.

Svenungsson, J. (2023). "From Apocalyptic Demonization to Theological Responsibility". *Streit-Kultur. Journal für Theologie*.

Taylor, C. (2007). *A Secular Age*. Cambridge, MA: Belknap Press of Harvard University Press.

Terzyan, A. (2023). "The state of religious freedom in Russia: towards Orthodox monopoly". *Journal of Liberty and International Affairs* 9, no. 2: 507–519

Vagramenko, T., and F. Arqueros. (2023). "Criminotheology: Persecution of Jehovah's Witnesses in Putin's Russia". *International Journal for Religious Freedom* 16, no. 2: 83–103.

Van der Tol, M.D.C., and P.S. Gorski. (2022). "Secularisation as the fragmentation of the sacred and of sacred space". *Religion, State and Society* 50, no. 5: 495–512.

Van der Tol, M.D.C. (2025). *Constitutional Intolerance: The Fashioning of the Other in Europe's constitutional Repertoires*. Cambridge: Cambridge University Press.

Volf, M. (2021). *The end of memory: Remembering rightly in a violent world*. Wm. B. Eerdmans Publishing.

Volf, M., and R. McAnnally-Linz. (2017). *Public faith in action: How to engage with commitment, conviction, and courage*. Brazos Press.

Whyte, J. "The postliberal confusion." *Economic Affairs* 43, no. 1: 109–114.

APPENDIX 1

A Declaration on the "Russian World" (Russkii Mir) Teaching

Coordinators of the Drafting Committee: Brandon Gallaher and Pantelis Kalaitzidis

The Russian invasion of Ukraine on February 24, 2022, is a historic threat to a people of Orthodox Christian tradition. More troubling still for Orthodox believers, the senior hierarchy of the Russian Orthodox Church has refused to acknowledge this invasion, issuing instead vague statements about the necessity for peace in light of "events" and "hostilities" in Ukraine, while emphasizing the fraternal nature of the Ukrainian and Russian peoples as part of "Holy Rus'," blaming the hostilities on the evil "West", and even directing their communities to pray in ways that actively encourage hostility.

The support of many of the hierarchy of the Moscow Patriarchate for President Vladimir Putin's war against Ukraine is rooted in a form of Orthodox ethnophyletist religious fundamentalism, totalitarian in character, called *Russkii mir* or the *Russian world*, a false teaching which is attracting many in the Orthodox Church and has even been taken up by the Far Right and Catholic and Protestant fundamentalists.

The speeches of President Vladimir Putin and Patriarch Kirill (Gundiaev) of Moscow (Moscow Patriarchate) have repeatedly invoked and developed *Russian world* ideology over the last 20 years. In 2014, when Russia annexed the Crimea and initiated a proxy war in the Donbas area of Ukraine, right up until the beginning of the full-fledged war against Ukraine and afterwards, Putin and Patriarch Kirill have used *Russian world* ideology as a principal justification for the invasion. The teaching states that there is a transnational Russian sphere or civilization, called Holy Russia or Holy Rus', which includes Russia, Ukraine and Belarus (and sometimes Moldova and Kazakhstan), as well as ethnic Russians and Russian-speaking people throughout the world. It holds that this "Russian world" has a common political centre (Moscow), a common spiritual centre (Kyiv as the "mother of all Rus"), a common language (Russian), a common church (the Russian Orthodox Church, Moscow Patriarchate), and a common patriarch (the Patriarch of Moscow), who works in 'symphony' with a common president/national leader (Putin) to govern this Russian world, as well as upholding a common distinctive spirituality, morality, and culture.

Against this "Russian world" (so the teaching goes) stands the corrupt West, led by the United States and Western European nations, which has capitulated to "liberalism", "globalization", "Christianophobia", "homosexual rights" promoted in gay parades, and "militant secularism". Over and against the West and those Orthodox who have fallen into schism and error (such as Ecumenical Patriarch Bartholomew and other local Orthodox churches that support him) stands the Moscow Patriarchate, along with Vladimir Putin, as the true defenders of Orthodox teaching, which they view in terms of traditional morality, a rigorist and inflexible understanding of tradition, and veneration of Holy Russia.

Since the enthronement of Patriarch Kirill in 2009, the leading figures of the Moscow Patriarchate, as well as spokespersons of the Russian State, have continually drawn on these principles to thwart the theological basis of Orthodox unity. The principle of the ethnic organization of the Church was condemned at the Council of Constantinople in 1872. The false teaching of ethno-phyletism is the basis for "Russian world" ideology. If we hold such false principles as valid, then the Orthodox Church ceases to be the Church of the Gospel of Jesus Christ, the Apostles, the Nicene-Constantinopolitan Creed, the Ecumenical Councils, and the Fathers of the Church. Unity becomes intrinsically impossible.

Therefore, we reject the "Russian world" heresy and the shameful actions of the Government of Russia in unleashing war against Ukraine which flows from this vile and indefensible teaching with the connivance of the Russian Orthodox Church, as profoundly un-Orthodox, un-Christian and against humanity, which is called to be "justified … illumined … and washed in the Name of our Lord Jesus Christ and by the Spirit of God" (Baptismal Rite). Just as Russia has invaded Ukraine, so too the Moscow Patriarchate of Patriarch Kirill has invaded the Orthodox Church, for example in Africa, causing division and strife, with untold casualties not just to the body but to the soul, endangering the salvation of the faithful.

In view of the "Russian world" teaching that is devastating and dividing the Church, we are inspired by the Gospel of Our Lord Jesus Christ and the Holy Tradition of His Living Body, the Orthodox Church, to proclaim and confess the following truths:

1   **"My kingdom is not of this world. If my kingdom were of this world, my servants would fight, so that I should not be delivered to the Jews; but now my kingdom ss not from here." (John 18:36)**

WE AFFIRM that the divinely-appointed purpose and accomplishment of history, its *telos*, is the coming of the Kingdom of our Lord Jesus Christ, a Kingdom of righteousness, peace and joy in the Holy Spirit, a Kingdom attested by Holy Scripture as authoritatively interpreted by the Fathers. This is the Kingdom we participate in through a foretaste at every Holy Liturgy: "Blessed is the kingdom of the Father, the Son and the Holy Spirit, now and ever and unto ages of ages!" (Divine Liturgy). This Kingdom is the sole foundation and authority for Orthodox, indeed for all Christians. There is no separate source of revelation, no basis for community, society, state, law, personal identity and teaching, for Orthodoxy as the Body of the Living Christ than that which is revealed in, by, and through our Lord Jesus Christ and the Spirit of God.

WE THEREFORE CONDEMN AS NON-ORTHODOX AND REJECT any teaching that seeks to replace the Kingdom of God seen by the prophets, proclaimed and inaugurated by Christ, taught by the apostles, received as wisdom by the Church, set forth as dogma by the Fathers, and experienced in every Holy Liturgy, with a kingdom of this world, be that Holy Rus', Sacred Byzantium, or any other earthly kingdom, thereby usurping Christ's own authority to deliver the Kingdom to God the Father (1 Corinthians 15:24), and denying God's power to wipe away every tear from every eye (Revelation 21:4). We firmly condemn every form of theology that denies that Christians are migrants and refugees in this world (Hebrews 13:14), that is, the fact that "our citizenship is in heaven, and it is from there that we are expecting a Saviour, the Lord Jesus Christ," (Philippians 3:20) and that Christians "reside in their respective countries, but only as sojourners. They take part in everything as citizens and put up with everything as foreigners. Every foreign land is their home, and every home a foreign land" (*The Epistle to Diognetus*, 5).

2 "Render therefore to Caesar the things that are Caesar's, and to God the things that are God's." (Matthew 22:21)

WE AFFIRM that in anticipation of the final triumph of the Kingdom of God we acknowledge the sole and ultimate authority of our Lord Jesus Christ. In this age, earthly rulers provide peace, so that God's people might live "calm and ordered lives, in all godliness and sanctity" (Divine Liturgy). Yet, there is no nation, state or order of human life that can make a higher claim on us than Jesus Christ, at whose name "every knee should bow, in heaven and on earth and under the earth" (Philippians 2:10).

WE THEREFORE CONDEMN AS NON-ORTHODOX AND REJECT any teaching which would subordinate the Kingdom of God, manifested in the One Holy Church of God, to any kingdom of this world seeking other churchly or secular lords who can justify and redeem us. We firmly reject all forms of government that deify the state (theocracy) and absorb the Church, depriving the Church of its freedom to stand prophetically against all injustice. We also rebuke all those who affirm caesaropapism, replacing their ultimate obedience to the crucified and resurrected Lord with that of any leader vested with ruling powers and claiming to be God's anointed, whether known by the title of "Caesar," "Emperor," "Tsar," or "President."

3   "There is no longer Jew or Greek, there is no longer slave or free, there is no longer male and female; for all of you are one in Christ Jesus." (Galatians 3:28)

WE AFFIRM that division of humanity into groups based on race, religion, language, ethnicity or any other secondary feature of human existence is a characteristic of this imperfect and sinful world, which, following the patristic tradition are characterized as "distinctions of the flesh" (St. Gregory of Nazianzus, *Oration* 7, 23). Assertion of superiority of one group over others is a characteristic evil of such divisions, which are entirely contrary to the Gospel, where all are one and equal in Christ, all must answer to him for their actions, and all have access to his love and forgiveness, not as members of particular social or ethnic groups, but as persons created and born equally in the image and likeness of God (Genesis 1:26).

WE THEREFORE CONDEMN AS NON-ORTHODOX AND REJECT any teaching that attributes divine establishment or authority, special sacredness or purity to any single local, national, or ethnic identity, or characterizes any particular culture as special or divinely ordained, whether Greek, Romanian, Russian, Ukrainian, or any other.

4   "You have heard that it was said, 'You shall love your neighbour and hate your enemy.' But I say to you, love your enemies and pray for those who persecute you, so that you may be children of your Father in Heaven." (Matthew 5:43–45)

Following the commandment of our Lord, WE AFFIRM that as St Silouan the Athonite declares, "The grace of God is not in the man who does not love his enemies", and that we cannot know peace until we love our enemies. As such, the making of war is the ultimate failure of Christ's law of love.

WE THEREFORE CONDEMN AS NON-ORTHODOX AND REJECT any teaching that encourages division, mistrust, hatred, and violence among peoples, religions, confessions, nations, or states. We further condemn as non-Orthodox and reject any teaching that demonizes or encourages the demonization of those that the state or society deems "other," including foreigners, political and religious dissenters and other stigmatized social minorities. We reject any Manichean and Gnostic division that would elevate a holy Orthodox Eastern culture and its Orthodox peoples above a debased and immoral "West". It is particularly wicked to condemn other nations through special liturgical petitions of the Church, elevating the members of the Orthodox Church and its cultures as spiritually sanctified in comparison to the fleshly, secular "Heterodox".

5 "Go and learn what this means, 'I desire mercy, and not sacrifice.' For I came not to call the righteous, but sinners." (Matthew 9:13; Cf. Hosea 6:6 And Isaiah 1:11–17)

WE AFFIRM that Christ calls us to exercise personal and communal charity to the poor, the hungry, the homeless, the refugees, the migrants, the sick and suffering, and seeking justice for the persecuted, the afflicted, and the needy. If we refuse the call of our neighbour; indeed if instead we beat and rob, and leave our neighbour to suffer and die by the wayside (Parable of the Good Samaritan, Luke 10:25–37), then we are not in Christ's love on the path to the Kingdom of God, but have made ourselves enemies of Christ and his Church. We are called to not merely pray for peace, but to actively and prophetically stand up and condemn injustice, to *make peace* even at the cost of our lives. "Blessed are the peacemakers, for they shall be called sons of God." (Matthew 5:9). Offering the sacrifice of liturgy and prayer while refusing to *act* sacrificially constitutes a sacrifice to condemnation at odds with what is offered in Christ (Matthew 5:22–26 and 1 Corinthians 11:27–32).

WE THEREFORE CONDEMN AS NON-ORTHODOX AND REJECT any promotion of spiritual "quietism" among the faithful and clergy of the Church, from the highest Patriarch down to most humble layperson. We rebuke those who pray for peace while failing to actively make peace, whether out of fear or lack of faith.

6 "If you continue in my word, you are truly my disciples; and you will know the truth, and the truth will make you free." (John 8:31–32)

WE AFFIRM that Jesus calls his disciples not only to know the truth but to speak the truth: "Let your word be 'Yes, Yes' or 'No, No'; anything more than this comes from the evil one." (Matthew 5:37). A full-scale invasion of a neighbouring country by the world's second largest military power is not just a "special military operation", "events" or "conflict" or any other euphemism chosen to deny the reality of the situation. It is, rather, *in fact* a full-scale military invasion that has already resulted in numerous civilian and military deaths, the violent disruption of the lives of over forty-four million people, and the displacement and exile of over two million people (as of March 13, 2022). This truth must be told, however painful it may be.

WE THEREFORE CONDEMN AS NON-ORTHODOX AND REJECT any teaching or action which refuses to speak the truth, or actively suppresses the truth about evils that are perpetrated against the Gospel of Christ in Ukraine. We utterly condemn all talk of "fratricidal war", "repetition of the sin of Cain, who killed his own brother out of envy" if it does not explicitly acknowledge the murderous intent and culpability of one party over another (Revelation 3:15–16).

We declare that the truths that we have affirmed and the errors which we have condemned as non-Orthodox and rejected are founded on the Gospel of Jesus Christ and the Holy Tradition of the Orthodox Christian faith. We call all who accept this declaration to be mindful of these theological principles in their decisions in church politics. We entreat all whom this declaration concerns to return to "the unity of the Spirit in the bond of peace" (Ephesians 4:3).

APPENDIX 2

A Statement of Solidarity with the Orthodox Declaration on the "Russian World" (russkii mir) Teaching, and against Christian Nationalism and New Totalitarianism

Following the invasion of Ukraine by the Russian Federation in February 2022, Orthodox voices have thoroughly rebutted the use of the "Russian World" (russkii mir) teaching, which claims that there is an organically unified transnational orthodox Christian Russian civilization that includes the territories and people of Russia, Ukraine, Belarus and sometimes other nations, to justify the current war. This statement seeks a) to facilitate support from among non-Orthodox Christian scholars for the rejection of the "russkii mir" teaching; b) to reject unholy alliances between Christian identity and political power which have also emerged in the context of Christian Nationalism; and c) to call for the development of an ecumenical "Theology after Christendom". We invite support from Christian scholars and clergy, and are open to those who do not share the Christian language of this statement, but who share its purpose.

> There is no Holy One like the Lord,
> no one besides you; there is no Rock like our God.
> Talk no more so very proudly,
> Let not arrogance come from your mouth;
> For the Lord is a God of knowledge,
> And by him actions are weighed
> *From Hannah's Prayer, 1 Samuel 2*

1 **We recognise that Christian traditions historically ascribe holiness to God alone. Neither nation or state, nor any political community can legitimately claim intrinsic holiness**

Christian identity is not singularly, exclusively, or supremely held by a nation, a race, or a civilisation. The integrity of the Christian witness is distorted where it is used to create separation between people and people, between race and race, between nation and nation, and between civilisation and civilisation.

2   **We therefore stand against "Christian Nationalism", "Christian Europe" and the "Russian World"**

Russia and wider Europe have historically been home to a plurality of religious, ethnic, and linguistic communities. The integrity of the Christian witness is distorted by political aggression, the infliction of bodily harm, suffering, and disadvantage, or the denial of the rights and integrity of communities with whom we coexist – be it in name of Christian Nationalism or in name of the so-called Russian World (Holy Rus).

3   **We remember that Christianity has often been slow to recognise the danger of its complicity in political violence**

Christian identity has been misused against both Christians and non-Christians: in outbursts of sectarian violence, in the horrific persecution of Jewish and other minorities, and against the peoples of the world who Christian colonisers sought to forcibly convert. The integrity of the Christian witness is distorted by the use of aggression in matters of religion and by the use of religion in matters of aggression.

4   **We call on other Christian scholars in Europe and beyond to speak out against unholy alliances between Christian identity and political power**

Christian scholars must be ready and willing to speak out against unholy alliances of Christianity and political power, and especially in the context of nationalism, populism, and new forms of totalitarianism. The integrity of the Christian witness is distorted when the appropriation of Christian identity remains uncontested from within Christian traditions.

5   **We laud the 'Declaration on the "Russian World" (Russkii Mir) Teaching' from within parts of the international Orthodox community**

The abuse of the Russian World teaching has been thoroughly rebutted as *non-Orthodox* by international Orthodox voices. Orthodox theologians have not hesitated to condemn the fratricidal war against Ukraine as "the repetition of the sin of Cain". The integrity of the Christian witness is honoured by Christian solidarity with those who speak truth to power.

6   We call for the development of an Ecumenical "Theology after Christendom"

Drawing upon Scripture, reason, and the rich traditions of the Christian churches around the world, 21st-century Christianity needs to nourish its reflection on theology and political thought, specifically investing in an ecumenical "Theology after Christendom". Orthodox, Catholic and Protestant scholars must support one another in resisting the sacralisation of political communities, and in offering resources to articulate a theology committed to the common good, to truthfulness, and to justice.

Index

Ancient Rus'   6, 87, 117, 118, 120, 122
Anglicanism (Anglican)   14, 296, 297, 304, 306, 308–312, 314, 316–319, 322–324
Antichrist   31, 74, 126, 143, 145–149, 152–154, 158–161, 163–166
anti-democratic politics   2, 3, 6, 260, 326
anti-gender   12, 55, 64, 65, 78, 169, 171–175, 177–180, 182–193
anti-LGBT   6, 197, 326
anti-liberal   3, 6, 8, 13, 18, 19, 21, 22, 90, 95, 101, 212, 226, 326, 330
anti-Semitism   257, 258
anti-western   6, 11, 13, 107, 112, 113, 117–120, 126, 127, 136, 178, 226, 326
apocalyptic (apocalypse)   5, 7, 8, 12, 15, 16, 96, 125, 143–145, 147, 151, 153, 159, 160, 164, 167, 326, 332–334
Arendt, Hannah   118, 120, 122
atheism   108, 150, 151, 211, 216–218, 228, 238, 310, 322, 329
authoritarianism (authoritarian)   VII, 23, 28, 40, 74, 91, 93, 102, 105, 125, 141, 149, 154, 162, 163, 167, 170, 178, 189, 225, 226

Barth, Karl   10, 41–47, 49, 50, 52, 53, 56–59, 62, 232, 247, 263, 264, 267, 268,
belonging   7, 10, 12, 14, 15, 18, 36, 41, 43–45, 47, 48, 51–53, 55–57, 59, 63, 82, 83, 91, 116, 187, 192, 196, 197, 211, 212–217, 227–229, 231, 241, 246, 274, 288, 290–293, 297–306, 312, 316–319, 321, 323, 330
belonging without attending   13, 210, 211, 217, 222, 223, 225, 226, 275
Brexit   34, 35, 274, 277, 278, 288

capitalism   22, 41, 59, 67, 69, 91, 105, 154, 160, 300
Catholic Church   25, 29, 38, 42, 48, 55, 57, 58, 61, 63–65, 68, 73, 77, 138, 170, 172, 174, 176, 189, 193, 213, 216, 256, 273–275, 287, 289, 314
Catholicism (Catholic)   XIII, XIV, 9, 11–14, 24, 25, 32, 38, 39, 42, 43, 48, 50, 54, 55, 58, 59, 62–65, 71, 73–79, 135, 138, 147, 168–170, 173, 174, 176, 177, 179, 181–183, 187, 210, 216, 228, 240, 253–257, 259, 260, 263, 265, 266, 271, 273–277, 280–286, 318, 329, 331, 337, 344
Christen-Democratisch Appèl (CDA)   251, 252, 259–264, 266–269, 271–272
Christian democracy   8, 10, 13, 54, 250–253, 259, 260, 263–267, 269, 270, 274, 286, 287
Christian Democratic Appeal. See Christen-Democratisch Appèl
Christian Democratic parties   250–253, 259, 263–267
Christian Democratic Union (CDU). See Christlich Demokratische Union
Christian nationalism   X, 10, 42, 61, 66, 75, 95, 103, 230, 231, 234, 237, 239, 241–243, 331, 333, 342, 343
Christian Right   3, 16, 57, 58, 83, 90, 95, 104, 171, 172, 190, 193, 329, 334
Christianism (Christianist)   VII, X, 1, 6–9, 12, 14, 19, 28, 29, 33, 39, 326, 327, 330, 332
Christlich Demokratische Union (CDU)   251–259, 261, 264, 266–270
Christlich Soziale Union (CSU)   253–255, 257, 258, 267, 268
Church of England   XV, 286, 291, 295–298, 303, 305, 308, 309, 310–319, 321–324
church-state   XIII, 211, 212, 225, 291, 295–297, 302, 304, 305, 309, 312, 332, 333
civilisationalism   6, 15, 90, 101, 326, 330, 331, 333
climate crisis   18, 285
conservatism   2, 10, 28, 143, 168, 169, 171, 172, 176, 185, 186, 230, 236, 248, 325, 329
constitution (constitutional)   XII, 11, 20, 23, 30, 40, 81, 92–96, 103–105, 108, 111, 143, 154, 164, 177, 244, 245, 248, 274, 302, 307, 330, 332, 333, 335
Covid-19   126, 198, 206
crusade   1, 2, 12, 64, 84, 127, 140
cultural Christianity   29, 81, 93, 230, 233, 330
culture war   3, 5, 16, 64, 83, 95, 105, 113, 124, 155, 214, 228, 329, 334

Danish Peoples Party (DPP)   13, 230, 231, 233–239, 241, 242, 244–246

discrimination   73, 188, 258, 261
diversity   175, 214, 229, 286, 291, 295, 297, 306, 308, 311, 312, 314, 316, 323, 327
Dugin, Aleksandr   5, 12, 15, 125, 143, 144, 149, 150, 155–167, 326, 333

equality   6, 20, 21, 28, 29, 64, 72, 155, 169, 172, 177, 186, 191, 326
eschatology (eschatological)   7, 12, 16, 34, 35, 37, 40, 89, 96, 106, 119, 143–146, 148, 154, 159, 160, 163, 164
ethnicity (ethnic)   3, 6, 12, 15, 24, 28, 38, 44, 45, 47, 48, 51, 52, 54–57, 61, 63, 77, 78, 82, 90–94, 105, 113, 123, 127, 128, 131, 133, 170, 174, 176, 196, 207, 212–214, 224, 228, 246, 247, 261, 295, 326, 333, 336, 337, 339, 343
ethnonationalism   12, 13, 48, 54, 58, 90, 170, 171, 174, 175, 183, 186, 187, 188, 300
European Union (EU)   4, 5, 13, 14, 22, 93, 103, 117, 177, 178, 194, 224, 233, 237, 251, 264, 265, 267, 269, 270, 273–289, 327
euroscepticism (Eurosceptic)   XIV, 274, 275, 282, 285–287, 289
Evangelicals   3, 61, 85, 95, 96, 101, 174, 187, 317
evil   7, 12, 30, 74, 88–90, 93, 95, 96, 97, 99, 101, 112, 121, 126, 135, 139, 143, 145–148, 152–154, 164, 166, 328, 337, 339, 341
exceptionalism   8, 11, 12, 91, 101, 129, 130, 135
exclusion (exclusionary)   20, 22, 39, 73, 186, 187, 198, 200, 290, 296, 304, 310, 312, 332

family policies   2, 113, 180
family values   XV, 61, 162, 171–174, 178–181, 183–187, 190, 206
Far Right   IX, XIV, 2, 3, 5, 14–16, 61, 78, 84, 90, 105, 156, 162, 187–189, 275, 287, 325, 326, 328–331, 333, 334, 337
feminism (feminist)   119, 172, 187, 190, 299, 306, 322, 324
Fidesz   61, 68, 102, 244
Fratelli Tutti   10, 60–62, 65–72, 75–78
fraternity   11, 61, 62, 66, 68–72, 74, 76–78, 84, 104
freedom of religion. *See* religious freedom
freedom of speech   6, 24, 54, 160, 162

gender   XIV, XV, 6, 12, 28, 29, 64, 65, 67, 90, 95, 113, 170–174, 177, 179, 183, 186, 188–193, 201, 203–205, 212, 277, 280, 322, 324, 326, 327, 334
geopolitics (geopolitical)   XII, XIV, 5, 6, 12, 16, 61, 79, 82, 86–88, 105, 115,116, 121, 124, 127, 131, 133, 149, 150, 157, 166, 167, 213, 251, 265, 267, 284, 326, 329
globalism (globalisation)   1, 2, 7, 8, 34, 69, 153, 160, 198, 253, 275, 279, 300, 305, 326, 327, 337
Greek Solution party (GS)   12, 195–201, 203, 205–209

Holy Rus'   1, 6–8, 11, 87, 89, 107, 108, 112, 115–120, 122,124, 336, 338
humanism (humanist)   74, 134, 160, 233, 237
Hungarian World   4, 11, 80–84, 91, 92, 95, 100–102

identity politics   2, 15, 22, 39, 84, 103, 196, 208, 239, 241, 264, 268, 328, 333
illiberalism (illiberal)   3, 6, 8–10, 12, 16, 21, 23, 33, 37, 40, 83, 90, 92–94, 103–105, 169, 171–174, 176, 181, 186, 187, 189–191, 195, 208, 209, 265, 325, 326, 328, 329, 334
imagined communities   46, 50, 58, 81, 82, 102
immigration. *See* migration
incarnation   25, 38, 42, 43, 48, 51, 55, 57, 58, 166, 170, 315
inclusion   14, 290–295, 298–300, 302, 304, 305, 310
inculturation   57
Islam   XIII, 12, 28, 37, 54, 58, 60, 138, 150, 161, 169, 195, 196, 200, 206, 210, 213, 229, 243, 245, 246, 257, 295, 306, 309

Jewish   X, 147, 148, 154, 166, 199, 211, 258, 307, 343

Karol Józef Wojtyła. *See* Pope John Paul II
Katechon   7, 12, 126, 143–155, 158–165, 167
Krarup, Søren   231, 233–242, 244–247
Kremlin   1, 3, 16, 80, 87, 88, 111, 112, 117, 122, 124–126, 128, 129, 140, 141, 149, 157, 166, 329, 330

Law and Justice Party (PiS)   24, 61, 68
LGBT+   28, 29, 88–90, 160, 162, 171, 172, 174, 177, 179, 197, 208, 224, 280, 326, 327, 333
liberal democracy   17–20, 23, 24, 27, 35–39, 61, 68, 295

INDEX

liberalism   8, 17–23, 27, 29, 30, 32, 35–40, 64, 68, 82, 93–95, 101, 157, 160, 163, 173, 230, 233, 252, 278, 287, 297, 326, 337

Make America Great Again (MAGA)   8, 11, 34, 80–84, 91, 95–97, 100–102
Meloni, Georgia   28, 61, 65
Messerschmidt, Morten   13, 231, 238–246, 248
migrant   7, 28, 61, 65, 67, 68, 82, 95, 97, 171, 174, 195, 198, 201, 202, 236, 237, 243, 338, 340
migration   1–3, 12, 29, 60, 61, 65, 68, 71–73, 80, 92, 97, 195, 196, 201, 230, 231, 233–235, 249, 302, 306, 320, 327
minorities   18, 20, 22, 24, 73, 83, 90, 94, 105, 169, 171, 172, 192, 308, 323, 330, 340, 343
modernism (modernity)   7, 42, 46, 58, 59, 119, 155, 156, 245, 246, 281, 287
moralism   130, 134–136
Moscow Patriarchate   1, 8, 61, 89, 109, 112, 114, 124, 126, 141, 164, 168, 200, 336, 337
multiculturalism   64, 68, 160, 231, 233, 234, 237, 245, 275
multipolar world   1, 5, 158, 165, 328
Muslim   XV, 28, 29, 54, 60, 97, 159, 171, 195, 201, 202, 213, 214, 229, 256, 257, 261, 266, 310, 314, 316, 319–324

nation state   46, 54–56, 59, 68, 74, 81, 173, 212, 294, 295
national belonging. *See* belonging
national identity   XIII, 9, 10, 13, 15, 41–48, 52, 53, 56, 57, 62–65, 73, 88, 92, 103, 113, 116, 140, 155, 173, 184, 186, 195, 210–212, 214, 217, 224, 225, 228, 241, 242, 246, 274, 289–291, 295, 309
nationalism   X, XV, 6, 9, 10, 12, 13, 15, 24, 27, 28, 35, 38, 41–44, 46, 52, 54–56, 58–63, 66, 67, 69, 71, 75–78, 80, 93, 95, 102, 103, 126, 140, 149, 157, 160, 166, 168–171, 173, 174, 176–178, 180, 182–187, 190, 192, 196, 199, 207, 208, 212, 213, 228, 230, 231, 234, 237, 239–243, 246, 247, 249, 291, 294, 295, 306, 326, 330, 331, 333, 342, 343
NATO   4, 5, 87, 88, 89, 114, 143, 160, 194
natural law   32, 38, 40, 63

Orbán, Viktor   2, 4, 5, 11, 21, 33, 35, 65, 68, 80, 83, 85, 86, 91–95, 102, 274, 287, 327, 329, 330, 333

orders of creation   46, 52, 56, 57
Orthodox Church   90, 119, 147, 156, 160, 163, 183, 186, 200, 217, 225, 226, 336–338, 340
Orthodox Church of Greece (OCG)   12, 194, 195, 197
Orthodoxy   IX, XIII, XVI, 6, 9, 11, 15, 16, 54, 58, 85, 88–90, 103, 104, 109, 110, 114–117, 119–126, 129, 133, 135, 138, 141, 143, 147, 156, 159, 161–164, 167, 169, 170, 176, 178, 179, 186, 187, 193, 197–201, 206, 208–213, 216, 217, 224–229, 257, 302, 329–334, 336–344

Patriarch Kirill   1, 8, 11, 87, 89, 90, 108, 111, 112, 114, 116, 121, 123, 124, 126, 141, 163, 168, 336, 337
patriotism   43, 49, 50, 55, 63, 139, 182, 183, 185
Pax Americana   5, 6, 86, 88
pluralism   12, 20, 32, 77, 170, 181, 186, 252, 310, 323, 324
political imaginary   8, 10, 11, 14, 15, 80–86, 89–91, 95, 101–105, 122, 244, 286, 291
political realism   86, 105
political theology   XIV, 5, 9, 12, 14, 15, 18, 19, 37–39, 42, 58, 66, 73–76, 79, 84, 88–90, 103, 105, 119, 123, 143, 149, 150, 154, 158, 164, 168, 169, 188, 196, 208, 231, 241, 249, 294–297, 302, 305, 306, 325, 327, 328, 331–333,
Pope Benedict   XVI, 11, 62–64, 78,
Pope Francis   10, 29, 61, 62, 64–72, 75–78
Pope John Paul II   10, 11, 41–44, 47–57, 59, 62–64, 78
populism   XV, 1, 3, 8–10, 13, 16–32, 34–40, 42, 43, 52, 56–58, 60, 61, 68, 76, 78–80, 83–85, 93, 95, 96, 103–105, 171, 172, 174, 177, 191, 193, 196, 199, 206, 208, 212, 231, 236, 238, 242–249, 264, 268, 270, 274, 287, 288, 325, 326, 343
Protestantism (Protestant)   XII–XIV, 9, 41, 43, 59, 138, 186, 210, 251, 253, 254, 256, 257, 259, 260, 263, 266, 269, 271, 311, 331, 336, 344
protests   4, 179, 225, 303
public space   31, 33, 81, 108, 109, 183, 213, 242, 243, 278

Putin, Vladimir 1, 5, 8, 11, 12, 15, 18, 23, 40, 61, 82, 83, 85–91, 93–95, 102–105, 108–111, 113, 114, 116, 117, 120–129, 140–145, 155–157, 159–165, 167, 168, 226, 329, 330, 334, 336, 337

race 44, 53, 56, 63, 92, 93, 322, 324, 327, 339, 342
Radical Right 3, 12, 15, 25, 38, 39, 170–172, 176, 187, 191, 192, 195, 197, 199, 203–206, 208, 238
Redemptor hominis 48, 59, 62, 63, 78
religion-state. *See* church-state
religious freedom 32, 39, 81, 112, 279, 330, 334
religious nationalism 12, 13, 54, 55, 59, 169–171, 173, 174, 176, 178–180, 184–186, 206, 213
rule of law 10, 86, 90, 93, 103, 260, 261, 265
Russian Orthodox Church 1, 6, 8, 11, 15, 16, 61, 79, 87, 89, 101, 102, 103, 105, 107–118, 120–122, 124–127, 138, 143, 158, 166, 211, 329, 336, 337
Russian Orthodoxy 6, 11, 15, 61, 79, 89, 109, 111, 115, 119, 123, 136, 138, 159, 161, 211, 329, 334,
Russian World 1, 5, 6, 8–12, 16, 80–84, 86–91, 93, 94, 101–103, 105, 107, 115, 116, 120–124, 126, 143, 163, 164, 168, 213, 225, 322, 326–328, 331, 333, 336, 337, 342, 343
Russkii Mir. *See* Russian World

sacralisation 7, 8, 11, 16, 30, 31, 34–37, 40, 80, 83, 84, 88, 91, 96, 100–102, 106, 231, 242, 330, 344
sacred 7–11, 16, 19, 22, 26, 27, 29–31, 33, 35, 36, 40, 80, 81, 84, 85, 88, 99, 102, 103, 106, 117, 161, 183, 193, 210, 213, 228, 229, 231, 242–244, 249, 271, 279, 286, 289, 303, 323, 324, 330–332, 335, 338, 339
sacred space 7, 16, 31, 40, 80, 81, 84, 88, 98, 99, 100, 106, 116, 183, 193, 213, 229, 242, 249, 271, 279, 286, 289, 310, 323, 324, 331, 335,
Salvini, Matteo 24, 61, 65, 69, 78
Schmitt, Carl 12, 73–76, 78, 79, 143, 144, 147, 149–155, 157, 158, 164, 166–168
Second Vatican Council (Vatican II) 57, 62

secular XIII, 7, 8, 14, 15, 16, 19, 25, 29, 31, 34, 35, 39, 40, 81, 84, 85, 88, 96, 101, 102, 106, 108, 119, 124, 149, 153, 158, 160, 162, 176, 179, 182, 183, 186, 210, 213, 216, 228, 231, 235, 242–246, 250, 256, 263, 267, 269, 274, 279, 286, 287, 299, 306, 325, 327–332, 334, 338, 340,
secularism (secularisation) 6–9, 13, 14, 16, 20, 25, 27, 29, 31, 35, 36, 40, 63, 65, 72, 74, 75, 76, 78, 80, 81, 84, 85, 96, 102, 104, 106, 130, 144, 153, 158, 164, 172, 173, 182, 183, 185, 187, 193, 210, 213, 229, 242–245, 248–250, 252, 255, 260, 261, 265, 268, 271, 279, 286, 289, 295, 306, 323–326, 329–331, 335, 337
secular-sacred 6, 7, 11, 15, 31, 85, 102, 242, 279, 327, 330
Serbian Orthodox Church (SOC) 13, 170, 174, 176, 178, 211–214, 221–226
Serbian Orthodoxy 13, 48, 54, 58, 169, 170, 173, 174, 184, 185, 189
social media 68, 158, 258, 266
social movement organisations (SMOs) 177, 179, 180, 183, 185, 186
social networks. *See* social media
Solzhenitsyn, Alexander 11, 12, 125, 127–142
Soviet Union 42, 112, 118, 127, 131, 132, 137, 139, 143, 154, 156, 157, 163, 165, 266, 281
special military operation 7, 12, 83, 89, 95, 144, 158, 159, 341
spirituality XIII, XIV, 77, 83, 84, 99, 100, 121, 123, 336

terrorism 60, 97, 114, 281, 287
Tidehverv 13, 230–242, 244–249
traditional values 2, 21, 29, 36, 68, 80, 90, 93, 111–113, 126, 171, 183, 206, 303, 307
traditionalism (traditionalist) 9, 64, 83, 113, 119, 156, 163, 177, 326, 329
Trump, Donald 2, 3, 8, 11, 34, 35, 61, 65, 80, 85, 86, 95–103, 106

Ukraine 3–6, 82, 83, 86–88, 90, 93, 104, 107, 108, 112, 115, 117, 118, 121, 126–128, 131, 133, 140, 143, 159–161, 163–165, 167, 194, 200, 207, 211, 265, 278, 336, 341, 342

violence   66, 77, 83, 90, 95, 99, 100, 118, 129, 131, 135, 178, 187, 190, 285, 303, 306, 332, 334, 339, 343
Vučić, Aleksandar   65, 178, 225

war crimes   88, 101, 144, 165, 168
war in Ukraine   VII, IX, 1, 4, 5, 8, 11, 12, 61, 83, 86–89, 103, 104, 107, 110, 112, 113, 115, 117, 121–123, 125, 127, 129, 140, 143, 144, 149, 158, 160, 163–166, 168, 206, 217, 224–226, 266, 278, 279, 327–330, 332, 334, 336, 337, 342, 343
Wilders, Geert   2, 3

xenophobia (xenophobic)   66, 71, 77, 194, 206, 244

www.ingramcontent.com/pod-product-compliance
Lightning Source LLC
Chambersburg PA
CBHW070745020526
44116CB00032B/1973